D1328387

THE ONE SHIP FLEET

U.S. Navy Hymn

Eternal Father, strong to save,
whose arm hath bound the restless wave,
Who bidd'st the mighty ocean deep,
Its own appointed limits keep.
Oh, hear us when we cry to Thee,
For those in peril on the sea!.

Eternal Father, lend Thy grace
To those with wings who fly thro' space,
Thro' wind and storm, thro' sun and rain,
Oh bring them safely home again.
Oh Father, hear a humble prayer,
For those in peril in the air!

Oh, Trinity of love and pow'r,
Our brethren shield in danger's hour,
From rock and tempest, fire and foe,
Protect them where so e'er they go.
Thus, evermore shall rise to Thee
Glad hymns of praise from land and sea! Amen.

THE ONE SHIP FLEET

The USS *Boise*—WWII Naval Legend 1938–45

PHILLIP T. PARKERSON

CASEMATE

Philadelphia & Oxford

Published in the United States of America and Great Britain in 2023 by
CASEMATE PUBLISHERS
1950 Lawrence Road, Havertown, PA 19083, USA
and
The Old Music Hall, 106–108 Cowley Road, Oxford OX4 1JE, UK

Copyright © 2023 Phillip T. Parkerson

Hardcover Edition: ISBN 978-1-63624-299-6
Digital Edition: ISBN 978-1-63624-300-9

A CIP record for this book is available from the British Library

Printed and bound in United Kingdom by CPI Group (UK) Ltd, Croydon, CR0 4YY
Typeset in India by DiTech Publishing Services

For a complete list of Casemate titles, please contact:

CASEMATE PUBLISHERS (US)
Telephone (610) 853-9131
Fax (610) 853-9146
Email: casemate@casematepublishers.com
www.casematepublishers.com

CASEMATE PUBLISHERS (UK)
Telephone (0)1226 734350
Email: casemate-uk@casematepublishers.co.uk
www.casematepublishers.co.uk

Front cover image: USS Boise *(CL-47) shelling the beach, Gela Sicily, July 1943 (USNARA, 80-G-54550).*
Back cover image: USS Boise *(CL-47) at sea 1943 (USNARA, 80-G-68105).*

In memory of Electrician's Mate First Class Avery F. Parkerson, and all of the men who served on the USS *Boise* during World War II. With selfless courage, they helped to save the world from fascism. I salute them for their dedication to duty and country and wish them "fair winds and calm seas" for all eternity.

This book is for my grandson, Avery Parkerson, in the hopes that it will inspire him to become a brave and honorable man like his great-grandfather.

"May God be with you and your magnificent ship until we meet again."
Final words of General Douglas MacArthur to Captain W. M. Downes on
leaving the *Boise*, 16 June 1945.

Contents

Prologue

A Georgia "Cracker" Joins the USS *Boise*

I have heard many sea stories in my life, especially when I was in the U.S. Navy. Sailors say that a sea story is similar to a fairy tale, the only difference being that instead of beginning with "Once upon a time," a sea story begins with "This ain't no shit." What you are about to read is a sea story, but unlike so many, this one is actually true. It is the story of the light cruiser USS *Boise* (CL-47), one of the most famous American combat ships of World War II that literally became a legend in its own time. I first heard the *Boise's* story as a young boy from my father, Avery F. Parkerson, who served aboard the cruiser as an Electrician's Mate (EM) from April 1943 until October 1945. It is also his story, and he told it very well. I hope my retelling of it here does justice to him and his magnificent ship.

The story begins with a young sailor from rural South Georgia, my father, standing on a pier at the Norfolk Navy Yard in April 1943 gaping open-mouthed at the huge cruiser that loomed high above him. The *Boise* was much larger than he had imagined and literally bristled with big guns. The ship was long and sleek, longer he guessed than two football fields set end to end. His heart swelled with pride knowing that he was about to report aboard one of the U.S. Navy's most celebrated warships and soon would be riding her into combat against his nation's enemies. At the same time, however, he could not tear his thoughts away from his pretty, young wife and how painful it had been to say goodbye to her when he had boarded the train down in Georgia at the end of his home leave just a few days before. But there was a war on, and Avery had to return to duty.

My father already knew something about the USS *Boise*; the ship had already become famous even though the United States had been at war for less than 18 months. Part of what he knew he had learned from his uncle, Ben Wade, a former U.S. Marine. Ben had been right; it was a big, modern warship, a true "queen." Avery had also heard the stories about the ship during his naval training, and had read newspaper and magazine articles about its outstanding performance in a major shootout with the Imperial Japanese Navy (IJN) in October 1942 in the Solomon Islands, in which it was credited with sinking, or assisting in sinking,

USS *Boise* (CL-47) off Philadelphia Navy Yard, 22 April 1943. (US National Archives [USNARA], 19-N-43829)

six Japanese warships. The nationwide press coverage that the *Boise* received had made her a navy legend, and its name had become a household word at home and abroad. Avery also knew that the cruiser had suffered severe damage and heavy loss of life among her gallant crew in that battle. In fact, he was acutely aware that he was replacing a sailor who was killed in the night engagement. Thus, he could not help wondering whether rejecting the navy's offer of shore duty in Brazil and putting in for a shipboard assignment instead had really been such a good idea. Well, he made that request, the navy had granted it, and had assigned him to the cruiser's electrical division (E Division). So now, here he stood, staring in awe at the magnificent ship that was about to become his new seagoing home. So, there was nothing to do but shoulder his sea bag, walk up the gangplank, salute both the flag on the fantail and the Officer of the Deck (OOD), and report aboard. Seaman Second Class Avery Parkerson's seafaring adventure aboard one of the navy's most fabled fighting ships was about to begin.

Avery was born on 9 March 1916 in Eastman, Georgia, the county seat of Dodge County, which is located in the heartland of the state some 60 miles southeast of Macon. His family were true "crackers," being the direct descendants of Jacob Parkerson, a Revolutionary War veteran from the Eastern Shore of Virginia, who had moved his family into the "Wiregrass" region, between the Oconee and Ocmulgee Rivers, when it was first opened to white settlement after the Creek Indians were forced to cede the territory to the state in 1805.

Times were hard in rural Georgia when my parents were growing up in the 1920s and 1930s, and Avery always worked to help out his parents who had six children to feed and clothe. His father owned a small service station in the town, and his mother was a homemaker who took in sewing to help make ends meet. Avery was the third of four brothers and had two younger sisters. He always complained that he was the one who had to do all the household chores while his siblings got away with doing little or nothing. As a young boy, Avery had a paper route, delivering newspapers each morning before going to school. He remembered trembling with fear when distributing papers through the dark, silent county courthouse in the pre-dawn hours. Avery was affable and upbeat. He had a lively sense of humor and enjoyed being with people. As a result, he was well-liked by almost everyone who knew him, young and old.

After graduating from Eastman High School in 1932, my dad worked for a time as a farm laborer for his uncle, "plowing a mule for fifty cents a day." Jobs were nearly impossible to find in rural Georgia during the Great Depression. With the family struggling to feed so many mouths, Avery joined the Civilian Conservation Corps (CCC) on 11 January 1935 at Folkston, Georgia, near the Florida border. The CCC was a New Deal public relief program that put young, unmarried men back to work during the Great Depression. Administered by U.S. Army Reserve officers, it not only required hard manual labor, but also heavy physical exercise and military training and discipline, aimed at preparing young American men for war, which was then looming on the horizon.

The CCC put Avery to work in a reforestation project in Georgia's great Okefenokee Swamp. Among other tasks, he had to cut fire breaks through the forest by hand, always keeping an eye out for the highly venomous water moccasins and huge alligators that inhabited the swamp. Clearing brush and cutting trees with axe and crosscut saw was hard, back-breaking labor, but it got the 19-year-old into the best physical shape of his young life. After a stint in the Okefenokee, he was transferred to Savannah, Georgia, to work in the cleanup and restoration of Fort Pulaski, the old Civil War fort that sits out in the coastal marshes guarding the approach to the city a few miles upstream from where the Savannah River empties into the Atlantic Ocean at Tybee Island. Here again, the work of clearing the brush and trees out of the old fort was physically demanding. When his hitch was up after some 13 months in the CCC, Avery decided not to re-enlist and was discharged at Fort Pulaski on 31 March 1936. He performed well during his service and his supervising officer's final evaluation commended him for his irreproachable manner and actions, honesty, trustworthiness, and hard work.

Returning home to Eastman, Avery got a job managing the soda fountain at College Street Pharmacy, which was owned by his father's brother. He soon began courting Anne Taylor, a pretty, dark-haired girl whose father owned a large farm in the Dubois community located in the northern end of Dodge County. Anne had an older sister, Ruby, who was killed in a buggy accident in 1933 when she was only 19, and a younger brother, Wendell (aka "Skinny"), who worked the farm with my grandfather for most of his life before dying at age 42 in an automobile accident in 1966. My grandfather was a successful farmer who was able to send Anne to college during the Great Depression, although she dropped out after completing her third year at Birmingham Southern College in 1937. Returning to Dodge County, Anne took a teaching position at the Cottondale Elementary School where she was known as "Miss Anne" to her second-grade students. The school was located in the mill village where the workers at the local cotton mill lived with their families. In those days, the children of the mill workers were disparagingly referred to as "lint heads" by the middle-class children of the town.

After a period of courtship, the young couple were married before a justice of the peace in nearby Dublin, Georgia, on Christmas Day, 1938. The newlyweds struggled to make a living during the dark days of the Great Depression, just like all their friends and neighbors. Anne continued in her teaching job, and Avery eventually got a break on 1 September 1939, when he was hired as a linesman by the Ocmulgee Electric Membership Cooperative (or REA as it was popularly known at the time). He worked at that job, climbing poles to build and repair power lines, until he joined the U.S. Navy in August 1942.

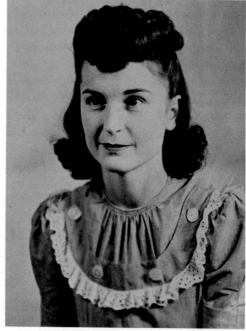

Avery Parkerson, circa 1943. (Author)   Anne Taylor, circa 1942. (Author)

My parents scrimped and saved while postponing their plans to have children (they always wanted two, a boy and a girl) for better days, which they believed would surely come. Before things improved very much, however, the United States was finally drawn into the war that was raging in Europe, Asia and Africa, by the Japanese attack on the U.S. Navy Base at Pearl Harbor, Hawaii, on 7 December 1941.

Avery enlisted in the navy on 17 August 1942, just six months after his youngest brother, Signalman Third Class Clifford Harrison "Bo" Parkerson, USN, was killed in the wreck of the USS *Truxtun* (DD-229), which ran aground, broke apart, and sank in the icy waters off Newfoundland on 18 February 1942. This tragedy, in which the navy transport ship USS *Pollux* (AKS-2) also grounded and sank, was the worst noncombat-related disaster in U.S. Navy history, claiming the lives of over 200 sailors. It was the result of navigational errors complicated by a major winter storm in the North Atlantic. At the time, Avery and his family did not know the details of what had happened to their 20-year-old son and brother. The navy informed them that he had drowned, but we learned 70 years later that he died of hypothermia while working with rescuers to save as many of his shipmates as possible. Avery had been very close to Bo, six years his junior, and loved him very much. The two were practically inseparable. Bo Parkerson was a handsome, friendly young man, a star athlete in high school, and a great dancer, all of which made him very popular in their hometown, especially with the young women. Mother always said that her brother-in-law was the nicest boy she ever knew. His brother's death devastated Avery, who never completely got over it.

Dad did not tell my mother that he was volunteering for the navy. Instead, he slipped off with several other boys from Eastman to go to the Navy Recruiting Office in the nearby city of Macon to enlist. After signing up, the young men went out to eat before driving the 60 miles back home. During their meal, the waitress stopped by to ask if they wanted dessert. One good ole boy in the group, who was called "Toofy" Nicholson and was known for his country witticisms, replied that he wanted a piece of pie. When the waitress asked what kind of pie he wanted, Toofy drawled back, "'Tater, fool. What else kinda pie is they?" Nicholson was of course referring to sweet potatoes, a staple of the southern diet during the tough economic times of the 1930s, which make a delicious pie that many connoisseurs prefer to pumpkin pie. Avery always got a good laugh out of recalling that story in the years after the war.

Mother was furious because he enlisted without consulting her beforehand. She never really forgave him for it, always insisting that he would not have been drafted into service because of his critical job as a lineman for the OEMC. But Avery, like so many young men of his generation in the aftermath of Pearl Harbor, was determined to get into the war, which in its early stages was not going all that well for the United States and its allies. Caught up in the tidal wave of patriotism that swept the nation after the Japanese attacked Pearl Harbor, Avery felt it was his duty to fight for his country. Moreover, he was out to avenge his younger brother's death. Despite the fact that the enemy had played no direct role in the shipwreck that took Bo's life, Avery still held them responsible and wanted "to kill 'em all," as my mom put it.

The navy sent Avery to Norfolk, Virginia, for six weeks of basic training. Upon completion of boot camp, the new able seamen were asked by their chief petty officer (CPO) if anyone wanted to volunteer for the submarine service. One of the first lessons a recruit learns in the navy is never to volunteer for anything, so Avery held back along with everyone else. Seeing that no one stepped forward, the chief sent the entire class over to take the physical exam for submarine duty. Avery was rejected due to some minor problem with his eyesight or hearing and breathed a big sigh of relief. Although he had joined up to fight, Avery said he had no desire whatsoever to go to war in a "sewer pipe," as submarines were often called at the time.

After basic training, my father was granted two weeks of home leave during the second half of October 1942. At that point, Avery had been assigned to attend a naval electrical training program at Purdue University, but for some reason, known perhaps only to the "Puzzle Palace," the U.S. Navy's Bureau of Personnel, his orders were changed. Instead, he was reassigned to the navy's Class A Electrical School at Newport, Rhode Island, where he trained from 1 November 1942 until 14 February 1943. Although Avery never made it to Purdue, he somehow felt a special connection to the university and would always review the college football scores on Sunday mornings to see if Purdue had won its games. During the time he attended electrical school, Avery came down with the mumps, a common childhood malady that can be much more complicated when it strikes adults, and was briefly hospitalized at the Newport Naval Hospital. This disease turned out to be the most serious physical ailment he would suffer during his wartime naval service.

Upon completing electrical school with excellent scores, Avery was offered an assignment to the U.S. Navy Air Facility at Natal, Brazil, which recently had been opened to funnel supplies to Allied forces in North Africa. Brazil had begun cooperating with the United States in early 1942 and declared war on the Axis powers in August of that same year. Later in the war, some 27,500 Brazilian soldiers were sent to Italy in 1944 where they gave a good account of themselves in the fight against Germany. Avery, who wanted to get into the war, asked for sea duty instead and was given orders to report for duty aboard the USS *Boise* (CL-47), which was then undergoing repairs in the Philadelphia Navy Yard. Before joining his ship, however, he was granted another home leave during March 1943 while repairs to the cruiser were being completed and it was being made ready to return to the fleet. On the train ride south, Avery conversed with the conductor, a distinguished African-American man. The morning after leaving New York on the Southern Crescent, which ran from New York City to New Orleans, the conductor shook Avery awake with a big smile on his face to inform him that they had crossed the Mason-Dixon line so that they were serving grits for breakfast in the dining car.

This news made the Georgia sailor very hungry. While he liked hash-brown potatoes, they are a poor substitute for grits to the Southern palate. In Atlanta, Avery changed trains to continue on down to Macon and then home to Dodge County, where he spent a few wonderful days with his wife and family.

When his leave ended, Avery returned to duty and reported aboard ship immediately upon arrival at the Navy Receiving Station in Norfolk, Virginia, on 3 April 1943. For Avery, those precious few days he had spent at home with Anne were the happiest days of his life. He wrote to her later from Philadelphia, promising that "This war will be over soon and then I can come home and take up where I left off. I felt like crying when I got on that train to leave you that day. I love you so much."

After he joined the ship, the *Boise* spent the next week at sea conducting test runs and gunnery practice in preparation for deployment. Avery quickly fell in love with the magnificent cruiser and every day he grew prouder that he was serving on such a famous warship. He assured Anne that there was no need to worry about him because he was serving on "one of the best ships in the fleet," and boasted proudly, "Boy, she is plenty fast and got enough guns to blast the Axis off the face of the earth. She is as big as a battleship and faster than most of them."

He would soon find out just how right he was about the USS *Boise*. This is where Avery's sea story actually began. The adventure would take him and his shipmates nearly three quarters of the way around the world and into both major theaters of war, from North Africa and Italy to Australia, New Guinea and the Philippine Islands. Little did they know that they were also entering into the annals of naval history.

The research for this book drew on hundreds of original documents from the U.S. National Archives and U.S. Navy sources, primarily *Boise*'s monthly war diaries December 1941–October 1945) and action reports (1943–1945), as well as some that were in my father's wartime scrapbook. In addition, I conducted personal interviews with two surviving crew members and consulted numerous printed and electronic primary and secondary sources I could locate. I chose not to include endnotes in the text for the sake of readability, but all sources consulted are listed in the bibliography. I have also used military time (24-hour clock) and included a glossary of naval terms, slang, and acronyms.

CHAPTER ONE

The USS *Boise* (CL-47), 1938–42

The ship that became Seaman Second Class Avery Parkerson's new seagoing home in April 1943 was christened with the name of the capital city of the state of Idaho at its launching on 3 December 1936. Construction of the new cruiser was completed two years later, and the USS *Boise* was commissioned and joined the fleet with the hull number CL-47. It was the next to last ship of a class of 10,000-ton "treaty cruisers" that were built between the end of World War I and the outbreak of World War II in accordance with the terms of the multilateral naval treaties of Washington (1922) and London (1930). These naval treaties limited the numbers, displacement, and armament of certain types of warships, including heavy cruisers. The *Boise* was a light cruiser—that is, its main battery consisted of 6-inch guns rather than the 8-inch guns of a heavy cruiser—and therefore was not in the categories of ships whose numbers were limited by the naval treaties. The first of the class of American light cruisers built under the terms of the treaties was christened the USS *Brooklyn* (CL-40). Therefore, it and the other six built to the same basic design and specifications—*Philadelphia* (CL-41), *Savannah* (CL-42), *Nashville* (CL-43), *Phoenix* (CL-46), *Boise* (CL-47), and *Honolulu* (CL-48)—became known as *Brooklyn* class light cruisers. The basic design for these fast, powerful ships became the model for all American cruisers, both light and heavy, built during the war with slight modifications.

The USS *Boise* was a sleek, beautiful, head-turner of a vessel. Its twin raked stacks, sweeping bow, teakwood decks, highly polished brass fittings, and two rows of portholes below the main deck gave it an elegant look reminiscent of a luxury, ocean-going yacht. A peculiar design characteristic of the *Brooklyn* class cruisers was their squared-off stern, which differed strikingly from the more common, oval-shaped fantails of most other warships. This distinctive-looking rear end, which resulted from housing the aviation hangar one deck below the aircraft launching area on the fantail, led many sailors to dub them "bobtails."

Boise was also a large, powerful craft. Stretching over 608 feet from stem to stern and 62 feet wide at the beam, its displacement was over 11,000 tons once wartime modifications and new armament were added. Four powerful steam turbines

USS *Boise* shortly after commissioning, circa 1938–39. (Naval History and Heritage Command [NHHC], NH97779)

developed 100,000 shaft horsepower (SHP) that allowed it to hit speeds of up to 33.5 knots (38.6 mph), which was extremely fast for such a large ship. The *Brooklyn* class cruisers, designed to roam far and wide over large expanses of the Pacific Ocean, where the United States had few naval bases, had a range of 10,000 nautical miles (11,500 statute miles) at a speed of 15 knots (see details in Appendix I).

Avery joined the ship's company of over 1,000 men. Among them was a 30-man Fleet Marine detachment who served as guards for the brig and the ship's commanding officer as well as participating in boarding and landing parties, the original functions of the U.S. Marine Corps. A Marine always accompanied the skipper wherever he went and stood guard outside his cabin during the night. In combat, "leathernecks" manned Turret III of the big cruiser's main battery as well as some of the 40- and 20-mm antiaircraft (AA) guns. For their fabled proficiency and marksmanship, the Marine gunners earned the unwavering gratitude, sincere admiration, and profound respect of their shipmates.

The *Boise* was equipped and appointed well enough to accommodate its officers and crew in adequate fashion. For feeding such a large number of hungry mouths, there were three separate dining facilities or mess halls: one general mess for the enlisted ratings, another exclusively for CPOs, and a wardroom for the commissioned officers. The officers' wardroom was by far the nicest of the dining facilities; the CPO mess was a bit more spartan. Staffed by African-American and Filipino sailors who served as cooks and mess stewards, the wardroom and messes dished up good food in hearty amounts that was the envy of every Marine or GI who ever set foot on its decks. The *Boise*'s storage compartments and coolers carried enough provisions to feed the crew for up to a year.

Avery rated the food served to the sailors on the *Boise* as pretty good, but complained that the cooks tended to serve creamed-chipped-beef on toast, known in navy slang as "shit on a shingle," a bit too often for his taste. Also, he claimed that on at least one occasion they were served horsemeat when supplies ran low in the Southwest Pacific, but he did not seem to have been greatly put off by it.

The commissioned officers' living quarters, although small, were far more comfortable than the crowded spaces that housed the enlisted men, who slept in "racks" (bunks) or, in some cases, hammocks strung wherever space could be found. All in all, Avery found life aboard the *Boise* to be tolerable. The heads always had plenty of hot water for showers, and the sailors at least got "three hots and a cot" instead of living in a muddy foxhole or a trench and eating K-rations like soldiers. Among the ship's creature comforts and amenities were a library, a post office, a barber shop, a general store, a laundry, a tailor shop and even an ice cream parlor, or canteen. The latter feature, commonly known as the "Geedunk Bar," was immensely popular with the crew as the canteen made its own ice cream and served ice cream sodas and sundaes as well as coffee and other snacks at practically any hour of the day or night. Although the *Boise* lacked air conditioning, with the exception of the captain's cabin, there was a system for circulating fresh air below decks that helped make life somewhat more bearable in such close quarters. Even so, in tropical climates, Avery, like many other sailors, often chose to sleep on deck whenever possible to escape the intense heat belowdecks. Another essential feature that enhanced the quality-of-life aboard ship was the *Boise*'s sophisticated evaporation equipment that produced 140,000 gallons of desalinated water for steam power as well as for bathing and consumption by the crew. Cold-water drinking fountains, known as scuttlebutts, were conveniently placed throughout the ship.

To keep all hands informed and entertained, the ship's radio shack had three AM receivers that were constantly tuned to three separate stations. By means of speakers installed throughout the ship, listeners could choose from among the three stations that were on the air at any given moment. Avery and his shipmates enjoyed listening to news broadcasts as well as music programs while they worked or relaxed. Ironically, much of the programming was provided courtesy of their enemies' propaganda networks. Avery mentioned that they frequently listened to "Tokyo Rose," "Axis Sally," and "Lord Haw Haw," scoffing at the grossly exaggerated or completely false claims of major defeats suffered by the Allies at the hands of their victorious forces, and because they played the latest, most popular tunes of the day. Although *Boise* lacked a movie projection room like those found on many modern warships, feature films were shown on the fantail in the evenings when the ship was in port, weather and combat conditions permitting. Finally, to care for the men's health, the light cruiser had a 20-bed sick bay, which was constantly manned by a pharmacist mate (hospital corpsman) and where a medical officer held sick call every morning. The suite contained a small operating room as well as a fully equipped dentist's office. The medical department staff consisted of two surgeons, a dentist, and 14 corpsmen.

Despite such creature comforts, the *Boise* was a combat ship, not a passenger liner. A light cruiser was designed to function primarily as a floating artillery platform and packed a tremendous amount of firepower. The main battery consisted of 15 6-inch (150-mm) guns, or rifles as they were known in the navy, which were triple-mounted in five armored turrets, three forward and two aft, weighing some 70 tons apiece. The turrets were rotated and their gun barrels were elevated by powerful electric motors. The long rifles' aim was radar-controlled, giving them deadly accuracy, and they could be fired electronically or manually. The three guns in a turret could be fired simultaneously or individually as soon as it was loaded and ready when the main battery was operating in continuous-fire mode. The gunnery officer could also fire a broadside of all 15 6-inch guns if battle conditions warranted. The recoil from a broadside was so powerful that the big cruiser rolled enough to throw a man off his feet unless he was holding onto something. Each turret was manned by a gun crew of three officers and 52 enlisted men who were rigorously trained to hone their skills and maximize efficiency, speed, and accuracy.

Although armed with smaller-bore rifles than a heavy cruiser's nine 8-inch (203-mm) guns that fired projectiles weighing about twice as much, the *Brooklyn* class light cruisers still packed a mighty punch. *Boise*'s 6-inch rifles could hurl a 130-pound armor-piercing (AP) projectile capable of penetrating up to five inches of hardened steel armor plating at a distance of 13 miles. Maximum range was 26,000 yards (about 14.5 statute miles). Whatever they lacked in throw weight, they easily made up for in rapidity of fire. The main battery guns could pour out shells at lightning speed, kicking out one round about every six seconds, which translates to 150 rounds of AP projectiles (combined throw weight of 9.75 tons of high explosives) at an enemy warship or shore installation every minute This amazingly rapid rate of fire, which was about twice that of the 8-inch guns, was commonly attained by adept gun crews like *Boise*'s. The deafening thunder from all 15 rifles in the main battery operating in rapid continuous fire mode was compared by friend and foe alike to the staccato bark of a heavy automatic weapon, and led the Japanese to refer to the American light cruisers in official battle reports as "machine gun cruisers."

Avery proudly boasted of his ship's excellent gunnery, and bragged that other than running out of ammunition, the only factor limiting the *Boise*'s furious pace of fire was the possibility that its gun barrels might warp from the intense heat generated during firing. The *Boise* perfected its gunnery and other combat-related functions to the point that she emerged as a legend in her own time, earning herself the sobriquet of "The One Ship Fleet." She was also known to some as the "Noisy *Boise*" for this ability to fire her guns so rapidly and effectively.

Backing up the main battery was a secondary battery of eight, single-mount, 5-inch (130-mm) 25-caliber cannon distributed four on each side of the ship. These dual-purpose deck guns were used for shooting it out with enemy ships or shore bombardment, as well as for defense against enemy aircraft. The gun's short barrel made it fairly easy to train manually against fast-moving targets, and the 54-pound projectile packed a heavy punch that could swat an enemy aircraft out of the sky at a maximum altitude of 27,400 feet, while it was still miles away from the point where it could launch an attack on the ship. Hence, the 5-inch guns were sometimes referred to as the AA battery.

For locating and identifying enemy surface targets and aircraft, as well as for directing the fire of the main and secondary batteries, *Boise* had the most complete array of state-of-the-art radar systems of any ship in the fleet. These systems, coupled with the ship's new computer (rudimentary though it was), permitted tracking and shooting at two surface targets simultaneously using full radar control on all main and secondary battery guns. This top-secret technology was continuously upgraded with the latest and most sophisticated equipment every time the cruiser returned to the United States for repair and refitting during the war. The technology helped make its gunnery amazingly accurate and gave it a distinct advantage over any Japanese warship afloat as well as other American combat ships not yet fitted with these high-tech systems.

Rounding out its armament for AA defense, *Boise* sported numerous (exact number undetermined) single-mount, Oerlikon 20-mm cannon. According to the U.S. Navy's 1943 Service Manual for the 20-mm cannon, the gun had a rate of fire of 450 rounds per minute, which was limited somewhat by the need to change the 60-round magazines when emptied, at a muzzle velocity of 2,800 feet per second. The 20-mm shell was 110 mm (7 inches) long and weighed half a pound; some shells carried an explosive charge, with or without tracer, while some did not. The maximum range of the 20-mm cannon was 4,800 yards at a 45-degree elevation. When fitted with the MIT-developed electronic gunsight, the 20-mm became one of the most effective AA weapons of the war. Although it lacked the punch of the 40-mm cannon, which could knock down a kamikaze suicide plane with a single round, it was far more maneuverable, making it highly effective at close range. It has been said that these guns shot down about one-third of all Japanese aircraft over the Pacific.

After weapons upgrades were performed in 1942 and 1943, two quad-mount and four dual-mount Bofors 40-mm cannon were added. The Bofors 40-mm, known as the "pom-pom" gun because of the distinctive sound it made when fired, was a highly effective, rapid-fire AA weapon capable of shooting 160 rounds of high explosive (HE) AA shells per minute that could reach altitudes of over 22,000 feet. With this blistering fire power, the pom-pom guns could throw up a deadly curtain of steel that literally knocked attacking aircraft out of the sky. The "forties" could also fling a 4-pound AP projectile against enemy ships that closed to within 6,000 yards. (See Appendix I for a general description of the *Boise*, including her armament.)

Avery was particularly proud of the expert marksmanship of his ship's AA gunners who manned the twenties and the forties. He often bragged: "Those boys could really knock." During air attacks, the 5-inch guns could reach out and smack enemy planes that were miles away from the ship. As the "bandits" (hostile planes) got in closer, the 40-mm cannon took over and then, if they were able to get past all of that and were barreling right down on the ship, the twenties opened up on them. Avery realized that as long as the 5-inch and even the forties were firing there was no need for concern, but when the twenties cut loose, he knew things were getting hot, and, whenever possible, would have to go out on deck to have a look and watch the action.

Like other American cruisers and battleships, *Boise* had an aviation division made up of small floatplanes that served as the ship's eyes-in-the-sky for reconnaissance, artillery spotting, and anti-submarine patrol. The spotter planes were of two types—the Curtiss SOC Seagull biplane, which entered service in 1935, and the

Curtiss SOC "Seagull" ready for launching from the catapults of a *Brooklyn* class light cruiser. (USNARA, 80-G-470115)

more modern Vought OS2U (or OS2N if built by the navy) Kingfisher monoplane, which joined the fleet in 1940. Although both aircraft were underpowered and slow, the latter was faster than the Seagull with its cloth and tubular construction. Both types could be launched from the two catapults, or "slingshots" to the sailors, mounted on the ship's fantail, or take off in the water. The tiny floatplanes landed on the water next to the ship after she had executed a special sweeping maneuver to smooth out the ocean's surface. The aircraft were then hoisted aboard by means of a large crane fixed to the stern between the catapults. Both the Seagull and the Kingfisher were lightly armed with two .30-caliber machine guns and could carry up to 650 pounds of bombs or depth charges. Each type was manned by two naval aviators—a pilot and an enlisted rate crewman who served as radio operator and gunner. (See Appendix VI for Allied and Axis aircraft designations.)

The *Boise* and its sister ships could carry up to four SOC Seagulls in the hangar deck, which was located in the stern section of the ship just beneath the high, squared-off fantail. The Kingfishers, however, could not be stowed in the hangar deck because their wings did not fold; they had to remain on the catapults, leaving them exposed and vulnerable to damage during combat or bad weather. When *Boise* deployed to the Mediterranean Theater in mid-1943, she carried two Seagulls and one OS2N Kingfisher. When she was transferred to the Southwest Pacific later that same year, two Kingfishers were carried.

Vought OS2U "Kingfisher" floatplane of Observation Squadron One (VO-1) taxiing beside the ship. (USNARA, 80-G-66108)

The Reluctant Dragon: *Boise's* Early Years, 1938–42

After commissioning and initial sea trials were successfully completed, *Boise* made a shakedown cruise to Cape Town, South Africa, and Monrovia, Liberia, during October–November 1938. Upon passing final acceptance trials in January 1939, the new cruiser joined the Pacific Fleet at Long Beach, California, and began operating on the West Coast and out of Pearl Harbor, Hawaii.

Boise's first encounter with the Imperial Japanese Navy (IJN) came just a few weeks before war was declared on 8 December 1941. On 18 November, the cruiser left Pearl Harbor escorting a troopship convoy bound for the Philippine Islands. While steaming through the strait between Guam and the Japanese-mandate island of Rota in the early days of December, *Boise* crossed paths with a group of Japanese warships that was most likely a scouting force for the IJN fleet that launched the surprise attack on Pearl Harbor. That, at least, was the assumption drawn by three crewmen on the *Boise* at the time—Radioman Vincent Langelo, Electrician's Mate Garnett Moneymaker, and Sergeant Jesse Glenn Cressy, who served as a Marine gunner in the main battery. Although the United States was not yet at war with Japan, the *Boise* went to general quarters (GQ, battle stations or high alert) just in case. The tension in the air was so thick it could have been cut with a knife, as everyone anxiously waited to see if the Japanese ships would open fire. Neither side, however, even waggled a gun, and both groups of ships continued on course in opposite directions. The chance encounter might have erupted into a gunfight if the *Boise* had broken radio silence to alert the Pacific Fleet Headquarters at Pearl Harbor. One must wonder whether the *Boise's* skipper reported this incident with the Japanese ships when he reached Manila on the morning of 4 December. Perhaps he did, and if so, no action was taken. Glenn Cressy, whose article on the standoff is based on the version his father told him, is probably correct in concluding that it fit into the plan to allow the Japanese to carry out their "sneak" attack in order to galvanize American public opinion in favor of war at a time when isolationist sentiment gripped the nation. It is now known that the United States was aware of an impending attack on its major Pacific naval base because the Americans had recently broken the secret Japanese diplomatic code.

After only two days in Manila, *Boise* was suddenly ordered to sea again and got underway to rendezvous with a large convoy of warships and transports that were headed for ports in the Dutch East Indies. As it steamed through the Sulu Sea towards the island of Cebu on 8 December 1941 (Philippines time), a radio dispatch informed them that the IJN had attacked Pearl Harbor that very morning (7 December Hawaii time). They also monitored reports that Manila and other points in the Philippine Islands had been bombed as well. The news that the United States was at war with Japan shocked the crew. Most took it in their stride, while a few of the men were visibly upset.

Life aboard changed instantly as the big cruiser abandoned the peacetime routine and assumed a war footing. The *Boise* shed something of its yacht-like appearance as it stripped down to fighting weight. The crew painted over the gleaming teakwood decks and shiny brass fittings with dull gray paint to make them less visible to enemy aircraft. Unnecessary objects that might splinter or catch fire, including furniture and some of the lifeboats, were removed and tossed over the side. The strip down was accomplished quickly with all hands turning to, leaving the big cruiser ready for action.

The *Boise* then joined the U.S. Asiatic Fleet, whose ships had plied the rivers of China and the seas off mainland China, Japan, Southeast Asia, and the Dutch East Indies since the early years of the 20th century. Until the Japanese invaded the Philippines the Asiatic Fleet was headquartered in Manila, the home port of the "China Sailors," men who spent their entire careers in the Orient and often retired out there. Avery described them as a breed apart, salty types who sported Chinese dragons and other colorful Asian motifs embroidered in the linings of their jackets and on the underside of the cuffs of their blouses that matched the tattoos decorating their bodies, all of which were strictly non-regulation. Many wore an earring for each hitch they had served in the Asiatic Fleet, and some older men had a number of them looped together hanging nearly to their shoulders. While the salty behavior and non-regulation attire of the China sailors would not have been tolerated in the more formal, tradition-bound fleets of the U.S. Navy, they were generally overlooked in the decidedly more relaxed Asiatic Fleet.

Boise's primary duty was to escort convoys of Allied merchant vessels, but on 21 January 1942, she struck an unchartered reef off the island of Timor, ripping a huge gash in the hull. Thus, the cruiser had to put into Colombo, British Ceylon (modern-day Sri Lanka) for repairs. While en route to Colombo, the ship made a stop at the Javanese port of Tjilatjap (current spelling Cilacap) on 28 January 1942. There, the executive officer, Commander Edward. J. "Iron Mike" Moran, USN, was promoted to captain and relieved Captain S. B. Robinson, USN, as the *Boise*'s commanding officer (CO). The ship then proceeded to British Ceylon where it remained for 11 days (9–18 February) awaiting a berth for repairs. When no room for her was found in Colombo, *Boise* departed on 18 February for Bombay (Mumbai), British India, where she went into dry dock.

When temporary repairs were completed, *Boise* got underway from Bombay on 4 April 1942 and made for Mare Island Navy Yard at San Francisco, California, where she underwent an overhaul and refitting for war. *Boise*'s departure from the Southwest Pacific Area (SWPA) without having gotten into the fight earned her the disparaging moniker "the Reluctant Dragon," a slur the crew greatly resented.

While undergoing the overhaul, *Boise* received upgrades to its AA defenses. The improvements included replacement of older types of AA guns with 40-mm and 20-mm cannon, and installation of the latest versions of the FC and FD fire control radars and SC-1 air search and SG-1 surface search systems, that greatly extended their reach. By 20 June 1942 the overhaul was completed, and the ship was again ready for sea. Two days later, *Boise* sailed from San Francisco as escort for a troop convoy bound for New Zealand and put into port at Auckland on 14 July 1942. After four days in New Zealand, she made her way back to Pearl Harbor, arriving there one week later.

By now, it seemed to some of the crew that they were destined to spend the entire war sitting on the sidelines. The "Reluctant Dragon," however, soon got a chance to do something other than playing nursemaid to transport ships. After a quick turnaround at Pearl Harbor, she put to sea on 27 July 1942 to conduct a solitary feint into Japanese home waters aimed at drawing the attention of the IJN away from the Solomon Islands, where U.S. Marines made an amphibious assault on Guadalcanal and Tulagi on 7 August. As part of a clever subterfuge, *Boise* pretended to act as the scout for a nonexistent American naval task force on a mission to raid the Japanese coast. The plans were broadcast by radio so that the enemy would intercept them and hopefully pull some of their warships away from the Solomons to protect their own coast.

Operating alone, the cruiser steamed across the Pacific to within 750 miles of Tokyo. Under orders to attract as much attention as possible to its presence in the area, *Boise* broke radio silence and turned on all her lights at night so the Japanese would know her location. Some of the crew feared this ruse was a bit too risky; operating without destroyer escort could be suicidal if a Japanese submarine or scout planes were to discover a lone cruiser instead of an entire task force. One night at around midnight, four planes flew over, and the crew held their breath until the aircraft passed by and continued on their way without attacking the ship. The cruiser returned to Pearl Harbor on 10 August 1942 without having engaged any Japanese ships or planes. Nevertheless, the crew hoped that by distracting the enemy's attention, they had taken some of the pressure off the Marines landing on Guadalcanal. The only major misfortune suffered during the operation was that *Boise* lost two of her scout planes that failed to return from a reconnaissance flight on 5 August. All hands prayed that the aircrews would be picked up by American submarines before the Japanese could find them. Nothing was ever heard again of the four aviators, so it was assumed that they had perished.

While *Boise* was steaming back to Pearl Harbor, the Japanese fleet handed the U.S. Navy a major defeat in the Solomon Islands. In a night action off Savo Island on 9 August 1942, four Allied heavy cruisers (three American and one Australian) and two destroyers were sunk and another cruiser was damaged. In addition to the loss of these valuable combat ships, over 1,000 men were killed. Two weeks later, a carrier duel in the Eastern Solomons on 24 August resulted in a tactical draw. One Japanese light carrier was sunk and the USS *Enterprise* (CV-6) was damaged and had to withdraw to Pearl Harbor for repairs. A week later, the USS *Saratoga* (CV-3)

USS *Boise* at Espiritu Santo, New Hebrides, August 1942. (USNARA, 80-G-K-558)

was struck by a torpedo from a Japanese submarine that caused sufficient damage that it too had to be pulled back for repairs. These losses compounded an already difficult situation for the Allies, leaving them with only one American aircraft carrier, the USS *Wasp* (CV-7), and one battleship in operable condition in the entire South Pacific. The fight was therefore left up to the so called "light forces," namely cruisers and destroyers. In near desperation, the U.S. Navy now turned to a group of battle-minded skippers to take the fight to the Japanese on the high seas of the South Pacific. One of these seagoing gunslingers was Captain Edward J. Moran, CO of the USS *Boise*, which now deployed to reinforce the task group defending the Marines on Guadalcanal from the IJN.

During part of August and September 1942, *Boise* took part in operations in the SWPA primarily in the New Hebrides and Solomon Islands. From 14–18 September 1942 she joined Rear Admiral Norman Scott's Task Force 64 (TF-64) which was providing cover and support for landing the US Seventh Marines to serve as reinforcements for their fellow leathernecks who were already on Guadalcanal. After this, she returned to Espiritu Santo Island in the New Hebrides archipelago on 21 September. For the next couple of weeks, *Boise* operated in and out of Espiritu Santo, the island immortalized in fictional form in James Michener's *Tales of the South Pacific*.

The Night Brawl off Cape Esperance, 11–12 October 1942

All hands on the *Boise* were pumped with excitement when they put to sea again on 7 October 1942. At last, they were going to get their long-awaited chance to strike a blow against the Japanese fleet. *Boise* was deployed on a search and destroy mission with the cruiser task group TG-64.2 commanded by Admiral Norman Scott, USN.

TG-64.2 comprised the heavy cruisers USS *San Francisco* (CA-38) and *Salt Lake City* (CA-25), *Boise*, and four destroyers—*Buchanan* (DD-484), *Farenholt* (DD-491), *Laffey* (DD-459), and *McCalla* (DD-448). Scott's force was beefed up when it was joined by a Cleveland Class light cruiser and a destroyer, USS *Helena* (CL-50) and *Duncan* (DD-485), as TG-64.2 made its way northwest towards the Solomon Islands. Their specific mission was to strike hard against the "Tokyo Express," as the Allies called the nightly Japanese convoys that were reinforcing and resupplying the enemy garrison on Guadalcanal. The warships that escorted the convoys frequently shelled the beleaguered Marines that were trying to take the island, especially those leathernecks concentrated in the vicinity of the airstrip, Henderson Field. Admiral Scott intended not only to ambush the "Tokyo Express," but also to shoot it out with any IJN surface force that showed itself and get some payback for the heavy losses that the Americans had suffered in the disastrous defeat at Savo Island the previous August.

Although the men of the *Boise* knew they were headed into combat with the enemy against whom they were determined to fight with all their might, they could not have known that the cruiser was also sailing into U.S. Navy legend. The battle that loomed before them would be the first of two major surface actions in which the *Boise* would fight during the war. It would be a brief, bitterly fought, night engagement that would cover them with glory while also bringing them to the brink of disaster.

Twice on 11 October reconnaissance aircraft had reported sightings of an enemy task group said to comprise two heavy cruisers and six destroyers headed at high speed for the northeast point of Guadalcanal, where they were expected to arrive at about 2300. TG-64.2 was ordered to attack this enemy surface force and moved up to intercept them in Savo Sound (aka "the Slot"), the waters situated in the midst of the Solomon Islands group. According to naval historian James Hornfischer's excellent account of the battles in the Solomon Islands entitled *Neptune's Inferno: The U.S. Navy at Guadalcanal*, there were two groups of Japanese ships in the vicinity of Guadalcanal that night. One was the "Tokyo Express," a reinforcement group consisting of two large seaplane tenders and eight destroyers that were transporting troops and supplies to be landed on the island. A separate cruiser group under the command of Rear Admiral Aritomo Goto, IJN, is thought to have been made up of three heavy cruisers—*Aoba* (flag), *Furutaka*, and *Kinugasa*, with an escort of two destroyers—*Fubuki* and *Hatsuyuki*. Admiral Goto's main objective was to attack the Marines at Henderson Field. It appears, however, that there was at least one additional task group of Japanese warships present in Savo Sound that night, which went unreported.

The night was dark with a new moon. A light breeze was blowing, and the seas were calm with a gentle swell. Visibility was about 4,000–5,000 yards. As TG 64.2 moved up to engage the enemy at 2145, the cruisers were in a column with Admiral Scott's flagship *San Francisco* in the lead followed by *Boise, Salt Lake City,* and *Helena*. The five destroyers were in the screen ahead and on the flanks. *Boise* was at GQ and all hands were ready for a fight. Captain Moran and his men were tense and excited as they headed for what would be their first real taste of combat in the war. Everyone on the *Boise* was sick of their ship being derisively called "The Reluctant Dragon," and they were anxious to show the rest of the U.S. Navy, not to mention the Japanese, what they could do. Moran's cruiser was using her electronic eyes and ears to seek out the Japanese task group. According to *Boise* radar technician Vincent A. Langelo, she had the most complete array of state-of-the-art radar technology of any ship in the task group, although the *Helena* also had an SG-1 surface search radar that far outclassed the older SC sets on the heavy cruisers *San Francisco* and *Salt Lake City*. Indeed Scott, a traditional-minded commander who lacked confidence in the new technology, had ordered his flagship not to use its SC radar equipment for fear that the beams might be detected by the Japanese warships. The *San Francisco* also lacked the new electronic FC and FD fire control systems of the *Boise* and had to rely on optical range finders for aiming her guns. Therefore, the task group commander was essentially operating blind, electronically speaking, and was dependent upon *Boise* and *Helena* to report any radar contacts picked up by their superior SG sets.

At 2200, Admiral Scott ordered each cruiser to launch one scout plane to search for the Japanese ships that he believed must be close. *Salt Lake City*'s plane burst into flames on launch and crashed into the sea. The fire, caused by the accidental ignition of a flare on board the aircraft that burned so brightly and for such a long time that some men feared it would alert the enemy to their presence. As luck would have it, Japanese lookouts apparently did see the glow from the burning floatplane, but did not report it as coming from enemy ships.

The two scout planes that were airborne were ordered to seek out the enemy ships, report their position, and then land at Tulagi, one of the smaller islands in the Solomons group that had been occupied by the U.S. Marines. Eighteen minutes later, TG-64.2 moved into attack disposition with three destroyers—*Duncan, Farenholt,* and *Laffey*—in the van, and the other two, *Buchanan* and *McCalla*, bringing up the rear. The cruisers held their same stations in the column with the flagship in the lead, followed by *Boise, Salt Lake City,* and *Helena*.

"Pick out the biggest"

The cruisers' scout planes had no luck in locating the Japanese fleet. The first news *Boise* got of the location of Admiral Goto's cruiser force came at 2338 when its radar detected five ships at a range of 14,000 yards. When he was informed of the radar contact, Moran ordered his Fire Director I, which controlled the forward three turrets of the main battery, to begin tracking the largest ship in the enemy column. The director controlling the starboard 5-inch deck guns locked onto a destroyer on the left flank of the column of three cruisers. The Japanese ships steamed straight ahead apparently oblivious to the presence of TG-64.2. Unless Goto's task group changed course, the Americans would soon "cross his T" leaving them exposed to full broadsides from the American warships, a most unenviable position in which no naval commander ever wants to find himself. "Crossing the T" is a naval maneuver where a group of ships cuts across the heading of an enemy force and unleashes its broadside to strike on the advancing column, which finds itself at a distinct disadvantage in firepower that can be brought to bear.

James Starnes, who was in the *Boise's* chart house on the bridge level of the ship, affirmed in an interview videotaped years later that Moran advised the task group commander that his radar screen clearly showed the group of five Japanese ships and requested permission to open fire. Admiral Scott, however, hesitated. Unfortunately, a botched turn by the flagship a few minutes before the radar contact was reported had thrown the American column into disarray and left the three destroyers in the van steaming off in the dark on the original course to starboard of the cruisers. Unable to see the Japanese ships and not knowing the exact position of his destroyers, Scott feared that the *Boise's* radar might be tracking them instead. *Boise*, however, could clearly distinguish the blips bouncing back off the American destroyers, which were then scurrying past on the cruisers' starboard flank, from those of Admiral Goto's warships. Moran had good range on the enemy column and knew for certain that his own destroyers were much closer than the ships on the radar screen.

Admiral Scott, gripped by uncertainty, continued to wait. James Hornfischer's account of the naval battle of Guadalcanal reveals that Scott's battle plan had instructed his captains to open fire as soon as they had a confirmed fix on the enemy ships without waiting for permission to do so. Instead of complying with this order for some reason, the other cruisers held their fire while Scott made up his mind.

The American task group commander's lack of appreciation for the effectiveness of radar and the new electronic fire control systems led him to pass up the opportunity to strike the unsuspecting Japanese cruiser group when he had them with their pants down. The enemy task group was easily within range of his guns, but lacking sophisticated radar technology, was too blind and distant to be able to fight back effectively. Had the American admiral put his trust in his radar, the battle might have ended as an even greater victory at far less cost than the one he actually won.

As the minutes ticked by, the two opposing task groups approached closer to each other with the Americans "crossing the T" of the Japanese column, but no order to commence firing was forthcoming. The tension mounted as all hands watched the Japanese cruisers getting closer and closer until *Boise's* radar screens revealed them to be only 4,500 yards out. With the enemy vessels now visible even without binoculars, some sailors on the American warships began to wonder if the battle plan was to board them with pistols and cutlasses, as was the practice in the days of sail. The Japanese column still ignored the American warships bearing down on them and continued on the same heading. Finally, *Helena,* which was also tracking the enemy formation on its SG radar, could wait no longer and requested permission to commence firing. Receiving what was understood to be an affirmative reply, the American cruiser let loose a broadside at 2346. The *Salt Lake City* immediately followed suit and began blazing away at the lead enemy cruiser that now was at point-blank range.

Seeing the opening salvo from *Salt Lake City* just behind him, Moran barked an order to his gunnery officer: "Commence firing." Illuminating the lead enemy cruiser with its starboard searchlights and using full radar control, *Boise*'s main battery flung a broadside of 15 AP projectiles, several of which slammed into the Japanese heavy cruiser amidships, which was also taking hits in her superstructure from the *Salt Lake City.* Simultaneously, the 5-inch guns of the starboard secondary battery blasted away at the destroyer they had been tracking. After the initial salvo, both batteries went into continuous rapid-fire mode. The flames spouting from the gun barrels lit up the night, and their thunder was deafening. The recoil from the big guns rocked the ship violently enough to knock a man off his feet. Red tracer shells seemed to float across the water, but kicked up blinding flashes from the explosions as the projectiles found their mark. After only four minutes of pounding by the two American cruisers at nearly point-blank range (about 4,000 yards), the Japanese cruiser exploded, broke in two, and sank, "going down by the bows with her screws still turning, and her turrets apparently still trained in." The enemy destroyer that was hammered by *Boise*'s 5-inch guns also sank after being ripped apart by a several huge explosions.

At 2350, just four minutes after shooting began, both enemy targets disappeared from *Boise*'s radar screens, and the men on deck watched them slip beneath the waves. The cruiser then briefly checked fire, having expended about 300 6-inch and 120 5-inch rounds. According to Electrician's Mate First Class Garnett Moneymaker, stationed topside on the searchlights, *Boise* not only had done the illuminating, but also had done most of the shooting. *Salt Lake City* had fired only three salvos while the Japanese cruiser, which he described as "a pretty ship and large," never got off a shot.

Boise quickly shifted targets of which there were five still showing on the radar scopes. The men on deck celebrated having drawn first blood. Lieutenant Commander Thomas Wolverton, USN, the damage control officer, who was broadcasting a running account of the battle over the *Boise*'s PA system, passed the news throughout the ship, and the men below decks joined in the jubilant cheering. Boatswain's Mate (BM) Paul Wilkes from Macon, Georgia, told his hometown newspaper in a 1944 interview that when the shooting stopped after the first four minutes, he naively believed the battle to be over, thinking to himself that there really wasn't much to this whole combat thing.

The celebration abruptly ended when the skipper ordered the gunnery officer to shift target and resume firing. *Boise's* director was already locked on another Japanese destroyer in the vicinity of the one just sunk. Both batteries began pumping lead into the enemy tin can until a large explosion was seen on board, and it too disappeared from the radar screen after a two-minute pummeling.

Moneymaker, watching from his vantage point on the searchlights, described it thusly: "There is a large explosion (very red) on the four-stacker, she heels over and goes down. The Japs are wearing white uniforms." Paul Wilkes declared that once the action resumed following the brief interlude, things really "began to get hot."

After sinking the second enemy tin can, *Boise* again checked fire, but immediately shifted her guns to engage a larger ship to the right of where the second destroyer had gone down. The guns were still operating under full radar control, but now fired without illumination by the searchlights. Fires broke out on the bow of the target vessel, lighting up her midsection for a short time and revealing her to be a two-stacked cruiser, which Moran's action report described as "unmistakably Japanese, with the trunked forward stack and latticed tripod mainmast close to the after stack." The enemy cruiser returned fire, and several stations on *Boise* reported the shriek of large projectiles passing overhead. Subsequent salvos straddled, and shells splashed 50 feet short and to port of the American cruiser. The geysers kicked up by the shorts sprayed great quantities of water over the starboard AA battery and after superstructure, reaching high enough to drench Petty Officer Moneymaker at his battle station high up on the searchlights.

As *Boise* followed *San Francisco* into a turn at 2354, an 8-inch projectile struck her side armor, indenting the armor plate about three inches and penetrating the side plating just above the armor belt. That shell exploded in the *Boise's* forward mess hall causing minor damage. A moment later, the cruiser was hit again, this time by two or three smaller shells on the starboard side of the superstructure between the main deck and the communications platform. These hits caused minor personnel casualties in the area near deck gun number 5. Shell fragments riddled a 5-inch ready box and set off several rounds of ammunition. Other shells from the salvo demolished the captain's cabin, setting it on fire, and cutting all power and communications to 5-inch gun number 1 as well as knocking out *Boise's* TBS radio, which was used to talk with other ships in the task group.

Deck gun number 1 was temporarily silenced by a blast from a shell that knocked the gun crew to their knees and wounded several men in the immediate vicinity. A piece of shrapnel badly mangled one sailor's knee, and he had to be carried away to a medical aid station. A gunner on 5-inch gun number 3 also was hit in the leg by shrapnel, but remained in the fight to the end. When the sailor finally collapsed, he was taken to the sick bay where the surgeons dug 32 shell fragments out of his leg and showed him a two-inch hole in his steel helmet made by another. Two men stationed up in the searchlights were also wounded by shrapnel. Moneymaker was struck near the corner of his right eye and another sailor caught one in the leg. Fortunately, their injuries were not serious, and everyone else up there was all right.

The men of the *Boise* were so busy doing their jobs that it apparently never occurred to them that their own ship might get hit. When the first enemy barrage slammed into the ship, a salty CPO who served as a trainer in the forward director roared indignantly, "What the hell! The '*sonuvabitches*' are shooting back at us!"

Despite several 8-inch hits, *Boise* continued blasting the enemy heavy cruiser, which soon burst into flames and burned brightly. The starboard side deck gunners, who had been knocked down by the exploding shells that destroyed the skipper's cabin, quickly regained their feet and resumed firing. Even deck gun number 1 got back into the fight. The gun captain, realizing that his communications with the fire director had been cut, quickly checked his gun and informed the secondary battery officer and the chief boatswain's mate who was his immediate superior that he thought the gun could be fired manually and wanted to give it try. Although attempting to fire a damaged gun could be extremely dangerous—it could explode killing everyone around it—both the battery officer and the chief, who had complete confidence in the skills of the gun captain and his crew, gave their consent. The young lieutenant sweated it out as he watched the first shell being loaded by hand. The first shot was a direct hit on the Japanese heavy cruiser, and two more followed as the deck gun manually pumped out round after round. Near the end of the four-minute gun duel, the Japanese ship was enveloped in smoke. According to Moran's action report, several huge explosions ripped through her at 2357 "and she was not seen again."

An enemy destroyer that was already ablaze became *Boise*'s next victim. The wounded cruiser's guns poured tracer shells into the tin can for two minutes until it too disappeared from the radar screens shortly after midnight (now 12 October).

As the American formation was completing a series of three turns, a sharp-eyed signalman spotted a torpedo wake running "hot and true" at the *Boise*. The skipper immediately threw the big ship into a hard-right turn at breakneck speed to parallel the course of the torpedo, which narrowly missed the port bow. A second torpedo wake was also seen passing aft along the starboard side as the cruiser's stern swung clear of it by barely 50 yards.

Tom Wolverton, who continued his play-by-play broadcast of the action over the PA system, reported the torpedo sightings throughout the ship. Everyone held their breath for seconds that seemed like hours until the news came that the deadly fish had missed them. That most welcome news was met with a great sigh of relief by all hands, especially those stationed below-decks. Everyone knew that a single one of these deadly "fish"—the Type 93 torpedo, known to the Americans as a Long Lance—could sink a cruiser with its 490 kg (1,100 lb.) warhead if it struck the ship in the right place.

Once the torpedoes had sped harmlessly by, *Boise* turned back hard left to retake her position in the cruiser column and bring her guns to bear on the enemy once again. Meanwhile, the fire in the captain's cabin had been extinguished, the hole in the side at the waterline had been patched with mattresses, and members of the gun crews of the starboard 5-inch battery, who had been assisting the damage control party, returned to their guns.

At that moment (0009), the search radar revealed a new enemy target. After illuminating it with the searchlights, *Boise* began pouring effective, continuous fire into what was identified as a Japanese destroyer. Fires broke out on the tin can, which returned fire scoring four hits on the American cruiser between the second and third decks.

At this point in the battle, Iron Mike's Irish luck ran out. Almost simultaneously, *Boise* was engaged by a heavy cruiser that suddenly appeared some distance from the original position of the enemy column and just forward of *Boise*'s beam. The enemy ship's abrupt appearance on that bearing led Moran to conclude that this attacker had not been part of the original Japanese formation. The big cruiser fired on *Boise* unopposed for about three minutes (0009–0012), "shooting beautifully" from twin 8-inch gun mounts with "rapid control and good dispersion," according to Moran. The enemy projectiles straddled the American cruiser repeatedly along the forward half of her forecastle, scoring several hits; one shell slammed into the barbette of turret 1 and exploded in the gun room starting a fire at 0010. Another projectile blasted turret 3's faceplate. Despite the huge explosion from the shell, which caused considerable damage and filled the turret with smoke, the Marines manning it were able to fire two more rounds from each of their three guns before they ran out of ammunition after another Japanese shell hit their magazine.

In the shootout with the heavy cruiser, the stricken *Boise* was clearly outmatched by the enemy's 8-inch guns. Given her course, that took her headlong at her attacker, she was only able to engage the enemy with her forward turrets until they were knocked out of action. The two after turrets and the starboard secondary battery continued concentrating fire on the Japanese destroyer that was attacking their ship from astern.

The enemy tin can then put two 5-inch shells into the hull of the beleaguered *Boise*, but they passed all the way through and exited the port side without detonating, thus causing only minimal damage. Then, at 0011, *Boise* received a crippling blow. An 8-inch shell from the Japanese heavy cruiser penetrated her hull nine feet below the waterline and exploded in the large, 6-inch magazine located between the handling rooms of turrets 1 and 2. The tremendous blast tore through all forward main battery magazines and handling rooms, except for those of turret 3, although the interior of that turret was filled with flames that were entering through the forward scuttle. Burning gases swept through turrets 1 and 2 setting them afire as well. Quick action by the officer in charge of turret 1 got some of the men out of the gun room before the shell exploded. But all the men in the handling rooms and magazines (mostly African-American and Guamanian sailors) as well as the entire gun crew of turret 2 and those who were unable to get out of turret 1 were killed immediately. This spectacular explosion brightly lit up the surrounding area. Burning gases poured from turrets 1 and 2, starting fires on the forecastle deck and burning the men who seconds before had managed to escape from turret 1's gun room.

Seeing the stunning explosions and flames on the *Boise*, the other American ships thought that the gallant ship had been dealt a death blow. But the intrepid light cruiser was not done for yet and turned to major damage control even as it continued to fight. An order to flood the magazines could not be carried out because the power had been cut, and the men on the control panel were dead. One sailor heroically attempted to carry out the order, but he was overcome by toxic gases, dying before he could reach the valves. Although it was impossible to flood the magazines deliberately, these areas were flooded by seawater pouring in through the gaping hole the shell had punched in the hull as well as the breaches in various watertight seals caused by the huge explosion. This accidental flooding put out the fires before the *Boise*'s own ammunition could be set off, which surely would have doomed the ship and sent her to the bottom of the sound.

At 0012 the Japanese tin can, firing from the aft position, put two 5-inch rounds through *Boise*'s hull near the waterline, causing further extensive flooding below decks. These hits sent a strong "wave motion" sweeping through the cruiser, leading some sailors to believe they had taken a torpedo somewhere in the forward section of the ship. Up in the CIC and radio shack, *Boise*'s radar expert, Vince Langelo, thought the ship was sinking, so he put on his life vest and went out on deck, remaining there to watch the final minutes of the battle.

Caught in a punishing crossfire between two Japanese assailants, one forward and one aft, Moran had to take quick evasive action, even at the risk of losing sight of his flagship and becoming separated from the column. To escape the deadly barrages, the skipper threw *Boise* into a hard-left turn, broke out of the column, and rammed the speed up to 30 knots. This sudden, high-speed course change came not a minute too soon. The next 8-inch salvo from the heavy cruiser fell short by 50–100 yards, or just about where the *Boise* would have been had she maintained the same heading. As the embattled light cruiser turned, her after 6-inch and starboard secondary batteries continued shooting for as long as possible; they ceased firing only when they were no longer able to train the guns on their attackers (0013). The enemy destroyer they had been targeting was seen to explode moments later after taking hits from both *Boise* and *Salt Lake City*. As *Boise* veered away, the *Salt Lake City* moved up into a position that effectively shielded the badly burning *Boise* from the enemy cruiser's guns, but the conflagration on the stricken light cruiser perfectly silhouetted the American heavy cruiser for the Japanese gunners to score several hits on her. Moran later had high praise for the skipper of the *Salt Lake City,* Captain Ernest G. Small, USN, whose gallant act saved his crippled warship even though it put his own ship at risk. Moran also asserted that together they were able to silence and sink the Japanese cruiser, but the American heavy cruiser also suffered considerable damage in the process.

Boise sustained severe damage and heavy casualties. All three forward turrets were knocked out of action, and turrets 1 and 2 were consumed in flames. The fires topside could be seen for miles in dark night. With her hull punctured in several places, the cruiser was flooding extensively. Iron Mike urgently needed a more complete damage assessment. Therefore, he rounded his course to move away from the battle and give his men a chance to complete the assessment and undertake damage control to keep the ship afloat.

The light cruiser was down by the bow and listing pronouncedly to starboard; both list and trim were increasing as the flooding progressed. It was obvious that the ship's combat capabilities had been critically reduced. Under no circumstances would the crew be able to get back into the fight. It made little difference, however, because by then the battle was over, and the remnants of the bloodied Japanese task group were retiring. The night went black once again, and an eerie silence fell over the dark waters of the Slot, which ultimately became known as Iron Bottom Sound because of all the ships sunk there during the Solomons' campaign.

Boise remained on a heading away from the scene of the battle while all hands turned to fighting fires, controlling flooding, and rescuing trapped personnel as well as tending to their wounded. The heroism displayed by her crew in the fight with the Japanese was now equaled in their struggle to keep their ship afloat, assist their less fortunate shipmates, and recover the dead. This grim work continued on through the following days.

BM Paul Wilkes later described the combat off Guadalcanal on the night of 11–12 October 1942 as "hotter" than the Normandy invasion of 6 June 1944, in which he also participated. Wilkes was hit by shrapnel during the Cape Esperance gunfight while manning one of the starboard 5-inch guns, which he did not realize until the fighting ceased. With flames pouring from the ship all around, all hands able to do so had to turn to firefighting. After about two hours, the conflagration was finally brought under control, and Wilkes went down to the sick bay to seek medical attention for a shoulder wound. Upon seeing so many of his shipmates being treated for far more serious wounds, he decided that his own injury was little more than a scratch. The young boatswain's mate, who had joined the navy in 1938, served on the *Boise* for four years; he was reassigned to another ship when the cruiser returned to Philadelphia for repairs after the Battle of Cape Esperance.

By 0240, all fires had been extinguished. The ship was seven feet down at the bow, but all flooding was now under control. Thanks to superhuman efforts spearheaded by damage control officer Tom Wolverton, *Boise* was still afloat and able to proceed under her own power. When she finally reappeared from out of the darkness to rejoin the column at 0245, to those on the other American ships, who feared she had been sunk, her reappearance seemed almost miraculous. They were happy to see her.

Two of Admiral Scott's tin cans, *Duncan* and *Farenholt*, had been heavily damaged by friendly fire from the heavy cruisers as well as by Japanese ordnance. According to Moneymaker, the *Boise* herself poured eight rounds into the *Duncan* when the latter ship suddenly crossed her line of fire. Vince Langelo, however, believed that it was the *San Francisco*'s 8-inch shells that hit the hapless destroyer, judging from the dye stains found all over the tin can's main decks, which were the same color used in the *San Francisco*'s shells. In the first naval battle of Guadalcanal on 13 November 1942, the *Frisco* also accidently hit the anti-aircraft cruiser *Atlanta* (CLAA-51), which was lost in that night engagement. At any rate, the *McCalla* was left behind to try to salvage the *Duncan* and rescue survivors. The destroyer picked up 195 men, nearly the entire crew, but the little tin can was damaged beyond repair and had to be scuttled. The *Farenholt*, like the *Boise*, withdrew from the fight to conduct damage control and finally was able to limp back to Espiritu Santo Island some 50 miles behind the rest of TG-64.2.

Boise's participation in what naval historian James Hornfischer (*Neptune's Inferno*) has called a "shot-guns across the table" gun fight lasted a mere 27 minutes, during which time she took on six enemy ships, scoring direct hits on each and every one of them. Using automatic-continuous mode, both she and *Helena* were firing so hot and heavy that American sailors on a nearby destroyer compared the staccato sound of their salvos to machine-gun fire, while the Japanese captains on the receiving end of these blistering barrages later reported the appearance of "machine gun cruisers" at Cape Esperance. At one point in the thick of the fighting, Admiral Scott called for a cease fire, fearing that his destroyers might be targeted by the "blow-torching" light cruisers. *Boise* and several other ships never let up, however, fearing that to check fire would be too risky. According to Langelo, the *Boise*, at least, always knew which ships she was targeting with deadly barrages thanks to Moran's constant, expert use of radar during the night battle.

In his action report dated 22 October 1942, Moran asserted that the Japanese force that TG-64.2 actually engaged on the night of 11–12 October was "considerably more powerful" than the two cruisers and six destroyers that had been reported by the search aircraft earlier in the day. The *Boise*'s skipper was convinced that there were three groups of Japanese warships at Cape Esperance. By his count, the first group attacked by TG-64.2 consisted of three cruisers and three destroyers. The second group that appeared during the gun duel was of unknown composition, but Moran believed the heavy cruiser that crippled his cruiser with 8-inch gunfire was part of this unreported force.

A third group of three ships was first sighted by *San Francisco*'s scout plane at 2250, and later identified by the *Boise* senior aviator, Lieutenant R.C. Bartlett, after he had put his SOC floatplane down on the water close to the shore of Guadalcanal at 2330 because of an oil pressure problem. The Seagull pilot and his air crewman were close enough to watch the action during the battle, but in the dark, they could not always distinguish with absolute certainty which ships were which. They picked out one ship in the left-hand column that they took to be the *Boise,* because of the rapidity of her salvos, which lit up the night. They saw this cruiser take several hits before coming under attack from another ship that joined the enemy column on the right. The target ship was then fighting two vessels to its right, and the devastating effect of the double pounding was apparent to the two flyers. Suddenly, the bow of the target ship exploded shooting flames high above her masts. The burning cruiser then turned to port, and it was obvious that her part in the battle was over. As it turned, it continued firing, but with only a few of its guns; those in her forward section were silent. The sea then suddenly grew quiet, and the dark closed in again as the shootout ended.

Bartlett and his radioman discussed the fierce gun battle that they had witnessed and wondered which side had won. They were fairly certain that the light cruiser they had been observing was the *Boise*. They fell silent, however, when they heard the sound of a diesel engine through the night and made out the shape of a vessel passing them to the west. It was part of a third group of three Japanese ships, which passed the American flyers at about 200 yards, close enough for their wakes to cause the little biplane to bob about, but fortunately the enemy lookouts did not spot them in the dark. Bartlett identified the three vessels as a small, single stack cruiser or large minelayer, a diesel-powered ship with a widely separated bridge and stack that he believed to be the minelayer *Itsukushima*, and a small destroyer or destroyer escort.

After the enemy ships passed, Bartlett decided to get the hell out of there before he was seen by Japanese soldiers on the nearby beach or those on the sea. He cranked up his SOC floatplane and took off, putting down again in the water between Tulagi and Florida islands, which he knew were in the hands of the U.S. Marines, and waited for sunrise. Just after daylight, the *Boise* airmen were picked up by a landing barge, and their plane was towed to Tulagi, where they spent the rest of the day with the Marines while the Seagull's oil line problem was repaired. The following day (13 October) they flew off to rejoin the task group, but had to be picked up by one of the other cruisers since the *Boise* was in no condition to receive them back aboard.

At final count, *Boise* lost 107 men (including three officers) killed, and 45 enlisted personnel were severely wounded. Among the cruiser's casualties were not only those wounded in body, but several who were wounded in spirit, or, as Moneymaker phrased it, had gone "batty." Captain Moran stated in his action report that he took some consolation from the fact that all of his men who died did so knowing that they had sunk at least three enemy ships and others were soon to follow.

During the voyage back to Espiritu Santo on the morning after the battle (12 October) the cleanup proceeded, wounded continued to be pulled from the wreckage, and the bodies of dead sailors and Marines were collected for burial. Sixty-seven bodies were recovered from areas that were accessible during the voyage, and were sewn into canvas shrouds with a 6-inch shell between their legs in preparation for burial at sea. With permission from Admiral Scott, who detached a destroyer to protect her from enemy submarines, *Boise* dropped out of the formation in order to commit the bodies of these brave warriors to the sea on 13 October 1942. Burial of the remaining 40 dead had to wait until their remains could be pulled from the wrecked and flooded areas of the ship once the hull had been temporarily patched and the seawater pumped out. Nineteen of them were recovered and buried on Espiritu Santo Island two days after the battle, while the final 21, all unidentified, were interred at Noumea, New Caledonia, on 21 October once further repairs had been made.

After the moving burial service, *Boise* limped into Espiritu Santo several hours behind the rest of TF 64.2. When the badly mauled cruiser stood into the harbor, the other ships in the anchorage saluted as it passed, hoisting the signal flags for "Well done." Their crews manned the rails and gave a rousing cheer for the now not-so "Reluctant Dragon." *Boise*'s communicators were kept busy all day receiving congratulatory messages sent by the COs of other ships in the harbor. One message from Admiral Scott's flagship, the *San Francisco*, expressed the admiration of the officers and crew for their "spirit and fighting ability." In this manner, the other warships of Vice Admiral William F. Halsey's fleet demonstrated their full appreciation for the fierce and determined fight that the men of the "Noisy *Boise*" put up against the IJN, and also for the following hours and days when they struggled to save their crippled ship. The day after *Boise* arrived at Espiritu Santo, a debriefing was held by Admiral Scott on board the *San Francisco*. Vince Langelo wrote in his history of the *Boise* that the consensus at the meeting was that the task group had sunk six Japanese ships, for which his ship was given most of the credit.

Moran's action report estimated that of the six Japanese ships his cruiser fired on during the engagement, three destroyers and two heavy cruisers were sunk and another heavy cruiser was severely damaged and probably sunk. Moran speculated that perhaps as many as 2,000–3,000 Japanese crewmen on these ships might have been killed. In the brief gunfight, *Boise* expended 803 6-inch and 605 5-inch rounds, with all guns firing on full radar control. Since her participation in the close-range gun duel lasted only 27 minutes, this was the equivalent of 9–12 rounds per gun per minute. Moran proudly noted that his 5-inch battery had sunk one Japanese destroyer totally unaided. The skipper was extremely proud of his ship's gunnery performance, which he declared to be:

… above our highest expectations in every particular. Rapidity and accuracy of fire, fire discipline, and absence of material casualties were all without precedence in target practice. Perfect fire discipline was an especially conspicuous feature. At the orders "Commence Firing" continuous fire began instantly. When ordered to cease or check fire, the batteries responded at once. In an action involving relatively brief bursts of fire and frequent target shifts, the importance of such positive control can scarcely be overemphasized.

The *Boise's* skipper also had high praise for his officers and men. Allowing for the normal confusion of a night action, the heavy damage sustained, and the large number of casualties, there were "no personnel failures." He went on: "Except as the direct result of enemy hits, the ship's organization functioned smoothly, effectively, and without a break throughout the action and during the difficult and dangerous damage control work which followed."

The skipper's report lauding his gunnery division's performance in the battle caught the attention of, and garnered praise from, the senior naval leadership in the Pacific, who began to see the advantages provided by radar. Admiral "Bull" Halsey, a scrappy old seadog who appreciated a seagoing gunslinger when he saw one, was greatly impressed by Moran's recounting of how the *Boise* used her radar systems to control her lethal, rapid-fire barrages and, in his endorsement of the report, commended both the skipper and crew for their "brilliant battle performance." Admiral Chester W. Nimitz, Commander in Chief Pacific Fleet (CINCPAC), later praised the *Boise's* "excellent" gunnery and damage control and pointed out that radar was the big advantage for the American task force. Nimitz added that Scott's "clear-cut victory" off Guadalcanal showed that our "light forces" are "equal or superior" to those of the enemy. It should be noted, however, that while the Americans won a tactical victory at the Battle of Cape Esperance, and spared the Marines at Henderson Field from yet another naval bombardment that night, TG-64.2 failed to stop the "Tokyo Express" from reinforcing the Japanese garrison on Guadalcanal. The battle for control of the Solomon Islands raged on for several more months on both land and sea.

While the *Boise* was at Noumea, Admiral Halsey held a ceremony on board to decorate members of the crew for their performance in the Battle of Cape Esperance. Fourteen officers and four enlisted men received medals that day. Moneymaker was so irked by what he saw as unfair favoritism shown the officers that he penned a protest in his war diary. The Electrician's Mate was especially disgusted by the fact that two officers killed in turrets 1 and 2 were given the Navy Cross while no mention was made of the enlisted men who died with them. He argued convincingly that if a medal were awarded to one, then all should have received the same distinction.

After completing repairs at Noumea, the crippled *Boise* got underway on 24 October 1942 for California to undergo further repairs and overhaul. En route, however, her orders were changed, and the cruiser was sent instead to the Philadelphia Navy Yard where the work load was lighter. She limped across the Pacific under

USS *Boise* arriving at Philadelphia Navy Yard for repairs, November 1942. (USNARA, 80-G-300235)

her own steam, transited the Panama Canal (13 November), and arrived at Philadelphia on 19 November 1942. There the damaged cruiser received another rousing reception complete with a brass band playing as it docked. In his welcome home speech, Chief of Naval Operations Admiral Ernest J. King, USN, referred to the scrappy cruiser as "A One Ship Fleet." The phrase was picked up by the press from a publicity campaign aimed at boosting the morale of the American people by hyping this naval victory over the heretofore seemingly invincible IJN. *Boise* received so much press attention crediting her with sinking six Japanese warships in 27 minutes that she literally became a legend in her own time, both at home and abroad. One key piece of that PR campaign was Frank D. Morris's highly readable book entitled *Pick out the Biggest* (1943), which lauded the *Boise*'s performance in the Battle of Cape Esperance.

The actual number of Japanese ships sunk in the night battle later became a bone of contention. Admiral Scott's task group believed that they had sunk six Japanese ships. While the *Boise* skipper's action report for the Battle of Cape Esperance indicates that he believed his ship sank at least five ships (two cruisers and three destroyers), Moran openly admitted that in some cases other American ships were also firing on the same enemy vessel as the *Boise*. At the time, she sported six Japanese flags with their corresponding ships' silhouettes on the "scoreboard"

USS *Boise* scoreboard showing six Japanese flags for enemy ships sunk at Cape Esperance, 1942. (USNARA, 80-G-36229)

painted on her superstructure. Nevertheless, official navy documents prepared after the war credited *Boise* with having sunk only three ships: one enemy cruiser and two destroyers.

Captain Tameichi Hara, IJN, in his history of the Japanese navy claims that his fleet lost only one cruiser and a destroyer that night. James Hornfischer, who consulted Japanese as well as American sources, credits Admiral Scott's TF-64 with sinking one Japanese heavy cruiser and three destroyers as well as severely damaging a second heavy cruiser, the *Aoba*, flagship of Admiral Goto, who was himself killed in the battle. It should be noted, however, that Hornfischer identifies two of the Japanese destroyers as ships belonging to the "Tokyo Express" reinforcement group, so evidently there were at least seven enemy ships, rather than just the five said to have been in Goto's bombardment group, that took part in the night action. Hornfischer appears not to have consulted *Boise*'s action report as it is not listed among his sources. A word of caution is perhaps in order here. Although the U.S. Navy sometimes inflated the numbers of enemy ships sunk or damaged in battle, the Japanese were notorious for consistently underreporting their own losses while grossly exaggerating American losses in every major naval battle of the war. Therefore, it would be inadvisable to give too much credibility to the Japanese statistics from this particular engagement.

The day after the battle, the American media reported that the U.S. Navy had been victorious in an engagement with a Japanese fleet off Guadalcanal on the night of 11–12 October, in which they had sunk seven enemy ships and damaged one. Of nine American ships participating in the battle, one was reported to have been severely damaged. No names of any of the ships or further details were given, nor was any mention made of the destroyer that had to be abandoned and scuttled. On the other hand, Tokyo Rose lambasted TG-64.2 as a group of pirates that had cowardly and savagely attacked the Japanese fleet at the Battle of Cape Esperance. Nevertheless, she boasted with her usual hyperbole that the Japanese sank all of the American ships in yet another glorious victory.

Boise radar technician Vince Langelo, who was in the CIC and the transmitter room on the cruiser's signal bridge from the outset of the battle, tells it differently in his history of the *Boise*. For a while, Langelo watched the action on the radar scopes while listening to Wolverton's play-by-play broadcast over the ship's PA system. Later, after his cruiser had dodged a couple of torpedoes and had been hit twice by large-caliber projectiles, thinking the ship was sinking, he put on his life jacket and went out on deck from where he watched the final minutes of the battle. His dramatic, firsthand account of the brief, but ferocious, night action asserts that the *Boise* sank at least five IJN warships—one heavy cruiser, three destroyers, and a fifth, unidentified ship. In addition, he also declared that *Boise* fired on another Japanese cruiser until violent explosions were seen on board her, at which point his ship ceased firing, apparently believing the enemy vessel was sinking. Moneymaker, who witnessed the battle from his battle station on the searchlights high up on the *Boise*'s superstructure, recorded in his memoirs that his ship sank two Japanese cruisers and three destroyers. His war journal referred to the press campaign as a "big gooey spill in the papers." In a telephone interview with the author (14 July 2013), he declared that the claim of six ships sunk was inflated to boost American public morale, but he knew that the cruiser sank, or helped to sink, three or four enemy ships.

The media attention given to the *Boise* sparked jealousy among some who had served on the other ships that fought at Cape Esperance. This may have influenced the navy's decision to give her credit for sinking only three enemy warships. Perhaps in reacting to post-war attempts to tarnish *Boise*'s legend, Langelo affirmed that she had indeed outperformed the other American warships, and marshaled considerable evidence to back up his assertion. His firsthand account sets forth a well-documented, detailed analysis of why the *Boise* performed so well and outshone the other cruisers in the battle. He attributes her superior performance to four fundamental factors: training, proficiency, teamwork, and superior radar and fire control technology. Langelo, who was one of the U.S. Navy's top radar experts in 1942, points out that the latest and most sophisticated air and surface search radar and fire director systems in the world were installed on the *Boise*. No other ship in the task group, not even the *Helena*, had such a complete array of state-of-the-art technology. As *Boise*'s radar systems were top secret, photographs of the ship and news reports of her performance in the battle were tightly censored by the U.S. Navy. More than 50 years after the war ended, and with the promulgation of the Freedom of Information Act that saw many important documents declassified, Langelo decided that the time had come to publish the "true story" of the *Boise* in the Battle of Cape Esperance.

With electronic warfare still in its infancy, Admiral Scott, like many senior naval officers of the day who were reluctant to rely on radar in night engagements, preferred to stick to the traditional practice of waiting for visual contact with the enemy, thus until his ships were almost on top of the enemy flotilla before attacking them. In the Battle of Savo Island on 9 August 1942, such adherence to accepted naval doctrine led American commanders to surrender the advantage afforded by the element of surprise, resulting in a tragic, costly defeat for their forces. On the other hand, Japanese naval commanders were quick to recognize the technological superiority in radar-controlled gunfire that had given the Americans an important edge at Cape Esperance, declaring that it had a "bad influence" on their crews' morale. These failures to take advantage of superior technology bring to mind a wisecrack that was often repeated among sailors when this author served in the U.S. Navy in the late 1960s: "The Navy: 200 years of tradition totally unhampered by progress."

On the other hand, Moran, the *Boise*'s more progressive-minded CO, was a firm believer in the value of technology and made sure that his men were well-trained and highly proficient in its use. "Iron Mike" Moran was a tough skipper who ran a very tight ship, but he was fair and had a deep appreciation of the abilities of his men. He encouraged the development of a winning, can-do attitude in his crew and made sure they were trained to the point of maximum efficiency. Langelo was unequivocal in stating that Moran's use of radar direction for controlling his guns, and his expert ship handling, were key to the *Boise*'s success and survival in the night action. Instead of wasting time collecting data from reports of the enemy's position changes and plotting the information on charts, Moran and his gunnery officer were glued to an SG monitor on the *Boise*'s bridge, and their orders were based on the up-to-the-minute data displayed on the screen. Thus, they were able to finish off one enemy ship while simultaneously picking out their next victim.

Thanks to such judicious use of technology and the high level of proficiency of her gun crews, *Boise* was able to maintain an accurate, blistering rate of fire of up to 12 rounds per minute per gun during the Battle of Cape Esperance. From studying the action reports of the ships that participated in the engagement, Langelo found that the *Helena* fired only 900 rounds while *Boise* spit out 1,405 shells. The heavy cruisers shot only about a third as many shells—471 rounds for the *Salt Lake City* and 462 rounds for the *San Francisco*. He deduces that the "Old Noisy *Boise*" fired the greatest number of projectiles because of its proficient tracking team, who constantly had accurate radar ranges and bearings and thus knew exactly which ships they were targeting.

From Langelo's analysis, it is clear that radar gave his ship "an ace in the hole" in the night shootout off Cape Esperance. She not only had the edge on the enemy, but also had an advantage over the other ships in the task force with the possible exception of the *Helena*. The U.S. Navy apparently learned a lesson from the disastrous surface battles in the Solomon Islands campaign and began installing the latest and best radar on more and more of its warships. After 1942, the Americans never fought another surface battle without it, and never again suffered another disaster like those in the Solomons.

Refitted and Ready for Action

The now famous *Boise*—the "One Ship Fleet"—remained at Philadelphia until refitting was completed on 20 March 1943. As part of the upgrades, she was given the latest AA guns available, including two quad-mount Bofors 40mm guns (one on each side), and wherever space could be found, an additional number of single-mount 20mm cannons on both sides of the ship. In addition to the new guns, the latest generation of top-secret radar equipment was installed allowing her to positively identify as friend or foe any ship that appeared on her radar screens. All of this new technology made her a formidable, modern warship that posed a deadly threat to any enemy that crossed her path.

From 20 March through 23 April 1943, under command of her new skipper, Captain Leo Hewlett Thebaud, USN, *Boise* conducted training and sea trials out of Norfolk in the Chesapeake Bay and nearby areas of the Atlantic Ocean, with a return visit to Philadelphia during 11–22 April. During these sea trials, the *Boise* tested her new AA weapons as well as her main battery and the new fire control and AA radar equipment. One innovation they practiced was the use of the 6-inch battery to defend against air attack, which the new equipment now made practicable. For target practice they used a remote-controlled drone. Thanks to their new radar and guns, the drone was knocked down after only two salvos. The efforts to perfect the use of the main battery for AA defense would later pay off for the *Boise* when she had to confront Japanese suicide planes in the Philippines (1944–45). The intensive training exercises continued through the month of May until all divisions on the ship were as well-prepared as possible for whatever their respective assignments and responsibilities would be when they went back into combat.

Avery, who had been serving aboard *Boise* since 3 April 1943, was happy to be involved in preparing the ship to return to combat duty. Even though the crew was busy with training drills and other duties, there was time to dwell on thoughts of family and friends back home. Avery wrote letters home whenever he could, but they spent a lot of time at sea and often had to wait for the chance to send or receive mail, which at times was accomplished by using one of the ship's floatplanes. As the moment approached for the cruiser to return to sea duty, he repeatedly reassured his wife, telling her not to worry about him because the scuttlebutt was that they would be assigned to convoy duty in the Atlantic, where they would only have German U-boats (submarines) to contend with. In his letters he always asked her to send him all the news from home. On May 4, 1943, he pointedly asked: "Did they draft any of the married men yet? I guess all the boys are getting worried now. It looks like their numbers are coming up soon. I don't care though. I'll be glad to see some of them have to go. They tried so hard to keep from going."

He told Anne that he preferred she not go to work in the nearby city of Macon during her vacation, but recommended that she stay home and rest instead. He closed this particular letter, as he often did, with the query, "I just wonder if you miss me just as much as I miss you. I love you very much."

It should be noted that Anne did not follow Avery's wishes and later that year went to work in the Quartermaster's office at the US Army Air Force (USAAF) base in Warner Robins, Georgia. For her valuable service to the USAAF, she was awarded a certificate of appreciation. In 1943, both Anne and Avery were doing their part for the war effort; she on the home front and her husband in the Mediterranean Sea.

CHAPTER TWO

Operation *Husky*: The Invasion of Sicily

Just two months after reporting aboard ship, Avery's long-awaited chance to get into the war was suddenly thrust upon him. The *Boise* was deploying, but they were not going to be escorting convoys to England, as the scuttlebutt had it. Instead, on 8 June 1943, *Boise* steamed out of Norfolk with Task Force 65 (TF-65) bound for the Mediterranean Sea, where the Allies were mopping up after defeating the Germans and Italians in North Africa and preparing to invade southern Europe through Italy. They were going to take part in the invasion of Sicily. TF-65 was led by one of *Boise's* *Brooklyn* class sister ships, the USS *Philadelphia* (CL-41), and included a brand-new *Cleveland* class light cruiser, the USS *Birmingham* (CL-62), the communications and headquarters ship USS *Ancon* (AGC-4), the attack transport *Leonard Wood* (APA-12), an oiler *Chemung* (AO-30), and the destroyers *Knight* (DD-633), *Nelson* (DD-623), and *Glennon* (DD-620). The warships of TF-65 would join Vice Admiral Henry Kent Hewitt's U.S. Eighth Fleet, which was then operating with the Royal Navy in the North Africa, Mediterranean and Middle Eastern Theater. A British admiral had overall command of naval operations in the theater as the Royal Navy had a much greater presence in the Mediterranean. The light cruisers would be the U.S. Navy's largest and most powerful warships in this theater of operations as Admiral Hewitt had no capital ships or heavy cruisers under his command. As it turned out, collaboration and coordination between the two major Allied navies in the Mediterranean Theater proved to be excellent.

Boise and TF-65 joined a much larger convoy of merchantmen, which were escorted by their own destroyer screen across the Atlantic Ocean. German U-boats (submarines) that constantly prowled the Atlantic posed an ever-present danger during the voyage. On the second day out of Norfolk, the men of the *Boise* began noting the presence of numerous enemy subs in the sea lanes that the convoys followed to the Strait of Gibraltar. In his war journal entry for 9 June, Moneymaker commented that as many as three "wolf packs" of 15–20 U-boats each had been reported "just about straddle our course" about halfway across the Atlantic between North America and Morocco. While this news caused anxious apprehension among

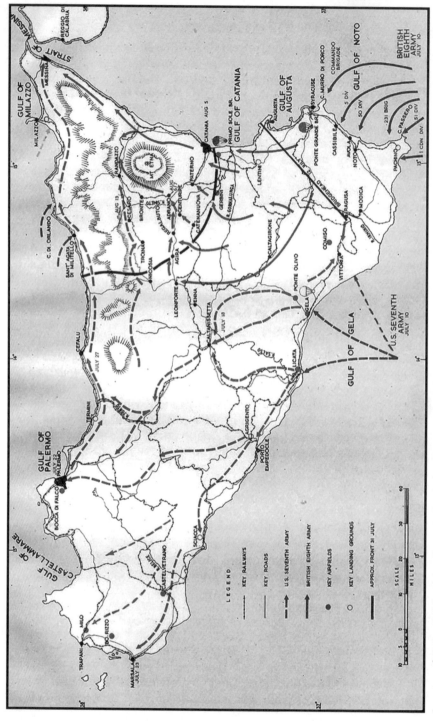

Invasion of Sicily, 10 July 1943. (Denis Richards & Hilary St. George Saunders, *Royal Air Force 1939–1945, The Fight Avails, Vol. II*, London: HMSO, 1954, p. 386)

some crew members, an "old salt" like Moneymaker claimed he was not the least bit worried by it. Two days later (11 June), the destroyers escorting the convoy detected a U-boat at 32°N 59°W, which they quickly sank with depth charges. U-boats were also reported to be harassing another convoy about two days ahead of the *Boise*, but no American ships had been sunk. Although U-boats did come snooping around from time to time, they never attacked the ships in the *Boise*'s convoy.

Convoys were primarily protected from submarine attack by screens of destroyers that could sink the U-boats with their "ash cans" (depth charges). Anti-submarine (ASW) aircraft, such as dirigibles and long-range, twin-engine PBM Mariner patrol bombers also accompanied the ships for the portion of the voyage that was within their range. Moneymaker noted the presence of a number of blimps and Mariners patrolling the area around Bermuda on 10 June.

The *Boise*'s reconnaissance planes also flew daily patrols to search for enemy submarines and surface ships. On 13 June, one of the little floatplanes failed to return to the ship after going out on anti-submarine patrol. An air and surface search were mounted. The *Boise*'s senior aviator, Lieutenant C. G. Lewis, USNR, continued the air search until after nightfall, but had to give it up when it became too dark.

USS *Boise* at sea in the Atlantic, 6 May 1943. Photo taken from USS *Yorktown* (CV-10). Note the Grumman F6F-3 "Hellcat" on carrier's deck-edge elevator. (NHHC, NH97780)

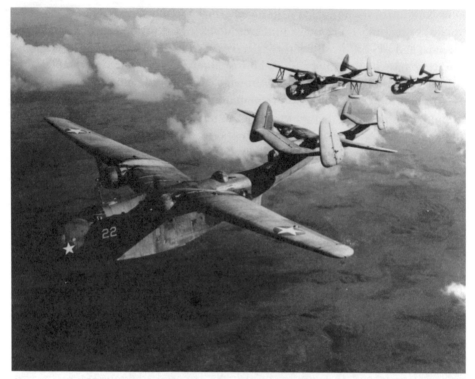

PBM Martin Mariner patrol bombers, 1943. (NHHC, NH85535)

The surface search, conducted by destroyers from the convoy's screen, went on until midnight, but also failed to locate the missing aircraft, which just seemed to have vanished. The lost pilot, Ensign Eugene Farley, USNR, and his radioman/gunner, Aviation Radioman Third Class P.O. Gibson, were listed as missing in action. Their shipmates hated having to leave them behind, but everyone hoped they would be found by the next convoy that came through or by one of the search-and-rescue patrol planes. Twelve days later (25 June), when the *Boise* was at Algiers, they got the good news that Farley and Gibson had indeed been rescued and were reported to be in good condition. Their little floatplane was reportedly sunk by gunfire (most likely on purpose by the rescue vessel), but no further details were given. The type of aircraft that was lost was unspecified in the incident report. With the loss of this scout plane, the *Boise* was left with only one Kingfisher and one Seagull during her Mediterranean tour. Mindful of the cruiser's previous loss of two of her aircraft in the Pacific in 1942, Moneymaker wrote: "We are back to two planes. Just as long as we keep two planes, we are OK. But soon as we get over two, we always manage to lose enough to bring us back to two."

Except for the loss of the scout plane, the crossing was fairly pleasant. The weather was good, and the seas were normal. Fortunately, the convoy did not run into any storms; the Atlantic hurricane season got off to a late start in 1943 and the first tropical system did not appear until late July. Thus, the new men, as well as the old salts, had an easy first crossing of the Atlantic Ocean, which Avery described as "always rolling," making sea travel a bit uncomfortable.

In addition to their regular duties, Avery and the men of the electrical gang received additional training (always a high priority on the *Boise*) from Moneymaker to improve their knowledge of electricity and related subjects, such as mathematics. Some of the men failed to appreciate this opportunity and grumbled about having to solve math problems or to learn about alternating current. But Moneymaker knew that there was more to electricity than just being able to work with it, and confessed in his journal that he himself was learning a great deal from teaching his men.

The Electrical Division was also assigned several special projects during the voyage. One of these was to make a set of lights that could be dimmed to simulate the rising of the sun and the moon. These lights were to be installed in the captain's cabin to illuminate the contour maps of the place where the cruiser would be supporting an amphibious assault. While working on the lights, Moneymaker speculated that the landing site might be somewhere in Italy and vowed to confirm this when he got into the skipper's cabin to install them. A couple of days later, he and another electrician installed the lights over the maps and charts, but only determined that they would be attacking a beach area below a small town that he believed to be located somewhere in Sicily, or perhaps Greece. The electricians also had to make a rheostat to replace the dimmers mistakenly removed from the *Boise*'s running lights by the Philadelphia Navy Yard, a slip-up that had become a joke among the men about the navy's efficiency. With this fix, the cruiser was finally able to dim her running lights for the first time since returning to sea.

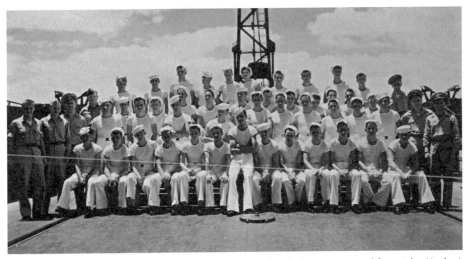

USS *Boise*, "E" Division, circa 1943. Avery Parkerson is seated in the front row, second from right. (Author)

In their free time, the men exercised, read, attended lectures by the chaplain, played cards, slept, and engaged in other leisure activities. Moneymaker noted that several reservists, whom the regular navy men complained about because of their lack of experience, were caught smoking on deck one night after lights out and were court-martialed for their serious breach of security.

On 14 June, *Boise* and the destroyers *Glennon* and *Nelson* were ordered to separate from the convoy and proceed to Algiers in French North Africa. They passed through the Strait of Gibraltar on the late afternoon of 19 June, with all hands keeping a sharp lookout for signs of U-boats that customarily prowled around the approaches to the Strait, waiting to pounce on Allied ships. The men of the *Boise* gazed upon the famous "Rock" as they passed through the "Gates of Hercules" into the Mediterranean Sea; some fellows commented that it looked just like the picture in the Prudential Insurance Company's advertisements.

After a brief stop at Oran, the cruiser and her two destroyers pulled into Algiers on 21 June to join the U.S. Eighth Fleet for duty in Task Force 81, which was under the command of Rear Admiral J. L. Hall, USN. They found the harbor filled with American and Allied ships as they docked alongside their *Brooklyn* class twin, the USS *Savannah* (CL-42). Preparations were well underway for the invasion of Sicily, the first phase of the Allies' initial assault on Hitler's "Fortress Europe." *Boise* immediately joined in the preparations by participating in a one-day, joint army-navy, practice exercise with a mock invasion force on 23–24 June. This nighttime exercise kept the crew at GQ from 0115 until 0730 on the 24th. Moneymaker scoffed at this "foolish" exercise that merely kept all hands running around in circles. He knew the men needed training, but frankly doubted that they could be trained to go without sleep.

Following the practice exercise, the *Boise* remained at Algiers for the next two weeks. During this layover, Avery was promoted to Electrician's Mate Third Class on 30 June.

The men were granted liberty to visit Algiers, which offered a variety of diversions. Wine was plentiful,

Avery Parkerson, circa 1944. (Author)

and most of the women were "well built," as one sailor put it. While speaking French helped in meeting women, some found other ways to communicate. One sailor carried several pairs of women's panties with him and when he spotted an attractive female he would approach and offer her a choice of the panties, a tactic that apparently worked well enough. Algiers, like most ports around the world, also offered a selection of brothels. One of the more famous establishments was *Le Sphinx*, notorious for its live sex shows. After visiting *Le Sphinx* while on shore patrol duty, a shocked Moneymaker described the show as "awful." He further commented, "Isn't any wonder the French get such a name. No police restrictions either. Will turn your stomach!"

Despite such attractions, some sailors perhaps would have agreed with the Chief that Algiers was not a great liberty port. Moneymaker, who complained that there was nothing to buy and was unimpressed by the food and wine, preferred shore patrol duty to liberty in Algiers. As far as he was concerned, the city was dangerous and seemed to be an ideal place for spies to operate. The old Arab quarter, the Casbah, was off limits to American sailors, but some men slipped past the patrols to go in there anyway. Sometimes sailors returned from liberty with knife wounds, while a few did not return to their ships at all. Once there were reports that two "swabbies" (sailors) had thrown an Arab over a cliff after which the two Americans were never seen again. On one patrol, the Chief found a man who had ignored the restrictions on visiting the Casbah only to run into serious trouble. Later, he noted in his journal: "Don't know what he was doing and he can't tell us. He is in one devil of a fix. His lips were sewn up and you can imagine what was inside his mouth. What a way to die and embarrassing too, Ugh! A few come back all cut up but some people just can't be told."

Day after day of waiting around for something to happen grated on the men's nerves. The navy, of course, does not believe in leaving sailors idle for long, so a great deal of time was spent in training and teaching the new guys the ropes. The officers also held frequent personnel inspections that required the men to stand for long hours under the hot North African sun, a highly unpopular way to pass the time.

From time to time, the German *Luftwaffe* came calling as if to remind the U.S. Navy that there was still a war on. In an afternoon raid on 26 July, the men of the *Boise* scrambled to GQ to join the other ships in the harbor in throwing up an AA barrage that knocked down three of the attacking planes. A near-miss from a bomb sprayed shrapnel across the *Boise*'s deck, wounding one of her gunners. With so many ships present in the harbor, Algiers was a most inviting target, which led some to wonder why they weren't bombed more often.

On 4 July 1943, the Americans were honored by a 48-gun salute from the Royal Navy ships in Algiers harbor to commemorate Independence Day. Some of the men on the *Boise* were surprised by this unusual act of courtesy on the part of the British. Moneymaker quipped sarcastically: "This is the first time I ever heard of England giving us official recognition of our independence. War is wonderful, isn't it?!!! Brings out brotherly love. One politician for another. Still think this is a politician's war and I do not think it is a war to end wars."

The 4 July celebration was rounded out with a nice happy hour for the crew on the *Boise*'s squared-off fantail. After the happy hour, refreshments of pineapple juice and cake were served.

Two days later, a large number of British ships arrived in port, including four battleships, an aircraft carrier, and many transports. This served as a signal to careful observers that an invasion of something was eminent. *Boise*'s chief electrician correctly deduced that they were about to shove off to invade Sicily.

Sicily: "Killing" Tanks on the Plains of Gela

Allied strategists had agreed on a plan to invade Sicily in January 1943. As originally conceived, the Sicily operation was seen as an end in itself with clear, specific objectives, rather than a prelude to an invasion of Italy, although it would turn out to be just that. Code-named Operation *Husky*, the invasion was aimed at protecting the sea lanes of the Mediterranean, taking some of the pressure off the Soviet Red Army by opening a second front against Germany, forcing Italy to withdraw from the war, and persuading Turkey to join the Allies against the Axis powers. British Prime Minister Winston Churchill expected Sicily to pave the way for additional thrusts into what he called the "soft underbelly of Europe." His expectations were correct, but the underbelly proved to be anything but soft. As the distinguished naval historian Admiral Samuel Eliot Morison so eloquently put it, the Italian peninsula was "… boned with the Apennines, plated with the hard scales of [Field Marshal Albert] Kesselring's armor, and shadowed by the wings of the *Luftwaffe*." Indeed, Italy proved to be a tough nut to crack.

British intelligence helped to weaken the German forces occupying Sicily through a clever deception that fooled the enemy into believing the invasion would take place in Greece. In an operation known as *Mincemeat*, a cadaver disguised as a British naval intelligence officer carrying top secret documents was dropped off by submarine on the coast of Spain near Cadiz. When the fake documents made their way into German hands, the enemy transferred some of their forces from Sicily to Greece to combat the invasion they believed was coming.

The plan for Operation *Husky* called for landing two Allied armies to take Sicily. These invading armies, one American and the other British and Canadian, were supported by two naval task forces as well as the combined Allied air forces that would provide strategic and tactical bombing as well as close air support. The Royal Navy formed the Eastern Task Force that transported the British and Canadian landing forces, which were assigned the southeastern corner of the island as their point of attack. The Western Task Force was formed around the U.S. Eighth Fleet, whose job was to deliver Lieutenant General George S. Patton's U.S. Seventh Army to its landing sites and support the soldiers once they got there. The American forces were to invade the Gulf of Gela, a 37-mile stretch of coast on the south of the island between Torre di Gaffe and Punta Brackett to the west of where the British and Canadians would be landing. D-day was set for 10 July 1943.

Although part of the U.S. Navy's role in Operation *Husky* was to support the troops after they disembarked, the army had no idea just how crucial that support would prove to be at Gela. Heretofore, the U.S. Army had generally dismissed naval gunfire as being inferior to its own artillery, considering it useful only for pre-invasion bombardment to soften up beach defenses. In the Sicily invasion, however, the army foolishly prohibited the navy from shelling the beaches prior to the landings in the laughable hopes of conserving the element of surprise, as if the enemy would not spot the enormous invasion fleets crossing the Mediterranean Sea from North Africa.

Despite army skepticism, a new aspect of naval warfare was introduced at Gela— the use of naval gunfire to support the troops after they got ashore. Preparations and training for this had been conducted in North Africa. Shore Fire Control Parties (SFCP) were formed, each with its own navy liaison officer, to coordinate gunfire from the cruisers and destroyers whenever and wherever it might be needed. The U.S. Navy had introduced new technology that stabilized the guns so that in normal seas they could fire as accurately as if they were set on solid ground instead of the rolling, pitching deck of a ship. In addition, important advances in radar and improvements in optical rangefinders had been adopted. These innovations, together with operational procedures recently developed by the navy and Marine Corps, made naval gunfire far more precise than army commanders imagined at the time of the Sicily landings.

At Gela, the navy unveiled its new role in amphibious warfare when its cruisers and destroyers saved the GIs' bacon by beating back major counterattacks by massed enemy tanks that otherwise would have overrun the Gela beachhead. The senior army "brass" was amazed, and their skepticism towards the value of naval gunfire in supporting troops on land flew right out the window. To a great extent, it was the *Brooklyn* class light cruisers—especially *Boise* and *Savannah*—that wrote this new page in the annals of American naval warfare, with their highly accurate and effective barrages in defense of those indomitable American soldiers clinging doggedly to the beaches of Gela.

On 7 July 1943, *Boise* departed Algiers with TG-80.7, which included her *Brooklyn* class sister ships the USS *Philadelphia* (CL-41) and USS *Savannah* (CL-42) and several destroyers to support the amphibious invasion. For its initial mission, TG-80.7 was to seek out and interdict any German and Italian naval forces, so they were constantly on the lookout for enemy ships and submarines. As it turned out, there was little excitement during the trip except for some enemy aircraft that suddenly appeared out of the sun one evening, forcing the men of the *Boise* to rush to battle stations. The air raid did not amount to much, but it clearly demonstrated that the enemy knew the invasion force was on its way. So much for the element of surprise, but even so, no change was made in the battle plan.

For the most part, the voyage was placid and the crew remained calm, going about their duties as normal. The recently promoted Moneymaker, who took advantage of the time to read and continue his study of calculus, noted in his diary that this operation was very different from what he had experienced in the Pacific: "So far, no strain and no pain." He commented further: "Just feel like we are going out to do a job. There doesn't seem to be any tension on the crew yet. Everyone, very optimistic." Unbeknownst to the Chief and his shipmates, that feeling was about to change drastically.

Arriving off the southern Sicilian coast on 9 July, the cruiser squadron rendezvoused with the main invasion force in very rough seas. In all, there were some 2,500 ships involved in the amphibious invasion, which made it one of the largest in history. *Boise* Radioman Chalmers Hallman exclaimed "What a sight! I didn't even know the Navy had half this many." He and his shipmates sympathized with the "dog faces" (soldiers) in the flat-bottomed LSTs and LCIs that took quite a beating in the heavy seas. These smaller craft were sometimes completely covered by the large waves. The sailors worried about how seasick the soldiers in the landing craft must have been and what shape they would be in for the invasion the next morning. Luckily, the sea calmed a bit during the night so that the landing operations were somewhat easier for the soldiers.

Although enemy aircraft had sighted the Allied convoys a couple of days before D-day, nothing could have prepared the Italian troops on the beaches for what some later described as the "imposing and terrifying spectacle" that greeted them at daylight on 10 July; thousands of ships blotted out the horizon, and what seemed like thousands of Allied soldiers were digging in on the beaches while hundreds more were storming ashore every minute. When deployed to their assigned attack areas, the ships of this vast armada formed a steel fence around nearly one-third of Sicily's southern coastline. Admiral Morison wrote in his treatise on the Gela operation that the awe and panic this spectacle inspired in the enemy was even better than the element of surprise. To the defenders on the shore, it must have seemed that only a miracle could prevent this huge armada from landing.

Although the enemy was not caught unawares, he had very little time to prepare beach defenses. There were a few field pieces, AA batteries and concrete pill boxes scattered about, and some stretches of beach had been heavily mined, but these were pitifully inadequate against such a massive invasion force. Thus, the Italian and German commanders decided to mass their forces, including armored divisions and motorized infantry, for an all-out, go-for-broke counterattack intended to drive the invaders back into the sea.

The twin light cruisers *Boise* and *Savannah* were assigned to the Fire Support Group of TG-81.5. Their mission was to provide gunfire support for the GIs of the American 1st Infantry Division that would land at Gela. The "Fighting First" was General "Blackjack" Pershing's old outfit that had first chased "Pancho" Villa around northern Mexico in 1916 before winning fame and glory in World War I. The GIs had been prepared for amphibious assaults by training with the 1st Marine Division two years earlier, and had waded ashore in North Africa after additional practice in England.

The landing zone assigned to *Boise*'s task group, code-named DIME, was a 5,000-yard stretch of beach east of the seaside town of Gela. The town itself sits up on an elevated plain behind cliffs rising some 150 feet above the sea. The DIME landing zone was in the center of the Americans' target area and would be the scene of the fiercest fighting that the Allies would encounter. Another task group would land troops to the west of DIME in the area around Licata; this area was code-named JOSS. A third task group would land to the east in the CENT area around the small village of Scaglietti. The British and Canadians were simultaneously invading the southeast corner of Sicily from Cape Passero up to the beautiful, old Greek city of Siracusa.

The ancient town of Gela, which was founded by the Greeks in 688 BC, was surrounded by olive groves, vineyards and wheat fields. It lacks a natural harbor, but in 1943 there was a concrete and steel pier extending out into the water and connected to the town by a road winding up the cliff. The first wave in the amphibious assault in the DIME area would be made by the Rangers, whose objective was to take the town, which would require them to go up and over the steep cliffs after disembarking on the beach. It would be a difficult task, but the stalwart Rangers were undaunted by the challenge.

At around 2200 on the night of 9 July, TG-81.5 approached the Sicilian coast with DIME Force. The men of the *Boise* could see fires breaking out on the beach in the vicinity of Gela, followed by heavy AA fire as the Allied bombers made their first strike. Hallman, who watched the action from the cruiser's communication deck just outside the radio shack, remarked on all the AA fire over the island describing the sight as "very beautiful... Just like the fourth of July."

Trailing just behind the tails of the bombers, paratroopers of the 1st Airborne Division began jumping onto the island, officially kicking off the invasion with the Allies' first major air drop of World War II. In thousands of years of warfare in the Mediterranean, the people of Sicily had seen just about everything at one time or another, but never before had they witnessed anything like the sight of thousands of American and Allied soldiers floating down on them from out of the night sky. The sudden appearance of those paratroopers not only shocked the locals, but also threw many Italian soldiers into a panic, many of whom abandoned their defensive positions near the beaches.

Just after midnight on 10 July, *Boise* took her station in the Right Flank Fire Support Area some six miles off shore. At 0245, the first wave of American troops began landing on the beach, where they met some resistance. Machine-gun fire on shore could be plainly heard on the ship. The *Boise* stood by with the other fire support ships to provide call-fire. When the order to commence firing was given just over an hour later (0351), the flashes from the barrels of her big guns lit up the night. Her gunners, who were firing "in anger" for the first time since the Battle of Cape Esperance in October 1942, knocked out an "annoying" search light with their

USS *Boise* off the southern coast of Sicily, 10 July 1943. Note the OS2U "Kingfisher" on catapult. (USNARA, 80-G-74832)

first shot, a 5-inch salvo. Next, they blasted an AA battery, another searchlight, and a fortified mortar position that was firing at the American GIs on the beach. In the predawn hours, they also shelled assigned targets such as roads and shore batteries as well as other targets of opportunity.

Covering fire from the cruisers and destroyers forced the Italian defenders to keep their heads down while the American troops grabbed a foothold on the long, sandy beaches of Gela. These beaches were less than ideal landing sites as they were fronted by numerous sandbars and backed by large dunes and cliffs. The sands of the beaches, dunes, and access points were generally too soft to support vehicular traffic without the use of steel webbing. Moreover, much of the area was mined. These problems, coupled with choppy seas, enemy air attacks, and shore battery fire, made the going tough and contributed to delays in landing tanks and artillery to defend the beachhead and backup the Fighting First's push inland. In fact, not a single American tank was landed on D-day, but fortunately for the GIs on shore, the *Boise* and her sister ships, with their destroyer screens, were there to back them up.

Shortly after sunrise, *Boise* launched both of her scout planes to conduct reconnaissance and spotting for the main battery's long rifles. The planes, flying

USS *Boise* shelling the beach at Gela, Sicily, July 1943. (USNARA, 80-G-54550)

totally without fighter cover, identified targets that included field artillery, tanks and AA batteries, and helped her to home in on them while occasionally taking fire themselves when they flew too far inland. It soon became impossible for them to remain over the targets for long, because the tanks would radio for help and soon German *Messerschmitt* Me-109 fighters would swoop in to attack the little spotter planes. In fact, this first day at Gela turned out to be the deadliest that the intrepid "slingshot" flyboys would face in the entire war. The USAAF did not provide a combat air patrol (CAP) to protect the ships or cover the troops on shore during the operation, and it was not until the third day (12 July) that Royal Air Force (RAF) fighters showed up in sufficient numbers to provide effective help in defending the navy ships against enemy air attack.

At 0600 on 10 July, *Boise's* senior aviator, Lieutenant Lewis, catapulted off the ship in the Kingfisher accompanied by Lieutenant Junior Grade Harding in the Seagull. The two little scout planes flew out and spotted several targets, occasionally dodging flak that greeted them when they ventured within range. Later in the morning, after giving the ship the coordinates of an AA battery that had been shooting at them, Lewis and Harding flew to the east end of the DIME area and then, upon encountering no AA fire, headed inland to a point just south of the town of Niscemi, where they observed a column of military vehicles rolling down the road towards Gela. After reporting the sighting, the two navy pilots dived on the column to get a closer look and identified several Italian heavy tanks and numerous light-armored vehicles that were moving up to join the enemy counterattack on the beachhead. The Italian armor fired at the two spotter planes each time they passed overhead. About a half hour later, Lewis and Harding discovered another group of Italian tanks on the road about three miles from the coast. Several of these tanks were deployed along a nearby ridge from where they were firing on American troop positions.

Upon receiving the enemy tanks' coordinates from her reconnaissance aircraft, with a request for one turret salvos, *Boise* opened up on them at a range of about 10,000 yards (5.7 miles). Her first salvo of 6-inch, HE projectiles landed smack on target at 0910, not only scaring the Italian tankers out of their wits, but also surprising a group of American paratroopers that were engaging them. Neither the Americans nor the Italians had any idea where the deadly barrage was coming from. The big cruiser continued shooting for two minutes, firing as rapidly as possible with just one turret. The cruiser's precise shooting stopped the advance of the enemy column and won her the eternal gratitude of the airborne troopers when they learned that it was the navy who had saved their bacon. The destroyer USS *Jeffers* (DD-621), responding to a call from an SFCP, dropped 19 5-inch rounds on the same road. On 14 July, *Boise's* CO, Captain Hewlett Thebaud, and his gunnery officer, visited this site where they saw firsthand the results of their handiwork. Burned-out shells and pieces of smashed Italian tanks were scattered all about the area. The skipper later commented that had he known precisely what they were shooting at he would have "cut loose with the whole 15-gun battery." Had they done so, it is unlikely that a single one of those Italian tanks would have survived to fight another day.

Boise's aviators, Lewis and Harding, could not stick around to help spot the fall of shot for the ship. They were suddenly jumped by two *Messerschmitt* Me 109s and had to make a run for it. Luckily, both spotter planes managed to escape undamaged. Lewis radioed the ship that he had two enemy fighters hot on his tail and requested that she standby to pick him up. A moment later, however, he called in again, advising with typical naval aviator wit, "Belay that, they've gone back for reinforcements."

At 0940, Lewis, whose aircraft was low on fuel, returned to the ship leaving Harding behind to carry on the reconnaissance work. When the Kingfisher had been gassed up and armed with bombs, the junior *Boise* pilot, Ensign Roher, was sent in the plane to relieve Harding. The latter was already on his way back to the ship when he was suddenly attacked again by Me-109s, but the young aviator was able to evade his pursuers and made it home in one piece. The German fighters flew away, but later that day shot down a scout plane from the USS *Savannah* that was also spotting in the area.

Meanwhile, Roher continued flying alone while scouring the area for enemy targets. Just after calling in the position of yet another group of Italian tanks and dropping his bombs on them, his radio suddenly conked out. He then flew back to the ship, touching down in the "slick" behind the cruiser at 1130, safe and sound.

The enemy counterattack by tanks and infantry continued throughout the morning. Another group of 25 light tanks moving down the road from Ponte Olivo came under fire from the destroyer USS *Shubrick* (DD-639) at around 0830. The SFCP credited the little tin can with knocking out three of the Italian tanks and slowing down the rest. At around 1030, a group of nine or ten of these tanks broke into the town of Gela, but the American Rangers, who had captured the town earlier that morning, drove them off with bazookas, dynamite charges and a captured anti-tank gun. Two of the tanks were destroyed, one surrendered, and the rest withdrew after the brief dust-up with the Rangers.

Throughout the morning, *Boise* and *Jeffers* were not only smashing enemy tanks, but were also knocking out shore batteries that had been shelling the landing areas. At one point, *Boise* was ordered in close to take out a gun emplacement that was shooting at American troops on the beach. She moved up to within 3,000 yards of the shore, located the battery hidden in the sand dunes, and silenced it. Samuel Eliot Morison writes that the accuracy of the cruiser's fire amazed an American brigadier general of artillery positioned about 500 yards away from the enemy battery who praised the cruiser's "terrific" shooting.

At 1102, the *Savannah* was ordered in to help the *Boise* repel the enemy tanks that were threatening to overrun the American lines and break through to the beach. *Savannah* arrived on the scene around 1120 to find that her sister ship, which was firing on a shore battery, had the situation well in hand. She followed *Boise* down the beach trying to find the enemy guns, but could not locate them. *Savannah* changed course and retook her position astern of *Boise*, which continued shelling the beach along with the British monitor HMS *Abercrombie* (F-109). At 1145, *Boise* reported that she had knocked out the shore battery, so the *Savannah*, seeing that she was not needed, returned to her assigned area.

One of Avery's favorite sea stories was about the scout planes evading the two, faster, more powerful, and heavily armed Me-109s. He stood on the deck watching, with his heart in his throat. The Seagull was much slower than its powerful attackers—a veteran naval aviator once said that the plane could reach its top speed of 150 mph only in a "fatal crash dive"—but it was highly maneuverable. In such an unequal contest, the seemingly doomed navy pilot kept his wits about him, however, and used his own aircraft's maneuverability and the Me-109's great speed to foil his German assailants' attacks. Avery held his breath on every pass made by the enemy fighters. At the last instant, the Seagull would turn quickly and fly in the opposite direction, bobbing and weaving like a halfback dodging the opposing defense on a downfield run, all the while maneuvering nearer and nearer to the shoreline. The enemy fighters would bank around sharply in pursuit of their elusive prey, but their great speed caused the Me-109s to slide for several miles before they could complete the turn. Meanwhile, the young American pilot was skillfully twisting and turning while edging closer and closer to the ship. Finally, he got close enough for the cruiser's AA batteries to throw up a wall of covering fire and quickly slipped behind it. Avery let out a sigh of relief and joined in the rousing cheer that spontaneously welled up from the men observing the unequal contest from the *Boise*'s decks when the frustrated German pilots, who wanted no part of that deadly AA barrage, turned away and high-tailed it out of range.

Avery's David and Goliath sea story is confirmed by the action report preserved in the U.S. National Archives. The fox-and-hounds' confrontations are related in thrilling detail in a report to the skipper written by the cruiser's senior aviator, the same pilot who eluded the German fighter planes while Avery and others cheered him on from the deck of the ship. (See Appendix III for transcript of LT C. G. Lewis' report on his confrontation with the Me-109s.)

Lewis's description of his encounter with the Me-109s relates that, after hurriedly eating lunch, he went up again at 1215 in the Seagull and discovered more enemy tanks. While flying directly over them at 4,000 feet, he began taking AA fire that sent tracers streaking through the Seagull's cloth-covered wings. Rolling into an erratic dive, Lewis observed several guns firing at him. Some of the shells were coming hair-raisingly close. He called in the tanks' coordinates, and *Boise* opened fire on them with single-gun salvos. After the third salvo, two Me-109s plunged down on Lewis from above, and he had to make a run for it. Kicking the Seagull into a quick turn just inside the oncoming enemy fighters, he headed for the ship, which was patrolling about five miles off the coast, advising her that he was under attack. Lewis was still some five miles inland. Knowing that he could not outrun the more powerful German fighters, he used his attackers' phenomenal speed against them. On each pass they made, he executed a turn, keeping them in sight as long as possible, and when he sensed they were in position to fire, he would feint in one direction and then turn sharply in the opposite while continuing to dive. The German pilots fired long bursts from their 20-mm cannons on each pass, all of which fortunately missed. Then, the 109s dropped down to come up from below in the Seagull's blind spot. Lewis watched them climbing toward him for as long as he dared, and when he sensed they were just about in firing position, he kicked his plane into a right Split S (a half roll to inverted flight followed by a descending half loop), pulling out beneath his assailants at a mere 700 feet off the deck and flying in the opposite direction. As he was rolling into the maneuver his aircraft was hit by explosive shells which blew away a piece of the lower wing, but fortunately did not seriously damage the aircraft. By the time the young naval aviator emerged from the Split S, he found himself quite close to the coastline and high-tailed it for his ship. Just as Avery recounted in his sea story, the pursuing German fighter aircraft were discouraged by the withering AA barrage thrown up by the *Boise* and wisely decided to give up the chase.

Luckily, neither the pilot or his crewman was injured in the dogfight. The gunner managed to get off a few bursts from his machine guns at the enemy fighters, but the guns kept jamming, and he claimed no hits. Lewis radioed the cruiser that his plane had been damaged and was ordered to return to the ship. Before heading for home, he unloaded his bombs on a shore battery that was being shelled by an American destroyer. Back aboard the *Boise*, the aviators learned that the same attackers that jumped them had shot down a second scout plane from the *Savannah*, killing that cruiser's senior pilot. In his incident report, Lewis wrote:

> All I got was a scare, a stiff neck from my heavy binoculars jumping around on my neck while taking evading action, and a slight scratch on the first finger on my right hand. Also, an intense desire to fly a plane in which I can do something besides run when attacked or at least have adequate armor protection.

Lewis observed that the Seagull was too vulnerable to carry out its mission if it came under attack from AA batteries or fighter aircraft. Without flak protection and armoring around its gas tanks, it was nothing but "a flying coffin with opposition of any kind."

The *Boise*'s skipper later complained bitterly about the lack of fighter cover for the spotter planes during the first day of the landing operation, which nearly cost him two aircraft. But Thebaud highly praised his brave pilots. In the skipper's words, the planes ". . . were merely lucky, had the 'breaks', and were flown by pilots of great skill, determination and courage." The *Savannah*'s pilots were much less fortunate, however. Three of that ship's reconnaissance planes were shot down on the first day of the invasion.

During the early afternoon, the cruisers were informed that fighter cover could only be provided for their scout planes if flights were coordinated with those of the scarce fighter aircraft, whose principal mission was to protect the transport ships and support the landings on the beaches. It was, of course, impractical for the reconnaissance aircraft to fly spotting missions only on the rare occasions when Allied fighters were going to be over the beachhead, because they might be needed at any time an enemy threat arose. The British and American air force commanders had decided at the outset of the operation that combat air cover by fighter aircraft would not be provided, a decision that greatly angered General Patton, who asked the navy to send an escort carrier to Sicily for this purpose since he could get no help from the air force. Unfortunately, for the troops and the cruisers' spotter planes, the navy's "baby flat tops" (escort aircraft carriers, CVEs) were in use elsewhere so that none were available to support the invasion.

Rear Admiral J. L. Hall, Commander of U.S. Naval Forces in Northwest African Waters, heartily concurred with the *Boise* skipper's praise of the gallant "slingshot" aviators, noting that their contribution to the success of the invasion while flying obsolete aircraft against first-line enemy fighter planes was well recognized and appreciated. The admiral did not agree, however, with Thebaud's opinion that the scout planes should not have been used without fighter escort, and defended the decision to do so as "sound and justified." Since the Navy Department had decided that it was impractical to use naval aviators to fly land-based aircraft for spotting naval gunfire in the Mediterranean theater, Hall informed the Commander in Chief (CINC) of the U.S. Fleet that arrangements were being made to train USAAF pilots to carry out this function in future amphibious operations. The cruisers' scout planes were deemed to be too vulnerable after that disastrous first day of flying without adequate combat air patrol (CAP) protection, so they were not flown again during Operation *Husky*, leaving the warships entirely dependent upon the SFCPs for spotting gunfire.

Although the counterattacks on D-day were beaten back with the help of the big naval guns, at nightfall the situation on the beach remained tenuous at best. Difficulties in beaching and unloading landing craft due to surf conditions and sandbars, as well as enemy air raids, interfered with the Allies' efforts to get tanks and artillery ashore until the late afternoon of 10 July. At 1800, unloading began and some vehicles and supplies finally reached the shore, but the effort was suspended at 0200 (11 July). In his writing about the Sicily invasion, Samuel Eliot Morison commented that unless artillery and tanks could be brought in quickly the next morning, or naval gunfire could again work a miracle, it seemed likely that another counteroffensive by enemy tanks might drive the invasion force back into the sea.

In the early morning hours of 11 July (D+1), German tanks of the Hermann Goering Panzer Division began rolling toward Gela from Niscemi in the north and from Biscari to the east to renew the counterattack of the day before, in which German armor had participated only marginally. Without their eyes in the sky, the American cruisers and destroyers were unaware of the advancing German tanks for several hours. This delay allowed the enemy armored columns to move down out of the hills and reach the coastal plain unopposed by naval gunfire.

One column of Panzers attacked American troops on the plain near the Ponte Olivo airfield at 0700. With few tanks or artillery yet ashore, the main burden of beating back the enemy tanks again fell on the navy. *Savannah* and *Boise* with their destroyers were standing by to fire when needed, but for whatever reason, no call for naval gunfire from the SFCP reached the warships for over an hour and a half. Just after 0830, *Savannah* received a request for fire support and she immediately began laying it down on tanks moving along the Ponte Olivo Road near Gela. Fifteen minutes later, the USS *Glennon* responded to a call for fire on an armored column proceeding south on the Niscemi road and poured 193 5-inch rounds into the target area. Despite this pounding by naval guns, by 0930 some of the German tanks had pushed to within four miles of Gela and were charging at high speed across the plain toward the beach.

Some 60 German Panzers overran American positions and threatened to break through and push the GIs back to the beach. The Rangers once again requested fire support from the ships to stop the German armor attacking their advanced position. According to Radioman Third Class Hallman, *Boise* responded to an urgent call from the SFCP at around 1100 for immediate fire on German tanks that were threatening the beachhead (*Boise*'s action report states that she began firing on tanks at 1040). Once they had the tanks' coordinates, the twin bobtails *Boise* and *Savannah* poured out death-dealing salvos of 6-inch projectiles at the Panzers for more than half an hour. The astonishing precision of the big naval guns smashed the tank column, enabling the Rangers to hold the line just 2,000 yards short of the beach. About half the enemy tanks were destroyed before they broke off the attack, and beat a hasty retreat to get out of range of the incoming shells. The army SFCPs radioed kudos to the *Boise* for her excellent shooting that stopped the German armor's advance cold.

General Patton, CO of the U.S. Seventh Army, was making an inspection tour of the beachhead that morning during the German counteroffensive. Patton arrived at the Rangers' HQ in the town of Gela to find their commander, Colonel William O. Darby, firing a captured Italian field piece at the advancing German armor. Admiral Morison relates that the general, watching the enemy tanks bearing down on his troops, let fly with one of his famous strings of vehement profanity. A young naval liaison officer with the SFCP asked the general if he could be of any help. Patton barked back, "Sure, if you can connect with your [expletive deleted] Navy, tell them for [expletive deleted] sake to drop some shellfire on that road." The naval officer somehow managed to raise the *Boise* with his walkie-talkie, and the cruiser pounded the German tanks with 38 6-inch AP shells, stopping the attacking tanks in their tracks. Morison writes that at that moment, "Old Blood & Guts" Patton became a firm believer in the effectiveness of naval gunfire support. Darby's Rangers, who had been fighting off charging tanks since the day before, had reached that same conclusion well before their commanding general did.

Boise's gunners, who started work at 0810 on the morning of 11 July, continued pouring it on tanks, roads, bridges, AA batteries, and field pieces up until 1142, expending a total of 376 6-inch and 150 5-inch rounds. Morison's account of the battle reveals that, at 1119, *Boise* blasted a group of enemy tanks leaving Niscemi and moving south to join in the attack on American infantry positions. About an hour later, the first Sherman tanks and a "cannon company" moved up from the beach to back up the GIs, knocking out 10–15 enemy tanks and causing the rest to turn tail and run for the hills. *Boise* helped chase off the remnants of that tank group with 18 6-inch rounds that slammed into the upper part of the Niscemi road, throwing the retreating Panzers into a headlong rout. Morison not only credits *Boise* with having turned back the tanks, but also with helping to hasten the departure of the commanding general of all German forces in Sicily, who had driven down to observe the battle. After seeing the thousands of ships in the invasion force and witnessing the withering fire from the cruisers and destroyers smashing his tanks and artillery, the general understood that it would be impossible to stop the invasion. Thus, he got back into his car and sped away.

The blistering fire power of the twin light cruisers amazed even naval observers. Frank Krall, an AA gunner on the USS *Shubrick*, a destroyer in their screen that also firing on the tanks, noted in his personal war diary, "The *Savannah* and *Boise* have been shelling hell out of the hills all morning. Boy, they sure can lay it down!"

The *Brooklyn* class twin cruisers continued "laying it down" in the afternoon and evening of 11 July whenever the SFCPs requested their help. In the afternoon, the Germans launched a second armor attack, although this time with fewer tanks. Once again, the Panzers were ripped apart by salvo after salvo of 6-inch HE shells until their commander "wisely concluded that 26-ton Mark IVs were no match for cruisers." According to the Naval Command North Africa (COMNAVNAW) war diary, the army reported that 13 enemy tanks attacking in the Gela area that afternoon were completely destroyed. Hallman, who was manning the radio shack, wrote that the troops on shore later reported "that it was the most amazing piece of shooting they had ever seen," and informed them that they had knocked out 18 of the 36 tanks in the attack. Between 1404 and 1658 that afternoon, *Boise* fired 111 6-inch rounds at tanks on a crossroads and others in a pass through the hills behind Gela. At one point in the afternoon, she moved in so close to the beach that sailors had to be positioned on deck to take soundings to avoid grounding. Once in position, she hammered targets near Ponte Olivo that included tanks

USS *Boise's* pre-invasion bombardment, Gela, Sicily, July 1943. Note the heavily loaded troop transport in the foreground. (USNARA, SC 175981)

and roads and ended her day's work day at 1937 after dropping 51 6-inch rounds on enemy troops and tanks at a crossroads near Niscemi, over eight miles inland from the coast.

Chief Moneymaker also related that his cruiser shelled the beach continually during the day, generally firing deliberately with one or two turrets. The chief bragged that the *Boise's* gunners were really on the ball and did more damage with one turret than the *Savannah* did with all five of hers. In fact, the Naval Gunfire Liaison Officer (NGLO) with the army SFCP asked *Boise* to take on a couple of targets originally assigned to her sister ship. During the second day of the invasion, the cruiser not only smashed tanks and helped stop the enemy counterattack, she also knocked out AA batteries and field guns, and shelled enemy troop concentrations as well as blowing up roads and bridges. The light cruiser's excellent work contributed significantly to the soldiers' determined struggle to consolidate the beachhead.

In the landings at Gela, naval gunnery was used to support troops on shore for the first time ever in actual combat. Planning for Operation *Husky* had called for close coordination of naval gunfire as if it were being provided by the army's own artillery, although there many who doubted that it would work. Navy personnel practiced with the army on shore, army artillery officers were deployed on the warships, while navy officers were part of the SFCPs, so both services understood the other's needs and language. When the time came, the naval gunfire support was well coordinated, worked exactly as planned, and was much better than expected. Morison deemed this tank battle on the Gela plain to have been, "… a milestone in the development of naval gunfire support, and a shining example of Army-Navy cooperation."

The U.S. Navy's warships proved conclusively that they could provide timely and effective fire support for troops fighting a land battle. American GIs quickly learned to appreciate the lethal fire from the cruisers' long rifles, while their enemies came to fear it. Dazed tankers from the Hermann Goering Panzer Division taken prisoner during the battle asked their captors what was this terrible new anti-tank weapon that the Americans possessed. They had never experienced anything like it and could not imagine that the devastating barrages that ripped their tanks to shreds had come from cruisers and destroyers firing on them from miles off-shore. German officers grudgingly admitted that the warships' gunfire broke up their counterattack and forced them to retreat; many of their soldiers threw down their weapons and equipment while "running to the rear hysterically crying." The Hermann Goering Panzer Division lost 30 officers, 600 men, and some 40–50 tanks on the second day of the invasion.

Over the first three days of the invasion (10–12 July), *Boise* provided highly effective fire support for Patton's Seventh Army while repeatedly fighting off fierce enemy air attacks. One of her major roles in the invasion was to defend the transport ships anchored off the coast against enemy planes. Her first direct encounter with hostile aircraft came when she was buzzed by four planes attacking from "ahead on bows" around mid-morning on 10 July. Her formidable 20- and 40-mm AA fusillades gave the German pilots much to think about, even if no direct hits were made on the attackers.

At 0649 on 11 July, the ships were surprised by a raid from high-level enemy bombers approaching from the northwest. The USS *Barnett* (APA-5), a transport ship, was hit while three bombs fell about 200 yards from the *Boise*, fortunately causing no damage or casualties. The cruiser's AA batteries pounded away at the enemy bombers, but again claimed no hits. At 1113, two Me-210 twin-engine fighter-bombers swept in low over the land to get under the radar and dropped two bombs that missed the *Boise* by scarcely 200 yards. Her AA batteries fired at the attackers, which came in so low and fast that neither was hit.

The air raids continued into the afternoon of 11 July in coordination with the counterattacks by enemy tanks. At 1438, *Junkers* Ju-88 high-level bombers again flew over the DIME area and explosions were also seen in the JOSS area some distance away. An hour later, the bombers returned for another run; this time some 30 *Heinkel* He-111 aircraft appeared at 16,000 feet. At first, some ships mistook them for American B-17s until they started dropping bombs and were close enough to see the black cross markings on their wings. The *Boise* opened fire with her AA batteries and increased her speed to 25 knots while taking evasive action. The cruiser was bracketed by near misses from bombs that exploded within 75 yards of the ship. The explosions shook the warship so violently that men on some of the gun mounts and searchlights were drenched and water splashed over the fantail, and Hallman thought the ship had been hit. But luckily no one was injured, although some men below decks were knocked down by the bomb blasts. Moneymaker grumbled that *Boise's* AA battery "proved exactly useless" in these air raids. He blamed the electronic gunsights, saying he could not understand why the gunners were not allowed to use their optical sights on enemy planes that swooped in low and fast.

At 1604, another group of bombers, identified by the *Boise* as He-111s, come over and bombed the transport ships. Withering AA fire from the *Boise* and other ships forced the enemy planes to drop their bombs hastily. Even so, the SS *Robert Rowan*, an American liberty ship loaded with ammunition, was struck by three 500 kg bombs that started major fires on board. Minutes later, the munitions ship blew up in a spectacular explosion and sank. A large troop transport off *Boise's* port beam and several other warships, transports and landing craft were also damaged in the raid, but the enemy air attacks failed to deter the operations.

Avery often recalled a tragic mistake that occurred during an air raid that came after dark on 11 July. Some 144 C-47 transport planes flew over to drop paratroopers from the 82d Airborne Division to reinforce the American center. The navy was notified about the air drop only minutes before it happened, but it came too late to pass the word to all the ships. Unfortunately, in the confusion of the air raid, the troop transport planes were fired on by some of the warships and by army AA batteries on shore. Twenty-four of the aircraft were shot down and 37 were damaged, while eight of the C-47s returned to base without unloading their paratroopers. There were 229 casualties including 81 dead in the air drop, mostly as a result of "friendly fire." Avery was deeply upset by this tragic mishap, and always recalled it with great sadness. His voice would always break with emotion whenever he mentioned it in later years. Such are the fortunes of war.

The air attacks continued into the evening, striking now a bit closer to home. Just after 2230, the *Boise* was suddenly bracketed by flares dropped from an undetected aircraft that completely illuminated the ship. She fired her AA guns to extinguish the flares and increased her speed to 20 knots. Minutes later, four heavy bombs (1,000 pounders) exploded dead ahead, but the enemy plane got away without being seen.

After sunrise on Monday, 12 July, *Boise* resumed bombarding targets on shore as the enemy was retreating from the plain around Gela. She knocked out an AA battery at 0645 and continued firing at enemy tanks until 0730. During the naval bombardment, two British warships pulled into the DIME area at 0705. One of them, HMS *Petard*, was carrying General Dwight D. Eisenhower, Supreme Allied

Commander, who came to personally observe the progress of the landings. After meeting with the task force commander aboard the command ship, followed by a quick observation tour ashore, all of which took just under two hours, "Ike" departed the area. The RAF began flying fighter cover over the ships and the beachhead on 12 July so the air raids finally began to dissipate somewhat.

Later that morning, after capturing the Ponte Olivo airstrip, the army pursued the enemy into the hills behind Gela. Once again, *Boise* and *Savannah* lent their fire support, responding to calls from the SFCP to silence enemy artillery batteries in the hills and blast troop concentrations situated far back from the coast. *Savannah* shelled the hill town of Butera, located on a high peak some 11,000 yards from the beach, while *Boise* lobbed 6-inch shells into Niscemi. The British monitor HMS *Abercrombie* joined with *Boise* in shooting up Niscemi, dropping her huge 15-inch shells into the town. The fine shooting by the Brooklyn twins and the *Abercrombie* was praised by U.S. Army Brigadier General Clift Andrus as being "remarkably accurate" and delivered in a "surprisingly short time." Andrus also commented: "First Division Artillery recognizes superior gunnery when it sees it, and we are unanimously stating that the support rendered by Admiral Hall's command has been more than we could have expected, even from the United States Navy."

At 2000, an LST came alongside the *Boise* to transfer 12 wounded American soldiers and four German POWs for medical treatment in the ship's sick bay. Three of the wounded Germans were from the 2d Panzer Regiment of the Herman Goering Panzer Division and the other was from an AA battery of the 5th Division, 53d Regiment. Quite possibly the POWs had been wounded in the merciless shelling from the same cruiser that now provided them medical attention. At any rate, these German prisoners got a close look at the Americans' secret anti-tank weapon, a *Brooklyn* class light cruiser. *Life* magazine's story on the incident reported that the wounded Germans asked for a bar of soap and a hot shower, which must have seemed like a great luxury after the terrible ordeal they had been through. After being treated and fed, five of the wounded American GIs were transferred to another ship for further treatment. The rest were given a place to sleep for the night, as were the Germans, who were placed under Marine guard. The remaining American wounded and the four POWs were transferred to an attack transport ship, USS *Charles Carroll* (APA-28), after breakfast the next morning (13 July). *Boise's* mission of mercy did not end there as two wounded soldiers, one American trooper and one Italian, were taken aboard for medical treatment just before midnight on Tuesday, 13 July.

By the morning of 14 July, the unloading of troops and equipment at Gela was completed, the beachhead was secured, and the fighting had moved far enough inland that fire support from the cruisers' rifles was no longer in much demand. Therefore, after transferring the wounded American soldier and the Italian POW

USS *Boise* receiving American wounded and German POWs, Gela, Sicily, 13 July 1943. (USNARA, 80-G-74837)

to the *Savannah*, *Boise* stood out of the DIME area at Gela and got underway for Algiers to resupply.

The success of Operation *Husky* was in no small measure due to the accurate and devastating gunfire from the Allied naval forces, especially from American cruisers and destroyers, in support of the army troops on shore. *Boise* certainly stood out in carrying out this mission. While acknowledging that her AA fire on Me-109s and other enemy aircraft passing over low and fast had been ineffective, her gunnery officer commented that the ship's indirect firing on shore targets at ranges of up to 18,000 yards (10 miles) had been recognized by the SFCP as being "very effective." He argued convincingly that their effectiveness would have been even greater if fighter cover had been provided for the ship's scout planes to allow them to remain over the targets on the first day of the invasion, when they could have destroyed and dispersed enemy tanks, troop concentrations and equipment in a timely manner. The gunnery officer's report complained that every time they tried this, their planes were driven off by the Me-109s. Even so, the SFCPs gave the *Boise* credit for breaking up several tank attacks and for destroying at least four heavy tanks and some field artillery. He wrote that the SFCP informed them that the 6-inch HC projectile with the Mark 29 fuse literally ripped the tanks apart. Rear Admiral Hall himself praised the *Boise,* saying that all reports from both army and navy sources indicate that her gunnery was timely, accurate, and highly effective against tanks and other targets onshore.

Captain Franklyn E. Dailey, Jr., USNR (ret), who was serving aboard the USS *Edison* (DD-439) at Gela, singled out *Boise* for her gunnery during the battle in which she and four destroyers demolished at least 14 enemy tanks during one enemy attack on the beachhead. With reference to the heavy shelling by the cruisers and destroyers, which broke up attacks by German and Italian armor and proved to be the crucial factor that forced the Axis forces to withdraw, Dailey wrote: "We earned our way into the full respect of Patton's army."

General Eisenhower praised the U.S. Navy's shooting during the invasion, calling it "devastating in its effectiveness." In his notes on the Sicilian campaign, General Patton wrote: "In daytime, Navy gunfire support is of immeasurable value, and the means now developed by the Navy for putting it on are extremely efficient."

Thus, it is clear that the *Boise* and her sister ships were critical to the success of Operation *Husky.* Without their devastating gunfire, Patton's "dogfaces" would have had a much worse time of it on the beaches of Gela and quite likely would even have been pushed back into the sea by Axis armor.

Back to Algiers

Boise steamed back to North Africa in the company of her sister ships *Brooklyn* and *Savannah* with a screen of five destroyers. The flotilla arrived at Algiers on Friday morning, 16 July 1943. At 1512, a Liberty ship suddenly exploded near the fuel docks setting two other ships ablaze and producing numerous casualties in the area. The cause of the disaster was unknown, but Moneymaker, from his vantage point on the *Boise's* fantail, saw and felt the huge explosion. He described the scene as "a gory mess," claiming that 1,800 men were killed by the blast that leveled an area of about five blocks.

Once she had refueled and replenished her ammunition stores, *Boise* was ready to return to Sicily. Together with the *Savannah* and four destroyers, she sailed out of Algiers just after noon on Saturday, 17 July, and was back on station at Gela by the 19th. Things had quieted down there to the point that *Boise's* daily shipboard routine became almost like peacetime. Although some of the crew felt almost as safe in Gela as in Algiers, they got underway in the evenings to spend the night running in circles to foil possible air attacks. After a couple of days of this routine, many were beginning to wonder what they were doing there. By 22 July, General Patton had pushed all the way up to Palermo, the Sicilian capital, on the north side of the island, and so *Boise* and *Savannah* once again returned to Algiers, where they arrived on 24 July after a brief stop the day before at Bizerte, Tunisia. Moneymaker noted in his war journal that there were five "bob tails" (American light cruisers including *Boise*) and two of the newest British battlewagons (*King George* class battleships) in the port of Algiers.

During the two weeks the *Boise* was anchored at Algiers, Avery and his shipmates got a welcome respite from the war. On Sunday, 25 July, the E Division was permitted to go ashore for a game of softball; they lost to an unidentified opposing team 13–12. The ship also screened movies on the fantail at night. That same day, the crew learned that the Italian dictator Benito Mussolini had stepped down. Moneymaker recorded the event in his journal, commenting that most of the men thought that venereal disease finally got the best of "*Il Duce*" and expressed the hope that his resignation would make the going a bit easier in Italy.

Some sailors from the *Boise* ran into friends stationed with the U.S. Army in Algiers. Moneymaker had a college buddy serving with the USAAF who visited him aboard the *Boise*. Another friend in the army also visited the chief and ate supper in the CPO mess. Moneymaker remarked that his buddy sure enjoyed the meal and speculated that even the army based in Algiers did not eat as well as they did on the cruiser.

On 2 August, at the Red Cross Club in Algiers, Avery ran into Sergeant Charles Harrell, a friend from back home in Eastman, Georgia. Charles was sitting around the club wishing he could see someone he knew, when down the stairs walked Avery. In a letter to Avery's wife Anne, he wrote, "Avery really looks good, and believe me, I was really glad to see him…." (See letter to Anne in Appendix IV.) In another letter published in their hometown newspaper, Charles related the story of bumping into Avery at the Red Cross Club: "Believe me, I thought I was seeing a mirage! He looked well and I'm sure he's doing a good job for the Navy."

The two old friends from Eastman were delighted by this chance meeting in Algiers—their hometown weekly assured its readers that "no sailor ever looked better to a soldier and vice versa." Before parting, the two men made plans to meet up again later in the week.

A couple of days later, the *Boise* CPOs invited a group of 25 members of the Women's Auxiliary Army Corps (WAAC) for dinner aboard ship. The chief of the E Division voiced strong disapproval of this invitation, arguing that a warship was no place for a woman even in peacetime, much less during a war. Moneymaker worried that bringing the women on board would cause trouble for the men in his part of the ship. He was outvoted, however, and the other chiefs decorated the mess with flowers and ribbons. The rather prudish Moneymaker quipped disgustedly that the place looked "like a bunch of pimps have taken over," and speculated that the next thing he would find would be colored toilet paper in the head. In the end, he finally attended the dinner, as did the captain and the XO, but left as soon as he had eaten. Despite grumbling that the whole thing went against the grain with him, the chief grudgingly admitted that the meal was really good—tender, juicy steaks, and lots of brandy.

"Patton's Navy": Clearing the Road to Messina

The interlude in Algiers came to an end on 8 August 1943 when *Boise* got underway for Palermo to join the other ships in taking the Sicilian capital. She and the *Savannah* put into Palermo on the morning of 9 August to find everything relatively quiet and largely under control. The *Brooklyn* twins were assigned to TF-88, along with all the remaining American warships in Sicilian waters. TF-88, under the command of Rear Admiral Lyle A. Davidson, USN, who flew his flag in their *Brooklyn* class sister ship *Philadelphia*, was created exclusively to support General Patton's Seventh Army in its drive on Messina. Indeed, TF-88 was just as much "Patton's Navy" as the Seventh Fleet would later become "MacArthur's Navy" in the Southwest Pacific theater. It was the *Boise's* fortune to serve in both.

Admiral Davidson's mission was: (1) to defend Palermo; (2) deliver gunfire support for the Seventh Army's advance along the north coast of Sicily; (3) provide amphibious landing craft for "leapfrogging" around enemy positions; and (4) transport artillery, vehicles and supplies. The *Boise* was assigned to patrol the stretch of the northern Sicilian coast between Cape Orlando and Palmi, a town situated at the north end of the Strait of Messina on the Italian mainland near the toe of the "boot," and standby to support the Seventh Army as required. Her principal duties were to provide artillery fire support when needed and patrol the approaches to the strait and the waters around Cape Orlando.

In the face of a combined, two-pronged offensive by the American and British forces driving towards Messina, the German army began withdrawing from Sicily to the Italian mainland on 1 August 1943. At first, the Germans staged a slow, deliberate withdrawal eastward towards Messina that incorporated a series of defensive actions designed to delay the advance of the American troops across Sicily's north coast. Afterwards, the enemy stepped up the speed of their withdrawal to the mainland in the period 11–17 August, which the Allies made little or no attempt to block. That later would prove to be a costly mistake when the Americans and the British had to face these same units again after they had linked up with the main concentration of German forces in Italy.

The narrow Strait of Messina that separates the island of Sicily from the Italian mainland was heavily defended by field artillery and AA batteries, making it a very dangerous place for both warships and aircraft. No concerted effort to take control of the strait was ever conducted, in part because of poor coordination between the U.S. Navy and the USAAF, which also forced the ships to operate without adequate fighter cover much of the time. In fact, Admiral Morison declares in his history of the Sicilian campaign that the ships were not even allowed to communicate directly with the USAAF aircraft, an error that was not missed by the Germans, who took full advantage of it. The enemy began using a few planes as decoys to lure away the Allied fighter cover, and then the main force would swoop in to attack the ships.

The ships' radar would pick up the attackers, but since they could not radio the combat air patrol (CAP) for help, they were left to defend themselves solely with their own AA guns, but did so exceedingly well. Indeed, the ships' gunners honed their aim and became quite expert due to the considerable combat experience they acquired during this operation.

To thwart the German retreat and beat the British in the race to Messina, General Patton made good use of his sea power. He had Admiral Davidson draw up a plan for a series of amphibious operations that would leapfrog the retreating Germans anytime they stopped to take a stand. This was similar to the strategy that General Douglas MacArthur would use the following year against the Japanese on the island of New Guinea. The first such landings were made to the west of *Boise*'s sector of the coast and were covered by the *Philadelphia* and the *Savannah* on 7–8 August, when American troops with tanks and artillery were successfully landed at Sant'Agata di Militello near Santo Stefano. The Americans disembarked too late to do much good, however, as the Germans had already begun evacuating their strong defensive position at Monte Fratello, a few miles east of Santo Stefano. As they were pulling back along the coastal highway, the Germans used self-propelled artillery and demolition teams to harass and slow the advancing Americans. A second amphibious operation was conducted at Brolo just west of Cape Orlando on 10–11 August, but this attack succeeded only in forcing the Germans out of Cape Orlando a day earlier than planned. No enemy forces were trapped in either of the two landings.

At first, *Boise* found things to be relatively quiet in her operations area, but on 12 August, while patrolling and shelling targets of opportunity around Cape Calavá, which lies between Gioisa Marea and Marina di Patti, the *Boise* came under sporadic fire from a German heavy artillery piece hiding in a highway tunnel in the hills behind the cape. Enemy self-propelled guns had been harassing American troops advancing along this area of the coast since 31 July and had inflicted a number of casualties. The men of the *Boise* watched nervously as the shell splashes kept walking closer to the cruiser while the spotters desperately tried to pinpoint the enemy battery's location. Finally, after a shell burst about 400 yards from the ship's starboard beam, one of the lookouts spotted a flash coming from the mouth of the highway tunnel in the side of the mountain right at the shoreline. After firing one salvo in return and closing to a range of 5,900 yards, the cruiser took a near-miss on the starboard beam. Shrapnel rained down from the blast causing minor damage to the ship and moderate damage to the Kingfisher that was sitting on the starboard catapult. Worse still, five crewmen were wounded, one of whom lost an eye, and two suffered broken legs. The harm caused to his men angered Captain Thebaud no end.

The shelling was coming from a mobile heavy gun (estimated by *Boise* to be about a 5-incher) that the Germans would roll out to the tunnel's mouth and fire, after which the recoil propelled the gun back into the mountainside. *Boise* responded with a barrage from the main battery of 6-inch rifled cannons that was aimed at the eastern mouth of the tunnel. With their fabled marksmanship, the ship's gunners in the rear turrets poured out 70 6-inch, high-capacity (HC) rounds at the tunnel in just four minutes (0852–0856), some of which were seen to fall directly into the eastern entrance. According to Avery, the shells exploding into the tunnel's mouth caused the hill to rise up and then settle back down like a fat woman failing in an attempt to get up out of a chair, and that was the last they heard from that German self-propelled artillery piece. In a 2013 telephone interview with the author, Dr. Garnett Moneymaker, a retired anesthesiologist who was in his nineties, confirmed that Avery's description of the effect of the ship's gunfire on that mountainside was absolutely accurate.

In his version of the incident, Avery related that once the enemy motorized gun had been silenced, the gunnery officer asked the captain if he had any other targets, to which the angry skipper replied, "Any damn target you want." The ship then fired a broadside into a small town located on the shore at the base of the mountain, and 15 6-inch HE shells flew across the water and cut through the main street of the town. The Sicilian townspeople began frantically waving white bedsheets out their windows desperately trying to deter another salvo. Moneymaker, who did not mention this incident in his journal, told the author in a 2013 telephone interview that the AP rounds bored into the earth, damaging the town's water system, but speculated that, fortunately, very few, if any, people were killed. He also said that he visited the place later and observed the damage firsthand, but amazingly encountered no animosity from the townspeople.

Avery always regretted this incident; a pained, shameful expression would come over his face every time he told the story. Perhaps for the same reason, the ship's war diary and other documents that have been consulted make no specific mention of this incident, so it is not clear which town was shelled. Unfortunately, Moneymaker could not recall the name of the village either. The unlucky target of the *Boise*'s wrath was most likely the tiny village of Calavá, which sits just below the western mouth of the highway tunnel. Another possibility, however, is Gioiosa Marea, a town that the *Boise* had shot up twice that morning, the first time from 0731–0750 and again from 0838–0843, the latter during the time she was taking sporadic fire from the German gun (0825–0852). Perhaps the 6-inch projectiles that ripped through the town were accounted for in the war diary as part of the 70 6-inch rounds that collapsed the tunnel. Since both eyewitnesses coincide that the shelling occurred immediately after they had silenced the German gun, the target was most likely Calavá. The village is situated on and slightly above the beach on the western flank of Cape Calavá and is much closer to the tunnel than Gioiosa Marea, which is some 10 km away and situated somewhat inland from the beach. The author also visited the area in 2014, but the tunnel and the collapsed portion of the coastal road have been rebuilt and there were no visible signs of the destruction that had occurred 71 years earlier.

During that same morning, the cruiser also blasted highway and railroad bridges, vehicles, and other targets along the coast. On the return voyage to Palermo, she fired another 21 6-inch rounds into the mouth of the Cape Calavá highway tunnel, just to make sure that the enemy gun would cause no further trouble, and then fired on the coastal highway and a train rolling down the railroad (see the bombardment schedule below). After this incident, there were no further reports of hostile fire from a large caliber gun in this area.

Boise was accompanied on the mission by two destroyers, USS *Gleaves* (DD-423) and USS *Rhind* (DD-404), but they apparently took no part in the shore bombardment. When the American ground forces arrived at the Cape Calavá tunnel, they found it partially collapsed, and the highway bridge, which was just beyond it on the eastern side, was completely destroyed. The U.S. Army engineers assumed that the destruction of the tunnel and the bridge had been the expert work of German demolition teams in the wake of their army's retreat, but, in this case, the expert demolition job was carried out by the "Old Noisy *Boise*." The engineers quickly cleared the tunnel and threw up a makeshift bridge over the collapsed portion of the roadbed on 13 August, so that heavy vehicles were passing through there within 24 hours.

Boise's excellent shooting at Cape Calavá on 12 August caught the attention of her superior officers. Admiral Davidson credited her with locating and eliminating

USS *Boise*—schedule of shore bombardment around Cape Calavá, 12 August 1943

TIME	TARGET	NUMBER of 6-inch shells fired
0731–0750	Buildings in Gioiosa Marea	Not given
0753–0757	Bridge on coastal highway	Not given
0804–0804	Buildings in Patti	17
0810	Culvert on coastal highway	3
0814	Vehicle on coastal highway	6
0819–0820	Bridge on coastal highway	6
0821–0825	Railroad bridge on coastal road	11
0838–0843	Buildings in Gioiosa Marea	30
0848	Masonry, curve on coastal highway	6
0852–0896 [sic]	Tunnel entrance, Cape Calava	70
0955–1000	Tunnel entrance, Cape Calava	21
1012–1019	Train on coastal railroad	24
1032–1033	Coastal highway	6
TOTAL		200*

*Total does not include shells fired in early morning at the town of Gioiosa Marea and a highway bridge.
Source: USS *Boise* War Diary for August 1943

at least one of the German motorized guns that had been harassing the cruisers and destroyers along this stretch of coastline since the first day of the operation (31 July). The commander of TF-88 also stressed that after *Boise* knocked out this self-propelled gun, there were no subsequent reports of shelling by artillery of this size and range in the area. The commander of U.S. Naval Forces in the Mediterranean, when forwarding the report of the action to the CINC-US Fleet, also praised *Boise*'s "noteworthy" silencing of an enemy mobile battery hidden in a tunnel.

General Patton was sufficiently impressed with the amphibious landings at Sant'Agata and Brolo that an even larger assault was planned for 15 August. As a preliminary, in the early morning hours of 14 August, *Boise* was sent out to Marina di Patti to support the landing of artillery for the U.S. Seventh Army's 3d Division on the beaches there. In the afternoon, she and two destroyers were dispatched to stop a reported enemy evacuation by sea from the port of Milazzo. But the Germans had already passed through, and no evacuation vessels were sighted. Nevertheless, the cruiser shelled targets in and around the city of Milazzo, including a radio tower and boats in the port area, while the tin cans went after several 88-mm gun emplacements in the area. At 1745, a shore battery on the coast southeast of Milazzo opened up on the *Boise,* splashing a round about 400 yards to starboard. The cruiser immediately began evasive maneuvers and returned fire on two separate artillery positions for about 30 minutes, walking 15-gun salvos back and forth through their locations that exploded their magazines before the order to cease fire was given. After that, nothing more was heard from those gun emplacements. The cruiser then returned to base at Palermo without being able to determine the specific results of the action, although it was believed that her shells caused serious discomfort to the German forces retiring overland from the area. On this occasion, at least, fighter aircraft from the Air Support Command provided good cover for the *Boise* throughout the day and repulsed at least one air attack by enemy planes. Moneymaker identified the CAP fighter planes as RAF Spitfires. The Chief had earlier seen Spitfires up close at Algiers and considered them to be excellent aircraft.

Boise continued to garner praise from the U.S. Army for her shooting. Moneymaker noted in his journal on 16 August that General Patton had sent a message reading: "Due to you, our army will be the first in Messina, well done." Being first to reach Messina ahead of Field Marshal Montgomery's British forces, which had fought their way up the east side of the island, was of utmost importance to "Old Blood & Guts" Patton. Moneymaker also wrote that the *Boise* seemed to be doing more than the *Philadelphia* and the *Savannah*, alleging that both had taken fire from the beach and beat a hasty retreat, sarcastically remarking, "Can't win a war that way, huh?"

On the night of 17 August, with the bulk of the German army already having withdrawn from Sicily to Italy, *Boise, Philadelphia,* and three destroyers were dispatched on a hit and run raid that took them through the Lipari Islands and down the southwest coast of Italy to the vicinity of the city of Palmi, near the northern end of the Messina Strait. They had hoped to intercept surface vessels evacuating German troops from Sicily, but none were seen. *Boise* and one destroyer went on to shell targets at Palmi while the *Philadelphia* did the same at Gioia Tauro, some ten miles to the north. At 0145, *Boise* opened fire on Palmi; the specific target was a railway power generation facility near the city. Although the exact location of the power station had not been pinpointed, she fired her main battery for 11 minutes, expending nearly 300 6-inch rounds. The crew believed they had hit the target, but this was impossible to confirm. Moneymaker recorded in his journal that they heard a large explosion and assumed they had hit an ammunition dump with their final salvo. At the same time, *Philadelphia* attached a bridge outside Gioia Tauro. The American ships observed a huge explosion in the area where the *Philadelphia* was firing, which clearly meant she had hit something significant, but exactly what it was is undetermined.

Despite the lack of confirmed results, this night raid was quite possibly the first time that American warships actually fired on the Italian mainland. Moneymaker expressed concern for the townspeople of Palmi, saying he hated to think what they must have felt when they were awakened by the shelling, but added, "Such is war!" He noted that the *Boise* had been firing 15-gun broadsides with the ship closed up, making it insufferably hot below decks and complained that the men of the E Division were so drenched with sweat that afterwards they had to wring it out of their clothes. Nevertheless, Moneymaker noted that firing the main battery with all the hatches battened down was better than firing with the ship open, as that wreaked havoc with the electrical equipment.

Meanwhile, the Germans made good their evacuation from Sicily across the Messina Strait to the mainland. The Allies' failure to block the German army's escape from Sicily proved to be a costly mistake once the invasion of mainland Italy began at Salerno a couple of months later. Nevertheless, TF-88 made a significant contribution to the liberation of Sicily, by patrolling along the northern coast of the island to block the enemy and by providing fire support to the Americans' advance towards Messina. General Patton praised the "generous and gallant support" provided by Admiral Davidson, whom he colorfully described as "a real fighting SOB." Morison wrote that he was told time and again by soldiers of the U.S. Seventh Army that "the sight of 'those beautiful ships' standing by, or spouting fire from their big guns, gave them a sense of security and a feeling of invincibility."

Algiers again

The fall of Messina on 17 August 1943 officially ended the Sicilian campaign, and the men of the *Boise* got another well-deserved break to resupply and rest for a few days (19–24 August) at Algiers. She departed Palermo on 18 August to cross the Mediterranean Sea to Algeria. Around midnight, as she was cruising through the Tunisian War Channel, the men on deck could see heavy AA fire rising above Bizerte, Tunisia, where Allied installations were being slammed in a major air raid by enemy bombers. Moneymaker wrote that a few German planes made runs on the *Boise*, but all of their bombs missed. Suddenly, the cruiser was attacked by a German dive bomber, which was detected by the ship's radar when it was only about eight miles out, coming in low and fast. One bomber dropped a glide bomb from an altitude of about 500 feet, which missed the cruiser's starboard bow by a mere 400 yards thanks to the fact that she was "making 30 knots and zigzagging like the devil." Fortunately, the large explosion caused no damage or casualties. The attacker swept on by so fast that the cruiser's AA guns had no chance to fire at him. It was all over in a matter of minutes, and the rest of the voyage was uneventful. The crew could see the flames from a ship that had been hit about two miles off to port. They docked at Algiers on the afternoon of 19 August.

It is often said that naval warfare is made up of brief, intense moments of fighting separated by long periods of paint-scraping boredom while waiting around for something to happen. For the U.S. Navy in the Mediterranean Theater in 1943, the lulls between engagements could be quite pleasant thanks to the close proximity to civilization. Like other American sailors and soldiers, Avery got a chance to see some of the marvelous sights of the ancient world in North Africa and Sicily, as well as experience the local culture and hospitality. On one visit to Algiers, Avery and a shipmate happened to meet an elderly French lady in a local market who kindly invited them to her luxurious home for a meal. The gracious lady took them down to her extensive, well-stocked wine cellar and invited the two young sailors to drink as much of anything they wanted. The warm hospitality she offered the two sailors was her way of showing her appreciation for American support in the war.

The crew took advantage of the time in Algiers to go on liberty, write letters, and visit friends on other ships or with the army. On 23 August, the E Division played softball. Moneymaker lamented that they lost again, but still had a "swell time."

On 24 August, *Boise* moved to the port of Mers el-Kebir at Oran to participate in a training exercise in preparation for the upcoming invasion of the Italian peninsula. The crew thought for a time that they were headed home, but they were mistaken. When not conducting maneuvers, they tied up in Mers el-Kebir harbor. Moneymaker complained in his war journal that all of this was "getting monotonous," adding, "Sure will be glad when I wake up and there is no more war. That is too far off to think about. Better start studying again."

According to Vincent Langelo, after five days of this exercise, on 29 August *Boise* returned to Algiers and tied up alongside HMS *King George V*, Britain's mightiest battleship. The gigantic, 42,000-ton ship dwarfed the *Boise* so that it appeared tiny next to her, leaving Avery and his shipmates open-mouthed in awe. Thebaud received a dispatch from the CO of the battleship stating that they were honored to have a U.S. warship with such a prestigious combat record sitting alongside.

The cruiser had operated with the *King George V* on several occasions, and the British were familiar with her fame. The men of the *Boise* were justly proud to receive such a high compliment from the Royal Navy's largest battleship.

All the days spent in Oran provided time for liberty. Oran was much cleaner than Algiers, and some men considered it to be a better liberty port as well. One hot day, Moneymaker and some buddies climbed a small mountain, which was about 3,100 feet high, located on the coast just outside the city. The Chief called it Mount Atlas, even though it was separated from the main chain of the Atlas Mountains in the interior by some 150 miles. There they found shore batteries, radar antennae and large searchlights put there for protecting the harbor.

All the waiting around for action weighed on people's nerves. When not on liberty they looked for ways to occupy their time—letter writing was always one way, as were cards and other games of chance. Grumbling was also popular. Some of the more intellectually minded men, like Moneymaker, spent time reading and studying—the Chief noted in his journal that he was making progress on learning Spanish. On the morning of 5 September, the A and E Divisions (Auxiliary and Electrical Divisions) played softball. Moneymaker speculated that the fact that he was the umpire might have had something to do with the E Division's 16–12 win. The softball victory marked the end of their respite from the war. That same afternoon, *Boise* departed Oran with a task group whose final destination was the Gulf of Salerno, where an invasion of the Italian mainland was scheduled to begin just four days later.

CHAPTER THREE

Operation *Avalanche*: The Invasion of Italy

Although the capture of Sicily precipitated the fall of Italy's fascist dictator, Benito Mussolini, and the new Italian government had begun secret peace negotiations with the Allies, the Germans were still occupying the country. The next step for the Allies was to defeat the Germans in mainland Italy, but it was clear to everyone that they would put up a hell of a fight. The Italian campaign, therefore, promised to be a major undertaking.

The first Allied invasion of the European mainland took place just south of Naples at the Gulf of Salerno, with two smaller assaults, one across the Strait of Messina to the "toe of the boot" and the other at Taranto in the heel, with all invading forces converging on the city of Naples (see map overleaf). The Salerno landings were code named Operation *Avalanche,* with D-day set for 9 September 1943. *Boise* sailed out of Oran on 5 September, and after a brief stop at Bizerte on 7 September operated with TF-81 to support the landings in the Gulf of Salerno. The task force consisted of the *Brooklyn* class cruisers *Philadelphia, Savannah*, and *Boise,* together with three destroyers. Less than an hour after shoving off, however, *Boise* received orders from the CO of the U.S. Eighth Fleet to return to Bizerte, where she was to report to CINC Mediterranean, Admiral of the Fleet Andrew Cunningham, RN. Upon arriving at Bizerte, *Boise* was assigned for duty with the Royal Navy's 12th Cruiser Squadron under the command of Commodore W. G. Agnew, RN, which was preparing to land British troops at the Italian port of Taranto. Thebaud, was given only a summary briefing for his new assignment by Admiral Cunningham, who traced out a chart of the operation in the dust coating the side of his official vehicle. This was the only plan for the upcoming operation, code named *Slapstick*, that the *Boise's* CO ever saw. Rear Admiral Lyle Davidson in the USS *Philadelphia* signaled Thebaud: "You should be an admiral when you get back. Good luck."

With Italy's formal surrender expected to be announced at any moment, the Allies hastily decided to seize and occupy the naval base in the port city of Taranto, where a number of Italian warships were anchored. One of the objectives of the move was to deny those assets to the Germans. Operation *Slapstick* was timed to coincide with the main event in the Gulf of Salerno. After securing Taranto, British airborne troops were to move on up to attack Naples from the rear. With the bulk of transport vessels dedicated to the Salerno operation, the British 12th Cruiser Squadron—composed of the cruisers HMS *Aurora* (flagship), *Penelope, Dido* and *Sirius*, and the 2,600-ton minelayer HMS *Abdiel*—was pressed into service to transport the British 1st Airborne Division's troops and equipment to Taranto on 9 September. Since the British cruisers lacked sufficient space in which to transport the entire division, the USS *Boise* was detailed to assist the 12th Cruiser Squadron in this crucial task.

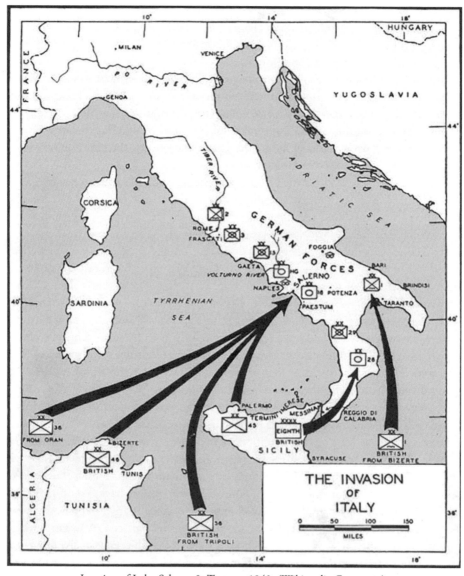

Invasion of Italy: Salerno & Taranto, 1943. (Wikimedia Commons)

Operation *Slapstick*: The Occupation of Taranto

The Allied warships loaded the British commandos and departed Bizerte on 8 September. To make room on board for 778 men with their 30 jeeps, light field pieces, and other equipment and supplies, the *Boise*'s scout planes were offloaded at Bizerte to make room on the hangar deck and fantail for vehicles and other equipment.

Moneymaker quipped that since the men were airborne troops, he wondered if the *Boise* would be flying them to their landing zone. More soberly, however, he reflected that the mission worried him because the ship would be forced to tie up to a pier in order to unload the jeeps and equipment. The Chief knew that the considerable amount of time required to do so would leave the *Boise* a sitting duck if the Germans attacked the landing force.

Among the American cruiser's passengers was a renowned British Special Forces demolition squadron commanded by Lieutenant Colonel Vladimir Peniakoff (aka "Popski," after a popular, and British newspaper, cartoon character), a Belgian of Russian Jewish extraction. The unit, formed in Egypt in 1942, had become known as "Popski's Private Army" (PPA). Its members were handpicked by Peniakoff, and

Operation *Slapstick*. British paratroopers bound for Taranto, Italy, on board USS *Boise*, 8 September 1943. (USNARA, 80-G-85580)

Operation *Slapstick*. British troops on board USS *Boise*, steaming towards Taranto, 8 September 1943. (USNARA, 80-G-85577)

it was said that he paid them from his own pocket. Avery described the British commandos as a "tough looking bunch—the kind you'd like to have on your side in a fight." Radioman Third Class Hallman had a similar impression, and recorded in his journal: "What a bunch of hardened guys they were. They had fought all through the North Africa Campaign. We carried about eight hundred and the decks were laden with jeeps, machine guns and even bicycles."

The *Boise* crewmen sympathized with the paratroopers, who had a hard row to hoe in combat, and the Chief Electrician's Mate wanted to help them as much as he could. During the crossing to Italy, the E Division repaired the voltage regulators on some of the British jeeps. They also made some funnels so that the commandos would not spill so much gasoline when refueling their vehicles. The British soldiers especially

Operation *Slapstick*. British commandos of "Popski's Army" on board USS *Boise*, heading for the occupation of Taranto, 8 September 1943. (USNARA, 80-G-85581)

appreciated the *Boise*'s showers and cold-water drinking fountains, creature comforts they had never found aboard the Royal Navy ships on which they had traveled previously. They were also favorably impressed with the cleanliness of the ship. Avery, who greatly admired the prowess and might of the Royal Navy, insisted that British warships were filthy in comparison to those of the U.S. Navy.

Late in the evening of 8 September, the cruiser squadron received a dispatch informing them of the unconditional surrender of all Italian armed forces; the Armistice of Cassibile had actually been signed on 3 September, but was kept secret for the next five days. To some extent perhaps, this bit of good news served to the detriment of Operation *Avalanche* because it led many soldiers to believe they would be welcomed ashore by the Italians and kept them from focusing their minds on the arduous and difficult fight they would have to wage against the Germans.

At 0600 the next morning, *Boise* and the British cruiser squadron rendezvoused northwest of Malta with the Royal Navy's Force Zebra, which was commanded by Vice Admiral Arthur Power, RN, and based in Malta. Zebra Force comprised two battleships—HMS *Howe* (flagship) and HMS *King George V*—and six destroyers. The combined force then proceeded to Taranto, arriving in the late afternoon of 9 September.

Admiral Cunningham dispatched Force Zebra to cover the cruisers to reduce the risk of a possible attack on the ships transporting the paratroopers by the Italian fleet anchored at Taranto, which he feared could prove to be a "jolly nuisance" as the cruisers were too heavily loaded with troops and equipment to defend themselves in a gunfight. After some delay resulting from the difficulty of navigating through the minefields and witnessing a major portion of the Italian fleet depart the port on their way to surrender to the Allies at Malta, *Boise*, following astern of the destroyer HMS *Jervis*, steamed into Taranto's Porto Mercantile ahead of the rest of the task force.

As the only American ship in an otherwise all-British operation, *Boise* was given the honor of being the first cruiser to enter the port while Force Zebra remained behind at a safe distance. Avery characterized the honor shown his ship as dubious; the Royal Navy was not taking any chances and preferred to let the Americans be the bait. He and his shipmates were plenty nervous as they looked back to see the British battlewagons and cruisers sitting on the horizon while two, giant Italian battleships, two cruisers and a destroyer were steaming past them headed out of the harbor. All hands on the American ship were sweating it out on their battle stations as they watched the Italian ships approaching. According to Avery, the skipper ran up an enormous American flag like the ones now flown over used car lots, to show everyone who was coming in and signaled the Italian warships to keep their guns trained straight ahead. Thebaud's radio message contained the warning that if any Italian ship so much as waggled a gun, he would commence firing. It would have been practically impossible for the *Boise* to make good on that threat, however, since the main deck was so crowded with vehicles and equipment that training their guns would have been difficult. Avery and his shipmates kept their eyes riveted on the big battlewagons that dwarfed the American light cruiser as they steamed past. Their fears were for naught, however, as the Italians were done with the war and stood out of the port without incident and proceeded to Malta where they surrendered according to the terms of the armistice. Only a handful of smaller warships and merchant vessels remained behind in Taranto harbor. These and other Italian warships that escaped destruction by the Germans then joined the Allied fleet. In his book on the Italian campaign, Morison points out that the Italian navy was the only branch of the armed forces that was able to comply fully with the terms of the treaty. The Italian army and air force simply dissolved.

Boise and the *Jervis* moored at quayside around dusk on 9 September. HMS *Penelope* pulled in soon afterwards and moored to starboard. Later they were joined by HMS *Howe* and the other ships of the cruiser squadron, and the cruisers began offloading the troops, equipment and supplies, with unloading operations completed in the predawn hours. Moneymaker and many other *Boise* hands pitched in to help the British commandos unload their jeeps, ammunition and equipment. The Chief wrote: "These soldiers will not have much of a chance to rest for a while so why not give them a hand." After disembarking, the paratroopers formed up and moved off smartly, boots rhythmically slapping the pier as they marched. The men of the *Boise* never saw them again and often wondered how they fared in the fight against the Germans in Italy.

Fortunately, the enemy did not oppose the Taranto landing, and the entire operation went smoothly, for the most part. The only tragic incident came a few minutes after midnight on 10 September when the minelayer HMS *Abdiel* suddenly exploded and sank from causes that were unknown at the time. The explosion killed some 58 paratroopers and wounded another 150 in addition to the loss of 48 of the ship's crew. There was much speculation as to what might have happened. Avery thought that although the harbor had been closed off with anti-submarine nets, it was possible a German U-boat had remained submerged on the bottom of the harbor and then torpedoed the British minelayer. British destroyers dropped a lot

USS *Boise* ties up at Taranto, July 1943. (USNARA, 80-G-85583)

of depth charges around the harbor, but no debris was sighted, so the results were unknown. The sinking of the *Abdiel* was later attributed to a floating mine dropped in the harbor by German motor torpedo boats a few hours before the Allies arrived, but Avery remained convinced that it was a sneak attack by a German submarine.

At 0625 on the morning of 10 September, the cruiser squadron departed Taranto for Bizerte to pick up more troops. Many of the *Boise*'s crew wondered why they had been the only American ship selected for this mission. While it is unclear who made the selection and why, the British were suitably impressed by her fame stemming from the Battle of Cape Esperance, so perhaps they preferred to have a fighting ship of her caliber join them for *Slapstick* instead of another American cruiser in Admiral Davidson's Cruiser Division 8.

Upon arriving at Bizerte on 11 September, the captain received immediate orders to rejoin her fire support group in the Gulf of Salerno. Operation *Avalanche*, which had begun on 9 September, was not going as well as expected and the old "Noisy *Boise*'s" firepower was sorely needed. While at Bizerte, they learned that their sister ship, the USS *Savannah*, had been knocked out of action by a German bomb in the Gulf of Salerno. The loading of British troops was immediately suspended,

Religious service on board USS *Boise*, Mediterranean Sea, 1943. (USNARA, 80-G-57184)

and the ship made ready to get underway for Salerno. Two American journalists, Dave Driscoll of the Metropolitan Broadcasting System and George Biddle of *Life* magazine, who had been on temporary assignment aboard *Boise*, left the ship before she departed Bizerte. Biddle was responsible for *Life's* article on the Sicily invasion that featured photographs taken aboard the *Boise*, which Avery's wife clipped and saved in her scrapbook.

Salerno Bay

When all British troops and equipment had been unloaded, the *Boise* pulled out of Bizerte and headed for Salerno Bay. Without destroyer escort, she raced alone across the Mediterranean Sea at 25 knots, zigzagging constantly to elude German U-boats, and arriving at the Gulf of Salerno at 0948 the next morning (12 September). When they pulled in, they could hear gunfire from the beach and guessed correctly that the "krauts" were putting up a determined fight.

The Salerno invasion was extremely hard fought. The Germans were well prepared for the invasion, and hotly contested the landings. They had set up formidable beach defenses with tanks, field artillery, land mines, and well-placed machine-gun nests. As in Sicily, the U.S. Army refused to allow a pre-invasion naval bombardment in the hope of maintaining the element of surprise, but once again surprise was merely a pipe dream. The commander of the German Tenth Army occupying the area had been expecting an invasion in the Gulf of Salerno for some time. His expectations were confirmed on 7 September when he received reports that large Allied convoys were steaming in his direction. The refusal to allow the navy to soften up the beachhead with its big guns prior to the landings proved to be a major mistake by the army. The troops on the beaches at Paestum and in the British sector encountered the heaviest, most determined resistance to any amphibious landing in the entire war. They not only faced the German ground troops and tanks, but also the *Luftwaffe* warplanes that bombed and strafed the landing beaches on a scale unparalleled in any other landing in the Mediterranean.

At first, it went so badly for the Americans and the British that some consideration was given to actually withdrawing. But here again, it was the fire support provided by the American and British warships in the roadstead that saved the day for the soldiers. *Boise's* absence during the opening days of the Salerno landings, while she was participating in Operation *Slapstick*, had created some problems for Admiral J. L. Hall, USN, commander of the Eighth Fleet's amphibious force. He complained that the loss of her firepower had been "keenly felt," and her absence had caused some confusion and "misunderstandings during the early stages of the attack." Nevertheless, the American light cruisers and destroyers, together with Royal Navy warships including the monitor HMS *Abercrombie* with her 15-inch guns, hammered enemy tanks, field artillery, troop concentrations, machine gun emplacements, and other targets identified by the SFCPs or spotted by the reconnaissance planes from the *Savannah* and the *Philadelphia*. Despite the heavy presence of enemy fighters, the little spotter planes were protected as they worked on the first day of the operation by a CAP of USAAF P-51 Mustangs that flew in pairs; one fighter assisted in spotting targets for the ships, while the others provided cover from the *Luftwaffe*. Both the "*Philly*" and the *Savannah* rained death and destruction on enemy tanks destroying a considerable number of them. The SFCP credited one destroyer with killing 11 tanks on its own.

Morison quotes the following message from the U.S. 36th Infantry Division's artillery commander, Brigadier General John W. Lange, sent to all the gun ships in the American sector by the naval gunfire liaison officer: "Thank God for the fire of the blue-belly Navy ships. Probably could not have stuck out blue and yellow beaches. Brave fellows these; tell them so."

The *Boise's* arrival in the Gulf of Salerno on the morning of 12 September came not a minute to soon, as the Germans launched a furious counterattack that day. The fighting on shore was fiercer than on any day previously. Her guns helped fill the gap left by the *Savannah*, which had been heavily damaged and was forced to retire from the operation. On 11 September, while operating off Salerno, the *Savannah* was struck by a radio-guided, 1,400 kg Fritz X glide bomb launched by a German bomber from 18,000 feet. The bomb scored a direct hit on her number 3 turret and exploded in the lower handling room. Despite heavy casualties her valiant crew saved the ship from sinking, but with a huge hole in her bottom she was no longer operational. The stricken cruiser had to withdraw to Malta for emergency repairs and from there returned to the United States for major repair and overhaul.

Avery said these "Buzz Bombs" (the nickname commonly given to the German V-1 flying bomb) were frequently used in the enemy air attacks against the Allied fleet at Salerno. One of his shipmates, James Starnes, declared in an interview that this threat truly put the *Boise* "in harm's way" for the first time in the Mediterranean campaign. He described the buzz bombs as frightening, because you could hear it coming, but had no way of knowing where it would hit. The Fritz X glide bomb was dropped from a bomber and guided to its target by an operator using a joystick and a radio transmitter.

Boise immediately jumped into the fight to help repel attacks by German armor that was pushing back the American Fifth Army. She took her station in the southern part of the gulf off the ancient Greek city of Paestum, with its magnificent temples that had withstood the ravages of time and warfare in near perfect condition for over 2,000 years. This was the area of the American sector where the fighting was fiercest, and the cruiser contributed substantially to throwing back the German advance on the beachhead. A gunner in *Boise's* main battery, Richard Plunkett, wrote: "The Fifth Army would have been pushed back into the ocean if it hadn't been for the Navy."

USS *Savannah* (CL-42) hit by a German radio-controlled glide bomb in Bay of Salerno, Italy, 11 September 1943. (NHHC, NH95562)

Fortunately, the heavy naval gunfire that hammered the Germans on shore during the battle caused no damage to the magnificent Greek temples as the ships took great care to avoid hitting them.

Boise spent the next four days providing fire support for the landing operations, shelling the Italian coast around the Gulf of Salerno wherever she was needed, and providing AA protection for the transport ships against frequent, heavy air attacks from the *Luftwaffe*. According to Admiral Davidson, commander of TF-86, gunfire from *Boise's* 6-inch and 5-inch batteries "played an important role "in repelling the enemy tank attacks against the American invasion force.

After seeing what the *Boise* and her bobtail sisters had done to their tanks at Gela, at Salerno the Germans singled out the cruisers for attacks by the *Luftwaffe*. Avery recalled that they were under almost constant air attack from the first day the ship arrived on station in the Gulf of Salerno until the day she left. He said that during air raids the skipper, an "old tin can sailor," would ring up full speed and begin cutting figure eights as if the big cruiser were a destroyer; the high-speed turns were so quick and tight that the deck crew had to hang on to keep from being thrown overboard.

Around 1800 on 12 September, as dusk fell over the gulf, three German dive bombers made a run at the *Boise*. She rammed up her speed and began firing her

AA guns at the attackers. The enemy planes dropped three bombs, all of which narrowly missed the ship—two fell within 100–150 yards off the port bow and another barely 100 feet off the starboard beam. In the words of Moneymaker, those near misses "jarred us up a little."

The German air raids continued almost without let up. During the night of 12–13 September, one of the three hospital ships in the gulf was bombed; the fires blazed on board her for about six hours. At around 1446 on the afternoon of 13 September, *Boise* fired her AA batteries at five *Focke Wulf* FW-190s that dived out of the sun and released their bombs, which failed to hit any of the ships. "They tried like hell to get us," said Richard Plunkett, but the *Boise* seemed to lead a charmed existence. Ten minutes later, the USS *Philadelphia* narrowly escaped the *Savannah*'s fate when a radio-controlled rocket bomb exploded close aboard. The nearly constant air raids failed to deter the cruisers from their fire support mission, and later that afternoon the *Boise* smashed an enemy tank attack and knocked out a gun emplacement with her main battery's rifles, letting up only when the SFCP advised that the German battery had been demolished. At 1928, after escaping unscathed from several more air attacks, she put to sea to pass the night, returning at dawn the next morning to take up her station.

During one of the many air raids at Salerno, the *Boise* was strafed by an Me-109. Avery was up in the superstructure during the attack, and on one of its passes the enemy fighter flew by the ship so close that he was able to look the German pilot in the eye. Avery said if he had been holding a potato in his hand, he could have hit the 109 with it, but the plane was flying so low and fast that the ship's AA guns were unable to draw a bead on it. He greatly admired the Me-109, which he described as "a sweet airplane," and had tremendous respect for the Germans as a formidable adversary. Moneymaker complained about all the air attacks and noted that the electronic sights on the 20mm guns were not "worth a damn." He wondered why they did not allow the gunners to fire tracer rounds instead.

At dawn on 14 September, the Germans renewed their counteroffensive against Allied positions with armor and infantry, making it another very busy day for the cruisers and other fire support ships. The German commander gave the naval guns significant credit for stopping his counterattack and preventing his troops from breaking through after the Germans were hammered by the heaviest shelling they had ever experienced. He grudgingly admitted, "With astonishing precision and freedom of maneuver, these ships shot at every recognized target with overwhelming effect."

Philadelphia had been shooting throughout the night in response to calls from her SFCP. *Boise* did not go to work that morning until 0846 after she received calls to fire on tanks and troop concentrations. She continued blasting away with her main battery almost continuously up until 1349, slamming 18 separate targets with hundreds of 6-inch rounds. After *Boise* blasted a tank group with a barrage of

German tank smashed by naval gunfire, Salerno, Italy, September 1943. (NHHC, NH95563)

83 shells, the SFCP signaled "well done." She then had a break from providing call fire while *Philadelphia* took over for the rest of the afternoon. It wasn't much of a break, however, as it was interrupted at least four times by air raid alerts. Plunkett wrote in his diary that while they were firing that day, the German planes "came at us again and dropped one radio-controlled bomb which exploded right off our fantail—missed us again (pretty lousy)." Plunkett claimed they shot down one of the attackers.

In one such bombing attack, Avery told of how a firefighting team was standing ready on the cruiser's fantail with their fire hoses hanging over the side so that their powerful streams were directed into the sea. Suddenly, a bomb exploded just astern of the ship, startling the men who took off running to escape the blast, leaving their hoses unattended. One of the fire hoses slipped back aboard and was slithering around the deck like a cobra dancing to the music from a flute with its head raised in the air. The nozzle whipped around, spraying its heavy stream with great force, until one young sailor ran up and tackled it like a linebacker slamming into a charging fullback. Unfortunately, in trying to bring the fire hose under control, the poor boy grabbed the hose with the nozzle beneath his chin, and the powerful force of the water almost tore his head off. With help from other firefighters, the hose was quickly restrained, and the kid suffered no major injuries, although he most likely had a sore neck for several days.

At 2126, *Boise* took another turn at bat; her first target was an enemy troop concentration. The SFCP requested rapid fire, and she responded quickly with 72 rounds as the spotters reported "No change" and "Straddle, straddle." At 2310, *Boise* laid down interdicting fire on German troops moving down from Eboli; the SFCP reported during the shoot, "You are doing well." By midnight, she had answered five requests for gunfire and expended 427 6-inch rounds. In less than 20 minutes, the cruiser was again responding to SFCP requests for artillery support, and continued to do so nine different times throughout the night and into the early morning of 15 September, expending 475 rounds from her main battery. She pounded various targets, but mostly hit enemy troop movements near Persano, northeast of Paestum. The first call from the SFCP at 0018 (15 September) was for four minutes of rapid fire, which *Boise* obligingly provided. After five more shoots, at 0347, the SFCP spotters radioed: "Your firing has won our praise. It has 'Jerry' puzzled. Well done. Will be back in 20 minutes for more." By 0425, the army was again asking for help from the bobtail cruiser, which she enthusiastically provided, firing three times up until 0531, when she was relieved by her twin, *Philadelphia*.

At 0745 on 15 September, a Ju-88 high-level bomber and six FW-190 fighters attacked the ships in the fire support area. The Ju-88 made a direct hit with a radio glide bomb on a transport ship a mere 700 yards off *Boise*'s port bow. Avery recalled seeing the "rocket bomb" slam into the transport ship, causing severe damage and inflicted heavy casualties. He said the Germans directed the bomb right down the transport's stack. Some men were blown into the water by the huge explosion while others jumped over the side. *Boise* was running flat out while taking evasive action so she could not stop to pick up survivors in the water, many of whom were wounded. She was cutting figure eights at high speed while firing on attacking FW-190s with her AA guns. The enemy fighters dropped two small bombs that missed by barely 150 yards to port.

The U.S. military's newspaper, *Stars and Stripes Algiers Daily*, on 10 October 1943 reported that on 15 September, the *Boise*, *Savannah*, *Philadelphia*, and their accompanying destroyers were joined by two British battleships—HMS *Valiant* and *Warspite*—in helping to turn the tide of battle when the Germans threatened to crack Lieutenant General Mark Clark's bridgehead. Withering fire from the big naval guns helped smash enemy resistance and open the road to Naples. While describing the big battlewagons' fire as spectacular, *Stars and Stripes* bragged that the job done by the cruisers and destroyers in laying down fire support was more crucial. "Their guns roared day and night while the operation was in progress." According to the armed forces newspaper, the legendary *Boise* was "acclaimed for her desperate engagements in the Pacific," fired 563 rounds at German troops and tanks near Persano that day (15 September). It should be noted that this *Stars and Stripes* report was mistaken, in that the *Savannah* had already been knocked out of action and had left Salerno four days earlier. Nevertheless, that gallant cruiser deserved high praise for an outstanding job well done during her participation in the invasion. *Boise* Radioman Chalmers Hallman commented in his journal that "The Army was being driven back and things looked bad. The turning point came… when the *Boise* plus *Philadelphia* started bombarding with everything we had. We blew a couple of ammunition dumps sky high and really played hell with their troops [Germans]. That was the turning point. The next morning, the Fifth Army started their big offensive." Avery greatly admired the might and firepower of the British warships, especially the battleships. But he was justly proud of his own ship's well-deserved reputation for excellent gunnery and bragged that she could "really knock" with her main and secondary batteries.

In the late afternoon (1700–1853) of 15 September, *Boise* shelled two enemy artillery batteries and one personnel concentration with 76 6-inch and 129 5-inch rounds. During these shoots, she also fought off attacking enemy planes with her AA guns. She closed out the day's shooting at 1940 after blowing up a German ammunition dump in what was a major display of pyrotechnics. By the end of the day on 15 September, the German counterattack had been stopped, and the situation seemed somewhat improved for the Allies. Plunkett wrote that they had been under constant air attack all day while they were firing on the beach. A couple of LSTs were hit and bombs fell all around the *Boise*. Plunkett nervously quipped, "What a hell of a place! Smoking too much." Moneymaker recorded that he saw two enemy planes get shot down that day, but complained that the *Boise* did not score a single hit.

The Germans were not yet finished, however, and made one final attempt to squash the landings. This last counterattack came along the entire front beginning at 0900 on 16 September. The ground attack was preceded by an enemy air raid at 0730 during which *Boise* fired her full panoply of AA guns at attacking aircraft. Their bombs missed the big cruiser, but hit an LCI and a Liberty ship. When the German forces began to advance, she blasted away at them with both her main and secondary batteries four different times until 1127. About an hour later, she lobbed 58 6-inch rounds into another target under the SFCP's direction. In the early afternoon (1426–1429), six FW-190s made a dive-bombing run at the *Boise*, which she repelled with her 40- and 20-mm AA guns. Late in the afternoon, she fired parting shots at the retreating German troops and tanks for two hours beginning at 1750. Once again, she drove off a raid by enemy aircraft, this time using her 5-inch guns loaded with AA ammo as the bandits flew over at high altitude (1825–1827). Plunkett recorded, "We are very lucky, furious fighting on beach."

The situation by the end of 16 September had improved considerably for the Americans and the British. According to Morison, the Germans had lost any hope of retaking Salerno's beaches and began to pull back from the coast. In his memoirs,

Field Marshal Kesselring admitted, "On 16 September, in order to evade the effective shelling of warships, I authorized a disengagement on the coastal front…"

After wrapping up her last call-fire assignment of the day, *Boise* pulled out of the Gulf of Salerno at 1915 bound for Bizerte. After four days of heavy bombardment, her magazines were almost depleted; she had expended a total of 1,939 6-inch and 1,161 5-inch rounds during the four days she participated in the Salerno operation. Therefore, she was sent back to Bizerte to replenish her ammunition and other necessary supplies. The skipper's action report for Operation *Avalanche* indicates that his ship bombarded many different targets on call from the SFCPs at ranges of 8,000 to 22,000 yards. Her fire was indirect and could not be observed from the ship, but its effectiveness was attested to by artillery observers ashore. *Boise* had aided materially in repelling one major enemy counterattack, and in one instance a large explosion in the area they were pounding was seen from the ship, which according to the SFCP came from an enemy ammunition dump that was blown up by a direct hit from the *Boise*. Despite the constant air raids and the new "rocket bombs" she so deftly dodged, the cruiser suffered no damage or casualties during the invasion. Admiral Davidson's endorsement of the ship's action report for the invasion stated that during the operation, she had fired "against troops and tanks and in interdiction with telling effect." Vice Admiral Hall commented that the "quality of fire support she is capable of providing is demonstrated by [Davidson's] Endorsement…."

A report on naval cooperation with the U.S. Army in the European Theater, prepared in 1945 and preserved in army records, attests to the important contribution made by the U.S. Navy cruisers and destroyers at Salerno. It stresses that the data on the amount of ammunition expended by the ships during the operation provide little sense of the "intensity" or "deadly accuracy" of their shelling, but "the covering and supporting gunfire from the warships played an immense part in the eventual success of the operation…"

On the night of 16–17 September, German bombers again attacked Allied installations at Bizerte as the *Boise* was speeding her way there. It was a dark night, and the ship was blacked out to avoid being spotted by German aircraft and zigzagging to foil a possible submarine attack. One of her escorting destroyers suddenly reported two enemy planes approaching at 2,000 feet from about two miles out. No sooner had the alarm been given that a loud noise was heard that some described as an explosion. The big warship was shaken so violently that Radioman Hallman was thrown to the deck. At first, Hallman assumed they had been struck by a torpedo, but later was told there had been a near-miss astern by a German bomb.

Avery, on the other hand, thought the *Boise* had run over something, possibly a submarine, smack in the middle of the Mediterranean Sea that night. He said the big cruiser rose up so high out of the water that he was thrown from his bunk, where he was sleeping below decks, and there was a loud scraping noise as her keel passed over the unidentified object and then dropped back into the water on the other side. The cruiser suffered some damage to the bow and one of her screws was bent, which caused a heavy vibration when she was underway. A night or two later, Avery was again sleeping in his bunk when he was awakened by the captain, who asked him when he had first noticed the vibration that could be distinctly felt aft, almost directly underneath where he slept. Avery told the skipper that it had begun right after the ship ran over whatever it was they had hit on the night of 16–17 September. The CO thanked him and told him to go back to sleep. As the incident had occurred in deep water where the charts showed no rocks or shoals, Avery always insisted that they had run over a German submarine probably sitting on the surface to serve as a navigational aid to guide the enemy bombers on their flight over to the North African coast.

Boise's war diary entry for the night of 16–17 September makes no mention of this incident, but when the cruiser returned to Palermo on 20 September, divers were sent down to inspect the screw. They found that one of its blades was badly nicked and bent while a second blade also had a slight nick. The war diary entry for 20 September gives the cause of the damage as "apparently striking an underwater object while underway on 17 September—position 37°21'N and 10°41'E in 135 fathoms depth." This entry in the ship's war diary would seem to confirm Avery's version of the story that the cruiser ran over something quite large in the middle of the Mediterranean Sea, and it is not unreasonable to assume that it could have been a German U-boat. No reference was made to damage to the bow in the record, however, which Avery claimed was pushed back several inches. Moneymaker's journal (21 September) records that the No. 4 screw was so badly bent that they would have to go somewhere to get a new one and to have a great deal more work done. He speculated that this might mean they would return to the United States. In a telephone interview with the author on 23 July 2013, he said he remembered them running over something that night of 16–17 September 1943, but could not be certain what it was—it could have been a submarine or perhaps an uncharted rock or shoal. Moneymaker did not recall that the cruiser suffered any damage to her bow in the incident.

Boise continued on into Bizerte without further incident, arriving at 1058 on the morning of 17 September. She quickly loaded ammunition and supplies and returned to the Gulf of Salerno. By the time she arrived back on station on 18 September, the Allied invasion force had pushed so far inland that cruiser fire support was no longer needed. Thus, on 19 September *Boise* was ordered to stand down and. was sent to Palermo to await further orders. Most of the crew probably shared gunner Plunkett's feelings about leaving Salerno when he wrote: "Very glad to get out of here, [I] am very tired." Upon reaching Palermo, Moneymaker noted in his journal, "What a relief."

Palermo - Piazza stazione Centrale e via Roma.

Postcard, Palermo, Sicily, 1943. (Author)

During an extended stay at Palermo from 19 September to 5 October, Avery and his shipmates were granted liberty, giving them the opportunity to see the sights in the Sicilian capital, much of which dated from medieval times. As a small-town boy from rural Georgia, he had never seen anything like it, and was very impressed by the old city despite the ravages of war it had suffered. Avery and others of his shipmates were especially struck with the catacombs, the old cathedral, and several other beautiful churches (see postcard above that he sent home). He remembered that the cathedral's beautiful dome had been perforated by a bomb that also penetrated the floor, but fortunately did not explode. Vince Langelo recalled that the Red Cross canteen in the city served up delicious ice-cold lemonade made with fresh lemons donated by Sicilian farmers in gratitude for their liberation from German domination. Lemons and oranges, together with grapes and olives, were the island's principal crops. Some of the crews were saddened to think of how many acres of orchards that produced those delicious lemons had been destroyed by their shelling during the shore bombardments of Operation *Husky*.

At Palermo on 25 September 1943, Captain J. S. Roberts, USN, replaced Captain Hewlett Thebaud as the *Boise*'s CO. Thebaud, who was later promoted to rear admiral, was awarded the Legion of Merit with Combat V and a Gold Star as well as a Bronze Oak Leaf Cluster in lieu of a second and third Legion of Merit for his leadership and the cruiser's outstanding performance during Operations *Husky* and *Avalanche*. The men's first impression of their new skipper was that he seemed like

Captain Hewlett Thebaud bidding farewell to the officers of USS *Boise* during the change of command at Palermo, Sicily, 25 September 1943. (USNARA, 80-G-57183)

"a pretty good old bird," although for Moneymaker, at least, this impression would change for the worse as time went by.

From the Mediterranean to the Southwest Pacific

No further missions were assigned to the *Boise* in the Mediterranean, and she was released from the Eighth Fleet to return to the United States before heading out to the Pacific. She departed Palermo on 5 October 1943, and after a brief stop at Malta on 6 October, where the crew saw the *Savannah,* continued on to Algiers. Moneymaker declared that 206 of *Savannah*'s crew (about one in five) had been killed at Salerno and guessed that she would probably have to remain at Malta for a couple of months before getting underway for the United States.

On 7 October, *Boise* began a 16-day visit at Algiers, where the crew enjoyed good liberties. Hallman wrote in his memoirs that the best one was the chaplain's wine party:

> The afternoon beach party . . . was organized by the Chaplain of the ship, and what a party that turned out to be. We bought a couple of barrels of good wine and rolled it out on the beach.

USS *Boise* at sea, 1943. (USNARA, 80-G-68105)

Everyone got drunk as hell and the Chaplain himself took quite a beating as he was thrown in the water, clothes and all! We got a good poker game going, [in] which our chief radioman Wang Ju and myself cleaned up. We came out a couple hundred dollars on top. It was sunset before we got back to the ship. Everyone stinken [sic] drunk, but happy as hell.

One day, Moneymaker and several other CPOs went on a day trip to the town of Medea, about 40 miles inland from Algiers. The outing took them across a small mountain range that was part of the Atlas chain. They had a pretty good time, and everyone got drunk except Moneymaker and a few others. Two men cracked their skulls when they fell off the truck, and so Moneymaker and another sober CPO had to take their injured companions to the hospital in an ambulance. Moneymaker, who was disgusted by raucous, drunken behavior, summed up his feelings about the whole affair with the exclamation "Nuts!!!"

Before departing Algiers on 23 October 1943, an awards ceremony was held aboard the *Boise*. Twelve crewmen received Purple Hearts and five were awarded the Distinguished Flying Cross (DFC) for their flying on the first day of the Gela invasion. Moneymaker scoffed at the number of awards handed out saying that good money could be made from selling medals for a dime a dozen. He griped that it was becoming disgraceful to wear a medal in the navy and that he would be ashamed to do so. He particularly ridiculed the pharmacist mates who received Purple Hearts for being "gassed," sarcastically suggesting that it was most likely from their own flatulence.

On the voyage back to the United States *Boise* stopped briefly at Oran (24–28 October) and then Casablanca (29 October–7 November) before crossing the Atlantic to New York, where she arrived on 15 November. During the crossing she was escorted by two destroyers, the USS *Nicholson* (DD-442) and the USS *Rhind* (DD-404). Once they reached the open ocean, the crew was ordered to batten down the ship for a hurricane. The storm turned out to be a big one, and the seas, with 20-foot waves crashing over the main deck, were so rough that tables could not be set up in the mess, so the sailors had to eat sitting on the deck. Avery recalled that he sat down on the deck for a meal and just as he set his coffee cup down, the ship rolled sending the cup flying, and it smashed into the bulkhead on the other side of the mess. Indeed, at times the ship was listing so extremely that just a few more degrees and her gun turrets could have fallen over the side into the sea. Hallman records that during the trip across the "wild Atlantic" the *Boise* sprung a leak and had about three feet of seawater in one of her compartments. Avery observed that the Atlantic was always rolling, tossing the big cruiser around and making navigation uncomfortable. He much preferred to sail the Pacific, which in good weather generally lived up to its name.

Even the old salt Moneymaker wrote in his journal that this voyage was one of the roughest he had ever made. The storm lasted several days, making sleep impossible so that everyone was exhausted and looking "like the devil." One morning, the ship was rolling so badly that the salty old chief, while heading for GQ, was thrown against a bulkhead and cracked his left ankle. The hurricane jostled them around much of the way to the extent that no church service was held on Sunday 14 November. Interestingly, there is no mention of the hurricane in the *Boise*'s war diary; as far as the official record is concerned it was business as usual in the U.S. Navy. For sure, though, all hands were greatly relieved and happy when they finally anchored in Gravesend Bay, New York, the next morning.

In New York, *Boise* went into the Brooklyn Navy Yard for repairs and refitting for its new assignment with the U.S. Seventh Fleet in the Southwest Pacific Theater. The legendary cruiser had earned two battle stars during her service in the Mediterranean Sea: one for her participation in the occupation of Sicily and the other for the Salerno landings. She helped to write a new page in the history of naval warfare by proving that naval gunfire could be as devastatingly effective, if not more so, than land-based artillery in supporting troops in the field, something which the U.S. Army had come to appreciate most highly.

While the cruiser was undergoing repairs, Avery and his shipmates got a chance to go home on leave for a short while. After the terrific stress and strain of fighting the Germans in Sicily and Italy, this was a most welcome break. It would be Avery's last chance to get home until July 1945. The fighting that awaited them in Southwest Pacific, especially in the Philippines, would make the action in the Mediterranean look tame by comparison.

.*i*

Leapfrogging the Japanese in New Guinea, 1943–44

While the crew of the USS *Boise* was fighting the Germans and Italians in the Mediterranean Theater, the United States and its allies were rolling back Japanese advances in the Pacific and Southeast Asia. Imperial Japanese forces had pushed into Southeast Asia and the Dutch East Indies to secure oil, rubber, and other natural resources vital to their war industries. Fearing that the United States would eventually come to the defense of Great Britain, Imperial Japanese forces had attacked American bases in Hawaii, the Philippine Islands, and elsewhere in the Pacific in December 1941. By early 1942, the Commonwealth of the Philippines, an American protectorate, had fallen to the invaders, and General Douglas MacArthur, under presidential order, was evacuated from the Philippines to Australia. The Japanese thrust into New Guinea, which was almost evenly divided into two territories controlled by Great Britain and the Netherlands, and elsewhere in the SWPA, threatened Australia, but the Japanese steamroller was finally halted by mid-1942, in great part thanks to the U.S. Navy's victory in the Battle of the Coral Sea (4–8 May 1942), southeast of New Guinea and northeast of Australia.

The Allied Counteroffensive in the South Pacific, 1942–43

From their base in Australia, Allied forces—primarily American, Australian, and New Zealand, with some participation by the British and the Dutch—under the command of General MacArthur launched a counteroffensive to roll back the Japanese in New Guinea, while the U.S. Navy and Marine Corps were doing the same in their island-hopping drive across the Central Pacific. In March 1942, the Allied Combined Chiefs of Staff created the Southwest Pacific Area (SWPA) as a distinct theater of war, naming MacArthur as Supreme Commander (CINCSWPA) in charge of all land and naval forces in the area. SWPA included the Philippine Islands, Borneo, the Dutch East Indies, New Guinea, Australia, the western Solomon Islands and a few other island groups (see map below). By the beginning of 1943, the Japanese had lost the initiative in the South Pacific, and MacArthur was preparing to advance along the northern coast of New Guinea as the preliminary stage of the campaign

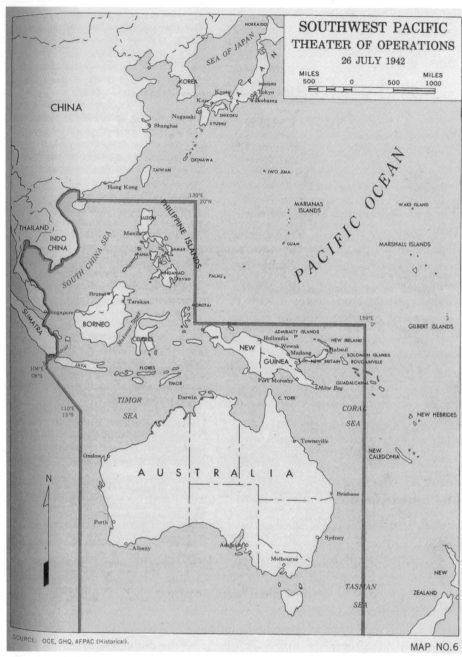

Southwest Pacific Theater (University of Texas Library, Perry Castañeda Library Map Collection, "Engineers of the Southwest Pacific, 1941–1945, Vol. 1," p. 38)

to recapture the Philippine Islands, the major Japanese stronghold in the region. In preparation for this offensive, the U.S. Seventh Fleet was formed from remnants of the old Asiatic Fleet on 15 March 1943, under the command of Vice Admiral Arthur S. Carpender, USN, to support Allied land forces.

At first, the Seventh Fleet, which became popularly known as "MacArthur's Navy," was primarily a submarine force. It had no capital ships, i.e., battleships and fleet aircraft carriers; its true workhorses were two *Brooklyn* class light cruisers, USS *Phoenix* (CL-46) and USS *Nashville* (CL-43), as well as a number of destroyers, PT-boats, and small, slow escort carriers, also known as jeep carriers or "baby flat tops." Warships of the Royal Australian Navy (RAN)—primarily two heavy cruisers and several destroyers—under the command of Rear Admiral Victor A. C. Crutchley, RN, reinforced the Seventh Fleet as did a handful of ships from the navies of New Zealand, Great Britain, and the Netherlands.

Through the summer of 1943 American submarines preyed on Japanese shipping in the region, ferried supplies to Filipino guerrillas and resistance forces on other islands, and brought back valuable intelligence about enemy positions and activities. Rear Admiral Daniel E. Barbey, USN, assumed command the Seventh Fleet's Amphibious Force of LSTs and LCIs with the job of transporting American and Australian troops to invasion sites and protecting them until beachheads were secure. During the summer and fall of 1943, Barbey began practicing amphibious landings, which rapidly improved his force's proficiency. Later in the fall, Vice Admiral Thomas C. Kinkaid, USN, relieved Admiral Carpender as Commander Seventh Fleet. The latter was an overly cautious commander who would not put his warships, which were in short supply in the South Pacific, at risk. Such timidity irritated General MacArthur no end, and Kinkaid, an aggressive fighter, was much more to the CINC's liking. In late 1943 and early 1944, the Seventh Fleet was beefed up and began to take on the appearance of a true fighting force. Kinkaid even got his own air arm of B-24 heavy bombers and PBY Catalinas. The deployment of the *Boise* to the SWPA was part of this Seventh Fleet build-up in the campaign to give the boot to the Japanese occupation forces in New Guinea and the Philippine Islands.

A South Pacific Cruise, 1943

On 6 December 1943, *Boise* departed New York for the Southwest Pacific, passing through the Panama Canal four days later. After a day and two nights anchored at Balboa on the Pacific side of the isthmus, she got underway on 12 December bound for Milne Bay, Territory of Papua, which lay some 7,800 nautical miles (8,978 statute miles) away across the South Pacific. The 18-day voyage was peaceful, and the weather was good. In fact, her Pacific crossing would have been almost as pleasant as sailing aboard a cruise liner had it not been for the daily drills and gunnery practice exercises. Even so, the men had time to enjoy the cruise and reflect on the wonderful time they had spent at home, as well as to speculate on what lay ahead. While most of the men on the *Boise* could not know what the future held in store, to quote one who did, veteran Radioman Vince Langelo, they "were ready to do their duty."

The intense training and gunnery practice revealed problems that had to be solved before the big cruiser went back into combat. One of the more serious was that some of the main battery's new guns were not completely ejecting shells, so the jams had to be dislodged by hand. Despite the numerous exercises, some of the more experienced hands complained that not enough attention was being given to training the new crew members for combat. Moneymaker noted in his journal that efforts to teach damage control to the men of the electrical gang at times seemed hopeless. The Chief also griped about the shortage of electrical supplies on board. Remembering the Battle of Cape Esperance, he added, "By golly, if we get hit this time it sure is going to be a different story, and we may tie up alongside the *Helena.*" (The USS *Helena* (CL-50) was sunk by Japanese torpedoes in the Battle of Kula Gulf (New Georgia Island) on 5 July 1943.) Moneymaker bitterly grumbled "If we are sent into battle any time soon, it will be suicide."

The *Boise*'s formidable firepower was sorely needed in the SWPA, where many American warships had been lost in combat with the IJN, so there was no time to waste. Therefore, she made only two, brief refueling stops on the voyage from Panama to the Territory of Papua, one at Bora Bora in the Society Islands (22 December) and another at Suva, Fiji Islands (26–27 December). When the cruiser crossed the Equator a few days out of Panama, Avery and the other "pollywogs" (novitiates) on board underwent the traditional naval baptism by the "shellbacks" who had crossed the line before. As with most sailors, it was an experience he never forgot.

An anonymous chronicle of the *Boise* in the SWPA, a copy of which was found in Avery's collection of navy memorabilia, relates that they made the voyage alone, without the protection of a destroyer screen. On the day the ship crossed into the southern hemisphere, the *Boise Chronicler* wrote: "We are alone, we are alone; no escort at all and it is 4,780 miles from Panama to Bora Bora. It sure is hot here and it sure tells on us after being used to a cool climate."

During the voyage across the South Pacific the men were awed by the beauty of the islands they passed. As *Boise* pulled into Bora Bora, she was greeted by a scene that had been repeated countless times throughout Polynesia over the previous four centuries—a flotilla of some 50 canoes paddled out to sell souvenirs to the sailors. Time was short so the crew were not granted shore leave on the island. Moneymaker complained that prices for shell necklaces had risen sharply since the ship's last visit to the island. The native vendors were asking one dollar for a shell necklace in December 1943, whereas before a quarter would have bought "all you wanted." The Chief blamed the Americans' generosity for the higher prices. Avery, the sailor

USS *Boise* Christmas card, 1943. (Author)

from Georgia who was seeing it all for the first time, was particularly struck with the natural beauty of Bora Bora, which he frequently recalled in later life.

Boise crossed the International Dateline at approximately 1000 on the morning of 25 December 1943, which made for a very short Christmas Day as it was already 26 December west of the line. Nevertheless, the men had their Christmas dinner with turkey and all the trimmings, and the chaplain passed out their Christmas stockings, which he had received before the ship sailed from New York.

Boise arrived at Suva at 1532 on 26 December, where they laid over until the next day, and the crew were granted liberty. Some men complained that there was not much to see and the weather was "torrid." It was hot, and rained off and on all day. The town's single small hotel had a bar, but the place was empty. Some guys picked up some nice souvenirs, such as grass skirts and shell beads, which according to Moneymaker were overpriced. According to the *Boise Chronicler*, the sailors did not think much of the local women, who were nothing like the Polynesians portrayed in the movies. "They are just plain colored people, and they don't appeal to us in the least." This racist appraisal was not shared by everyone in the ship's company. Avery's navy scrapbook contains a couple of photographs of two very attractive South Pacific women, the darker of whom is definitely Fijian and the other is Polynesian, most likely from Bora Bora. He was always absolutely non-discriminatory in his appreciation of female beauty.

At 2300 on 27 December the ship weighed anchor at Suva bound for the Territory of Papua, some 1,794 miles away. Steaming west, she passed the New Hebrides and Efate Island, and three days later arrived at Milne Bay, located at the southeastern tip of the Territory of Papua. The bay had been developed into an important base of operations since it was first occupied by Australian and American forces in September 1942. General MacArthur's forces were engaged in a desperate struggle against the Japanese, who had taken up strategic positions along the island's north coast in early 1942. The men of the *Boise* could hear the unmistakable sounds of combat not far up the coast as the ship dropped anchor in the harbor.

The crew gazed out almost in disbelief on the mountainous, "wild-looking" country around Milne Bay. There was no sign of a town of any description anywhere in sight. At the time, the Territories of Papua and New Guinea were indeed wild and wooly places. It consisted of some 152,000 square miles of rugged, mountainous terrain covered with dense jungle. Prior to the war, Papua was administered by Australia under a League of Nations mandate and the Netherlands' control of New Guinea was confined almost exclusively to a few points along the northern coast while the interior was populated almost entirely by different groups who Samuel Eliot Morison described as being among the "most savage and ferocious" of all Pacific islanders. Head hunting and cannibalism were still practiced, and some Japanese soldiers, who were hated by the islanders, may have ended up roasting over their cookfires. There were no urban areas of any consequence, and the 1936 census counted only 204 Europeans in the entire territory. Avery and his shipmates, therefore, could plainly see that they had come to a place far different from those they had visited in the Mediterranean. But many of them remained ignorant of the fact that they would now be fighting a vastly different kind of war against an enemy totally unlike the ones they had faced in Sicily and Italy.

Papua and New Guinea, January–September 1944

Just over a year after her trial by fire in the night engagement of Cape Esperance off Guadalcanal, *Boise* was back in the South Pacific again to do battle with the Japanese. She was assigned to the Seventh Fleet's Cruiser Division 15 (CRUDIV-15) commanded by Rear Admiral Russell S. "Count" Berkey, USN, in TF-74. Berkey's cruisers included *Boise's* sister ships *Phoenix* (CL-46) and *Nashville* CL-43), while TF-74 also included warships of the RAN including the heavy cruisers HMAS *Australia* and HMAS *Shropshire*, as well as other U.S. Navy vessels.

Initially, *Boise* was involved in helping to consolidate the Allies' recapture of the Territories of Papua and New Guinea, where the fighting was less intense than what she would encounter later on. In November 1942, Australian and American troops had launched an offensive against the major Japanese strong points at Buna, Sanananda and Gona on the northeast coast. It was a fiercely fought campaign that was only brought to an end in January 1943, 11 months before the *Boise* arrived on the scene. Thereafter, MacArthur adopted a strategy of bypassing the stronger enemy positions, cutting them off from supplies and reinforcements, and attacking the weaker ones in a leap-frog campaign similar to that being used by the U.S. Navy and Marines in the islands of the Central Pacific. On New Year's Day 1944, *Boise* left Milne Bay for Buna Roads to rendezvous with *Nashville* and *Phoenix*, which were anchored in Porlock Harbor. The Japanese forces sandwiched between Admiral Berkey's cruisers at Buna and the Allied base at Milne Bay had been cut off. The *Boise Chronicler* surely reflected his shipmates' feelings about the enemy troops left in such dire straits when he wrote "I hope they starve."

When *Boise* arrived at Porlock Harbor, Allied troops were still mopping up the remnants of the enemy garrison that had fled into the jungle. The fighting was near enough that smoke from artillery fire could be seen from the ship. The cruisers were ordered to stand by just in case their big guns were needed, but for the next two weeks no calls for fire support were received. The cruisers went out to Buna every morning and returned to Porlock Bay in the evening, a routine that soon became exceedingly monotonous. The waiting around was hell on the men's nerves, especially since no one bothered to tell them why they were waiting. From the main deck, the crew could see swarms of American planes flying overhead, coming and going on their bombing missions. The sailors baptized Porlock Harbor with the nickname "Maggot Bay" because the foul stench of death hung over it like a pestilent cloud. They finally discovered the source of the nauseating odor; some 3,000 Japanese had been killed in combat there, and their rotting corpses covered the harbor's bottom, producing patches of white scum and particles that floated on the waters' surface, preventing the sailors from swimming in the bay. The tropical heat and humidity were insufferable, and the men were convinced it was hot enough to fry an egg on the deck; some prankster would undoubtedly have tried to prove the point, if an opportunity could have been found when no officers or senior CPOs were around.

Discontent among the crew grew as the days wore on, and the heat punished them unmercifully. The ship's ventilation system provided little relief. Alterations made at the Brooklyn Navy Yard had only made the situation worse, to the point that the system was practically useless. Captain Roberts and his XO, Commander Thomas Wolverton, added insult to injury by holding personnel inspections that required the men to stand on deck in their white uniforms for hours in the hot sun, and the skipper's complaints that the air conditioner in his cabin was so noisy that it kept him awake at night severely irritated Avery and his buddies in the E Division. Moneymaker grumbled that they had rushed all the way out to New Guinea to sit around doing nothing in the stifling heat. He cursed the officers and the politicians for making them stand idle as if waiting for a Japanese submarine to attack, and scoffed, "Some people say there is a war going on, but you couldn't tell it by being aboard the *Boise*." For the Chief, the boredom of inaction was worse than the dangers of combat, and he longed for a transfer to PT boats or destroyers, which at least were doing something.

Boise finally left Buna on 14 January 1944, without having fired a shot, to return to Milne Bay, where she arrived the next day, and devoted the next two days to gunnery practice. The heat was as bad as it was at Buna, but at least the men could go ashore and play softball. They also had movies on the fantail. One evening an army band made up of African-American GIs performed on board ship. Moneymaker, who was increasingly hard to please, praised the band as very good.

The heat was so intense that the crew's quarters below decks were like an oven, and it played havoc with some of the ship's electrical motors. One burned out in the evaporators, which were essential equipment as they converted sea water into water for drinking and for generating steam to drive the ship. The electrical gang had to repair the motor, and on 19 January Moneymaker and some of his electricians began rewinding it, working all day and through the night until 0300 the next morning. Even so, they were unable to finish the job, and he and Avery completed the rewinding on the afternoon of 20 January while the other electricians went ashore.

On the positive side, the mail finally caught up with them at Milne Bay on 23 January, the first mail delivery since leaving the United States over a month earlier. All hands would have agreed with the *Boise Chronicler* that "It sure was welcome." Thereafter, it seems that mail began arriving on a more or less regular basis.

A few nights later, *Boise* was finally called into action along with the *Phoenix* and three destroyers. It would be her first real combat mission since rejoining the war against Japan, and everyone on board was anxious about how it would go. The Japanese were beefing up their presence in the Madang-Alexishafen area, and the task group's mission was to bombard enemy installations, supply dumps and troop concentrations near the shore. The attack, scheduled for the night of 25–26 January, was designed to facilitate future advances by Allied forces along the north coast to the west of the target area. *Boise* and one destroyer, the USS *Mullaney* (DD-528), were assigned to shell fuel dumps, barge landings, personnel concentrations, and other targets at Alexishafen, while *Phoenix* with two tin cans would strike Madang about eight miles away.

Unfortunately, *Boise*'s first shore bombardment in New Guinea did not go particularly well. Problems with her Mark-8 radar caused a delay of about 20 minutes in opening fire. Even so, she flung some 953 HE rounds (502 5-inch and 451 6-inch) at enemy positions on the island, but the radar glitches hampered correct identification of coastal targets, leading to miscalculations in determining the ship's true position. This complex set of issues threw off her aim to the point that she missed her targets at times by as much as five miles, according to the PBY "Black Cats" that provided aerial spotting for the night shoot.

During the attack, she took some light return fire from enemy shore batteries. Fortunately, their aim was not so good either; no incoming Japanese shells scored

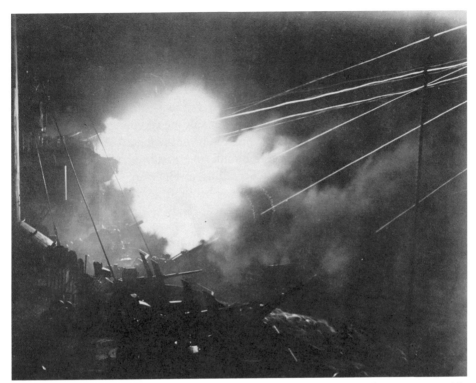

USS *Boise* shelling the New Guinea coast (probably at Madang-Alexishafen, January 1944). (USNARA, 80-G-213844)

a direct hit on the ship, although three sailors were slightly wounded by shrapnel from a near miss. While the mission's results may have disappointed their superiors, the crew were relieved that no one had been seriously injured and the ship had suffered no damage. Moneymaker could not resist a sarcastic dig at the officers for their having missed the target, noting in his journal: "It was either the Navigator's or gunnery officer's fault. If it had been an enlisted man, guess he would have been strung up, but since it was an officer, he will probably get a medal for knocking down the greatest number of coconut trees in the shortest time."

The month of February got off to a good start for Avery, who was promoted to Electrician's Mate Second Class. On 10 February, Admiral Berkey transferred his flag from the *Phoenix* to the *Boise*. After the Alexishafen mission, *Boise* returned to Milne Bay to refuel and resupply, remaining there while awaiting a new assignment. *Boise* took advantage of this time to conduct daily gunnery practice. She also performed radar maintenance and calibration exercises to avoid a recurrence of the embarrassing problems that were experienced during the Alexishafen mission. In their free time, the men were able to see some movies and enjoy beer parties on the beach when the weather permitted. One of the major complaints, other than the heat, was that it rained every day. Indeed, it was said that in New Guinea "it rains every day for nine months, and then the monsoons begin." Boredom also took a toll on morale. In his journal, Moneymaker quipped, "Well, looks like as far as the *Boise* is concerned the war is over," and sneered that "the *Boise* is now classified as a second line ship so we will probably get stuck with this kind of duty for D.O.W. [duration of the war]." At this point, the salty veteran made up his mind to request a transfer because "this business of laying around in a harbor does not suit me very much."

On 20 February, the ship held a Happy Hour on the fantail. Among the guests in attendance were two army nurses, a blonde and a redhead, who caused quite a stir of excitement among the sailors. According to Hallman, "The fellows almost went crazy." Some good boxing matches were held during the afternoon, and after the Happy Hour the crew enjoyed cake, punch, candy, and "smokes," followed by a movie.

As the days and weeks dragged on, the heat and inactivity continued to erode morale among the crew. Moneymaker especially seemed to sink deeper and deeper into discontent, becoming even more irritated with the conduct of the war and the cruiser's officers in particular. By this point, he was thoroughly disgusted with both the skipper and the XO, Commander Wolverton, who had become a pain in the neck since his promotion. The Chief derisively caricatured Wolverton, comparing him to Elsa Maxwell, a short, heavy-set celebrity of the day. He joked sarcastically that the XO looked exactly like her while running around in khaki shorts and pith helmet and giving orders through a megaphone during an abandon ship drill that forced the crew to jump over the side into the contaminated waters of Milne Bay, in which they were not allowed to go swimming.

Fortunately, before morale dropped to breaking point, the men of the *Boise* got a respite from the relentless heat and drudgery in the form of R&R in Australia. Before departing for Sydney, however, they joined the *Nashville*, HMAS *Shropshire*, five destroyers and a submarine for drills and simulated combat in the Coral Sea on 25 February. At 0600 the next morning, *Boise* separated from the task force and set a course for Sydney, traveling without a destroyer escort. All hands were excited about the visit and looking forward to drinking plenty of cold beer; the beer they could get at Milne Bay was hot. En route to Australia, the orders of the day on 27 February gave the crew an explanation of the country's currency—the exchange rate was US$3.23 per pound—together with detailed instructions on sexual hygiene and the proper use of condoms, which were available for purchase in the Ship's Service Store. According to the XO this was crucially important because some men, especially while under the influence of too much alcohol, would have sexual intercourse with "promiscuous women" who were infected with venereal diseases.

The big American cruiser docked at Woolloomooloo Wharf in Sydney at 0800 on 29 February. The excited sailors were most impressed with what they saw of the city on their way in. It was a beautiful place that reminded the crew of any large city back home, a welcome change from the wilds of Papua and New Guinea. A large crowd was on hand at the pier to welcome them; the atmosphere was festive with bands playing, and everyone in the crowd was smiling and waving. From what they could see, the women on the pier looked wonderful, leaving all hands chomping at the bit to go on liberty.

During their two weeks in Sydney, Avery and his shipmates tried to forget the war and enjoy themselves to the fullest. They went to the movies, ate steaks in expensive restaurants, visited amusement parks, and hit the bars. It was late summer in Australia, but there was plenty of good, ice-cold beer. There were few Australian servicemen around except for sailors, but the town was crawling with American soldiers, sailors, and Marines, many from nearby training camps. The locals were very friendly for the most part, and the men of the *Boise* put aside all thoughts of the war and really let their hair down.

Among the principal attractions in Australia for the American sailors were the women, who were beautiful, friendly and spoke English. During one of their port calls at Sydney, Avery met a pretty Australian woman whose husband was in the army and had been shipped overseas to fight, probably in New Guinea or perhaps Europe. The attractive young woman invited the sailor from Georgia to her home, fixed him a meal, and took him into her bed. A brief affair ensued. It was merely a wartime fling that was not intended to become anything serious. They were two young people caught up in the tragic circumstances of war that sorely missed their loved ones and sought a moment's solace in each other's arms. Avery was deeply in love with his wife and constantly longed for Anne throughout his service in the navy. He wrote her tender, loving letters in which he poured out his heart and dreams of the life they would build together once the war was over.

The bars and restaurants were crowded, and there were plenty of steak, eggs, lamb, and fresh vegetables to be had as well as abundant cold beer with which to wash them down. One day Avery stepped into a bar to have a beer where he overheard some men discussing the war. One of them expounded that Adolf Hitler might eventually take the United States, but the dictator would have to cut a deal with Ole Gene Talmadge before he got control of the state of Georgia. These men surely must have been Americans; it is highly unlikely that Aussies would have heard the fantastic tales talked about Eugene Talmadge, the colorful, populist governor of Georgia who became known as the "Wild Man from Sugar Creek."

While the majority of the boys spent their time and money dining, drinking, and chasing girls, some took the opportunity to sample the local culture. Moneymaker and some friends went to the symphony one evening, which the CPO rated as "pretty good." They also went out to the Sydney suburb of Epping one Sunday where they watched the locals play a few games of lawn bowling, which struck Moneymaker as a game that obviously required quite a bit of practice. They walked around the town, attended church, and visited the technological Institute and the World War I ANZAC Memorial, both of which impressed them deeply.

The Boise's brief respite from the war came to an end all too soon on 11 March. The port call at Sydney had been a truly wonderful time, almost like a dream, and the Boise boys said goodbye to Australia with tears in their eyes. Everyone hoped they would get a chance to return for another visit someday, as indeed they would. According to Hallman's detailed and highly entertaining recounting of the visit, many of the girls the sailors had met came down to the pier to see them off, waving farewell to the men whom they knew they might never see again. The Boise Chronicler wrote that any future mention of Sydney would certainly fill his mind with happy thoughts. This was definitely true for Avery, who celebrated his 28th birthday in Sydney on 9 March 1944. He fell in love with the country and its people and always wished later in life that he could return there for another visit.

When the Boise stood out of Sydney Harbour she was accompanied by the RAN heavy cruiser Australia. Together they conducted gunnery practice by day and night at Cape Moreton, east of Brisbane, on 12 March. Boise's two Kingfisher aircraft were used to spot for both ships since RAN cruisers did not carry reconnaissance planes. The night firing drills were conducted under full radar control on the main battery with outstanding results. Boise's Mark-8 equipment performed extremely well, demonstrating that the maintenance and calibration exercises conducted earlier had solved the radar problems experienced at Alexishafen on 26 January. According to Langelo, once those adjustments had been made, the Mark-8 radar never failed again during combat, and it gave the Boise a tremendous edge over her Japanese opponents, who lagged far behind the Americans in radar technology. The secondary battery's performance was less satisfactory, however, underscoring the need for yet more gunnery practice. Once the firing drills were completed, both cruisers set a course for Milne Bay.

The 1,500-mile voyage back to Papua turned out to be a rough ride lasting three days. The stormy seas violently tossed the cruiser about, and there were many seasick sailors on board, but they made it back in one piece, dropping anchor in Milne Bay on 14 March 1944. They hung around the base for a couple of weeks while everyone wondered what their next mission would be. During this period, Moneymaker got his much-desired transfer along with a promotion to the junior commissioned officer rank of ensign. He left the Boise on 22 March to spend the rest of the war in various postings in the United States. In one assignment, Moneymaker trained as a "frogman" with the elite underwater demolition teams, forerunners of today's Navy SEALs.

On 27 March, the Seventh Fleet was reorganized into two task forces. TF-74, under the command of Rear Admiral Crutchley, consisted of two Australian heavy cruisers, Australia and Shropshire, and four destroyers, two of which were American. TF-75, under the command of Admiral Russell Berkey, USN, had the three Brooklyn class light cruisers and six destroyers. TF-75 then shoved off on 29 March to conduct training operations for two days, returning to Milne Bay on 31 March.

Before *Boise* was ready to get back into the war, more training exercises were needed to hone her gunnery skills to a fine edge. This was especially true for AA defense, in which accuracy was of paramount importance, but exceedingly difficult to attain, as was seen during the air raids that the cruiser had undergone in Sicily and Italy. Unlike the 5-inch battery, the 20-mm and 40-mm guns were not radar controlled, but were fired independently. With constant practice to improve their aim and develop their skills, the ship's gun crews eventually became highly proficient at AA defense, which would become vitally important as the war continued.

While the *Boise* was in Australia, General MacArthur had proceeded to retake the Admiralty Islands, some 200 miles northeast of New Guinea, to use as a staging area for future operations in the area. The series of battles for the Admiralties began on 29 February 1944, and the two largest islands, Manus and Los Negros, were quickly occupied by the U.S. 1st Cavalry Division with the backing of the Seventh Fleet. This victory gave the Allies control of a major anchorage at Seeadler Harbor,

General Douglas MacArthur with Admiral Thomas Kinkaid on board USS *Phoenix* during the invasion of the Admiralty Islands, 28 February 1944. Note the quad-mount 40-mm gun in background. (USNARA, SC 188839)

which became a base for all future operations in the SWPA, including the invasion of the Philippine Islands in the fall of 1944.

MacArthur personally witnessed the invasion of Los Negros Island from the deck of the USS *Phoenix* in the company of Seventh Fleet commander, Vice Admiral Kinkaid. The CINC was profoundly impressed with the pre-landing shore bombardment, especially on the third shot when *Nashville* and *Phoenix* knocked out a large shore battery, which had made the fatal mistake of missing the twin cruisers with its opening salvos. The two senior commanders went ashore to visit the troops and observe the action first hand. At one stop on their tour, a young army officer, surprised to see the two flag officers so near the front lines, warned them that just minutes earlier his soldiers had killed a Japanese sniper in the area, to which MacArthur coolly responded, "That's the best thing to do with them, son."

After experiencing combat aboard the *Phoenix* at Los Negros, MacArthur was bitten by the bug, and thereafter always preferred to ride a *Brooklyn* class light cruiser into battle, using one of them as his headquarters afloat when attack transports or other vessels might have provided more suitable accommodations for the supreme commander of an entire theater of war. Following the capture of Seeadler Harbor, the campaign to complete the occupation of Manus Island and to take the smaller islands in the group continued on until May 1944.

Hollandia, Dutch New Guinea

In April 1944, the Allies launched their campaign against the Japanese occupation forces in Dutch New Guinea. New Guinea was the major stepping stone between Australia and the Philippine Islands, the retaking of which was MacArthur's ultimate objective in the SWPA. But first, he had to neutralize the enemy forces in New Guinea so as not to leave his rear exposed.

Dutch New Guinea was a wild area of dense jungle inhabited by tribes who lived by hunting and subsistence farming. It offered only one good harbor, Humboldt Bay, an area the Americans referred to as Hollandia (present-day Jayapura), after the name of the largest settlement in Dutch New Guinea, which then was little more than a small town situated on the bay. The Japanese invaded the place in early 1942 and built several airfields in the vicinity. A year later they also occupied Wewak, to the east of Humboldt Bay, and built up a sizeable military force and air assets at that location. In early 1944, the Japanese began pouring men and materiel into Hollandia, which they intended to develop into a major base to convert New Guinea into an integral part of their inner defense perimeter that ran from there up through the Dutch East Indies, the Marianas, and Palau. To thwart the enemy's intentions, the Allies aimed their first offensive at Humboldt Bay, bypassing the major Japanese stronghold at Wewak. The idea was to construct airfields, develop the area as a port for the navy, cut the supply lines to the Japanese forces at Wewak, and then starve them out.

As a unit of Admiral Berkey's TF-75, *Boise* participated in all the major operations of the campaign in Dutch New Guinea. The cruisers were primarily employed in shore bombardment and fire support for the amphibious landings. After her experience in the Mediterranean theater, this sort of thing was old hat to the *Boise*. Berkey's cruisers operated in the area between Buna Roads and Humboldt Bay during the week of 15–22 April 1944. They arrived at Buna, also known as Cape Sudest, at 1800 on 15 April, and remained there for the next three days. The time was spent conducting gunnery practice, primarily aimed at honing the skills of the AA gun crews.

At 1100 on 18 April, *Phoenix* and *Boise*, with their destroyer screen, got underway from Buna. With everything in the navy always kept on a need-to-know basis, the men of the *Boise* had no idea where they were headed. The next day, however, they learned that they were to take part in Operation *Reckless*, an amphibious landing around Hollandia where 45,000 American troops were to storm the beaches in the largest such assault on the island to date. They were warned to expect heavy enemy air attacks, possible shore batteries, and perhaps even submarines. The order was passed for all hands to sleep in their clothes, keep their eyes peeled, and be ready for anything at all times. A simultaneous, but smaller landing (Operation *Persecution*) was set to take place at Aitape, 125 miles to the east, in order to capture the enemy airfield and establish a position to block any westward movement by the large Japanese force based at Wewak.

When her sister ships left Buna Roads on 18 April, the *Nashville* remained behind to await General MacArthur, who had so enjoyed his experience aboard the *Phoenix* that he decided to continue the practice and selected the *Nashville* as his headquarters afloat. On 20 April, *Nashville*, with the CINC aboard, caught up and rejoined TF-75. They then rendezvoused with TF-77, the amphibious landing task force, to become part of an armada composed of four separate task forces with a total of over 150 vessels. TF-77 consisted of 24 transports, 60 landing craft, 18 destroyers, and the flagships USS *Blue Ridge* (AGC-2) and USS *Swanson* (DD-443). TF-78 was made up of eight escort carriers from the Seventh Fleet and 17 destroyers. The Pacific Fleet also lent MacArthur its TF-58 with 12 big fleet carriers, but Admiral Halsey could spare them for no more than a few days. TF-74 comprised two RAN heavy cruisers with their screen of two Australian and two American destroyers. The three American light cruisers and six destroyers of TF-75 became part of TF-77 and were assigned to the Central Attack Group (TG-77.2), which was to storm the beaches in the area around Hollandia and Humboldt Bay itself. The Western Attack Group (TG-77.1) was aimed at the area around Tanahmerah Bay, while TG-77.3 would invade the Aitape area east of Humboldt Bay. The baby flat tops of TF-78 and fleet carriers of TF-58 took up station 25 miles off the coast to provide air cover for the landings.

When Operation *Reckless* kicked off on 22 April 1944, surprise was complete and overwhelming. The Japanese occupation force had been fooled into believing the Allied strike would come at Wewak, which was bombed by sea and air for several days prior to D-day. Empty rubber boats were dropped around Wewak so the Japanese would discover the secret plans they were carrying for a bogus landing in that area. As a result, initial enemy resistance at Hollandia was light and the air threat to the ships and beachhead never materialized, although the latter was in great part due to good cover from land- and carrier-based aircraft that neutralized Japanese air power in the area.

With H-Hour set for 0700, the men of the *Boise* went to battle stations at 0430 and did not secure from GQ until the late afternoon. Their job was to provide covering fire for the landing and to support the GIs once they were on the beach. After launching both of her Kingfisher floatplanes to spot fire for the bombardment, she opened fire first with the main battery at 0605, followed by the secondary battery three minutes later. *Boise* gunners blasted their assigned targets for 25 minutes, pouring out a combined total of 763 shells before the first wave of landing craft shoved off for the beach at 0631. Meanwhile, *Nashville* and *Phoenix* also shelled their assigned target areas. American aircraft swept in over the beaches to destroy anti-landing craft barriers and blow-up land mines buried in the sand. When the cruisers wrapped up their bombardment, the destroyers moved up to within 1,000 yards of the beach and proceeded to work over the same targets with their 5-inch guns. While the first wave of landing craft was moving in, their approach was covered by blistering rocket barrages launched from two LCIs to make sure the

Cruisers firing on beach in the Hollandia operation, Humboldt Bay, Dutch New Guinea, 22 April 1944. Note USS *Boise* firing tracer rounds as LVTs head in to land troops. The ship ahead of *Boise* in the background is USS *Phoenix* (CL-46). (USNARA, SC 264436)

Japanese kept their heads down. The dazzling pyrotechnics of these rocket launches were often likened to 4th of July fireworks by those who witnessed one first hand, although the enemy on the receiving end no doubt found them to be a great deal less entertaining and far more deadly.

Thanks largely to this massive concentration of naval firepower, the Hollandia landings became a walk in the park for the soldiers. The first wave of troops encountered no opposition when they hit the beach at 0700. When the first big shells from the naval bombardment began raining down, the panicked Japanese defenders, who had been going about their regular morning routine, fled the beaches and headed for the hills. The American GIs found tea and food being warmed for breakfast in the enemy's positions, indicating that they had departed in great haste. Some light AA fire was observed in the hills behind the beaches, but strafing runs by American fighter planes quickly silenced those enemy guns.

Shortly after the first wave hit the beach, *Boise* began slowly firing her 5-inch guns on assigned targets and kept it up for the next two and a half hours. At 0815, one of her scout planes dropped two 100-pound bombs on a small cargo vessel near the shore, but was unable to determine the damage caused. After she ceased fire (0943), the cruiser stood by awaiting calls for fire support from the SFCP, but as the soldiers continued to meet only light resistance, none were received.

At 1000, General MacArthur went ashore to get a personal look at how the battle was progressing. By mid-afternoon the GIs had taken all the objectives set for D-day, and by 1745 the landing phase of the operation was over. The landings had gone smoothly and the beachhead was firmly established. *Boise*'s job was finished as D-day drew to a close, although mopping up operations at Hollandia would continue for several weeks until the area was completely secured. The American invasion force met only minimum resistance and did not have to face a single air attack. Nevertheless, it had been a long, exhausting day for the men of the *Boise*; the gun crews of TF-75's cruisers and destroyers poured 1,600 6-inch and 3,700 5-inch rounds into enemy positions on shore during the landing. After securing from battle stations at 1800, *Boise*'s task group 77.2 headed for Manus Island in the Admiralty group, a short distance to the northeast of New Guinea.

Operation *Reckless* was well conceived and carefully planned, drawing on excellent intelligence on Japanese positions and defenses from several sources. Among the most important sources of information were MacArthur's spies on the island, many of whom were Australian coast watchers. These were men who owned plantations in New Guinea and other islands in the South Pacific region. They knew the terrain like the back of their hands and had good relations with the native peoples of the islands. When the Japanese invaded, these stout-hearted fellows withdrew into the mountains with their native workers to keep close tabs on the enemy. The Aussie coast watchers communicated with MacArthur's headquarters by portable radios supplied by the Allies that were often delivered, along with other supplies, by American submarines. The intelligence on the enemy gathered by these daring coast watchers proved invaluable at Hollandia and in other operations in the SWPA.

After the Hollandia operation, MacArthur's strategy called for continuing strikes at selected points along the coast in short order until he reached the northwestern tip of Dutch New Guinea's Vogelkop Peninsula, some 550 miles west of Hollandia. The Allies accomplished this feat in just over three months, always keeping in mind the target date of 15 November for the invasion of the Philippine Islands. This campaign involved four operations: Wakde, Biak, Noemfoor, and Sansapor. The SWPA forces always traveled from one landing site to the next by sea, and in each and every operation, Admiral Berkey's cruisers and destroyers were there to deliver gunfire support, a task at which they became increasingly adept.

Before undertaking the next mission, *Boise* returned to Manus Island and put into Seeadler Harbor on April 23 where she got a short breather after refueling and taking on ammunition. The *Boise Chronicler* described the bay as a very beautiful place, one of the best natural harbors to be found anywhere. The harbor is formed by the main island of Manus and the other smaller islands spreading around to make an almost complete circle. The cruiser remained at Seeadler Harbor until 26 April when she returned to New Guinea, arriving off Hollandia on 27 April, to relieve TF-74 and TF-78.2. *Boise* began patrolling with four escort carriers from TG-78.1 to protect the Allied forces at Hollandia from Japanese air or sea attack and to prevent enemy evacuations from points along the coast between Humboldt Bay and Madang.

Wakde-Sarmi, May 1944

As it turned out, the swampy terrain around Hollandia proved to be less suitable for an airbase than expected. The Japanese-built airstrips would not support American heavy bombers, so a better site was needed. Therefore, a spot on the coast 120 miles west around Maffin Bay was selected for this purpose, which was essential to the plans for continued operations along New Guinea's north coast. The Japanese had already built two airstrips in the area, one on Wakde Island and another between Maffin Bay and the nearby town of Sawar; a third aerodrome was under construction close by the bay itself. Morison comments in his history of the New Guinea campaign that it was soon agreed, however, that Biak Island was the best place in Dutch New Guinea for basing heavy bombers. MacArthur thus decided to scale down the Wakde operation and push ahead to Biak as soon as possible, which is to say as soon as the Wakde airstrips could be captured and put into operation for American fighter aircraft. Morison speculates that if the Seventh Fleet had possessed large aircraft carriers whose squadrons could have provided adequate air cover for amphibious landings, the entire Wakde operation could have been foregone. Both the CINC and Admiral Kinkaid repeatedly asked for carriers, but none were ever made available on a permanent basis. There simply were not enough big flat tops in the Pacific to go around, so SWPA was left to make do with a handful of escort carriers that belonged to the Seventh Fleet, and the USAAF units assigned to the area.

Before the main event, a preliminary strike was made on the Japanese airfields around Wakde—the naval equivalent of a nocturnal drive-by shooting. Leaving their "baby bird farms" behind on station off Humboldt Bay, on 29 April "Count" Berkey's cruisers *Boise, Nashville,* and *Phoenix* were dispatched with two destroyers to coordinate with USAAF bombers in destroying the Japanese air bases on Wakde Island and at Sawar. The warships struck first at the Sawar airstrip just after midnight on 30 April. *Boise* poured 400 rounds from the secondary battery and 150 6-inch rounds onto assigned targets in each area. This time, the night bombardment was pulled off without a hitch. At Sawar, her salvos were dead on target, and large explosions and fires on shore, presumed to be from an ammunition dump, were seen from the cruiser's decks. After pounding Sawar, the bobtails and tin cans moved on to Wakde, where they gave a repeat performance beginning at 0130 on 30 April. *Boise* fired on assigned targets, including enemy personnel concentrations and barracks, a materiel depot, and the airstrip. Her initial salvos were spot on, and here again fires and explosions were observed from the ship and confirmed by a spotter plane. Hallman bragged in his memoirs that it was "one of the most effective jobs of bombarding" he had ever seen, while the *Boise Chronicler* agreed that they had done "a pretty good job." The next day, Admiral Berkey informed his ships that aerial photographs taken by carrier planes earlier that morning confirmed that both enemy airstrips were heavily pockmarked and had been rendered unserviceable by the shelling. The TF-75 cruisers and destroyers then shoved off for Humboldt Bay to resume patrolling with the escort carriers. These preliminary air strikes and the raid by the cruisers and destroyers on the airstrips around Wakde-Sawar-Sarmi neutralized the threat from enemy aircraft for the upcoming amphibious assault on the area scheduled for 17 May.

On 3 May, Berkey's Cruiser Division (CRUDIV) 15 accompanied the four baby flat tops of TG-78.1 to Seeadler Harbor, where they dropped anchor two days later. While there, the crew enjoyed beer parties on a small island, skinny dipped in the crystal-clear waters of the bay, and sunbathed on the beautiful beaches. Not all was fun and games, however, as Admiral Berkey relentlessly insisted that his cruiser division work on improving the accuracy of their AA fire, so several days were dedicated to target practice on high and low-flying runs. The gun crews performed well during these exercises, and the captain was highly pleased with the results of the drills that would help prepare them to fight off the enemy air raids that were sure to come.

Leaving Manus Island at 1400 on 15 May with an army fire control team riding aboard *Boise,* CRUDIV 15 headed once again to Wakde Island to support the invasion of the Maffin Bay area of Dutch New Guinea. The objective was to take the area for a base of operations and isolate the Japanese forces situated to the east of that location. Although the Allied invasion force had only limited intelligence on the beach defenses, the positions of some coastal batteries had been identified and marked. On the night of 16 May, *Boise's* crew went to battle stations at 2300 and remained at GQ all night. As *Boise* approached her station in the Fire Support Area at around 0500 the next morning, bomb flashes were seen first around the Maffin airstrip and then on the beach to the west of the small town of Maffin. These explosions were caused by aerial bombing raids by the USAAF.

At 0540 she hoisted out two aircraft to spot fire, then at 0605 was the first ship to commence firing when she opened up with both her main and secondary batteries at a range of 11,000 yards, with the other cruisers following suit in short order. One minute later, four shell explosions were seen near her target at the eastern end of Wakde Island, and her spotter planes reported that the salvo had blanketed the target area. *Boise* also blasted assigned targets in the Yellow Beach landing area to the east of Maffin Bay, while the *Nashville* concentrated on Wakde Island. *Boise's* 5-inch battery continued shelling until 0643 when the first wave of landing craft headed for the beach; the main battery ceased fire five minutes later. At that point, the destroyers moved in close to the shore to provide covering fire for the soldiers. Navy spotter planes dropped red smoke grenades to mark the western edge of Yellow Beach, and then three LCIs fired spectacular rocket barrages into the area directly behind the landing zone. Just before the first wave of troops disembarked from the landing craft at 0730, several A-20 Havocs, B-24 Liberators, and B-25 Mitchells from the Fifth Air Force bombed and strafed the beach area, and continued their bombing and strafing runs on targets there and on the Maffin air field during the rest of the morning.

The first troops to hit the beach met no opposition and proceeded to move inland right on schedule. The succeeding waves of GIs also made their landings according to plan. Some light AA fire over the Maffin and Wakde airfields was observed, but these batteries were quickly silenced by the American warplanes. *Boise* stood by to provide supporting fire if needed, but no calls came in for the rest of the morning. At 0840, she ordered her spotter aircraft to drop their bombs on appropriate targets and return to the ship. The destroyers fired on several enemy barges that appeared near Maffin Bay, blowing them out of the water, while another exploded a large ammunition dump near Sarmi, and an A-20 strafed a fuel storage area triggering large explosions and fires. Later in the morning, after the CINC's flagship, *Nashville*, reported that all significant targets had been eliminated on Wakde Island, smaller landings were made there and on another nearby island. At noon, the commander of Task Group 77.2 released Admiral Berkey's cruisers from their assignment, thanking them for a "splendid job," whereupon they formed a column and stood out of the area bound for Humboldt Bay.

While at Hollandia, they suffered through several nights and days with frequent air raid alerts, which kept the crew from getting much sleep, although no actual

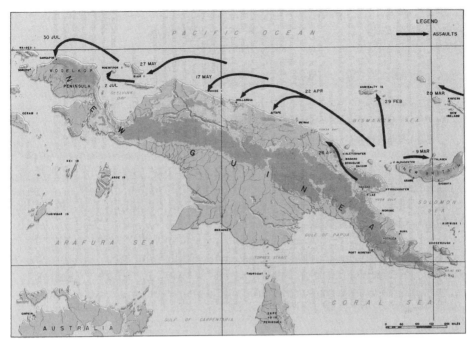

MacArthur's campaign in New Guinea. (U.S. Army Center for Military History. *Reports of General MacArthur: The campaigns of MacArthur in the Pacific, Vol. I*, p. 135)

attacks ever came. Finally, at 1830 on 20 May, they departed with TF-75 to relieve the Australian cruisers and destroyers of TF-74 that had remained on station as a covering force at Wakde-Sarmi. Intelligence reports indicated that the Japanese were planning to land reinforcements at Wakde in an attempt to retake the island from the Allies. From 21–23 May, TF-75 patrolled in an area north of Wakde Island, always remaining within range of fighter cover from the 8th Fighter Group based at Hollandia. At night, they made sweeps as far west as Cape D'Urberville searching for enemy ships and submarines. The only contact came just before 0100 on 22 May, when a destroyer picked up a sonar contact at 1,000 yards dead ahead, but nothing eventuated. On 23 May, some civilian radar technicians came aboard to inspect and tune the *Boise*'s sophisticated, top-secret radar systems.

By midday on 21 May, flight operations began at the Wakde airstrip. The runway was extended to accommodate heavy bombers, and it became a base for two bomber and two fighter groups as well as a B-25 reconnaissance squadron and a Navy PB4Y long-range bomber squadron. For a time, Wakde served as a key air base in the Southwest Pacific campaign until it was replaced by new bases closer to the Philippine Islands, and its usefulness declined. Fighting to neutralize the 10,000 Japanese troops in the jungles in the area continued until early September 1944.

Over 4,000 enemy soldiers were killed, and the survivors remained in hiding deep in the jungles around Sarmi, some until the end of the war.

Biak Island, 27 May 1944

General MacArthur's Southwest Pacific forces continued their relentless push along the northern coast of Dutch New Guinea, much to the consternation of the Japanese who were helpless to stop it. The Allies' next objective was Biak Island, one of the Schouten Islands near the northwestern end, which the general planned to hit a mere 10 days after the Wakde operation. Biak was strategically important to Japan. It was located close to their main supply lines for oil, rubber, and other necessary resources for their war industries. *Boise* therefore returned quickly to Hollandia on 24 May to refuel and replenish her ammunition and supplies. The next day she departed with TF-75 to rendezvous with a convoy of LSTs and LCIs (TG-77.4) for the attack on Biak. The island, which is practically solid coral and ringed with reefs, is strategically located at the entrance to Geelvink Bay, the key to control of the Vogelkop Peninsula that anchors the southeastern end of the axis leading from Dutch New Guinea to the intended target for the Allied invasion of the Philippines, Mindanao Island.

The intelligence experts grossly underestimated the Biak garrison to be no more than 2,000 men, while in reality it was closer to 11,000 well-entrenched Japanese troops. Several airfields were located on the island, and intelligence reports showed a concentration of dual-purpose guns (guns that could be used for AA defense or for shelling ground forces) around the landing strip at Mokmer. The Japanese supply base at Bosnik was also reported to have good AA defenses and possibly several shore batteries. Thus, a heavy shelling of the area by Berkey's cruisers and destroyers was deemed necessary prior to the landing operation, although MacArthur's planners did not anticipate a determined defense of major proportions. The objective of the mission was to seize and occupy Biak Island for use as an air and naval base for future operations on the road to the Philippines. The invasion was set to begin at 0715 on 27 May 1944.

The enemy had set up a defense perimeter around the Mokmer airfield consisting of three consecutive lines. The first was formed by shore batteries just inland from the beach. The second defensive line ran along a ledge behind the airfield and then followed along a ridge that rose behind the village. This line was well fortified, armed with AA guns, small field artillery, mortars, and machine guns. The final line of defense was a system of caves linked by tunnels and trenches capable of sheltering thousands of soldiers. The Japanese commander therefore had a "well-balanced force" that also included some light tanks. After the landings at Hollandia, the Japanese high command correctly deduced that the Allies would move against Biak, which was an important link in their strategic perimeter defense line. However, on 9 May the

Japanese announced that the line would be pulled back to Sarong and Halmahera, leaving Biak Island as an outpost to be defended to the last man. Although the enemy commander expected an assault on Biak and set up a formidable defense, the attack actually came much sooner than expected and caught the defenders off balance. Even so, they were able to deny the Allies use of the Biak airfields for nearly a month.

At 0437 on Z-day (27 May), *Boise* went to GQ and arrived on station in the fire support area 30 minutes later along with the other ships of TG-77.3 (CRUDIV-15). About an hour later, she hoisted out both Kingfisher aircraft to spot fire for her and HMAS *Australia*, and the planes flew spotting flights throughout the morning. From 0630–0715 *Boise's* main battery pounded the Borokoe airfield and other assigned targets at ranges of 12,700–13,900 yards. Although the spotter aircraft were unable to observe the first salvo on the airfield, they confirmed that the second fell squarely on the landing strip, and firing during the barrage was reported as "good." Meanwhile, the 5-inch guns fired on targets of opportunity, including some enemy barges that appeared just off shore and were quickly obliterated, and a flight of B-24 Liberators made the first air strike on the airfields at 0650. The destroyers laid down fire on their assigned targets nearer the beaches, while the cruisers were blasting others further inland.

Enemy shore batteries returned fire, scoring a hit on one of TG-77.3's destroyers, the USS *Hutchins* (DD-476), at 0721, but she reported only light damage and casualties. In his memoirs, Hallman wrote that the *Hutchins* lost her mast and radar and had a hole punched in her bottom. Admiral Berkey's flagship, the *Phoenix,* reported that the fire came from guns located near the Mokmer airfield, but she was unable to pinpoint their exact location. At 0755 Lieutenant William M. Laird, USNR, flying one of *Boise's* Kingfishers and spotting for TG-77.2 near the Mokmer airfield, began taking heavy AA fire from a 40-mm battery located near the airstrip. Laird took evasive action and looked for the guns, and spotted a cluster of 75-mm guns shooting at the task group's destroyers. One American destroyer, the USS *Bache* (DD-470), was hit by fire from those guns; later she reported that one man was wounded by shrapnel, but the ship itself was not damaged.

TG-77.2 ships were assigned to cover the area where the gun emplacement was located, but were not in position to fire on it, so the pilot radioed the *Boise* for help. Berkey gave permission for the *Boise* to engage the enemy guns as soon as she as she could turn into firing position. Meanwhile, a TG-77.3 destroyer took a shot at the gun emplacement, but missed. Then at 0811 *Boise* zeroed in on the 75-mm guns with her 6-inch rifles, and the secondary battery joined in five minutes later. The cruiser's HE projectiles fell directly onto the nest of guns, silencing them for the remainder of the operation.

Later in the morning (0910–0925) and in the early afternoon (1254–1313), *Boise* again worked over her assigned targets. The spotter plane reported that the shells had fallen well within the designated areas, and both the pilot and gunner confirmed that the Borokoe airstrip and nearby targets had been hit repeatedly. They also reported that the *Phoenix* was doing a good job of shelling the Sorido airfield. At 1326 *Boise*'s 5-inch battery took aim at a truck and some Japanese personnel that were spotted on the beach. After blowing up the truck with the first salvo, she continued to slam the enemy troops for another five minutes. With these final shots, the cruiser concluded her fire support for the Biak landings.

Boise's reconnaissance floatplanes did more than just a good job of spotting fire for the ships that day. During its first flight of the morning, Lieutenant Laird's Kingfisher, while spotting fire for the *Phoenix* and HMAS *Australia*, observed a partly camouflaged Mitsubishi Ki-57 "Topsy" transport aircraft parked on the Mokmer airfield. Laird quickly climbed to 1,700 feet and dropped into a shallow dive. Pulling out at 1,300 feet, he released two 100-pound bombs, which missed the airplane but destroyed several huts located along the edge of the airstrip. The young pilot turned and came back around for a strafing run, opening fire with his .30 caliber machine gun at an altitude of 700 feet. The twin-engine Japanese transport plane, which had apparently just been fueled, exploded in flames and burned brightly for the next 30 minutes.

During the morning's bombardment, the *Brooklyn* class triplets, *Boise*, *Phoenix* and *Nashville*, fired over 1,000 6-inch shells into assigned targets and others that cropped up. By 1715, some 12,000 American soldiers, 12 Sherman tanks, 29 field guns, 500 vehicles and other equipment and supplies had been successfully put ashore. The initial stage of the landings at Biak had gone off smoothly, in great part thanks to the naval bombardment (which the enemy greatly feared), but the *Boise*'s war diary notes that enemy resistance stiffened as the GIs moved inland later in the day. The Japanese expected an Allied invasion, and had planned to allow the Americans to come ashore and then walk into a trap, so they concentrated their defenses around the Mokmer airfield. When the Americans moved into that area, the trap was sprung, and all hell broke loose. The advance then ground to a halt, and it took another 10 days of intense fighting for the Americans to capture the airstrip.

For the first time in the New Guinea campaign, there was some enemy air action during the Biak operation. The Allies had expected the Japanese to use their air strength in every previous operation, but the shortage of aircraft and adequately trained pilots, not to mention excellent air cover by American warplanes, prevented this. After realizing that abandoning Biak Island to its fate had been a serious mistake, the enemy began significantly beefing up his air defenses in the area. Morison contends that the invasion of Biak alarmed the Japanese "war lords" more than any other operation in the Southwest Pacific theater. To explain why, he points out that Admiral Nimitz's Pacific Fleet was then located at Eniwetok Island, 1,000 miles east of Guam, but at Biak, MacArthur had moved to within 800 miles from Davao on the southern Philippine Island of Mindanao. This put the Allied forces dangerously close to Japan's main supply lines and in a position to threaten the Philippines. Until Japanese reconnaissance aircraft discovered the U.S. Pacific Fleet moving toward

Saipan in the Marianas on 11 June 1944, the Japanese high command believed that the main Allied thrust was in New Guinea. At that point, the enemy began pulling back their forces, which gave General MacArthur's men a welcome break. The air raids at Biak began at around 1100 on 27 May and continued into the afternoon. The first Japanese aircraft to make an appearance were a group of Mitsubishi A6M Zero fighters, which the Americans called "Zekes," that swooped in low to attack some American medium bombers that were making an airstrike on the airfields and beach defenses. These same fighters also jumped a scout plane from the *Nashville*. Around 1620, incoming "bogies" (unidentified aircraft) were picked up on *Boise's* air search radar at a distance of 54 miles; they turned out to be four twin-engine bombers escorted by a couple of fighter aircraft. Arriving over the invasion area 20 minutes later, the enemy planes first attacked the Bosnik beachhead, about 15 miles northeast of the *Boise's* position. Then they went after the *Nashville*, General MacArthur's flagship, which suffered a near miss. The Zeros also strafed a destroyer, the USS *Sampson* (DD-394). It proved to be a costly raid for the Japanese, who were met with heavy AA fire from the warships and the beach. Three of the bombers were shot down, and the fourth limped away trailing smoke. One determined Japanese pilot attempted to crash his crippled plane into the *Sampson*, but AA fire blew away a wingtip causing him to miss and go cartwheeling across the water into a submarine chaser (SC-699). Although the *Boise* crewmen saw the incident, they could not tell how badly the 98-ton vessel was damaged, because she was engulfed in smoke and flames. In fact, the sub chaser was set afire, suffering two killed and eight wounded before the fires were extinguished, but she remained afloat. Not more than five minutes went by before two Aichi D3A "Val" dive-bombers were spotted high above the *Boise*. Her portside 5-inch guns fired 16 AA rounds at them. No hits on the planes were observed, but they beat a hasty retreat out of the area. By 1649, the radar screen showed the area to be clear of enemy aircraft.

Boise had done an excellent job in the shore bombardment at Biak Island, which by this time was becoming fairly routine. In his report to the captain, Wolverton showered praise on the secondary battery for its excellent shooting; they had sunk an enemy barge with a direct hit and blew up a truck on their first shot. The XO proudly noted that those gun crews were showing steady improvement. He also recommended recognition be given to senior aviator Lieutenant Laird and his rear-seat man, Aviation Radioman First Class Thomas W. Healy, USN, for outstanding spotting and for having destroyed a *Mitsubishi* Ki-57 "Topsy" transport aircraft on the ground at Mokmer field.

After being released at Biak Island, *Boise* and her task force returned to station off Wakde Island on 28 May, and continued their patrols during the day while making sweeps to the west during the night. Allied intelligence had been expecting the IJN to show up for some time, so the cruisers, jeep carriers and destroyers were assigned to defend the approaches to Biak Island against possible Japanese surface encroachments. The cruiser kept this up until 31 May when she returned to Hollandia.

Enter the Imperial Japanese Navy

Meanwhile, the Japanese navy, which needed Biak's air bases to help defend against an expected invasion of the Philippine Islands, was attacking Allied forces in the area by air while planning to reinforce the island garrison by sea. Allied intelligence learned of a large enemy naval and air buildup within striking distance of Biak, and predicted that on 1 June the enemy would attack the Seventh Fleet and American ground forces on the island. The very next day, the ships remaining at Biak came under the heaviest enemy air strike they had yet faced. At 1640, over 50 Japanese aircraft attacked the beachhead, LSTs, and warships off the coast. Unfortunately, bad weather at Hollandia and Wakde prevented American fighters from coming to their aid, so the Americans had to depend solely on their own AA defenses. The enemy planes pressed their attack for over an hour in the face of heavy AA fire from the ships. Since the attackers concentrated on the warships, only one LST was damaged. The Japanese lost a dozen aircraft in the raid.

On 3 June, a Japanese naval force was spotted by an American submarine and a PBY reconnaissance plane, which alerted the Seventh Fleet commander. Knowing the IJN's intentions, Vice Admiral Kinkaid had placed Rear Admiral Crutchley in command of the combined Allied cruiser forces (TF-74 and TF-75) with orders to intercept them. Thus, *Boise* sortied on 3 June with HMAS *Australia*, USS *Nashville*, USS *Phoenix,* and 10 destroyers (four of which were Australian warships) along the south and west coasts of Biak Island, hunting for the enemy ships. But knowing that they had lost the element of surprise, the Japanese surface force withdrew before Crutchley's ships arrived. At 1720 on 4 June, *Boise*'s radar detected bogies around 60 miles to the west of their position. Twenty minutes later, eight "Zeke" fighter-bombers attacked the column. The enemy planes fanned out and made a run at the cruisers. *Boise*'s starboard AA guns opened fire on a Zero attacking the *Phoenix*, while her port battery took on another attacker on the port bow, disrupting its bombing run so that his bomb splashed harmlessly astern on the port quarter. However, a near miss opened a hole in the side of the *Nashville* causing flooding in two compartments, while shrapnel from another killed one man and injured several others on board the *Phoenix*. The *Nashville* remained in the fight despite enemy claims that she had been sunk. The Japanese propagandists frequently claimed to have sunk that gallant cruiser, which they considered a priority target because she was MacArthur's flagship. They never succeeded in sinking her, which was nicknamed the "Brassville" by her crew because of all the "brass" (senior officers) from MacArthur's staff on board, although they came pretty close to doing so in the Philippines later in 1944.

Just before 0100 on 5 June, Japanese torpedo planes attacked Crutchley's task force again. *Boise* rammed her speed up to 25 knots and began fishtailing erratically to evade the attackers. The cruiser was shaken by a large explosion, but sustained no damage. It was assumed that a torpedo had missed the ship and exploded on the nearby coral reef. As the enemy planes came in for another pass, the destroyers and cruisers in the van opened up with their AA guns, throwing up a heavy curtain of steel against the attackers; *Boise* blasted away at the torpedo planes with her 5-inch and 40-mm gun batteries. Crutchley's flag ship, HMAS *Australia*, advised that the planes had dropped some torpedoes and, although the *Boise* never saw any of the "fish," a second violent explosion rocked the cruiser, which once again came through unscathed. One of the cruisers—most likely the *Boise*—shot down an attacking plane. The "kill" was observed by *Boise* lookouts and other crewmen on deck and confirmed by the USS *Abner Read* (DD-526), which reported seeing the plane splash into the sea as it passed abeam of the cruisers. After 12 long minutes, the shooting stopped, and *Boise's* radar showed the skies clear of bandits, but the enemy was still lurking silently beneath the waves. Shortly before 0200, the USS *Mullaney* (DD-528) picked up a strong sonar contact bearing 300 degrees True at 1,000 yards. The task force turned to 090 degrees and increased speed, while the *Mullaney* peeled off to attack the enemy submarine with depth charges. After dropping her ordnance on the sub and picking up nothing on sonar, the destroyer resumed her position in the screen around the task force. The historical sources that have been consulted do not reveal the outcome, but the enemy submarine was not heard from again.

After failing to locate the enemy surface force, the Allied task force returned to its station northeast of Biak. During the daylight hours, they patrolled off Cape D'Urberville within fighter cover range of Wakde Island, and as the enemy surface force was still expected to show up in the area, on the night of 5 June made another sweep off Biak. On 6 June *Boise* and other ships, after two days and nights of combat, remained at battle stations, while *Phoenix* buried at sea her men who had been killed in the air raids of 4 June. Everyone was saddened by the loss of their comrades from the *Phoenix*. After the burial ceremony, the *Boise Chronicler* quoted Civil War General William Tecumseh Sherman in his journal, "War is hell, and I do mean hell."

The next day (7 June), *Boise* and the other ships of the task force made a quick run to Hollandia to refuel and resupply. While there, the crew had enough time to watch a movie on board before shoving off again at 2319. They again went hunting for the elusive Japanese fleet, which was making a second attempt to land reinforcements on Biak Island. About an hour before midnight on 8 June, the Allied task force pounced on five Japanese destroyers that were towing barges loaded with soldiers toward Biak. They cut the barges loose and made a run for it when the *Boise* and the other Allied ships gave chase. The Japanese destroyers fired "Long Lance" torpedoes, one or two of which just missed the *Boise's* fantail, and sped away at top speed. After chasing the fleeing enemy warships for nearly 100 miles, the cruisers gave up the pursuit and left it to American destroyers, which were making 35 knots, but the Japanese destroyers managed to get away in the early morning hours of 9 June, heading in the direction of their base at Mapua Island. Meanwhile, Crutchley sent the Aussie destroyers back to attack the barges, all or most of which were sent to the bottom. After all the excitement, the task force returned to Hollandia on 10 June and went on to Manus Island the next day, where the men looked forward to a chance to rest and relax while drinking a few beers.

Upon arriving at Seeadler Harbor in the company of the *Phoenix* and eight destroyers, the crew of the *Boise* were able to get some rest, play some softball, go swimming, and drink beer. The weather was hot and the beer got warm pretty quickly. Some of the guys thought that the Manus Island beaches were not as nice as those at Hollandia, but the swimming was still pretty good, and the shell hunting was excellent. Avery brought home some beautiful seashells from his tour in the Southwest Pacific, some of which perhaps came from Manus Island.

All was not merely fun and games during the time they spent at Manus Island. The task force conducted gunnery practice, radar tracking exercises, and night battle simulations during several days they were in the Admiralties. *Boise* performed well in these exercises, and her CO was proud of the progress his crew was making. At sundown on 13 June, Crutchley hauled down his flag on HMAS *Australia* and was replaced as commander of TF-74 by Commodore J. A. Collins, RAN.

While *Boise* was at Seeadler Harbor, the U.S. Army was wrapping up the battle on Biak Island. The Japanese put up a determined defense of the strategically important island, which was located only 800 miles from the southernmost point of the Philippine Islands. Fortunately, the navy stopped the Japanese from significantly reinforcing their forces on Biak, and the island ultimately fell to the Allies. Thereafter, Biak became an important air base for MacArthur's main objective, the retaking of the Philippines.

Seeadler Harbor was also being developed into a major base for staging future operations. U.S. Naval Construction Battalions (CB or SEABEE) and army engineer units were busily repairing roads and airstrips as well as building port facilities. On 20 June, the news came in by radio of the major victory in the Philippine Sea in which the Japanese lost two aircraft carriers and hundreds of aircraft while the U.S. Fifth Fleet lost only a handful of planes (although one flat top, the USS *Intrepid* CV-11), was damaged). By 23 June the "dope," or scuttlebutt, going around was that another invasion was in the works for somewhere near the northern tip of New Guinea in the near future.

Wrapping it up in Dutch New Guinea: Noemfoor and Sansapor

Even before MacArthur's forces had landed on Biak Island, it was decided to take over some other small islands nearby in order to establish an air base to cover operations in the area and to protect the gains on Biak. Noemfoor Island was selected as one of the principal targets, because the Japanese were using it as a staging area to reinforce their troops on Biak, and it was the site of three Japanese airfields that could be used by American fighters and bombers. Noemfoor lay about midway between Biak and the Japanese base on Vogelkop peninsula in Dutch New Guinea, which was also on the schedule of future operations. Intelligence estimated the enemy's strength on Noemfoor to be about 3,000 men with perhaps 2,000 of those being combat infantry troops. For once, Allied intelligence overestimated the enemy's strength. In reality there were only about 2,000 troops in the garrison with perhaps half of them considered battle-ready. Moreover, the Japanese at Noemfoor were poorly fed and suffered from low morale. Noemfoor was the center of Japanese air power in the region, so it was decided that the place would receive a sound thrashing by combined naval and aerial bombardment. Here again, Admiral Berkey's cruiser division would be part of the naval covering force, that would pound the well-defended beach in conjunction with aerial bombardment to soften up the defenses prior to the troops heading for shore. In the days prior to the invasion, the Allied air forces dropped over 800 tons of bombs on the island as a prelude to what was coming. These air raids met little opposition from AA fire or enemy aircraft, almost all of which had by now been withdrawn to meet the American invasion of Saipan in the Marianas.

At 1200 on 29 June, *Boise* departed Manus Island with TF-74 and TF-75 "looking for trouble." The combined task force would provide cover and fire support for the Noemfoor landings that were scheduled for 2 July. Both the USS *Nashville* and HMAS *Shropshire* remained behind to undergo repairs. En route to the invasion site, *Boise*'s crew continued their AA gunnery drills and tests of her sophisticated radar systems. Berkey constantly drilled his crews to ensure that they performed smoothly and effectively when they went into combat. As a result, they were becoming increasingly proficient in radar tracking of targets and gunnery, especially for AA defense. Berkey wanted his cruisers to be ready for anything at any time. Practically every spare moment was given over to gunnery practice, radar tracking exercises and other combat-related drills. The results clearly demonstrated that the training was paying off. Langelo recounted that the AA gun crews were constantly improving their accuracy and rate of fire. The skipper was very pleased, and the crew was becoming much more confident about fighting off enemy air attacks. Langelo declared, "The men of the *Boise* took their jobs seriously and always did them well." This intense training regimen would prove invaluable in the major battles that were soon to come.

Weather conditions on D-day (2 July) turned out to be ideal for the invasion. At daybreak *Boise* and *Phoenix*, working as a unit with their six destroyers, began shelling targets in the area east of the landing zone that included enemy gun emplacements and the Kamiri airfield. HMAS *Australia* and four destroyers pounded the landing zone itself, which was designated Yellow Beach. Some 44 American bombers joined in the assault. After an hour of intense naval and aerial bombardment, the troops began hitting the beach, where they met no initial resistance. The destroyers moved in close to the shore to assist the troops advancing on the airstrip by knocking out specific targets such as machine-gun nests and AA gun emplacements. Despite extensive enemy defense preparations, thanks to the effective naval and aerial pounding of the area the landing force suffered very light casualties on the first day of the battle—three killed, 19 wounded and two injured. The U.S. Army was growing increasingly fond of the pre-landing naval bombardments and had no complaints at Noemfoor. In relating the events of the engagement, Morison commented:

> For the first time in the Pacific war, the defenders had been pounded into that desirable state known to pugilists as "punch drunk." Japanese encountered around the airfield were so stunned from the effects of the bombardment that all the fight was taken out of them; even those in the nearby caves were dazed and offered little resistance.

The hastily planned Noemfoor landing proved to be one of the best executed in the Southwest Pacific campaign. Everything went smoothly. Once the soldiers were ashore, *Boise* and the combined task force pulled out of the area at 1215 and headed back to Hollandia, leaving the landing force to mop up the remnants of the Japanese defenders on the island. As had come to be expected, *Boise's* shooting that morning had been very good; all her salvos fell well within the target areas, which were "well shot up." Berkey later rated her performance during the invasion as "very satisfactory."

From Hollandia, CRUDIV15 moved on to Manus Island, where they arrived on 3 July. *Boise* spent the next two weeks at Seeadler Harbor, where all hands once again got to enjoy beach parties with beer, softball, and swimming. Just as before, the fun and games were interrupted by several days of intense training exercises with special attention paid to AA gunnery practice and night battle simulation. This was a time when many veteran *Boise* crew members were transferred to new ships, many being commissioned by the navy almost daily, and were replaced by less experienced men. Also, the new proximity fuse AA ammunition (code named VT, for Variable Time, to disguise the fuse's true operating principle), which had been introduced in late 1942, had to be tried out by the ship's gun crews before they used it in combat.

The relaxed, easy days at Manus Island ended when the cruisers were called on to support another mission, which as it turned out did not amount to much. On 27 July, *Boise* and *Phoenix* with four destroyers were called on to support troop landings on the north coast of Dutch New Guinea at Cape Sansapor, Sarong. The Japanese had already evacuated the area, so the landing on 30 July took less than an hour and turned out to be a non-event for the cruisers. With no Japanese defenders to be found, the preliminary naval bombardment was deemed unnecessary; *Boise* completed the mission without firing a shot. Among the troops that landed were a group of engineers who went in to build an airstrip.

On 1 August, *Boise* stood into Woendi Anchorage in the Padaido Islands of Geelvink Bay. There were air alerts every night, but no attacks ever occurred.

The next day a group of sailors from the *Boise* went ashore to explore the island, where they came upon a group of natives. According to one crewman, they "had quite a time" with the locals. American sailors stole a couple of native canoes and "went through" their huts. Such callous disrespect surely won the U.S. Navy few friends among the local population.

After two days, the big cruiser, escorted by three destroyers, left Woendi for another port call at Sydney. The crew were eagerly looking forward to this second visit, which offered the chance for liberty and a "few more of those good cold beers at $16.00 a case," in the words of the *Boise Chronicler*. On 10 August 1944, *Boise* docked at Woolloomooloo Wharf, Sydney. Hallman's memoirs once again provide a vivid account of his exploits during this R&R, which were no doubt representative of the experiences of most of his shipmates. Certainly, all of the men enjoyed their stay in Sydney and wished they could have remained there longer. There was a war on, however, and although the leapfrog campaign in New Guinea reached a successful conclusion while they were in Australia, their presence was required to prepare for the next major phase of the offensive against Japan. Therefore, on the morning of 26 August, *Boise* left Sydney for Milne Bay. As the tugs were towing the cruiser out of the harbor, a line snapped, and one of the tugs rammed the ship causing minor damage. Most of the crew hoped this accident would prolong their stay in Sydney, but the sailing was delayed by no more than a few hours. She finally stood out of Sydney Harbour in the late afternoon.

Boise joined up with TF-74 and TF-75 to conduct various combat training exercises during the return voyage. The combined task force refueled at Milne Bay on 30 August and immediately pushed on to Seeadler Harbor, where they remained for 10 days (1–10 September). A number of veteran crewmen received transfer orders during this period. One who departed was her chief radarman, Vince Langelo, who left the ship on 8 September to attend the Navy Radio School in Chicago, Illinois. Langelo was sad to leave the *Boise*. She was a good ship, and he knew she would "finish the war with flying colors," but he later wrote that he never imagined just how well she would perform during that final year of World War II.

Sansapor was the last stop in New Guinea for General MacArthur's Southwest Pacific Forces, which had rolled over the hapless Japanese like a juggernaut. The leapfrog advance of 550 miles from Hollandia to Cape Sansapor had taken only a bit over three months, thanks to the loan of Admiral Halsey's carriers and the excellent cooperation and support provided by the US Seventh Fleet. The final objective in the Philippines was now within the Allies' reach, but before moving on to the main event, a base for USAAF heavy bombers and naval forces closer to the final objective was needed. The obvious choice was to take one of the northern Molucca Islands, the next stepping stone on the road to Manila. The Moluccas were once known as the Spice Islands because they had been the center of the lucrative spice trade for centuries. The northernmost islands in the group lie only 300 miles southeast of Mindanao Island, the southernmost island in the Philippine archipelago.

Morotai, 15–16 September 1944

The obvious choice for the air base would have been Halmahera Island, the largest in the northern Moluccas, which sits squarely astride the Equator. In early 1944, the Japanese beefed up their defenses on Halmahera Island to defend the southern approach to the Philippines. They had built, or had under construction, eight or nine airfields with a garrison of some 37,000 soldiers on the island. The Allies therefore selected the smaller, less well-defended Morotai, which lies just north of Halmahera, as the easier of the two islands to capture. MacArthur amassed land, sea, and air forces that would easily overwhelm the small enemy defenses on the island, but these Allied forces were actually being mustered in preparation for the major campaign to follow.

On 10 September, Berkey's TF-75 departed Seeadler Harbor for Hollandia, and after arriving for a brief refueling stop the next day, departed Hollandia to rendezvous with TF-77, which consisted of two amphibious attack groups, four reinforcement groups, a support group, and an escort carrier group. *Boise* was part of the support group, which consisted of two Australian heavy cruisers, three American light cruisers, and eight American and two Australian destroyers. The escort carrier group, composed of six baby flat tops and 10 destroyers, provided combat air and antisubmarine cover. On loan from Admiral Halsey's Third Fleet was Vice Admiral John S. McCain's fast carrier task group, TF-38.4, with two fleet carriers, one light carrier, one heavy cruiser, one light cruiser, and 13 destroyers. McCain's carriers would stand by 50 miles north of Morotai to help out if needed and to bomb Japanese airfields in the nearby Celebes Islands.

At sunrise on the morning of 13 September, the *Boise* took her position in a large convoy of troop transports and landing craft off Biak Island. The *Nashville* had completed repairs and rejoined TF-75, and brought along General MacArthur, who would personally direct the operation. During the afternoon, TF-77 then linked up with the task group that included the six escort aircraft carriers. All hands felt much better when the "baby bird farms" showed up because this time, finally, they would have air cover for the operation.

On the morning of the invasion (15 September), *Boise, Nashville, Phoenix,* and their destroyers were assigned to cover the landings by first attacking Japanese forces at Galela on nearby Halmahera Island. After blasting targets on the beach for an hour and drawing no return fire, the Brooklyn "bobtails" moved on to Morotai, just 12 miles away across the strait, to provide supporting fire for the troop landings there. No fire support was required, however, as the GIs went ashore without opposition. Later in the morning, the cruisers were sent out to provide protection for the carriers on station east of Morotai and to cover the invasion site against a possible attack by enemy surface ships swooping down from the north. On the afternoon of 16 September, there was little else for the cruisers to do, so they departed for

Morotai invasion, New Guinea, 15 September 1944. USS *Boise* firing on Halmahera Island. (USNARA 80-G-301528)

Woendi Anchorage in the Padaido Islands, arriving on 18 September and remaining there until 27 September.

The soldiers quickly secured Morotai in the face of only the feeblest resistance by the small Japanese garrison. By 4 October, 117 enemy soldiers had been killed or captured, and another 200 or so were wiped out by PT boats while they tried to escape by barge to Halmahera. The survivors, perhaps 200 men, fled into the mountains, where they posed no threat to the construction of the airfield. Morotai proved very useful as a base for bombing raids on the Philippines and the Dutch East Indies. It also served as a major base for PT boats, at least until February 1945, when most of the speedy little craft were moved north to the Philippines. The remaining PT boats on Morotai kept the Japanese forces on Halmahera and the Eastern Celebes at bay right up until the end of the war. They also rescued the Sultan of Ternate, the descendant of the lords of the spice trade, who had been chafing under Japanese domination. The Sultan, along with his harem and his court, was removed to safety from the small island of Ternate off the western coast of Halmahera in May 1945 aboard PT boats, but not long thereafter the Japanese were driven out, and he was able to return home once again.

USS *Boise*, "E" Division, circa 1944. Avery Parkerson is first from left in the second row from the top. (Author)

After nine days at Woendi, on 27 September *Boise* pulled out for Seeadler Harbor on Manus Island. Upon arriving there three days later, her crew were surprised to find the harbor packed with a huge gathering of warships, including large and small aircraft carriers, battleships, and cruisers from both the Third and Seventh Fleets. The *Boise Chronicler* exclaimed that he had never seen so many ships at one place in his life. This was the invasion force of some 100 combat ships that was being prepared for what was to be the largest operation yet mounted by the Americans in the Pacific—the retaking of the Philippine Islands, which Japan had wrested from American control in early 1942.

General MacArthur had brought the first phase of his campaign against the Empire of Japan in the Southwest Pacific to a swift and successful conclusion. In just over four months, he had swept across 1,600 miles of the north coast of New Guinea in a series of well-planned, smartly executed strikes that showed few of the glitches and mistakes that inevitably occur in military operations. Despite his flamboyant style and strong personality, which caused some politicians to grit their teeth, MacArthur had once again shown himself to be a master strategist. He earned the respect of every officer who served under him, regardless of branch of service or nationality, for his military judgment and leadership. He also enjoyed the loyalty, respect, and admiration of his GIs and the "blue-jackets" of the Seventh Fleet, who would have followed him practically anywhere, even through the gates of Hell had he chosen to lead them there. Now the underworld was not MacArthur's target, although there would be moments in the campaign to retake the Philippines when it would seem that all the furies of Hell had been unleashed against the Americans and Australians who had come to liberate the islands from Japanese occupation.

The huge Allied armada departed Seeadler Bay on 11 October, and after a brief stop at Hollandia, on 13 October proceeded for the Philippine archipelago, the keystone of Japan's South Pacific empire. A major chapter in the war in the Pacific was about to unfold. Noting that it was Friday the 13th, the *Boise Chronicler* quipped, "What a day to begin."

CHAPTER FIVE

Return to the Philippines: The Battle of Leyte Gulf

By mid-1944, the United States and its allies had driven the Japanese from many of the islands they had held in the central and southwestern Pacific Ocean, and cut off numerous enemy bases that were stranded in isolated places such as the Solomon Islands, the Admiralty Islands, New Guinea, the Marshall Islands, and Wake Island. In June, a series of amphibious landings captured most of the Marianas, which breached Japan's strategic inner defense perimeter and provided bases for long-range B-29 bombers to strike the Japanese home islands. The IJN's counterattack was foiled in the Battle of the Philippine Sea (19–20 June 1944), an engagement the U.S. Navy nicknamed the "Great Marianas Turkey Shoot" in which they inflicted heavy losses on the enemy, including three aircraft carriers and two oilers sunk, six other ships damaged, and some 600 aircraft destroyed. This stunning defeat virtually eliminated Japanese carrier-based airpower in addition to costing them most of their experienced pilots.

At this point, American strategists and senior commanders engaged in a major policy debate over what should be the next objective in the advance on Japan. The Joint Chiefs of Staff favored blockading the Philippine Islands and invading Formosa (Taiwan) in order to give the Allies control of the sea lanes linking Japan to Southeast Asia and the East Indies, which were vital sources for oil, rubber, and other resources necessary for Japan's war industries. Formosa, it was argued, could also serve as a platform for launching an invasion of China. General MacArthur championed an invasion of the Philippines, which also sat astride the enemy supply lines; he maintained that to abandon the Commonwealth and to renege on America's commitments to protect the Filipino people would damage American prestige. The recovery of the Philippines was an intensely personal matter for MacArthur, who had been ordered by President Franklin D. Roosevelt to leave the archipelago after the Japanese invaded in 1942. On that occasion, he swore his famous vow of "I shall return," a promise to the Filipino people that he felt honor-bound to fulfill. Other top-ranking American military officers, such as Admiral Nimitz (CINCPAC), also believed that bypassing the Philippines altogether would be unwise because of the heavy concentration of Japanese land-based airpower in the islands, which could not simply be left behind and forgotten.

General MacArthur, whose father had been Governor-General of the Philippines at the beginning of the 20th century, had served in the islands as a junior officer in 1903–04 and again in 1922–25 as commander of the Manila Military District. In 1928, he returned to Manila as the commander of the Philippine Department, with responsibility for defending the entire archipelago, a post he held until 1930. After retiring from the U.S. Army in 1937, MacArthur became chief military advisor to the Commonwealth's government and was given the rank of field marshal in the Philippine Army. Upon being recalled to active duty in the U.S. Army in 1941, he was appointed commander of U.S. Army forces in the Far East with his general headquarters at Manila. He remained in the Philippines until he was ordered to evacuate with his family just ahead of the advancing Japanese invaders in March 1942. Thanks to this long and intimate relationship, MacArthur knew the islands and the Filipino people, and felt very much at home there.

Eventually, after lengthy debate and a meeting of the senior military leadership in the Pacific Theater with President Franklin D. Roosevelt, it was decided to forego the Formosa invasion, and General MacArthur's plan to retake the Philippines was given the green light. The plan called for the invasion of the island of Leyte in the central Philippines by combined land, naval, and air forces under MacArthur's command. Amphibious units and close naval gunfire support were to be provided by the U.S. Seventh Fleet commanded by Vice Admiral Kinkaid. Although the Seventh Fleet was largely an American outfit, some of its warships were from the Australian, New Zealand and Dutch navies. Admiral Halsey's Third fleet, with the fast carrier task force (TF-38) as its main component, was under Nimitz's direct command, but would be on loan to provide more distant air cover and backup for MacArthur's assault on Leyte Island. Perhaps the major flaw in the American plan was that no single admiral had overall responsibility for the naval operations. This lack of unified command coupled with miscommunications would lead to faulty coordination and confusion in the plan's execution that could well have cost the Allies the victory.

Fortunately, Japan's strategy suffered from the same defects, and their senior commanders made many of the same mistakes as the Americans, but only worse, which contributed significantly to the enemy's overwhelming defeat in the campaign. The complex Japanese strategy was actually four plans: one for responding to an invasion of the Philippines, and three to defend against possible American attacks on Formosa, the Ryukyu and Kurile Islands respectively.

When it became clear that the Allies' objective was indeed the Philippines, the IJN implemented a desperate plan that would throw the combined bulk of its remaining combat ships into a go-for-broke effort to repel the Allied invasion force. The senior Japanese military leadership knew that if the Americans retook the

Philippine Islands, then the Empire would be cut off from its vital supplies of oil and other strategic resources in Southeast Asia and the East Indies. If that happened, then the war would be certainly lost. Therefore, the Japanese objective was to win a decisive victory over the Americans and their allies, something they had hoped for since the beginning of the war, or go down fighting in the attempt.

The Japanese plan to counter the American thrust into the Philippines divided the naval fleets that were committed to the campaign into three forces. A northern group with the IJN's six remaining aircraft carriers, none of which had more than a handful of airplanes left, would act as a decoy to draw Halsey's fast carrier groups away from the Philippines. Meanwhile, central and southern task forces, under the commands of Vice Admiral Takeo Kurita and Vice Admiral Shoji Nishimura respectively, were to converge on the invasion site from the west, with the southern force coming up through the Surigao Strait into Leyte Gulf and the central force dropping down through the San Bernardino Strait into the Philippine Sea and then south to Leyte Gulf. The desperate drive through the Surigao Strait by the southern task force was calculated to draw off the majority of the Americans' combat ships, thereby facilitating the attack by the central force on the transports, any remaining warships, and the beachhead in Leyte Gulf. If Nishimura successfully broke through the Seventh Fleet's blockade of the southern approach to the gulf, he would coordinate with Kurita in attacking the Allied invasion fleet from opposite directions. If not, then he would die in battle, covering himself and his task force in glory in the best tradition of Bushido, the Japanese samurai's code of conduct that commands death before the dishonor of surrender.

As a preliminary to MacArthur's foray into Leyte Gulf, on 12 October 1944, carrier planes from Halsey's Third Fleet began pounding Japanese airfields on Formosa, Luzon in the Philippines, and Okinawa in the Ryukyu Islands, to prevent enemy aircraft based on those islands from striking the invasion force, which was scheduled to hit Leyte Island about a week later. The big flat tops pressed their attacks the next day and fought off counterstrikes by large numbers of Japanese planes over the next three days. Halsey's carrier squadrons once again inflicted catastrophic losses on the enemy, destroying some 550–600 airplanes, and thereby seriously reduced the Japanese land-based airpower in the area. In addition, some 40 freighters and smaller vessels were sunk, and ammunition depots, airfield facilities, and industrial plants were destroyed. Despite grossly exaggerated Japanese claims to the contrary, American losses were slight—no ships were sunk, and only two cruisers and one carrier were damaged. Broadcasts by Radio Tokyo bragging about the destruction of the Third Fleet were the butt of jokes in the Allied forces that were busily preparing for the big invasion. One of the best laughs of the Pacific war came when Halsey, responding with characteristic biting wit to Japan's fantastic claims, radioed his boss, Admiral Nimitz, that he was "… retiring towards the enemy following the salvage of all the Third Fleet ships recently reported sunk by Radio Tokyo."

Three or four days before the Leyte invasion began, Halsey's carrier-based planes struck south to Luzon, Negros, Cebu, and Leyte islands to attack enemy air and surface forces in the northern and central Philippines. On 17 October (A-3 day), the 98th Ranger Battalion landed on Suluan, Homonhon, Hibuson, and Dinagat Islands to secure the entrance to Leyte Gulf. That same day, the Seventh Fleet began minesweeping operations and beach explorations in preparation for the upcoming landings in the gulf.

Meanwhile, *Boise* was steaming north towards the Philippines with Rear Admiral Berkey's cruiser division in the Allied invasion fleet, and crossed the Equator on 14 October 1944. The voyage was largely uneventful. The men were told little about where they were headed and were forbidden to say anything in the letters they wrote. For example, Avery wrote a letter to his wife dated 18 October in which the censors cut out what was perhaps a reference to where the ship was and what it was doing. What remained of that letter contained no war news; it was mostly personal about how much he loved and missed her and how badly he wanted to get home. Avery also mentioned that there was an officer on board ship who had been stationed in Newfoundland when the USS *Truxtun* (DD-229) ran aground and sank in a terrible North Atlantic storm on 18 February 1942. The officer told Avery about having visited the burial site of the *Truxtun* men who died in that shipwreck, one of whom was Avery's younger brother Bo, who had been a signalman on the ill-fated destroyer.

On A-day, 20 October 1944, the huge armada steamed into Leyte Gulf and initiated one of the deadliest campaigns of the entire war, especially as far as the U.S. Navy was concerned. At 0200, GQ sounded, and the *Boise* crew members took up their battle stations. MacArthur was in command of the invasion aboard his flagship, the *Nashville*, which was positioned in the middle of the fleet steaming into San Pedro Bay. The men of the *Boise* were told to expect air raids beginning around daybreak. The enemy knew the Americans were coming and were itching for a fight.

The ships of the Seventh Fleet came under intense air attacks, unlike anything they had ever witnessed; in fact, for a time it seemed that victory would be snatched from the Allies' grasp. The Japanese began striking the invasion fleet on the first day of the battle. The first wave of hostile aircraft, from bases in the islands, attacked a bit after 0600, but the raid amounted to very little. As the fight raged on, the air raids grew in size and frequency until they suddenly and unexpectedly took on a bizarre new form so horrific that it was unfathomable to the Western mind, filling the hearts of the brave sailors and Marines with terror. That unprecedented tactic was, of course, the systematic use of suicide planes known as *kamikaze*, or the Divine Wind.

The assault by the Allied Northern Attack Force against enemy positions on the island of Leyte began at 0700 with the "Big Boys"—the battleships *Mississippi*,

West Virginia, and *Maryland*—blasting the beaches of the northern landing area with their huge 14- and 16-inch guns. The men of the *Boise* could hear the thunderous reports from the battlewagons' barrages even from below decks, and having set "condition affirm," stood ready to enter the fight. Once the battleships, which had temporarily joined the Seventh Fleet for the Leyte invasion, finished their shoot at 0900, they were relieved by Berkey's cruisers. At 0908 *Boise,* on station two miles east of Camiris Point, got her turn to fire and over the next 42 minutes flung 886 6-inch and 448 5-inch rounds at the enemy. Her reconnaissance planes spotted fire for her and the heavy cruiser HMAS *Shropshire,* and the pilots reported that both cruisers covered their assigned target areas well during the bombardment. When the cruisers ceased firing, the destroyers and LCI gunboats took their turn at bat. Their barrages reached a "terrific peak" just prior to H-hour (1000), when the first troops began storming ashore. The landing craft were preceded by withering outpourings from 11 LCI rocket launchers that hurled 5,500 4.5-inch rockets onto the beaches while the cruisers and destroyers raised their fire to pound targets further inland. The troops met less opposition than expected, in part due to the heavy naval bombardment that had gone on for three hours prior to hitting the beaches.

Once ashore, the American GIs moved quickly towards their objectives, calling on the cruisers for fire support from time to time. At 1136, *Boise* responded to the first of several calls from the SFCPs by promptly taking out an enemy gun emplacement that had been targeting incoming landing craft. Immediately thereafter, her secondary battery knocked out another field gun. After the shelling stopped, no further activity was observed from either Japanese shore battery. At noon, LST-181

Leyte Island, the Philippines. USS *Boise* bombarding shore on 20 October 1944 during the Leyte invasion. Note HMAS *Shropshire* partially obscured by gun smoke in the background. (USNARA, 80-G-287103)

was hit by mortar fire from the heights of Mount Guinhandang, that rose some 400 feet behind the beaches. *Boise* and *Phoenix* responded by blasting the area with 200 HE projectiles. Their bombardment apparently took care of that problem as no further calls for fire in that area were received. Between 1200 and 1300, both the main and secondary batteries continued to shell various targets called in by the SFCPs. *Boise's* total expenditure of ammunition for the day was 1,119 6-inch and 569 5-inch rounds. The hard-slugging cruiser was complimented for her excellent gunnery on A-day by a grateful U.S. Army on 23 October.

From time to time throughout the first day of the battle, Japanese aircraft returned to attack the invasion armada, but they primarily targeted the beach area to try to sink the landing craft ferrying the troops ashore. But *Boise's* sistership, the USS *Honolulu* (CL-48), was struck by an aircraft-launched torpedo and was so badly damaged that she had to retire to Manus Island for temporary repairs. This was the second time that the "Blue Goose" had been torpedoed, but the battle-hardened cruiser stubbornly refused to sink. She later returned to Norfolk to undergo major repairs that were finally completed shortly before the war's end.

By 1330, American troops had the situation on the beaches of San Pedro Bay well enough in hand for MacArthur to wade ashore accompanied by the President of the Commonwealth of the Philippines, Sergio Osmeña, and dramatically announce his return to the Filipino people, assuring them that the hour of their liberation was at hand. In a special radio broadcast, the CINC proclaimed, "People of the Philippines, I have returned! By the grace of Almighty God our forces stand again on Philippine soil."

Over the next four days and nights, land-based Japanese warplanes launched almost constant strikes against the American forces on Leyte Island and the ships operating in the nearby waters of the gulf, giving the men little opportunity to catch their breath. *Boise's* men were called to battle stations 15 times to repel air raids, not counting the attacks that occurred while the crew was already at GQ. The U.S. Navy had anticipated the aerial assault, and Rear Admiral Thomas L. Sprague's escort carriers of TG-77.4 provided strong fighter cover to do battle with the attackers. These air raids were largely ineffectual in terms of damage inflicted on Allied ships or land forces; few enemy planes managed to get through the strong defense thrown up by the combat air patrols. The air raids did, however, have a considerable harassing affect, and by the third day were beginning to wear down the men, provoking the *Boise Chronicler* to complain, "We have to eat, sleep and write between times. Those Japs sure are trying to discourage us. I hope that tonight we get some sleep. I have not had my clothes off since before the invasion."

Hostile air attacks resumed early on the morning after the landings (21 October), with the *Boise* going to battle stations at 0525 to fend off an air raid. At 0600, she and the other ships threw up a hot-steel curtain of flak at a couple of IJN "Val" dive bombers that were plunging down on the battleship *West Virginia* (BB-48). One of the bandits was hit by the AA barrage and began trailing smoke before crashing into the foremast of the HMAS *Australia,* engulfing the heavy cruiser's bridge and forward superstructure in flames and debris. The Aussie warship suffered serious damage and many casualties, forcing her to retire to Manus Island for repairs.

Boise spent the next two days (21–22 October) on her firing station waiting for calls from the SFCPs that never came. Therefore, she had little to do except repel enemy air attacks, one of which came at 0651 on 22 October when an enemy dive bomber made a run at the cruiser, swooping in on her port bow. The attacker was driven off by a hail of AA fire. During the evenings, she patrolled the areas in Leyte Gulf where the transports were anchored.

The morning of 23 October started out much the same way for the *Boise* and the rest of the fleet. Except for taking some potshots at a couple of Japanese planes that flew overhead at very high altitude at 0535, she had very little to do until 1008 when she was ordered to proceed to a point some 2.5 miles south of Dio Island to support troops moving south along the coastal highway near the town of San Joaquin. By noon the cruiser was in position standing by, awaiting orders to commence firing. She launched one of her Kingfishers to spot for her guns, but the army indicated that its forward observers would direct the shooting as their units advanced, marking the front lines with green-star blinkers. The spotter plane was asked to make sure that shells did not fall north of the blinkers, where American soldiers would be positioned. Finally, at 1352 the SFCP called for supporting fire, and the big cruiser's main battery began raining death and destruction onto enemy troop concentrations and pill boxes on the east side of San Joaquin, blasting the target area for about 45 minutes. An hour later, fire was again requested, and the main battery lobbed a few salvos onto the targets, and then the secondary battery took over to finish the job. Cease fire was called at 1632, but the ship stood by, ready to fire again if needed. Thirty minutes later, the SFCP asked for help in knocking out some machine-gun nests and pill boxes that were firing on the advancing American GIs at the outskirts of San Joaquin, and the ship's 5-inch guns blasted that area for the next half hour. The gunners varied their pattern of fire to keep the fleeing Japanese soldiers from gauging where the next shots would fall, but concentrated fire especially on enemy campsites. When the shooting stopped, the army artillery spotters informed the *Boise* that the shelling had been excellent, exclaiming, "Two Japs were blown to bits as they ran."

The next morning, reports from the SFCP confirmed that *Boise* had covered the area around the town with barrages that were "very effective on exposed personnel." The only targets not destroyed by her salvos were some pill boxes that could only have been knocked out by direct hits. The ship's plane spotter described the bombardments on A-day and on A+3 as "the most effective firing he had ever witnessed."

Boise's skipper, Captain Roberts, expressed his appreciation for the army's compliments on his shooting, and was highly satisfied with the volume and accuracy of fire laid down by both batteries. The months of intensive drilling, together with the experience and practice they had gained during the New Guinea operations, had paid off. As Langelo asserted, the *Boise* had never been satisfied with a merely good performance, but always strove for perfection. Moreover, the ship's gunnery department had applied some good old American ingenuity in developing a rather simple gadget they called a "gyamo," that provided an "instantaneous and continuous means of determining range and deflection spot to place opening salvos on target areas." While admitting that the idea itself might not be original, Roberts believed that this was most likely the first time it had been applied to this particular problem. The gyamo was nothing more than the old Short-Range Battle Practice approach diagram etched onto a piece of Plexiglas laid out over the bombardment chart, with the point of origin placed on the ship's position. This allowed correct ranges and deflection spots to be read off at a glance, while corrections to range and bearing could be made from "observed values" as needed. The *Boise*'s impressive success with this rather simple device led to its adoption by the other cruisers in the task group. Her task group commander, Admiral Berkey, whose flagship *Phoenix* also participated in the bombardment, rated the performance of the *Boise* as "excellent." The commander of TF-78 added his own praise, saying that the ship's gunfire was always of "the highest order."

In the first letter he was able to write since the Leyte operation began, Avery gave his wife a brief summation of the landings. On 5 November 1944, he wrote:

> I imagine by this time that you have figured out where we are. We are operating in the Leyte Gulf Area. We participated in the invasion of the Philippines. Our gun fire knocked out shore batteries, etc. before our soldiers went in. In other words, we gave them hell before our soldiers went into the beaches. We covered them and gave them support after they got dug in. They called for our support many times in the days that followed. We also fought off Jap planes. We were in many air raids also, we practically stayed or lived on our battle stations.

On 23 October, while the navy gunships were shelling enemy targets to support the army, reports were coming in that two large groups of IJN surface ships had been detected moving into the central Philippines. At about 0016, two American submarines, USS *Darter* (SS-227) and USS *Dace* (SS-247), spotted Admiral Takeo Kurita's huge task force off Palawan Island. Kurita's force consisted of five battleships, 10 heavy cruisers, two light cruisers, and 15 destroyers. At about 0530, the two subs attacked the enemy ships with torpedoes, sinking two heavy cruisers, the *Maya* and the *Atago*, the latter of which served as the Japanese admiral's flagship. The *Atago* went down so fast that Kurita had to swim for it. He was quickly picked up by one of his destroyers and transferred his flag to the 74,000-ton *Yamato*, the world's largest, most powerful battleship. A third cruiser, the *Takao*, was also hit and had to turn back to the Japanese base at Brunei Bay, Borneo. The American submarines' torpedo attack was the opening round of what would be the greatest naval battle of World War II.

The Battle of Leyte Gulf

Japan made a desperate attempt to crush the Allied offensive in the Philippine Islands, which was vital to its ability to continue the war. Thus, they threw the bulk of their remaining naval and air power into an all-out attack on the American and allied naval and land forces in Leyte Gulf. The Japanese counteroffensive led to the Second Battle of the Philippine Sea, which later became known as the Battle of Leyte Gulf, one of the largest naval battles in history. In that epic confrontation, battleships faced off against each other for the last time in naval history, and the enemy made deliberate, coordinated use of kamikaze aircraft for the first time in the war. It was also the first time an American aircraft carrier was sunk by a Japanese surface ship since the war began.

The Battle of Leyte Gulf was actually a series of four major engagements between the U.S. Navy's combined Third and Seventh Fleets, the latter of which included some ships of the RAN, and the greater part of the remaining surface forces of the IJN. Although these actions occurred across a huge expanse of ocean and were separated in some cases by hundreds of miles, they were closely interrelated. The four principal clashes of the battle, fought between 23 and 26 October 1944, were: the air action in the Sibuyan Sea (24 October), the nighttime surface battle of Surigao Strait (24–25 October), the battle off Samar (25 October), and the battle off Cape Engaño (25–26 October). In addition, there were several smaller actions. One of these was the opening engagement in the battle, an American submarine attack in Palawan Passage that occurred on 23 October as the Japanese fleet approached Leyte Gulf. The four IJN task forces that took part in this battle mustered nearly all of its remaining major warships in a go-for-broke attempt to repel the invasion. They failed, and were themselves repulsed by the Americans, suffering such heavy losses that Japan was never again able to mount a major naval offensive for the remainder of the war.

Early on the morning of 24 October, the Japanese naval forces that were detected by American submarines the day before were confirmed by aerial sightings of various groups in the Sulu and Sibuyan Seas. Halsey's fast carriers of TF-38 launched several air strikes against Admiral Kurita's task force in the Sibuyan Sea. The navy warplanes struck the Japanese ships like a swarm of angry hornets, sending the "unsinkable" 74,000-ton *Musashi*, *Yamato*'s sister ship, to the bottom. The intrepid American aviators also crippled the heavy cruiser *Myoko* and damaged several other enemy ships, including the *Yamato* and an older battleship, the *Nagato*. Although this air

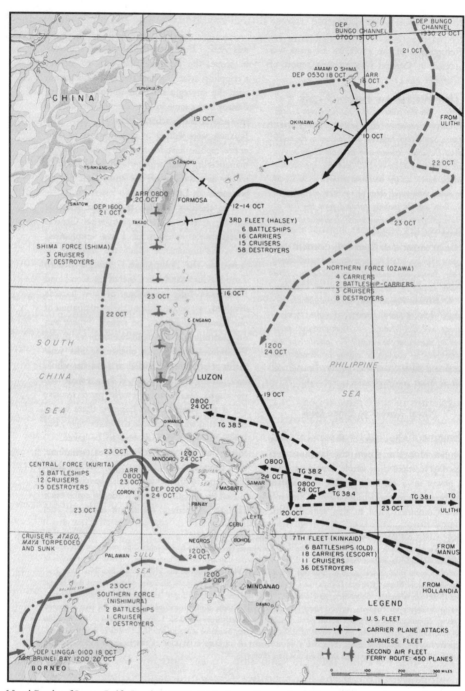

Naval Battle of Leyte Gulf, October 1944. (U.S. Army Center for Military History. *Reports of General MacArthur: The campaigns of MacArthur in the Pacific, Vol. I*, p. 204)

Battle of Leyte Gulf, Sibuyan Sea, 24 October 1944. Japanese battleship *Mushashi* under intense attack by carrier-based aircraft from Task Force 38. Note the enemy destroyer also being bombed, in the background. (USNARA 80-G-281764)

action, named the Battle of the Sibuyan Sea by the Allies, did not stop Kurita's advance, it did oblige him to retire back to the north to get out of range of Halsey's carrier planes. Kurita later turned south again and pushed down through the San Bernardino Strait during the night, planning to attack the Allied fleet in Leyte Gulf at dawn the next morning, in conjunction with the southern force under the command of Vice Admiral Shoji Nishimura.

At 0755 on the morning of 24 October, a large group of Japanese aircraft swooped down on Leyte Gulf from all directions, aiming primarily for the warships in an attempt to distract the Americans' attention from the approach of their surface forces. Most of the attacking planes were blocked by the CAP, but a few dive bombers managed to slip through. *Boise, Phoenix,* and *Louisville* took evasive action by steaming in a circle while fighting off the hostile aircraft. None of the warships in the transport area were hit, but an LCI was sunk, and a cargo ship was struck by bombs. Yet another air alert sounded at around 1112, interrupting the *Boise's* refueling operation, but this time no enemy planes got through the air defenses.

By noon on 24 October, Admiral Kinkaid was convinced that a Japanese incursion into Leyte Gulf was imminent, and set in motion a plan to intercept it. Admiral Berkey's cruisers were ordered to deploy with a large combined task group (TG-77.2 and 77.3) under the command of Rear Admiral Jesse B. Oldendorf, USN, to defend the southern approaches to Leyte Gulf against enemy warships that were expected to attempt to penetrate through the Surigao Strait during the night. Since General MacArthur was aboard the *Nashville* with a large number of senior officers in his entourage, she was not allowed to deploy with her sister ships, much to disappointment of her skipper and the general. MacArthur had never witnessed a major naval battle and so wanted to be on hand for this one, but Kinkaid would not hear of it. It was unthinkable to permit the supreme commander to put himself at risk by participating in what promised to be a major shootout with some of the IJN's largest and most powerful warships. *Nashville* therefore remained behind in San Pedro Bay with the three amphibious force flagships and the liberty ships, enclosed within a tight screen of destroyer escorts. *Phoenix, Boise,* and HMAS *Shropshire* began making ready for a nighttime gun battle with a major Japanese surface force.

"A Rugged Night" in the Surigao Strait, 24–25 October 1944

By 1600 on 24 October, *Boise* was refueled and headed out to sea. Racing along at 27 knots, she joined other Allied warships that were sent to intercept a large Japanese task force that according to intelligence reports consisted of two battleships, eight cruisers, and 14 destroyers. The Japanese were reported to be about 200 miles away and headed for a foray into Leyte Gulf via the Surigao Strait.

The Japanese naval forces were actually two separate groups, one commanded by Vice Admiral Shoji Nishimura and the other by Vice Admiral Kiyohide Shima. Nishimura commanded two *Fuso* class battleships, one heavy cruiser and four destroyers. Shima's group, which consisted of two heavy cruisers, a light cruiser, and four destroyers, was trailing some 25 nautical miles (29 statute miles) behind Nishimura when the latter entered the narrow Surigao Strait. Shima had been dispatched independently by the top naval brass in Tokyo to join with his colleagues in the attack, but was operating independently of Kurita's or Nishimura's command and had not participated in the pre-operation planning briefings. Moreover, the two task forces approaching from the south were maintaining strict radio silence in compliance with general orders, which made coordination impossible between them and Kurita's central force, which was approaching Leyte Gulf from the north through the San Bernardino Strait and the Philippine Sea.

It seems the task forces commanded by Nishimura and Shima had no idea of the ambush that awaited them in the Surigao Strait. Perhaps they anticipated another victory like the one they had won at the battle of Savo Island in 1942. If so, they

Leyte Gulf, map of the Battle of Surigao Strait, 24–25 October 1944. Note: Original map was pasted onto the inside of a window shade. (NHHC, NH79368)

failed to take into account the Americans' advances in radar technology and its game-changing use in night battles.

Knowing that they were going to slug it out with giant battleships and heavy cruisers, the men of the *Boise* were naturally anxious and scared, but they were determined to do their duty and battle the enemy with all their might. The *Boise Chronicler* wrote: "It is our job to stop them, and here goes nothing." The American ships suffered almost constant air attack on the run down to Surigao Strait. With enemy planes swooping in for the kill about every half hour, the *Boise* boys barely had time to eat their chow. The *Boise Chronicler* merely stated the obvious when he commented "I think they are trying to cripple our ships to make it easier for their ships when they get here." The air raids continued into the evening. One attack came at 1900 followed by another an hour later, but they failed to stop the American warships from arriving on station and into position at 2000. The *Boise* crew went to battle stations at 2300 in preparation to block the Japanese southern force as it traversed the strait. The anonymous chronicler reflected the hopes of all hands when he wrote: "Here is hoping we have lady luck with us."

Admiral Oldendorf, who had no intention of repeating another Savo Island fiasco, laid an ambush for the enemy fleet by positioning his ships and PT boats around the strait so that its narrow passage would hinder the enemy's ability to maneuver and make it impossible for them to evade the American trap. To pass through the narrows, the Japanese ships would first have to run the gauntlet of PT boats and destroyers arrayed along both sides of the channel after which they would run headlong into the heavy artillery of the battleships and cruisers. The battle line formed by six American battlewagons stretched across the entrance into Leyte Gulf. The cruisers were divided into two groups, one on each flank of the battle line. Morison extolled "Oley's" battle plan, which set up a textbook case of "crossing the T" of an enemy fleet that allows the battle line to bring the full force of its broadsides to bear on the advancing enemy ships. To accomplish such a feat is something every naval commander has dreamed of doing since the days of Admiral Lord Nelson. Oldendorf was set to hammer the Japanese intruders with everything he had, and like the legendary gambler of old, he had no intention of "giving a sucker an even break."

The ships of Oldendorf's combined Task Groups 77.2 and 77.3 substantially outnumbered and outgunned the approaching IJN forces. The battle line, under the command of Rear Admiral George L. Wyler, USN, consisted of six battleships—*West Virginia* (BB-48), *Maryland* (BB-46), *Mississippi* (BB-41), *Tennessee* (BB-43), *California* (BB-44) and *Pennsylvania* (BB-38). All with the exception of the *Mississippi* were "ghost ships," i.e., they had been raised after having been sunk or heavily damaged at Pearl Harbor. The battleships, with 14- and 16-inch guns in their main batteries, were flanked on the left by three American heavy cruisers—*Louisville* (CA-28), *Portland* (CA-33), and *Minneapolis* (CA-36)—and two light cruisers—*Columbia* (CL-56) and *Denver* (CL-58). Oldendorf flew his flag in the *Louisville*.

Boise was on the right flank in TG-77.3 with HMAS *Shropshire* and the *Phoenix*, Admiral Berkey's flagship. The four heavy cruisers sported batteries of 8- and 6-inch guns, while the four light cruisers bristled with 6- and 5-inch guns. In addition, "Oley" had 28 destroyers, some of which were Australian ships, armed with 10 torpedoes each as well as their 5-inch main batteries, and a swarm of 39 PT boats, the small, lightning-fast and highly maneuverable motor torpedo boats whose "fish" packed a deadly sting.

The principal concern of the American admirals was a shortage of AP ammunition. Their main battery magazines had been loaded primarily with high-capacity (HC) shells for shore bombardment, at least half of which had been expended in the landings at Leyte. Thus, there were precious few AP shells on hand, which were the only projectiles capable of piercing the thick, steel band of armor that protected the Japanese battleships and heavy cruisers, except at dangerously close range. Furthermore, there were no replacement torpedoes on hand for the destroyers, which were also critically short of 5-inch shells. Given the shortage of ammunition, the Americans and Aussies knew they had to fight smart and make every shot count.

All hands on the Allied warships spent a tense, sleepless night as they anticipated the coming clash. Avery no doubt expressed the concerns of all his shipmates on the *Boise* and of the sailors on every ship in the task group when he declared that he did not know whether he would see the sun come up the next morning. His thoughts were mostly with his young wife back in Georgia. Avery also worried about his parents, who had already lost one son in the war. His mind dwelt on Bo and other young friends from home who had been killed in the war, and he feared that perhaps he was about to join them. Avery prayed hard to set things right with his "Maker" in case he did not live through the battle.

Even the men on the transports and command ships back in San Pedro Bay were anxious and troubled. They were fully aware of their total dependence on "Oley's" ships; their prayers were with the admiral and their fellow bluejackets and Marines who were standing in harm's way in the Surigao Strait as their last line of defense.

As the Japanese ships drew closer and with the shooting about to start, the *Boise Chronicler* wrote:

> We are getting range from the Japs from time to time and … they are not getting any farther away. Well, I hope that us starting this campaign [in the Philippines] on Friday the thirteenth isn't an evil omen. I think if I live through this night, I will write a book about this day and call it "One Day of Hell."

It would indeed be a truly rough night. Nerves were on edge as all hands waited, straining their eyes in the darkness for a glimpse of the Japanese ships. The night was clear and dark with a light wind, which picked up slightly when a few rain squalls blew through the strait. The seas were smooth and glassy. The heat was scorching, with temperatures below decks climbing above 115°F, and the enemy's approach only made the night seem hotter. Just after midnight word came from the PT boats at the far entrance to the strait that they had made contact with the Japanese ships. Updates were passed to all hands over the *Boise*'s PA system. They now learned that there were two groups of enemy ships: one at 50,000 yards and the other at 70,000 yards. At 0252 (25 October), *Boise*'s radar made its first contact with the enemy column bearing 164°T, range 47,900 yards. The *Boise Chronicler* fretted, "That is getting pretty darn close to a big battlewagon."

The men of the *Boise* followed the early developments of the engagement by radio. Beginning around 2215 on 24 October, the valiant PT boats attacked Nishimura's column in waves for over four hours, dodging salvo after salvo from the big Japanese ships. Although they scored some hits with their torpedoes, for which they were given no credit, they certainly fulfilled their mission to provide the American commander with vital contact information. In the absence of radar-equipped, night patrol aircraft, the PTs served as the "eyes of the fleet." Avery had the greatest admiration for these tiny wooden boats whose only defenses were their high speed and the skill and daring of their crews. He was awestruck that they would run at the huge Japanese battleships through a hail of gunfire to get in at point-blank range before launching their torpedoes, then turn tail and haul ass, zigzagging like crazy, and making smoke in a desperate attempt to keep from being blown out of the water. The PT boys showed incredible courage and cool determination in pressing their attack, as well as proving their amazing toughness. Of the 30 boats that came under Japanese fire, only one was badly hit; it had to be beached by its crew, two of whom were killed and three were wounded, and it later sank with the rising tide. In all, only three PT sailors were killed and 20 wounded in the fight. Perhaps they did not inflict serious damage on the enemy ships or even slow their approach, but they certainly gave the Japanese something to think about. Nishimura may have erroneously concluded that the PTs were all the Americans had in the Surigao Strait, because he continued to plow ahead, straight on up the narrows as if he had a clear path all the way into Leyte Gulf.

After the PTs had done their best and alerted Oldendorf of the enemy's approach, the American and Australian destroyers jumped into the fight at about 0300 (25 October). For nearly an hour, they attacked the Japanese column from both flanks with spreads of deadly torpedoes, taking a devastating toll. Both battleships were hit, of which the 36,000-ton *Fuso* was sunk; two of Nishimura's four destroyers were also sunk, followed by a third later. The lead battleship, *Yamashiro*, Nishimura's flagship, although damaged remained underway, and followed by the heavy cruiser *Mogami* and the fourth destroyer, *Shigure,* plowed on north towards the American battle line, which remained hidden from view in the darkness thanks to the inferior Japanese radar. During the destroyers' attacks the flashes of gunfire, the detonations from torpedo hits, and the explosions and fires they caused could be seen from the Allied cruisers and battleships some 20 miles away. Avery said that he and others on the cruisers and battlewagons were so awed by the courage, audacity, and effective shooting displayed by the tin can sailors, that some began to fear the destroyers would sink all of the enemy ships before they got a chance to fire a single shot. No one knows exactly how many hits the destroyers scored during the battle, but they clearly had a field day. After delivering their punishing blows, the destroyers retired at full speed to get out of the way of the fiery hail of steel-shattering, heavy ordnance that they knew was about to come pouring down from the battleships and cruisers further up the strait.

The gunnery phase of the battle was fought in the classic style of formal battle line engagement with the American battleships and cruisers "crossing the T" of the advancing Japanese surface force. At 0350, when the three remaining ships of Nishimura's force reached a point only 15,600 yards distant from Oldendorf's flagship, *Louisville*, the American heavy cruisers stationed on the left flank opened fire. Seconds later, *Boise*, *Phoenix*, and HMAS *Shropshire* on the right received the order to open fire, and *Boise* cut loose with a broadside from her main battery on the *Yamashiro* at a range of 18,600 yards. With a deafening roar that reverberated for miles, the gun flashes lit up the dark night, and the tracers streaked red-hot to their targets. After the first spot up, *Boise's* gunnery officer, Lieutenant Commander William F. Cassidy, locked his guns into continuous rapid-fire mode, not even pausing to spot the fall of his 6-inch salvos on radar as he hammered away at Nishimura's flagship. *Boise* was blazing away so hot and heavy that after a few minutes Admiral Berkey ordered her to slow her rate of fire to conserve AP ammunition, which was in short supply. During the shootout, *Boise's* gun crews were working so furiously that a projectile man in turret II, Seaman First Class Clayton M. Boone, broke a bone in his left hand as he loaded a shell in the breech tray in the early minutes of the action, but continued to perform his duty throughout the gunfight, hardly missing a beat. On Berkey's order, she slowed her rate of fire, but continued to pour it on, slamming shells into the huge enemy dreadnaught with every salvo. *Phoenix* was firing 15-gun broadsides at 15-second intervals at the same target. *Shropshire*, having trouble with her fire control radar, did not open up with her 8-inch guns until 0356, when she began firing slowly and deliberately as Berkey had ordered.

In a night battle at sea—with the deafening noise, blinding muzzle flashes, and thick smoke from the big guns—there is inevitably a great deal of confusion. The battle of Surigao Strait was no exception, and the many ships' action reports from the shootout contain details that do not always coincide. For example, *Boise's* action report states that the battleships opened fire first with the cruisers following about a minute later. Later accounts by historians, which have analyzed all of the available documents, reverse this order. It seems the cruisers were the first big ships to open fire at 0351. Two minutes later (0353), the battleships jumped into the fight with their heavy guns. At 0353, from a range of 22,800 yards, the *West Virginia* began blasting away with her 16-inch guns, slamming the *Yamashiro* with her first broadside. The rest of the battle line quickly followed suit, their 14-inch and 16-inch guns belching smoke and flame that lit up the sea and the nearby islands.

The superior fire control radar of the American ships allowed them to reach out and swat the enemy at ranges from which the Japanese ships were unable to return fire in an effective manner. The American gunners were on top of their game that night, blasting the Japanese ships with deadly accurate barrages. The CO of DESRON-56 (Destroyer Squadron 56), whose destroyers were down range from

Cruisers firing at enemy task force during the night battle in Surigao Strait, 24–25 October 1944. (USNARA, 80-G-888493)

the cruisers and battleships, had a front row seat for observing the gun duel, which he described as the most beautiful sight he had ever seen, likening the big, glowing tracers to a "stream of lighted railroad cars going over a hill." The awed skipper added: "It seems as if every ship on the flank forces of the battle line opened up at once and there was a semicircle of fire which landed squarely on one point, the leading battleship [*Yamashiro*]."

From the battle line, the show was also spectacular when the cruisers' guns suddenly lit up the darkness. The USS *Maryland* reported:

> ... suddenly there was a great deal to see as all cruisers joined from both sides of the channel. The 6-inch cruisers fired so rapidly each kept four or five salvos in the air following one another in their beautifully curved trajectories. The 8-inch cruisers fire was more deliberate, but their intervals were amazingly brief.

Boise's action report gives her own perspective on the gun fight:

> While the enemy ships could never be seen ... until they began to burn, numerous hits were observed in the salvos from *Boise*. These could be noted by the sudden flashes of the shells exploding as the salvos fell. A bright glow persisted on the target for several seconds after some of these hits. The ship at which the *Boise* was shooting was observed to catch fire early in the action.

The light cruisers made up for their lack of armor and heavy artillery with a rapid, vicious rate of fire, and *Boise* showed no mercy as she laid it on the Japanese that night. Her guns blazed away like blow torches, hitting their target with every salvo. Avery specifically recounted that Gunnery Sergeant C. F. Martin (USMC), an old friend from Eastman, and his Marines in turret III really poured it out during the shootout. The Marines' gunnery skills were legendary, and "Gunny" Martin's turret proudly displayed a big white E for excellence, which they had been awarded for their outstanding shooting.

At 0357, *Phoenix* and *Boise* checked fire as their formation swung into a fast, tight turn to begin a run towards the west. HMAS *Shropshire* continued firing as she made the turn and switched to rapid fire when large Japanese projectiles suddenly splashed around her, kicking up enormous geysers. With the turn completed at 0400, the two American light cruisers resumed firing. Berkey's three right-flank cruisers poured out nearly 1,100 AP rounds and over 100 HC rounds before cease fire was called at 0410.

For much of the time the firestorm lasted, *Yamashiro* seems to have been the sole target of all the cruisers and battleships that joined in the shooting. After five or six minutes, however, some of the cruisers switched to other targets, one of which was the heavy cruiser *Mogami*. The Japanese battleship and heavy cruiser were crippled by the Allied projectiles, but they fought back gallantly. The *Yamashiro* eventually got into a broadside-to-broadside confrontation with the American battleships, and she gave a good account of herself in the type of fighting that the "Big Boys" were designed to do, despite the crippling damage she suffered. She scored no hits on her attackers, but as she came around managed to focus her fire on the right flank cruisers, first picking on HMAS *Shropshire*, straddling the Aussies with 14-inch rounds from her forward turrets. *Boise* also had a close call when the men topside heard several salvos from the enemy battleship pass screaming overhead before splashing into the water close aboard.

Admiral Berkey also managed to "cross the T" on the *Yamashiro* with his right-flank cruisers punishing her with hit after hit. Yet, she fought on, straddling the USS *Denver* and scoring multiple hits on the destroyer USS *Albert W. Grant*, which was down range from the battle line. By 0400 the enemy ships were so badly damaged that they halted their advance, and all units veered off to the west and south to escape the hammering blows they were taking. As they turned away down the strait, *Boise* could see fires blazing on the *Yamashiro* and other ships in the enemy column. At 0410, *Boise* received the order to cease fire, which was given to allow the USS *Grant* and other Allied destroyers a chance to get out of the line of fire.

The Japanese heavy cruiser *Mogami*, seeing the flagship *Yamashiro* burning fiercely and taking heavy fire herself, turned and prepared to launch her deadly Long Lance torpedoes. This turn, however, brought her face to face with American and Australian destroyers that were racing to get back into the melee while blasting away with their 5-inch guns. The tin cans' attack confused the *Mogami*'s skipper, and he delayed his torpedo launch. With fires blazing aboard, caused by the destroyers' salvos, the big cruiser was illuminated so well that she became a clear target for the American cruisers' 8-inch and 6-inch rifles, which poured shells into her mercilessly. The courageous Japanese skipper finally managed to launch four torpedoes just before he and everyone else on the bridge were obliterated by a direct hit from an 8-inch shell.

The feisty destroyers attacking the *Yamashiro* and *Mogami* got caught in the crossfire, but the *Grant* was the only one hit by both enemy and friendly fire. The *Yamashiro,* after being struck by more torpedoes from the destroyers, finally went down with Admiral Nishimura still aboard, slipping beneath the waves of the strait at around 0420. When Admiral Oldendorf gave the order to resume firing, there were no targets left on the American radars. The stricken *Mogami* took advantage of the 10-minute break to hightail it south along with the sole remaining destroyer *Shigure,* whose steering had been damaged by an 8-inch shell that failed to explode.

Those two ships were all that remained of Nishimura's task group, and they literally ran into Admiral Shima's column near the south end of the strait, where he was busy fighting off attacks from the American PT boats. After one of his light cruisers, the *Abukuma,* was knocked out of formation by a torpedo from PT-137, and seeing the two surviving ships from Nishimura's task group bearing down on him, Shima ordered a retreat, but his flagship, the heavy cruiser *Nachi,* collided head-on with the crippled *Mogami,* which was damaged further in the crash and was left behind on her own only to be jumped later that morning by Seventh Fleet carrier aircraft. Shima escaped with his column of ships, but all were sunk in the mop-up phase in Leyte Gulf or in later engagements. Of Nishimura's seven ships only the destroyer *Shigure* survived the Surigao Strait battle and its immediate aftermath, but she too was sunk by a U.S. Navy submarine later in the war.

At 0431, Admiral Oldendorf unleashed his destroyers like a pack of greyhounds to pursue the Japanese ships, and then moved out with his left-flank cruisers. Twenty minutes later (0451), Berkey's right-flank cruisers followed to help finish off the fleeing enemy ships. As *Boise* steamed south through the strait, the left-flank cruisers and destroyers began mopping up the disabled Japanese ships. At 0539, Oldendorf ordered a cease fire, so the cruisers turned about and headed back north towards Leyte Gulf.

By 0600 it was light enough to view the scene of the battle. Three large columns of heavy black smoke could be seen down the strait from the deck of the *Boise.* At 0625, the Allied ships again reversed course, and the left-flank force closed to polish off crippled Japanese ships. *Boise* could see a damaged enemy destroyer, hull down on the east side of the strait, taking blistering fire from the left-flank ships. The Japanese destroyer, perhaps the *Asagumo,* put up a fight, but was struck hard in the magazine and exploded at 0717. She sank just minutes later. The floundering heavy cruiser *Mogami* was attacked later in the morning by bombs and torpedoes dropped by Admiral Sprague's jeep carrier planes and her crew had to abandon ship. She was then scuttled and sent to the bottom by a torpedo launched from a Japanese destroyer.

The destroyers and PT boats were ordered to pick up survivors from the sunken enemy warships. There were hundreds of Japanese sailors in the water, many of them severely wounded, but most refused rescue by the Americans. In keeping with the Bushido code of the Japanese warrior, they preferred death to the dishonor of surrendering or capture. In one instance, a lifeboat loaded with Japanese sailors was approached by an American destroyer, and to a man, they all stood up, turned their backs on the Americans, and leapt into the water. At 0735, *Boise* monitored a radio transmission from the commander of one of the destroyer divisions informing Admiral Oldendorf that there were 300 to 400 "Nip survivors" in the water near his position and asking what he should do with them. The admiral's response was very direct and succinct: "Let 'em sink."

The "stunned and helpless" Japanese survivors who refused rescue faced dismal prospects. In the water they could become food for the sharks that always swarmed in a feeding frenzy after sea battles in the South Pacific. Even if they made it to land, they were still not guaranteed safety. Unless they happened into a Japanese-held area, they would likely fall victim to the sharp knives of Filipino guerrillas who hated the enemy with a deep, burning passion.

At 0732, Admiral Berkey's cruisers again hurried back to rejoin the battle line at the north end of the strait and concentrate at the entrance to Leyte Gulf. The ships

An American PT boat rescuing Japanese survivors after night battle in Surigao Strait, 25 October 1944. (USNARA, 285970)

were told to be ready to sortie if ordered to assist the escort carriers that were then under attack off Samar Island by a large Japanese surface force that had penetrated into the Philippine Sea through the San Bernardino Strait during the night. At 0800, Oldendorf's task group was nearly 70 miles from the battle between the escort carrier groups and Admiral Kurita's task force. It would have taken the battleships at least three hours to reach the scene of the action. With his ships all but out of AP ammunition and torpedoes, their best chance against Kurita seemed to be to rearm and wait for him to attempt to break into Leyte Gulf and try to pull off another ambush. Nevertheless, Admiral Kinkaid issued several countermanding orders over the course of the morning as the fighting off Samar ebbed and flowed, the next to last one was for Oldendorf to take half his force to assist the baby flat tops.

At 1153, *Boise* headed back into Leyte Gulf to replenish her ammunition, but 6-inch AP rounds were in short supply, and since other ships were in greater need she got no ammunition that day. At around 1300 Kinkaid cancelled the order for Oldendorf to deploy against Kurita, and his ships remained in the gulf. At 1730, *Boise* and the rest of her task group moved out to defend the approaches to Leyte Gulf from enemy forces that might still be lurking in the area. At this time, *Nashville*, *Shropshire*, and the destroyers rejoined the task group.

Boise's XO, Commander Wolverton, a veteran of *Boise's* first nighttime encounter with the IJN in the Battle of Cape Esperance in October 1942, wrote an account of the battle in the Surigao Strait that was couched as a transcription of a radio broadcast to the folks back home by what would today be called an imbedded reporter. His report, entitled "My Night," was copied and distributed among the crew. Avery sent it home telling Anne that if the humor was discarded, it was a pretty good account of what the battle had been like. (See Appendix IV.)

When he finally was allowed to write a letter home on 5 November, Avery commented on the engagement in the Surigao Straits, telling his wife:

> Well, I guess maybe you will be glad to hear from me again. I'm well and O.K. I hope you didn't worry about me or pay any attention to those wild Jap broadcasts about sinking the U.S. Navy. They claim they sunk us so many times I can't keep up with them. It was the other way around, we sunk them.
>
> We also engaged the Jap Navy in the battle of Surigao Straits. We fought Jap battleships, cruisers and destroyers. What a night that was. I didn't know whether or not I would see the sun come up the next morning, but the old *Boise* dished it out and come through with her colors flying and not a man hurt... The next morning when the sun came up, we could see smoke from the fires of the burning Jap ships. Our task force knocked hell out the Jap Navy that night.

He wrote again the next day, also referring to the battle on the night of 24–25 October:

> That was a rugged night, one I'll never forget. During that battle my thoughts were mostly of you.... I thought maybe I would join [Bo] and a few others, Buster Harrell and I. J. Williams

before the sun came up that morning, but I guess somebody heard my prayers. You can bet we beat hell out of the Jap navy that night. C. F. Martin is Gunnery Sgt. in turret III, and I mean those boys beat it out. Tell his mom he is well and that we are anxious to come home. We have been through the mill together out here.

Boise Radioman Chalmers Hallman wholeheartedly agreed with Avery and undoubtedly expressed the sentiments of all his shipmates when he wrote in his diary, "What a night! Hope to hell I never have to go through anything like it again."

The *Boise's* CO heaped praise on his crew, especially the gunnery department and CIC, declaring that "all hands performed their assigned duties magnificently." However, Admiral Berkey criticized the *Boise* for resorting to continuous fire after her first broadside on the battleship *Yamashiro*, which in his opinion was not in keeping with "sound radar spotting doctrine nor with the ammunition situation at the start of the action." Berkey was referring, of course, to the relatively short supply of AP projectiles since the U.S. Navy went to Leyte Gulf more prepared for shore bombardment than for surface action. For this reason, Admiral Oldendorf had ordered his ships to fire deliberately so as to conserve this ammunition for what might have been a prolonged gunfight. Berkey noted the excellent tracking of the enemy by the *Boise* CIC and almost grudgingly admitted that the cruiser had performed in a "creditable manner" during the action. Oldendorf, who had been in overall command at the Surigao Straits, of course agreed with his colleague's criticism, but emphasized that the *Boise* had made a significant contribution to the victory.

Vincent Langelo, who had served on the *Boise* during the Battle of Cape Esperance in 1942, defended her performance in the Surigao Strait shootout in his history of the ship. According to Langelo, her SG-1 microwave radar clearly showed the two Japanese columns with three or four ships in each. On the scope it appeared that the large ships leading each column were battleships. The *Boise* fire control team knew that if the lead ship were indeed a battleship, they would not be able to sink it because their 6-inch guns could not penetrate the dreadnaught's heavy armor. Thus, they had to aim for critical points in the superstructure to knock out vital navigation and fire control systems. The fire control team picked out the lead battlewagon as their first target. *Boise* had the latest in radar technology so she could see the enemy ships clearly through the darkness. When she opened fire on the *Yamashiro* under full radar control, her guns were shifted into continuous rapid-fire mode. After the first salvos, it became more difficult for the *Boise* to spot its own salvos due to the smoke from the fires that broke out on the target, so she shifted her guns into a "rocking ladder" for both range and elevation and resumed rapid-fire. This repeating sequence varied the gunfire up and down and right and left to cover the target. *Boise* continued punching the enemy battleship hard and fast until Berkey ordered her to slow her rate of fire. At that point the *Yamashiro*, burning fiercely, began a turn away from the battle line and slowed her speed,

Letter from Avery Parkerson to Anne Parkerson, Leyte Gulf, PI, 6 November 1944. Property of the author. The letter is incomplete and shows redaction by the censors to remove sensitive information. (Photograph by Enrique Menacho) apparently having lost all control. As the dreadnaught came about and headed in the opposite direction, she was struck a death blow by a spread of torpedoes from the American destroyers.

In Langelo's analysis, even though the *Boise* was aware of Oldendorf's order to conserve AP ammunition, she was the only ship in the combined task group that had fought a night engagement, and knew that her first salvos had to be accurate and decisive. In this detail, however, he was mistaken. Both the *Portland* and the *Minneapolis*, two of "Oley's" heavy cruisers on the left flank, had participated in night engagements off Guadalcanal in 1942. Be that as it may, the *Boise* fire control team knew they had to hit the battlewagon extremely hard and fast to disable her before she could sink any American ships. Therefore, she pumped 439 6-inch AP rounds into the *Yamashiro* in five minutes, the equivalent of 12 shells per minute from each of the 15 guns in her main battery. *Boise's* blistering barrage was, as Langelo colorfully expressed it, "so rapid and intense that even the bastions of hell would have screamed for succor."

One important detail that Langelo did not mention was that Commander Wolverton was a veteran of the Cape Esperance battle, where he served as her damage control officer. Wolverton, who may have been one of the few COs or XOs in Oldendorf's task group with that experience, undoubtedly knew that in a sea battle at night it was vitally important to strike the enemy first, hard and fast, before his bigger guns could draw a bead on you. The old "Noisy *Boise*" was ultimately given credit for disabling the *Yamashiro*, setting her up for the coup de grâce from the destroyers' torpedoes.

After the battle, Vice Admiral Kinkaid, commander of the Seventh Fleet, commented in a radio a message to the Commander of Cruiser Division 4:

> The courageous and aggressive action of all units … in the battle of Surigao Straits won a complete and sweeping victory over a large enemy taskforce. Sound tactics was implemented by excellent gunnery. The thorough thrashing administered to the enemy saved the day in Leyte Gulf and paved the way to Tokyo.

Official U.S. Navy reports dated five days after the engagement claimed that 10 Japanese warships were sunk—two battleships, two heavy cruisers, and six destroyers—and four were damaged. This count ultimately proved to be slightly exaggerated. Nishimura's southern force lost two battleships, one heavy cruiser, and three destroyers. Admiral Shima's support group lost one light cruiser and one destroyer. The Japanese therefore lost a total of eight warships in the Surigao Strait gunfight, while the Americans lost only one PT boat sunk and a destroyer that was heavily damaged.

The night battle marked the end of an era in naval combat. It was the last engagement in which a battle line slugged it out with enemy battleships and the last in which aircraft were totally absent (except in the final pursuit phase that began after daybreak). When the USS *Mississippi* fired the last broadside by a battleship in the Surigao Strait engagement, she was, to quote the eloquent words of Samuel Eliot Morison, "… firing a funeral salute to a finished era in naval warfare." It had been a ferocious fight and an overwhelming victory, one that General MacArthur undoubtedly regretted that he had not been present to witness personally.

Battle off Samar, 25 October 1944

After the victory in the Surigao Strait, two major confrontations in the Battle of Leyte Gulf were fought in which the *Boise* did not take part. The first of these took place in the Philippine Sea off Samar Island, while the cruiser was assisting in the mopping-up operation in the Surigao Strait and steaming back to San Pedro Bay on the morning of 25 October. After the commander of the Japanese center force, Vice Admiral Takeo Kurita, managed to overcome his initial indecisiveness, the force managed to penetrate through the San Bernardino Strait into the Philippine Sea unopposed, thanks to the fact that Admiral Halsey took the bait offered by Admiral Jisaburo Ozawa's decoy carrier force and struck off north in hot pursuit with his entire Third Fleet. In doing so, Halsey left the back door to Leyte Gulf wide open and practically unguarded. The only thing that stood between Kurita and the troop transports and supply ships in San Pedro Bay were the U.S. Seventh Fleet's escort carrier groups that were operating in the Philippine Sea under the command of Rear Admiral Thomas L. Sprague, USN, whose mission was to provide air cover for the amphibious assault in Leyte Gulf.

Admiral Kurita's large and powerful force of four battleships, including the 72,800-ton *Yamato* with its 18-inch guns, six heavy cruisers, two light cruisers, and 11 destroyers attacked Sprague's small forces of 6 escort carriers whose only defense were their small numbers of aircraft and their destroyer and destroyer escort screens. The northernmost carrier task unit, TU-77.4.3, under the command of Rear Admiral Clifton Sprague (no relation to Thomas Sprague) and known by its radio call sign Taffy-3, took the brunt of the Japanese attack. His destroyers put up a determined defense with their 5-inch guns and torpedoes backed by equally heroic support from the carriers' airplanes. The latter were armed mostly with bombs designed to attack ground troops and depth charges for use against submarines. They had precious few torpedoes or AP bombs, which were more effective against heavily armored ships like Kurita's battleships and heavy cruisers. Even after expending their ordnance, the carrier planes continued to make strafing runs and even dived on the enemy without ammunition in mock attacks that distracted the Japanese force and disrupted their battle formation. One navy pilot made a final pass while emptying his side arm on the enemy ships because his aircraft's machine guns had run out of bullets. The ferocious defense, which was beautifully and gallantly fought against overwhelming odds, gave five of Taffy-3's six escort carriers time to escape, although one was sunk by gunfire as were two destroyers and one destroyer escort.

A second Taffy-3 baby bird farm, USS *St. Lo* (CVE-63), was sunk later in the day after being hit by a suicide plane, becoming the first American carrier to be sunk by a kamikaze in the war.

In the running battle, the handful of American destroyers and tiny destroyer escorts (codename Little Wolves), in coordination with the aggressive attacks by their carrier planes, drove off the Japanese battleships, sank three enemy cruisers, and damaged several other enemy warships. Bewildered and demoralized by the fierce determination of the attack, the Japanese commander mistakenly assumed he was attacking a much larger and more powerful force. The bedazzled Japanese mistook the baby flat tops for fleet carriers and the destroyers for heavy cruisers. Disorganization and poor communications among his ships led to chaos, which reached the point that Kurita broke off the attack and withdrew, thereby snatching defeat from the jaws of victory. Thus, the largest and most powerful Japanese task force sent to destroy the American invasion force in Leyte Gulf failed to accomplish its mission. For the victory off Samar Island the U.S. Navy paid a high price in blood, planes and ships—two escort carriers, two destroyers, one destroyer escort, and dozens of carrier aircraft were lost. According to Morison's

Kamikaze attacks during the Battle of Leyte Gulf. USS *St. Lo* (CVE-63) hit by suicide plane off Samar Island, Philippines, 25 October 1944. (USNARA, 80-G-270516, Photograph taken by P. W. Neith)

estimates, the casualties suffered at Samar by Taffy-1 and Taffy-3 included 1,118 sailors and aviators killed and 913 wounded. An additional 12 aviators from TG-38.1 were killed during their air groups' attacks on Kurita's ships in the latter stage of the engagement.

Battle off Cape Engaño, 26 October 1944

While Admiral Sprague's jeep carriers and tin cans were facing off against Kurita's big guns, Admiral Halsey's fleet attacked Admiral Ozawa's force in the sea northeast of Luzon's Cape Engaño. Ozawa's four big carriers were truly a decoy, as they could muster only a combined total of some 108 aircraft with which to attack the American Third Fleet. Most of the first wave of 75 planes launched by the Japanese task force were shot down, and another 30 or so that were flying air cover for Ozawa's ships were destroyed by the first wave of American warplanes that attacked. American air strikes continued until evening, by which time three enemy aircraft carriers and a destroyer had been sunk, while another light carrier and a cruiser were damaged. A group of four cruisers and nine destroyers were deployed to pursue the fleeing Ozawa; they sank the crippled light carrier along with another destroyer. Later that night, another of Ozawa's cruisers was sunk by a torpedo from an American submarine that had been stalking his task force. The battle off Cape Engaño, the name of which was ironically appropriate (Engaño means deception or trick in Spanish, which is precisely what Ozawa's carriers had been), was the last of the four major engagements that made up the Battle of Leyte Gulf.

With the near annihilation of the Japanese navy's carrier force, the Battle of Leyte Gulf came to a victorious end. One historian has called the epic clash an "unmitigated disaster, a comprehensive defeat" for the IJN, which lost 26 combat vessels (three battleships, one fleet carrier, three light carriers, six heavy cruisers, four light cruisers, and nine destroyers) in the various engagements. The triumphant Americans also paid a high price for the victory, but their losses were significantly less than those of the enemy: one light carrier, two escort carriers, two destroyers, one destroyer escort, and one PT boat destroyed at the Surigao Strait. The IJN was left with only 36 warships, a fleet on the run that could do little against the might of the U.S. Navy and its allies. With what some historians have called their "improbable victory," the Americans won control of the seas and permitted them to retake the Philippine Islands and push on to Iwo Jima and Okinawa. Once they had taken those islands, which were positioned so close to Japan that American long-range bombers could strike the enemy's homeland at will, the end of the war was in sight, and an Allied victory was assured even without an atomic bomb, although the cost in casualties would have been incalculable.

Once the threat posed by the Japanese navy had been eliminated, the recapture of the Philippines became inevitable. Henceforth, the question became one of when, rather than if. After the war, the Japanese Naval Minister confessed, "Our defeat at Leyte was tantamount to the loss of the Philippines. When you took the Philippines, that was the end of our resources."

Recent historians' accounts of the Battle of Leyte Gulf point to the superiority in numbers enjoyed by the Americans and paint a picture of error and confusion on both sides. However, the Americans made fewer mistakes and capitalized on those of the Japanese. The errors made by policymakers and admirals do not diminish in the slightest the heroic efforts and great sacrifices made by the thousands of American sailors and Marines and their Australian allies at Leyte Gulf, which won them a victory that ranks among the greatest in the history of naval warfare. The same might also be said of the crews of the Japanese ships that fought bravely and gallantly in the battle. With their once-mighty navy reduced to little more than a coastal defense force, the Japanese now unleashed the Divine Wind, their Special Attack Force, in a desperate effort to hold the line against the American advance in the Philippines.

CHAPTER SIX

Kamikaze: The Divine Wind Sweeps Across the Philippines

After the failure of their go-for-broke attempt to destroy the Allied fleet in Leyte Gulf and block the invasion of the Philippine Islands, the Japanese high command resorted to a desperate strategy designed to rain death and destruction on their enemy from the skies as the last best hope for stopping, or at least delaying, the defeat of Japan. On the afternoon of 25 October 1944, the Japanese first unleashed their Special Attack Force of suicide planes, known as kamikazes (Divine Wind) against the U.S. Seventh Fleet's jeep carriers at sea and the Allied naval forces in Leyte Gulf.

Japanese suicide plane attempting to crash dive on USS *White Plains* (CVE-66) in Leyte Gulf on 25 October 1944. The "Zero" missed the carrier and splashed into the sea. (USNARA, 80-G-288882)

The enemy turned to the "special attack" (*Tokko*) tactics because American air and naval superiority was so overwhelming that kamikazes represented practically their only means of inflicting significant losses on the Allies. The Japanese naval and army air forces had lost so many aircraft and experienced pilots that they had to rely heavily on poorly trained replacements, many of them unexperienced and not much more than young boys who knew little but how to fly the airplanes. The suicide pilots were chosen from volunteers for the special attack squadrons and were selected for their unwavering dedication to Japan's cause and wholehearted devotion to the emperor. For the most part, the kamikaze pilots relentlessly pursued their objective of sacrificing themselves by crashing their aircraft into an enemy ship, with a fanatical zeal that was unfathomable to the Western mind. The suicide aircraft were not always front-line fighters or dive bombers, but older, obsolete planes, although when loaded with as much fuel and ordnance as they could carry and flown by a determined pilot, were converted into HE weapons capable of dealing a devastating, and frequently fatal, blow to a large ship. Their favored targets were aircraft carriers, and a lone kamikaze could sink one if it struck the flat top in the right place. When targeting a carrier, the suicide pilot generally aimed for the ship's elevators, or sought to dive straight down on the flight deck, in hopes of penetrating to the hangar deck where aviation fuel, bombs, torpedoes, and other ordnance were found as aircraft were being readied for flight operations. These highly flammable and explosive materials would multiply the power of the explosion and increase the possibilities of sinking or crippling the aircraft carrier.

The kamikazes usually flew in groups of two or more, escorted by a similar number of fighters to provide cover and with a single guide plane to direct them to their target areas. Whenever possible, the kamikazes would skim along just above the tree tops to avoid radar detection or being spotted by the American CAP. But once they crossed the beach and flew out over the water, they became exposed to view and could be fired upon by the ships' AA gun crews. Many of the unskilled pilots were not adept enough to maneuver their planes to avoid the flak, so they were not all that difficult to shoot down. Nevertheless, since their mission was intended to be a one-way trip they had to be knocked down, or else! A kamikaze pilot did not care if his aircraft were hit providing it would still fly long enough to give him time to look for the closest ship and attempt to crash into it.

Because of the pilots' unwavering determination to give their lives for the emperor, the suicide planes were a formidable, terrifying threat of the highest order. The American and Australian ships could do nothing but remain vigilant and ready to open fire when enemy aircraft appeared and then throw everything they had at their assailants. Once the element of surprise and shock were lost, however, the effectiveness of the suicide tactics steadily declined. As the Americans increased their air cover and the Allied ships improved their AA defenses, the Japanese had to send out more and more suicide planes and fighter escorts in the hopes of achieving significant results.

Battle of Leyte Gulf. USS *Suwanee* (CVE-27) hit by a kamikaze on 25 October 1944. Note the F6F "Hellcat" pulling out of dive directly above ship's bow after pursuing the enemy aircraft. (NHHC, 80-G-270516)

Historians have pointed out that American naval commanders were slow to pick up on the shift from the occasional random crash dives to the organized and deliberate suicide attacks. Even after they finally grasped that they were confronting a new and highly lethal threat, the U.S. Navy's top brass were unsure how to combat it. Tactics to counter the kamikazes had to be developed in combat, and this had to be done quickly before they destroyed too much of the Allies' sea power. The sailors and Marines on the ships immediately realized that something had suddenly changed for the worse, even if they could not comprehend why or how it fit into what they understood about warfare. Somehow, they had to fight off these relentless suicide attacks by what many came to call "devil birds," which caused such horrible carnage and death that they struck terror into the hearts of even the toughest, most courageous men. After witnessing the horror caused by the kamikazes, which seemed chillingly personal to the sailors, many men of the Seventh Fleet came to doubt that they would get through the war alive and in one piece. Avery frankly admitted that the kamikazes were the only enemy weapon or tactic that never failed to scare hell out of him. He echoed the sentiments of his shipmates and all the men of the

Seventh Fleet when he protested: "Those son-of-a-bitches were trying to kill me." The kamikaze attacks he and his shipmates had to confront were one of the main reasons why he passionately hated the Japanese until the day he died.

Avery and the men of the *Boise* first encountered the "Divine Wind" on 26 October 1944 in the skies over Leyte Gulf. *Boise* was in San Pedro Bay restocking her magazines with ammunition, but the operation was constantly interrupted by air raids that began at 0630 and continued throughout the day. Only once during the morning did enemy aircraft get close enough to the *Boise* for her AA gun crews to fire at them. At 0854, she opened up on two Japanese planes passing high overhead at 14,000 feet, but the hostiles made no attempt to attack her.

During the late afternoon and early evening things definitely heated up. The crew of the *Boise* scrambled to battle stations four times between 1800 and 2000. Although, once again, no Japanese planes came within range of their guns, at least one enemy aircraft was shot down by the battleships located northwest of her position. The *California* (BB-44) and the *Louisville* (CA-28) were struck by kamikazes that day, although neither ship suffered significant damage. Later in the evening, a different sort of threat appeared beneath the ocean's surface. At 2123, a TG-77.3 destroyer, the *Mullaney* (DD-528), picked up a sonar contact that appeared to be a submarine. The tin can moved-out to attack with depth charges, which she repeated three more times over the next hour. Another destroyer joined in the last two runs with the *Mullaney*, but the results of the "ash can" attacks were inconclusive. All sonar contact with the sub was eventually lost so it was either sunk or managed to slip away. After that incident, things were quiet for the remainder of the evening.

In the early morning hours of 27 October, *Boise*, *Nashville*, and several destroyers put to sea to relieve other ships that were protecting the escort carriers that had fought so heroically against Admiral Kurita's fleet two days earlier. MacArthur had transferred his headquarters ashore so the "Brassville" was now able to resume her regular duties with Berkey's cruiser division. A large tropical moon turned the night nearly as bright as day as the twin light cruisers and their destroyer screen sped out from Leyte Gulf to take up station with the jeep carriers. Being at sea with the "baby bird farms" gave the *Brooklyn* twins a brief two-day respite from the hot seat in Leyte Gulf.

Returning to San Pedro Bay on 29 October, *Boise* was finally able to finish replenishing her ammunition, and recovered her Kingfisher scout planes which had remained on the island since the afternoon prior to the night battle in the Surigao Straits. The U.S. Seventh Fleet underwent a major reorganization on 29 October with a number of ships being released to return to the Third Fleet or departing for other duties elsewhere. The ships that departed included the battleships *Maryland*, *West Virginia*, and *Tennessee*, and the cruisers *Louisville*, *Portland*, *Minneapolis*, *Denver*, and *Columbia*. Nine destroyers, including HMAS *Arunta*, were also released. A new task group (TG-77.1) was formed under the command of Rear Admiral G. L. Weyler,

USN, composed of Weyler's three remaining battlewagons—*Mississippi, California,* and *Pennsylvania*—as well as Berkey's cruisers, the *Phoenix, Nashville, Boise,* and HMAS *Shropshire.* TG-77.1 was rounded out with 12 destroyers from DESRONS 56 and 48. These warships, together with those on station with the remaining escort carriers in the Philippine Sea, were all that were left to the Seventh Fleet for the defense of Leyte Gulf.

As if fighting off the suicide planes was not enough, a tropical storm lashed the central Philippines with strong winds and heavy rain on the night of 29–30 October. Wind gusts of over 86mph were recorded. The *Boise* crew felt very sorry for the "dogfaces" fighting on Leyte Island who were caught out in the open during the huge storm. Mercifully, the cyclone blew on by quickly so that by morning, weather conditions had greatly improved. For the next two days, TG-77.1 spent the daylight hours on station in and around the transport area in San Pedro Bay. At night, *Boise* and other ships went back out to patrol in Leyte Gulf. There were several air-raid alerts each day, but no attacks materialized over *Boise*'s area. Elsewhere, however, the Divine Wind was blowing hot and heavy, and a number of ships of the Third Fleet, operating east of Leyte in the Philippine Sea, were struck by suicide planes.

Despite a temporary lull in the air action, the navy's situation at Leyte Gulf was not good. With several of the escort carriers en route to Manus Island for repairs, there were precious few fighter planes left to provide air cover for the ships in the gulf. As the kamikaze threat intensified, CAPs that could be mustered heroically defended the ships against the suicide planes. It should be noted that not all of the bandits that attacked the ships in and around Leyte Gulf were kamikazes. Conventional bombers, fighter aircraft, dive bombers, and torpedo planes also participated in the raids, making normal bombing and strafing runs on the Allied ships after escorting the suicide pilots to their target. But many of the hostile planes were being flown by aviators of the special attack force, and their numbers increased as the days passed. By flying in additional aircraft from Formosa and other locations, and with the reduced number of American carrier planes available, the Japanese practically regained control of the skies over Leyte in the final days of October.

For the next two weeks (1–16 November), *Boise* patrolled around San Pedro Bay and off Leyte Island during the daylight hours, frequently fighting off enemy aircraft. At 0928 on 1 November, a dozen Japanese dive bombers and torpedo planes jumped the *Boise*'s task group in Leyte Gulf like a swarm of angry yellow jackets. Two "Val" dive bombers attacked the *Boise*. She poured fire into one of the *Aichi D3A* "Vals" making a run on her starboard beam, forcing the plane to veer off and speed quickly out of range. At the same time, two low-flying enemy bombers crossing ahead of the formation came under heavy AA fire from the ships in the van. One of these bombers was hit and burst into flames. The Japanese pilot then tried to crash dive on the USS *Ammen* (DD-527), but overflew his mark and splashed into the

USS *Boise* firing on a kamikaze in Leyte Gulf, 31 October 1944. (USNARA, 80-G-288518)

sea after sheering off the tin can's stacks. Immediately thereafter, another "Helen" medium bomber intersecting the column's path was knocked down, splashing into the water off *Boise's* port bow. A third Japanese aircraft, also coming in low, ran into the heavy curtain of flak from the cruiser's AA batteries. The bandit was hit by the flak, which deterred him from pressing his attack, but the pilot still managed to fly away with smoke trailing from his plane. While *Boise* was busy fending off these aerial assaults, the USS *Killen* (DD-593) and USS *Claxton* (DD-571) were dive-bombed and damaged. After releasing its bomb, the assailant crashed into the *Claxton,* causing extensive damage. At 1012, another low-flying bomber made a run at the *Boise* on the port bow, but once again her ferocious AA barrage drove it off. For the next 45 minutes, Japanese planes continued to be spotted in the vicinity, but did not attack the ships. Except for sporadic AA fire from the destroyers in the screen, things in the gulf were fairly quiet for a time.

While there was a temporary let up in the air raids in the *Boise's* immediate area, the same was not true elsewhere. At 1100, the USS *Bush* (DD-529), on antisubmarine picket duty in the nearby southern Surigao Straits, came under attack by several dive bombers and torpedo planes. The *Bush* shot down two bandits and damaged two others while suffering only light damage and two casualties herself, thanks to her skipper's skillful seamanship. *Boise* later reported that the CAP was nowhere to be seen during these morning attacks, or the few available American fighters were incapable of handling the situation. Without effective air cover, the ships were left to defend themselves. Three destroyers were hit within a very short time period, two of them suffering heavy damage, leading *Boise*'s officers to speculate that the Japanese were intent on reducing the Americans' destroyer strength, which was vital for AA and anti-submarine defense. The destroyers were small enough to be sunk by a single suicide plane, far easier than a cruiser or battleship. In the case of the kamikaze that struck the *Claxton*, the Japanese pilot turned on the destroyer after attempting to crash dive on *Shropshire*, only to be driven off by the Aussies' blistering AA fusillades.

The lull in the air raids in Leyte Gulf was all too brief, because the devil birds showed up again in the early afternoon. At 1340, two *Aichi* D3A "Vals" slammed into the USS *Abner Read* (DD-526) as she was standing by the crippled *Claxton* about five miles west of the task group. The kamikazes set off a huge explosion in her magazine that turned the destroyer into a raging inferno. Some 20 minutes later, the torpedoes in the *Abner Read*'s tubes were accidentally discharged by the intense heat from the flames that were spreading out of control. The torpedoes were spotted running hot, straight and true at the concentration of ships in the task group. Only violent, evasive maneuvering by the *Phoenix, Nashville, Mississippi* and the *Pennsylvania* saved them from being struck by the torpedoes, which fortunately did not impact any of the Allied ships. The doomed *Abner Read* finally rolled over and sank at about 1417, thus becoming the first of many American destroyers to be sunk by kamikazes. In the midst of all this excitement, another "Val" dove on the USS *R.P. Leary* (DD-664), which was standing by the *Claxton* and the *Abner Read*, but the kamikaze was "splashed" before it could ram into the little ship. The rest of the day passed with no further kamikaze attacks, although the *Boise* crew remained at their battle stations all afternoon, finally securing from GQ at 1900. The U.S. Navy's losses were one destroyer sunk and five damaged in the suicide attacks on All Saints Day 1944, making it one of the worst days for the U.S. Navy in the Pacific war since the Guadalcanal campaign of 1942. As bad as it was, this was merely a taste of what was yet to come in the Philippines and at Okinawa in the weeks and months ahead.

Boise's November 1944 war diary does not refer to these attacking aircraft as suicide planes or kamikazes. The *Boise Chronicler*, in describing the All-Saints Day air raids, called them "crash divers." On the other hand, in his journal entry dated 2 November 1944, Radioman Third Class Hallman, who wished he were back home for the first day of hunting season, was absolutely clear about the nature of the kamikaze onslaught:

> All hell broke loose again yesterday. The Japs sent "suicide pilots" in one or two at a time yesterday on our Task Force. This force (special) is a suicide squadron, which deliberately dives into a ship for the Glory of dying for their country. They crashed five of our destroyers this way yesterday. The *Abner Read* was sunk in this manner shortly after noon yesterday.... We shot down quite a few planes yesterday, although the Japs really took a toll of our ships.

Thus, it appears that some *Boise* crewmen clearly perceived the significant change that had occurred in the enemy's aerial warfare tactics. Perhaps they could not be at home to hunt doves or quail that day, but they were shooting hot-and-heavy at the devil birds.

While the ships were fighting off the Divine Wind on 1 November, a Japanese surface force estimated to consist of two battleships, three heavy cruisers, and eight destroyers was reported moving east through the Sulu Sea. Shortly thereafter, another enemy force of heavy cruisers was reported standing south in the Camotes Sea west of Leyte Island's Ormoc Bay. These reports led the navy to conclude that another surface attack on Leyte Gulf was in the making and would likely come via the Surigao Straits at dawn on 2 November. Therefore, Admiral Weyler ordered TG-77.1 to deploy for battle. By 2030, all ships were in position with the battle line—*Boise* and *Nashville* were on the right flank with their destroyers, while *Phoenix* and *Shropshire*, accompanied by their destroyers, were on the left of the battleships. They stood ready to fight with every ounce of their strength, as they had on the night of 24–25 October, but this time no Japanese surface attack materialized.

The next morning, the navy learned that the first radio report of the sighting of a Japanese surface force had actually been a clever deception by the enemy. Nevertheless, this false radio report, coupled with the constant and heavy air raids, made it appear at the time that a real surface attack was looming. The second group of heavy cruisers in the Camotes Sea did turn out to be real, at least in part. On the morning of 2 November, a task group that was said to comprise two heavy cruisers, three destroyers, two transports, and six or seven barges was spotted in Ormoc Bay on the western side of Leyte Island, where they were attempting to reinforce Japanese ground forces on the island. According to Morison, this "Tokyo Express," which actually was made up of four cargo ships escorted by six destroyers and four other escort vessels, was attacked by USAAF P-38s from Tacloban field and B-24 Liberators from Morotai. One enemy cargo ship was sunk and several other vessels were damaged, but after unloading the troops and materiel, the three remaining cargo vessels and their escorts managed to flee back to Manila. During the course of the day (2 November) it became clear that there was no imminent threat of an enemy surface attack on Leyte Gulf. The IJN had been decimated during the engagements of the previous month and was, in fact, too weak to stage another attack on the Allied fleet.

During the night, *Boise*'s radars picked up occasional bogies but no attacks came. Before sunrise the next morning the devil birds were at it again. At 0510, a hostile aircraft was detected on radar at a range of 11,000 yards running directly at the *Boise*. When the aircraft was at a distance of 3,000 yards and an altitude of 1,500 feet, the cruiser threw a rapid barrage of 14 AA rounds from her starboard 5-inch guns that was apparently too much for the enemy pilot, for he veered away sharply and beat a hasty retreat. *Boise* patrolled in the eastern Leyte Gulf for the rest of the day, without incident, then after nightfall she moved into the Surigao Strait to guard the entrance to the gulf.

For the next week things seemed to be calming down a bit for the U.S. Seventh Fleet. There was a sharp reduction in Japanese air attacks over the gulf because Halsey's Third Fleet carrier squadrons bombed the Japanese airfields on Luzon and Mindoro Islands on 5 and 6 November, destroying 439 aircraft at a cost of 25 of their own planes. During this calm, Avery wrote to Anne on 5 November, "It looks like our troops on Leyte Island have everything under control. I will tell you about the air raids and the suicide dives they made on us when I see you again."

The next day, he wrote again stressing the relative quiet:

> Another day has passed and all has been quiet so far [*remainder of sentence and the next line and a half were blacked out by censors*]. It looks as if we have everything pretty well under control now. I'll bet before long we will be having movies on the fantail and be getting liberty . . . [*remainder blacked out*].

Halsey's carrier planes slowed down the suicide attacks for a time. But on the evening of 7 November, the weather turned foul due to another typhoon, the second to hit the Central Philippines in a week. The storm's center passed some 245 miles northeast of Leyte Gulf, but brought nasty weather that continued into the next day. On 8 November, the *Boise* deck crew saw a barge that contained the bodies of dead Japanese soldiers drift by the ship. No one knew where this barge had come from or what had happened to it, but it apparently had been ferrying troops to reinforce enemy forces on Leyte Island until it ran into trouble with the Americans.

After the typhoon passed by and the weather cleared, *Boise* continued patrolling in Leyte Gulf, fighting off air raids from time to time. For example, in the late afternoon and evening of 11 November there were three air raid alerts. During the last two, enemy aircraft closed near enough to draw flak from the destroyer screen around the *Boise*'s task group. Various groups of planes appeared to be making torpedo runs on the column of ships, but to everyone's relief, no wakes from torpedoes were sighted. Even so, the threat from the air was real, keeping the men of the *Boise* at their battle stations until 2205.

Early on 12 November, the Japanese planes returned, but this time they did not go after the ships. Instead, they bombed the area around Dulag and Tacloban where the USAAF airfield was located. Despite the darkness, *Boise* saw those nearby areas take a heavy pounding. Later, at 0700, the CAP reported a large group of enemy aircraft over northern Mindanao Island, south of the task group. *Boise* went to GQ in preparation for an attack that never came. They did see an enemy airplane splash into the sea and subsequently learned that American fighters had broken up a flight of six "Betty" medium bombers, shooting down five of the twin-engine aircraft in the process.

In the midst of all this terror and violence, some aspects of navy life and bureaucracy continued almost as if times were normal. Avery was promoted to the rating of Electrician's Mate First Class (a petty officer first class), on 10 November 1944. The young sailor was especially gratified by the pay raise that came with the promotion, as he was trying to save as much money as possible to make a new start after the war ended.

On 15 November, CRUDIV-12 returned to relieve *Boise* and her task group. The next day she departed for some R&R at Manus Island with *Phoenix, Nashville,* the battleship *Mississippi,* and *Shropshire,* under the protection of a destroyer screen. Once the column of ships had left the bay and headed into the open sea, Japanese warplanes dropped by to wish them bon voyage. All hands on the ships surely shared the *Boise Chronicler's* sentiments when he wrote, "I sure hope this is our last one for a long time."

TG-77.3 arrived at Seeadler Harbor on 21 November, remaining there for a week. While at Manus Island, *Boise's* skipper, Captain John S. Roberts, USN, suffered a heart attack on 28 November. The CO had to be relieved of command and was transferred to the U.S. Naval Hospital at Manus. Commander Wolverton, who had been relieved as XO by Commander E. T. Eves the day before, was then retained for duty and assumed command as the cruiser's temporary CO. On the afternoon of 28 November, *Boise, Nashville,* and four destroyers left Seeadler Harbor to return to the Philippines and get back in the war. While *Boise* was at Manus, the remaining ships in Leyte Gulf were frequently attacked by Japanese suicide planes—one cruiser was badly mauled and a battleship suffered minor damage.

Arriving back at Leyte Gulf on 2 December 1944, *Boise* and her task group relieved the cruisers and battleships of TG-77.2, which departed for the Admiralty Islands and Kossol Roads in the Palau group. The largest warships left at Leyte were the heavy cruiser *Portland* (CA-33) and Berkey's three light cruisers, screened by 15 destroyers. The four cruisers were divided into two groups with their assigned destroyers. One group patrolled in Leyte Gulf while the other remained in San Pedro Bay to protect the anchorage.

On the first night, *Boise* went out on patrol to cover the Surigao Strait entrances into the gulf. At 1847, she was attacked by an unidentified Japanese aircraft that swooped by at masthead height. The bandit came in so low that it was only five or six miles out when the radar picked it up, and the ship's AA guns had no time to fire on it. The Japanese pilot dropped a bomb or torpedo 3,000 yards on the *Boise's* port quarter before he was shot down by the destroyers in the screen. The next day (3 December), *Boise* made a quick refueling stop at San Pedro Bay and then returned to her station to patrol Leyte Gulf. There was an air raid alert at noon, but the attack was directed only against the ships in the anchorage. Another air raid followed at 1700, this time aimed at the *Boise's* group. Two enemy planes were shot down, at least one them by the *Boise*. That unlucky Japanese suicide pilot was diving on a destroyer, but the cruiser's AA guns knocked the plane down before it reached its target.

At 1630 that afternoon, the hospital ship USS *Hope* (AH-7), which had come to Leyte Gulf to evacuate wounded GIs and sailors, was attacked by a Japanese torpedo plane despite the fact that the big ship was clearly marked by enormous red crosses. Fortunately, the torpedo missed, passing astern and exploding harmlessly at the end of its run. Earlier that same day she had been hounded by a Japanese submarine. Three days later (6 December) while en route back to Manus Island, *Hope* was again attacked by an enemy dive bomber. That time the bomb fell close aboard, but luckily caused no damage.

After a couple of days of relative quiet, during which *Boise* remained on patrol, the Japanese launched a major aerial assault in the western area of Leyte Gulf at 1115 on 5 December. Kamikazes damaged several ships in that raid. The CAP shot down eight enemy aircraft that morning, and none made it into the area where the *Boise* was operating. Later in the afternoon, heavy flak was observed nine miles south of her position in the vicinity of Cabugan Grande Island, and at 1702, all hands rushed to battle stations as a group of enemy planes suddenly appeared nearby with eight to 12 fighters from the CAP in hot pursuit. A "meatball" (as the sailors and Marines called Japanese aircraft because of the large red circles that adorned their wings and fuselages) was spotted by *Boise's* lookouts some 4.5 miles out at an altitude of 4,000 feet as it began a run at the cruiser at 210 knots. When the kamikaze closed to 4,500 yards, heading straight for the ship's open bridge, it was met with a ferocious fusillade of AA fire. The "Val" dive bomber was blown out of the air by a direct hit from a 5-inch gun when it was only 1,200 yards away, and plunged harmlessly into the water. No sooner had she splashed the first kamikaze when another "Val" broke out of the clouds at 3,000 feet and about 6.5 miles out to begin a suicide attack, firing its machine guns as it swooped in. *Boise* opened up on this kamikaze when it reached 8,000 yards and began swatting it with 5-inch shells at 6,000 yards and with 40-mm fire when it closed to 3,000 yards. The suicide plane burst into flames at about 2,500 yards, still firing its machine guns as it veered away from the *Boise* and plummeted into the sea less than 50 yards off the port beam of the *Phoenix*. During this raid, friendly fighters knocked down two other enemy aircraft. No sooner had the attacks quieted down when the *Boise* spotted heavy AA fire coming from the ships near Cabugan Grande, and saw an explosion from a bomb or torpedo that hit the USS *Mugford* (DD-389). A few minutes later (1720), the CAP splashed a bandit near the *Boise*. The task group then rushed to the aid of the stricken *Mugford*, which was taken in tow by another destroyer for the return to San Pedro Bay. Afterwards, *Boise* and the rest of her task group resumed their patrol duties in Leyte Gulf.

Boise's new skipper, Captain Willard M. Downes, USN, came aboard on the morning of 6 December to relieve Commander Wolverton. In the afternoon, she resumed patrolling in the gulf with the *Phoenix* and three destroyers. At 1812, they sighted a "Val" dive bomber off Capines Point. General Quarters sounded, and the cruiser began high-speed evasive maneuvers to foil an air attack. Twenty minutes later, a Japanese torpedo plane made a run at the ship, screaming in from some 6,000 yards out, at no more than 100 feet off the water. As it was taking fire from the cruiser's port 5-inch battery, the plane dropped a torpedo aimed at the ship. The big cruiser quickly executed an emergency turn to starboard to avoid the torpedo and ceased firing at the plane, which beat a hasty retreat. During the face off with the enemy torpedo plane, heavy flak was seen from the beach at Dulag, and a burning airplane plummeted like a meteorite into the sea close to the *Boise's* position. No further air attacks occurred that evening, and the ships returned to their patrol station covering the Surigao Strait entrances into Leyte Gulf until the next morning, when *Boise* and *Phoenix* were relieved as the gulf defense patrol. After transferring the fire director team to the *Nashville*, the twin cruisers and their destroyers returned to San Pedro Bay for a brief rest and some "upkeep."

Boise spent the next two days anchored in San Pedro Bay. Although there was the occasional air raid alert, no enemy planes got through the CAP to attack the anchorage. On 9 December, she and the *Phoenix* went back out to resume patrolling the entrances to Leyte Gulf. Late in the afternoon of 10 December, a twin-engine *Kawasaki* Ki-45 "Nick" made an attack on the ship formation from the west. *Boise* opened fire with her starboard AA battery when the two-seat fighter closed to a distance of 4,500 yards. As it crossed ahead of the ship, her portside guns picked it up. When the "Nick" reached 16,000 yards, the pilot turned and came back in a suicide dive on the port quarter. *Boise's* port AA battery blazed away at the kamikaze until it crossed overhead and was picked up again by the starboard AA guns. The 40-mm guns were scoring hits on the kamikaze until it suddenly exploded into flames and splashed into the sea just 200 yards off the port bow of the *Phoenix*, which was steaming 1,000 yards off *Boise's* starboard beam. This was another close call for the bobtail cruisers and was, by the *Boise Chronicler's* count, his ship's third solo kill since the invasion of the Philippines began. Minutes later, a second "Nick" made a suicide run on the *Boise*, but a sharp-eyed lookout spotted the kamikaze about four miles out at 2,000 ft. She let loose with a furious barrage from her full array of AA guns, and the attacker slammed into the water after passing in flames within 400 yards of the ship. That made four solo kills.

After the clash with the devil birds, the formation received word that the USS *Hughes* (DD-410) had been badly damaged by a suicide crash in the Surigao Strait off Amagusan Point. They quickly moved out to assist the crippled destroyer, reaching her location at 1940 and forming a screen around her until another destroyer, the USS *Laffey* (DD-459), could take her in tow. The task group then escorted the damaged destroyer back to San Pedro Bay, where they arrived the next day and put in for refueling. The *Boise Chronicler* mentioned that another, unnamed destroyer had been sunk by kamikazes, going down before they could get to her.

Mindoro Island, 15 December 1944

The morning of 12 December was largely uneventful except when a PBY Catalina seaplane at anchor in San Pedro Bay suddenly exploded and burned. No one knew what caused the mysterious explosion. Later that afternoon, *Boise* sortied as part of TG -77.3, which also included *Phoenix* and the heavy cruiser *Portland* (CA-33), to support an amphibious assault around the town of San Jose, located near Mangarin Bay on the southwest corner of Mindoro Island. The island offered a good site for airfields from which to support the upcoming invasion of Luzon, the principal island in the Philippines and home to the capital city of Manila. The landings on Mindoro, which lies some 160 miles south of Manila, were scheduled for the morning of 15 December. The crew of the *Boise* were told to expect attacks by enemy aircraft, submarines, and PT boats all the way to Mindoro, although the convoy would have air cover during the entire voyage. Halsey's Third Fleet, which would be operating independently of the assault force, was tasked with intercepting any Japanese warships that might try to attack the convoy and block the landings. The Third Fleet aircraft carriers were also ordered to bomb all Japanese airfields in the area. As the *Boise* was leaving San Pedro Bay the first air raid occurred, convincing the crew that they would be in for it during the entire voyage since the enemy clearly knew that they were coming.

Yet the next morning (13 December) was surprisingly quiet, with only one air raid alert as they steamed through the Mindanao Sea. The afternoon was a bit more hectic. At 1457 off Negros Island, the convoy's flagship, USS *Nashville*, was struck by a kamikaze that wreaked horrible carnage and destruction aboard the light cruiser. The "devil bird" came in over Siquijor Island, skimming so low over the water that it was not picked up by radar or spotted by the lookouts until it was right on top of the ship. The kamikaze slammed into the cruiser's bridge, destroying the radio shack, killing 133 crewmen and maiming and wounding another 190, many of whom were not expected to live; the total number of casualties was nearly one third of the ship's complement. The scuttlebutt had it that the admiral commanding the assault force and two army generals were among those killed, but as it turned out, the only casualty among the brass hats on board was Brigadier General William C. Dunkel, commander of the landing force, who was wounded in the surprise attack. The dauntless cruiser was saved only by the courageous determination of her crew. While the brave men on the *Nashville* were fighting fires and tending to the wounded, another kamikaze tried to crash into her, but was driven off by AA fire from the destroyer screen and fighters from the CAP. At 1700, the admiral in charge of the convoy transferred his flag to the USS *Dashiell* (DD-659). Later that night, the crippled cruiser, unable to continue the voyage with the taskforce, dropped out of the column to return to Leyte Gulf.

Throughout the afternoon, the *Boise* lookouts sighted "meatballs" everywhere, and her crew remained at battle stations, although it was late in the afternoon before any attackers came within range of her AA guns. At 1741, a twin-engine "Nick" fighter passed high overhead, drawing fire from the cruiser's portside 5-inch guns, but the enemy plane got away. Less than 15 minutes later, a twin-engine "Lily" dove at the *Boise* from 10,000 feet at a range of 14,000 yards. Her AA gunners also fired briefly on this attacker, but ceased firing when the bomber was intercepted and shot down by two P-38s from the CAP. Another "Nick" fighter was seen diving on the destroyer screen, dropping its bombs from high altitude. The destroyers fired on it, but it too got away. More kamikazes attacked, and at 1805, two enemy planes were splashed on the opposite side of the formation. Minutes later, another "Nick" made a run at the *Boise,* but this suicide plane was also destroyed, by F-4U Corsairs, probably flown by Marine pilots operating from bases on Leyte Island. The inverted gullwing F-4U with its long snout was difficult to handle during carrier landings and at first was not much favored by navy pilots, who dubbed it "the bent-wing widow maker." The Marines, however, made good use of this fast, sturdy aircraft as a fighter, a fighter-bomber, and for close air support of troops on the ground. By April 1943, the difficulty with carrier operations was sorted out, and the Corsair became fully operational for the navy. With its 11:1 kill ratio, Japanese pilots respected the Corsair as a formidable opponent in aerial dogfights.

About 1850, *Boise*'s radar began tracking bandits closing on the convoy from 20 miles out. She fired on three "Lilies" passing overhead at 8,000 feet. One of the bombers peeled off, dropping down to 1,000 feet to make a strafing run. Her 5-inch guns first picked him up at 5,000 yards out, and then the 40-mms took over. As the enemy aircraft closed in, the 20-mms cut loose on it, forcing the pilot to climb hastily to 2,000 feet. The plane was shot up pretty good, but still managed to drop a bomb as it passed, which splashed in the cruiser's wake, missing her by nearly 1,000 yards thanks to expert ship handling by Captain Downes. After releasing his bombs, one Japanese pilot in the group tried to crash dive on a destroyer, but according to the *Boise Chronicler,* the destroyer "blew hell out of it" before the kamikaze could crash into her. There were several more alerts, but no additional suicide attacks came that evening, and the men of the *Boise* settled down to try to get some sleep. They were expecting the next day to be another bad one, but happily, 14 December turned out to be fairly quiet, with no enemy aircraft ever coming within range of their guns. The minesweepers were bombed, however, while they were clearing the channel through which the convoy had to approach the site for the amphibious landings.

Boise and TG-77.3 were on station to cover the operation by 1845. Her men figured that the air groups from their escort carriers, which were on station in the northern Sulu Sea, were mauling the enemy airfields. The crew hoped the next day would be just as quiet, but feared that was too much to expect.

On 15 December, after wolfing down their breakfast well before daybreak, the men of the *Boise* took their battle stations at 0500. The smoke watch reported fires on the beach off the port quarter that were believed to be from the American warplanes' bombing strikes on Japanese positions. At 0529, four destroyers were dispatched to sink some Japanese cargo vessels that were located about six miles away. Admiral Berkey's close covering group moved into position at 0600. *Boise* was assigned the role of fire support cruiser, to deliver call fire in case the GIs on shore encountered some special obstacle that had to be knocked out. At 0631, she and two destroyers, the USS *Moale* (DD-693) and the USS *O'Brien* (DD-725), moved into their fire support position about 3.5 miles off shore between the two landing beaches. With H-hour set for 0730, a destroyer reported that many Filipinos and carabao (water buffalo) had come out to the beaches to watch the fireworks. The destroyers were ordered to fire high over their heads to warn them off, but were cautioned not to endanger the people or their carabao. At 0710, after the sightseers were sent scurrying by four warning shots from the destroyers, Berkey's combat ships began softening up the enemy positions on the beach in preparation for the landing. The LSTs and LCIs were launching so many rockets that onlookers, as usual, were reminded of fireworks on the 4th of July. The destroyers had a field day with a 6,000-ton Japanese transport ship they caught in the harbor, pounding it mercilessly until it was engulfed in flames.

At 0715, an eerie silence fell suddenly as the intense naval bombardment ceased. Although it was well past daybreak, enemy aircraft had not shown themselves thus far. The first wave of troops went in at 0730 with the LSTs covering the smaller boats with blazing rocket barrages. Fifteen minutes later, the soldiers were ashore having met no opposition and without having suffered a single casualty. A formation of American fighter aircraft passed overhead. The CAP planes were always a thrilling sight to the men of the *Boise* who were glad to know they were around. The second wave of GIs headed for the beach at 0800, landing 10 minutes later, also meeting no opposition and suffering no losses.

One of *Boise's* reconnaissance planes reported what it first took to be a damaged Japanese cruiser lying dead in the water in Mangarin Bay, just 15,000 yards away from the ship's position. Closer investigation, however, revealed it to be an enemy destroyer that had grounded after being bombed by a carrier plane on 24 October. A destroyer was dispatched to take care of it, and her skipper later reported that he had "shelled hell out of it until it went under."

During the first days of the Mindoro operation, *Boise* saw primarily American planes in the skies. This was because the air groups of the Third Fleet's fast carriers had thrown a "big blue blanket" of protective fighter cover over the ships that kept most of the enemy aircraft at bay while the amphibious force moved into the Sulu Sea. The CAP maintained fairly effective control of the skies over the area until a large typhoon hit on 16 December.

Even so, some enemy planes managed to get through the air screen to attack the ships. Therefore, the lookouts and gun crews kept their eyes peeled, straining to spot the kamikazes before they could get too close.

At 0815 on 15 December, *Boise* learned that the escort carriers were under attack by enemy planes only a few miles out at sea, but they still had not seen a single one. Just a half hour later, however, her radar picked up the first bandits, a flight of 12 "Oscars" and "Zekes." All the ships' AA guns opened up on them when they swooped in just minutes later. The smoke watch reported the sky was full of meatballs as well as flak bursts. Within minutes, four enemy fighters had been swatted down by the

Crewmen of USS *Phoenix* strain their eyes to scan the skies for kamikazes during the Mindoro operation, 18 December 1944. (USNARA, 80-G-47471)

ships' AA barrages. *Boise* faced off with an "Oscar" that attacked from an altitude of 1,500 feet and screaming in at 280 knots. She and other ships fired their 5-inch guns, blowing it out of the sky; *Boise* claimed credit for an assist in splashing this devil bird only 2,000 yards off. Another suicide plane made a run at the cruiser while her AA fusillade was ripping it to pieces. The kamikaze burst into flames, but then banked sharply and slammed into a nearby LST that was heading into the beach on the cruiser's port side.

Although American fighter planes were up there doing what they could, the pilots found it difficult to go after the Japanese too aggressively for fear of getting hit by the thick curtain of flak from their own ships. Even so, the CAP managed to drive off most of the intruders. A pair of kamikazes crash-dived into two LSTs, both of which were badly damaged and later sank. Most of their personnel were rescued. By 0905, the air attack had been repelled, and all was quiet once again.

At noon the crew took turns getting chow with half the men eating while the others remained at battle stations. After receiving no calls for supporting fire, *Boise* moved out into the Mindoro Strait to patrol the approaches to the beachhead. In the afternoon there were more air raids, but no unfortunate incidents were reported. After nightfall the crew felt a bit safer as Japanese planes seldom attacked at night, yet at 1900, enemy planes again attacked the beach area. One meatball closed on the ships, but was driven off by intense AA fire from the destroyer screen.

The day after the landing on Mindoro (16 December), *Boise* was relieved on station by six battleships, and got underway that morning to cover the convoy of landing ships returning to Leyte Gulf. The cruiser spent the rest of the day waddling along with the convoy at seven knots; traveling at such slow speed always made cruiser sailors nervous as they were practically sitting ducks for air or submarine attack. There were several air-raid alerts during the day, but no enemy planes managed to get through the CAP to close on the ship formation—American fighters shot down a large number of Japanese aircraft. At midnight, *Boise* left the convoy and proceeded on to Leyte at 27 knots, arriving early the next morning. The crew had no idea how long they would remain at San Pedro Bay or what their next assignment might be.

Boise spent part of 17 December refueling. The *Nashville* was anchored about a mile away, too far for the men to determine how severely she had been damaged in the kamikaze attack a few days earlier. They could see only her burned smoke stack that stood out black against the blue camouflage paint of the ship. During the night, *Nashville* weighed anchor to return to the United States for repairs, radioing a parting salute to her sister ship, wishing all hands on the *Boise* a Merry Christmas. The crew of the *Boise* hated to see *Nashville* go. She was a great fighting ship and had been with them in every engagement since *Boise* joined the Seventh Fleet 12 months earlier, except for the shootout in the Surigao Strait.

A Hot Christmas in Leyte Gulf

Back at Leyte on 18 December, *Boise's* crew enjoyed a brief, welcome respite from Japanese air attacks. Early the next morning, they were told that kamikazes were to be expected up until noon, and the word was passed for all hands to keep their eyes peeled for them. General Quarters sounded four times that day, but no enemy planes came within range of their guns. The next day, however, was a different story. On 20 December, the devil birds made four raids on the ships in the gulf, but only once did they come close enough to the *Boise* for her gunners to shoot at them. At 1730, a formation of enemy planes was picked up on radar 70 miles north and heading east. *Boise* kept a constant radar track on the bandits and vectored the CAP to intercept them, but the American pilots were unable to make contact with the enemy in the dark. After circling around out of range for about an hour, the enemy aircraft began a run at the anchorage. Fifteen minutes later, heavy flak was seen about eight miles southwest of *Boise's* position. At 1849, two enemy "Nell" bombers plunged down on the *Boise* from about three miles distance. The cruiser's portside AA guns opened up on one of the kamikazes: first the 5-inch, then the 40-mms and finally the 20-mms when it got in close. All the other ships in the area were also firing on the crash-diving "Nells." The one that was under fire from the *Boise* closed rapidly, but overshot the cruiser and slammed into the water astern of her, close by the USS *Gansevoort* (DD-608).

In the afternoon of 20 December, a Filipino guerrilla paddled up in an outrigger canoe alongside the *Boise*. He tried to sell the sailors a Japanese soldier's head, which he said he took when his band killed 16 Japanese that came out of a cave to look for food. Avery related that one sailor lowered a bucket and hauled the head up, carrying it around the deck while holding it by the hair. The head was missing an ear, which the Filipino had already sold. The *Boise Chronicler* was convinced that someone would have bought the entire head, if such had been permitted and had there been somewhere to keep it. Neither Avery nor the *Boise Chronicler* specifically mentioned what finally became of the severed head, but presumably it was returned to the Filipino guerrilla. The beheading or slicing off of ears of an enemy soldier were rather typical of the treatment the guerrillas meted out to the Japanese, whom they detested intensely because of the many atrocities the occupation forces had committed against the Filipino people.

Just before Christmas, air raids occurred daily on San Pedro Bay during daylight hours. American fighters did an excellent job in intercepting the kamikazes, and only a few suicide planes were able to get anywhere near the *Boise*. Between sunset and midnight there were occasional "snoopers" (reconnaissance aircraft) and nuisance raids, but those attacks caused no harm to any of the ships in Leyte Gulf.

Christmas 1944 in the Philippine Islands was hardly a period of "Peace and Good Will towards Men," for the holiday meant nothing to the enemy. But even amidst the horror and carnage of war, the tough, resilient young sailors and Marines retained

Greetings for the holidays from somewhere in the South West Pacific U.S.S. Boise

USS *Boise* Christmas card, 1944. (Author)

their sense of humor and love of practical jokes. Avery told a story about some of his shipmates who slipped aboard the *Phoenix*, Rear Admiral Berkey's flagship, and pilfered a turkey that was being prepared in the officers' mess for Christmas dinner. Someone then draped a large canvas sign on the *Boise* that bragged: "We Stole Berkey's Turkey." Avery always had a good laugh when telling this story, but he never mentioned any names or said whether anyone was punished for the prank. Nor did he say whether he got a slice of the stolen turkey. But, be that as it may, the *Boise* crew had a nice Christmas dinner of their own, complete with turkey and all the trimmings.

The Japanese contributed fireworks to the Allies' holiday festivities by sending some bombers over during the evening, but their bombs failed to hit any of the ships. The *Boise Chronicler* noted that the crew went to GQ six times during those two days (24–25 December), making a total of 191 times since the invasion of the Philippines began, not counting Precautionary GQ.

The day after Christmas, the Seventh Fleet received a report that a Japanese task force consisting of one battleship, one heavy cruiser, and six destroyers had been sighted 100 miles west of San Jose, Mindoro Island. The enemy surface force had departed from Cam Ranh Bay in French Indochina (Vietnam) under cover of a huge weather front. Nevertheless, they were discovered and attacked by American aircraft, which damaged a battleship, a heavy cruiser, and one or more destroyers, but the air attack did not stop them. The enemy warships continued on course toward their objective, which was the American beachhead on Mindoro Island. *Boise* was ordered to sortie immediately with the *Louisville, Phoenix, Minneapolis,* and eight destroyers to intercept the flotilla. The task group set out for Mindoro via the Surigao Strait and the Mindanao Sea at high speed (27 knots), knowing they could never get there in time, but hoping the enemy task force would hang around the area and return the next night for another attack, thereby giving the Seventh Fleet warships a chance to engage them. The cruisers and destroyers arrived off Ilindo on Mindoro Island about 1530 on 27 December ready to mop up stragglers, but the Japanese flotilla had already cleared out after shelling the beachhead and airfields. It was obvious that the Americans on the beach had caught hell, but the *Boise* could not communicate with them to get more information because all their radios had been knocked out by the bombardment. Five or six fires were burning and two transport craft were on the beach, but damage to them appeared to have been light.

No enemy ships were in sight. Reports came in during the afternoon that a second enemy task force, consisting of one battleship, one heavy cruiser, one light cruiser, and four destroyers, was steaming 225 miles west of San Jose and 15 miles northwest of Palawan Passage. This group of ships was within striking distance of Mindoro, and *Boise* and the other warships were ready and waiting to get some payback if they showed up.

All Japanese surface forces in the area retreated off to the west, however, without making any further attempt to attack Mindoro, but at around 2113, enemy aircraft swooped in to bomb and strafe the beaches. *Boise* stood to battle stations, but no planes attacked the ships, although the air attacks on the beachhead continued throughout the night and into the early morning of 28 December. Still, the Japanese aircraft kept their distance from the warships, although several closed to within as little as three miles, most likely to scout the task group to ascertain its composition and strength. A tense moment occurred when a surface contact was made, but it turned out to be only two groups of enemy landing craft off Busuanga Island. American planes from the Mindoro airfields were dispatched to sink them, and the *Boise* secured from GQ at 0230 (28 December). They hung around Mindoro for the rest of the day just in case anything developed. At 1800, the task group departed for

Leyte Gulf, dropping anchor in San Pedro Bay at 1419 on 29 December without having had to face a single enemy air attack.

Boise spent the last two days of 1944 and the first three of 1945 anchored in San Pedro Bay. It was a relatively quiet period. A handful of enemy aircraft appeared in the area from time to time, but they made no attacks. During the lulls in the action, the crew had time to relax, talk, and write letters home. In a letter to Anne (the first page of which is missing), which seems to have come from this period, Avery wrote, "Hank [Labhart] and I just sit around and talk about you and Ann [Hank's wife] for hours sometimes. You know I love that boy as much as I do my brothers or more. We have been through the mill together."

The strain of war and the terror instilled by the kamikazes was beginning to wear him down. In a somewhat depressed and bitter tone he wrote:

> I'm sorry for writing that awful letter I sent to you last time but sometimes I get all wrong and just can't help it. We have to stay out here and work, slave and fight and can't even come home for a few days. For what? The people back there don't appreciate it, they don't even know there is a war going on. It is just a means of getting rich for them. That is the way I feel sometime.

Before closing, he assured Anne that he was doing his best to make sure she would never be ashamed of him or of anything he did. He was hoping the ship would be able to go home within a few months for some leave, adding, "I think we have done our part out here."

During the Leyte and Mindoro operations, the Divine Wind sank or damaged some 100 Allied ships and other vessels. The suicide planes were a fearsome, offensive weapon that the Japanese called upon in desperation and used with terrifying effect in the Philippines. By the end of 1944, however, it was apparent that the devil birds were actually the only offensive threat the enemy posed in the archipelago, and their numbers were rapidly depleting. Nevertheless, the special attack squadrons were far from done with the American and Australian ships. Instead, they were girding themselves to meet the next Allied offensive in the Philippines—the invasion of Luzon Island.

CHAPTER SEVEN

The Invasion of Luzon: The Battle of Lingayen Gulf, January 1945

The new year of 1945 began with the reorganization of the Seventh Fleet in preparation for the main event in the retaking of the Philippine Islands: the invasion of Luzon, the largest, most strategically important island in the archipelago and home to the capital city of Manila. After the *Nashville* was knocked out of action by a kamikaze during the Mindoro operation, the scuttlebutt was that General MacArthur had chosen the old "Noisy *Boise*" to carry him back to Luzon. The rumors were confirmed when Task Unit 77.1.2 was reconstituted with *Boise* designated as the supreme commander's flagship and two destroyers, USS *Edwards* (DD-619) and USS *Coghlan* (DD-609), as her escorts.

Following *Boise*'s return from Mindoro to Leyte Gulf, all hands spent the next few days readying the cruiser for the general to come aboard and the assault on the main island. One might ask why the CINC did not choose the USS *Wasatch* (AGC-9), Vice Admiral Kinkaid's Seventh Fleet flagship, for his new headquarters afloat. As an amphibious force command ship with sophisticated communications equipment, *Wasatch* would have been a much more suitable ship to host the command post for a large invasion force than a light cruiser. But MacArthur was an old warrior who wanted to be with his men in the thick of the fighting. Furthermore, he enjoyed riding into battle aboard a mighty warship, and *Boise* was one of the U.S. Navy's best. The fact that she was one of the most famous American warships of the war, and one with a proven reputation as a brawler, undoubtedly appealed to the general, who was always highly conscious of the image he projected. Thus *Boise,* among all the ships of the Seventh Fleet, was chosen to carry him back to Luzon so that he could finally realize his dream of liberating his beloved Philippine Islands from the Japanese occupation forces.

The Allies had gained an important foothold in the Philippines with the capture of Leyte Island, but the main concentration of enemy ground and air strength was based on Luzon. The IJN had been virtually eliminated as an offensive fighting force by its heavy losses suffered in the Battle of Leyte Gulf. Since then, USAAF aircraft and carrier-based navy warplanes had destroyed over 700 enemy aircraft in the air

General Douglas MacArthur and entourage boarding USS *Boise* bound for the invasion of Luzon Island, 5 January 1945. (NHHC, 80-G-304363)

and on the ground, severely reducing Japanese air power in the Philippines. Most of the remaining Japanese aircraft had been removed to Formosa. Thus, the only important offensive threat that the Japanese could muster against an invasion fleet were land-based suicide planes, most of which operated from airfields on Luzon. The capture of Mindoro Island, just south of Luzon, was important in large part because the Americans gained control of the Japanese airfields there, which could now be used to launch air strikes against the kamikazes before they could take off. Nevertheless, the presence of the Divine Wind would make the landings on Luzon anything but a routine operation and proved to be a far greater trial for the navy than the army.

The supreme commander hoisted his flag on the *Boise* on 4 January 1945, and came aboard with a large entourage consisting of three generals, 14 other army officers, nine enlisted men, as well as three civilian journalists. The reporters—Carl Mydans of *Life* magazine, Art Feldman of Blue Network, and Yates McDaniel of the Associated Press (AP)—were there to chronicle MacArthur's triumphant return to Luzon for the American public. That same afternoon at 1629, with the CINC's flag flying from her mainmast, *Boise* pulled out of Leyte Gulf with her two destroyers

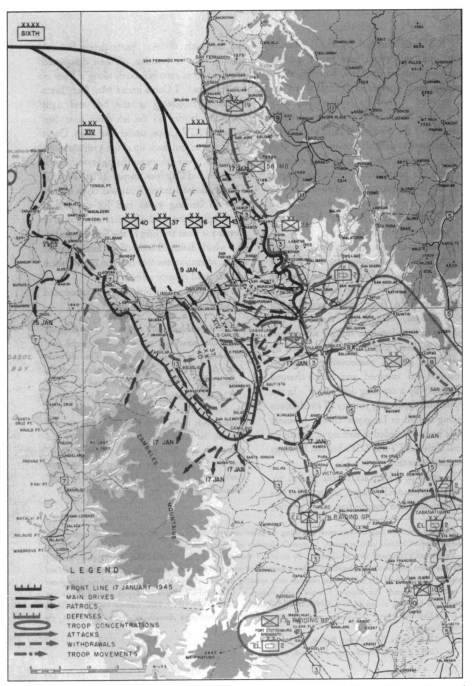

Invasion of Luzon, Lingayen Gulf landings, 1945. (U.S. Army Center for Military History. *Reports of General MacArthur: The campaigns of MacArthur in the Pacific, Vol. I*, p. 260)

in the company of Berkey's TG-77.3. They were to join up with a mighty armada of some 850 ships, one of the largest invasion forces ever assembled during the war in the Pacific. The several U.S. Army corps that would be landing troops had a combined total of some 280,000 men. The U.S. Navy's Close Covering Group (TG-77.3) consisted of Berkey's CRUDIV-15, which now had only one light cruiser (*Phoenix*), CRUDIV-12, with two light cruisers (*Denver* and *Montpelier*), and six destroyers of DESRON-21.

In keeping with the navy's tight security policy, the men of the *Boise* were never officially told where the armada was headed, but the scuttlebutt was that it would be someplace on Luzon. The invasion point turned out to be Lingayen Gulf on Luzon's west coast, about 112 miles (187 km) north-northwest of Manila. Opening onto the South China Sea, the gulf is 26 miles wide at its mouth and 36 miles long. MacArthur, who knew the Philippine Islands well, chose Lingayen Gulf because it offered a good landing area close to the principal roads and railways leading south across the central plains to Manila.

After establishing the beachhead, the plan called for the Americans to drive southward to capture the main objective of Manila Bay and the capital city. If they could quickly take the central core, they could dominate the island and make it difficult for the Japanese to coordinate their defense. Once again, the excellent intelligence provided by the Filipino guerrillas and coast watchers gave MacArthur's planners the exact locations where the enemy was concentrating his forces.

As in previous invasions, the Allies mounted dummy operations in an attempt to deceive the Japanese into believing the invasion would take place elsewhere, in this case at a point south of Manila. The enemy was not fooled by this deception, however. General Tomoyuki Yamashita, the commander in chief of all Japanese forces in the Philippines, was certain that the Allies' next target would be Luzon. He even guessed that it most likely would come around Lingayen Gulf, which was the same invasion point the Japanese themselves had used when they stormed ashore on the island in early 1942, but there was little he could do about it. With no naval and little air strength left, almost no artillery or armor, and with no possibility of help from outside the Philippines, General Yamashita decided to position his ground forces in three widely separated, remote, mountain strongholds from which they would fight a war of attrition against the invading forces.

The U.S. Seventh Fleet, by now commonly referred to as "MacArthur's Navy," continued its role of transporting and supporting the amphibious assault forces. In addition to a massive collection of transport ships, a sizeable number of escort carriers, battleships, cruisers, and destroyers served as the bombardment and covering force. This force included several RAN warships, primarily cruisers and destroyers, and the American sailors were glad to have them along because the Aussies had proved their mettle time and again in the New Guinea campaign and at Leyte Gulf. The battlewagons, along with some other warships, were on loan from the U.S.

Pacific Fleet, and their presence was also a comfort to the sailors who watched in admiration as the "Big Boys" plowed through the South China Sea. Halsey's Third Fleet, with its fleet carriers and fast battleships, was also on hand, to provide air cover and to deter any remaining Japanese surface forces that might approach the northern Philippines to support Yamashita. Five days before D-day, Halsey's carrier squadrons began bombing enemy airfields in northern Luzon, Formosa, Singapore, Borneo, and French Indochina.

Boise's role in the Lingayen operation was to serve as the CINC's headquarters afloat and deliver him safely to the invasion site, providing the support he required until he could transfer his headquarters ashore. During the voyage to Luzon, MacArthur and his staff frequently went up to the bridge to take the air and have a look around. Each time he did this, MacArthur would salute the skipper and request permission to come onto the bridge. Captain Downes explained to him that as CINCSWPA and the senior officer present, it was his right to be there at any time he chose. The general politely replied that he preferred to follow naval protocol and would not pull rank to impose his privileges upon the ship's captain.

Tokyo Rose and the Devil Birds of Luzon

The men of the armada learned from Japanese radio propaganda broadcasts that the enemy knew the invasion force was coming, where it was headed, and that it was being led by MacArthur who was riding on the *Boise*. Like all sailors in the Pacific, the *Boise* crew listened to "Tokyo Rose's" nightly broadcasts because they enjoyed the music she played, which consisted of the most popular tunes of the day, which reminded them of home—precisely the enemy's point. Indeed, the enemy propagandist would constantly taunt them by asking such things as what they were doing out there in a part of the world where they had no business, when they should be at home with their wives and sweethearts. At the end of her show, "Tokyo Rose" would address her *Boise* listeners directly, assuring them that the Japanese knew that MacArthur was on board and exactly where they were. She would threaten them, promising that at dawn the next day, the Japanese planes would sink the cruiser, killing MacArthur along with the entire crew. Then, after wishing them "sweet dreams," she would say good night and sign off. "Tokyo Rose" did not make idle threats. When the sun came up the next morning, kamikazes swarmed in like angry wasps, determined to fulfill her promise to send the supreme commander's flagship to the bottom of the ocean.

The CINCSWPA staff expected the Japanese to throw their remaining air power against the invasion force in the northern Philippines and anticipated that they would continue to use suicide tactics. Every aircraft that could be made available was flown in from Formosa and elsewhere to beef up the Japanese air defenses on Luzon. The kamikazes began attacking the ships of the assault force while they were streaming through the South China Sea en route to Luzon. The suicide attacks did not let up until after the Lingayen landings were completed (13 January 1945) and the enemy finally began to run out of airplanes.

Crash-diving suicide planes were not the only threat posed to the Allied armada by the Japanese, who desperately wanted to hang onto the Philippines. The ships were also stalked by enemy submarines, including a number of two-man midget subs, which began to harass the invasion fleet just after it pulled out of Leyte Gulf. While *Boise* and her task group were transiting the Mindanao Sea, at 1509 on 5 January, USS *Nicholas* (DD-449) reported torpedoes off her starboard bow. *Phoenix* immediately advised that she had spotted torpedo wakes headed directly at the *Boise,* and Admiral Berkey ordered his ships to make an emergency, high-speed, 20-degree turn. *Boise* sounded GQ as she sighted the two torpedoes headed straight at her at 6,000 yards. The skipper swerved the big cruiser sharply to starboard to evade the deadly "fish," which were running "hot, straight, and true." Her quick evasive action caused the torpedoes to pass on by and disappear harmlessly astern. At the time, MacArthur was out on deck conversing with the *Life* magazine reporter, Carl Mydans. The CINC commented to Mydans that they were retracing the exact same route he had taken when he left the Philippines aboard a PT boat in 1942. When the call to GQ rang out, the general, like many others on board, walked over to the rail to watch as the white torpedo wakes sped directly at the *Boise.* Through it all, MacArthur remained calm and composed, never uttering a word or showing the slightest concern. He merely nodded his head in appreciation of such an impressive display of skillful ship handling, for which *Boise* was renowned. It was but one of several attributes that made her the perfect choice to carry the supreme commander into battle.

The torpedoes were fired at the cruiser by a pair of Japanese midget submarines. Shortly afterwards, one of the little subs was spotted and bombed by a TBF Avenger. The USS *Taylor* (DD-468) moved in quickly and began dropping depth charges, forcing the minisub to surface about six miles off, whereupon the destroyer rammed it, sending it to the bottom. MacArthur, who had been observing the attack, again nodded his approval of the destroyer skipper's aggressive manner of dealing with the threat. The second minisub that participated in the attack got away.

The *Boise*, along with the assault forces convoy, got a brief respite from the kamikazes on 6 January, but only because the devil birds were busy mauling Admiral Oldendorf's fire support group of battleships and cruisers that had already pulled into Lingayen Gulf and were beginning the pre-invasion bombardment. That day, the largest and deadliest kamikaze attacks of the entire Luzon campaign swept across the gulf. According to Japanese sources, 58 suicide planes escorted by 17 fighter aircraft struck 15 or 16 of Oldendorf's warships, inflicting heavy casualties and causing extensive material damage. The light cruiser USS *Columbia* (CL-56), dubbed "The Gem of the Ocean" by her crew, was clobbered twice by

Suicide plane diving on USS *Columbia* (CL-56) in Lingayen Gulf, 6 January 1945. The "Zero" burst into flames after being hit by the cruiser's AA guns. It missed the cruiser, but splashed the superstructure with aviation gasoline. (NHHC, NH79448)

Kamikaze attacking USS *Columbia* in Lingayen Gulf, 6 January 1945. (NHHC, 80-G-301229)

USS *Columbia* struck by a kamikaze in Lingayen Gulf, 6 January 1945. The suicide plane slammed into the main deck, causing extensive damage and casualties. (NHHC, NH79450)

suicide planes that day. The second kamikaze penetrated two decks before it and the bomb it was carrying exploded, causing heavy damage, and killing 13 and wounding 45 of her crew. Superhuman damage control efforts saved the ship, and "The Gem" was able to continue her assignment in the bombardment.

Indeed, on 6 January 1945, the warships in Lingayen Gulf were crash dived by kamikazes attacking in force, making it the U.S. Navy's worst day of the war since 1942. Among the ships hit in the raids were the battleships *New Mexico* (BB-40) and *California* (BB-44), the latter was Oldendorf's flagship; the heavy cruisers *Minneapolis* (CA-36), *Louisville* (CA-28), and HMAS *Australia* (for the second time); as well as five destroyers and two minesweepers. During the day's attacks, six Allied ships sustained extensive to serious damage, and one minesweeper was sunk. The carnage caused by the suicide planes was horrible—a total of some 167 men were killed and 502 were maimed and wounded. Listed among the slain were Lieutenant General Herbert Lumsden, Royal Artillery, Winston Churchill's liaison to General MacArthur's command, and *Time* magazine correspondent William Chickering, both of whom were aboard the USS *New Mexico*. The big battlewagon's skipper, Captain R. W. Fleming, USN, was also killed in the blast.

So powerful was the onslaught of the Divine Wind that day that the Seventh Fleet's escort carrier squadrons were unable to cope with the overwhelming volume of enemy aircraft. Given the seriousness of the situation, Kinkaid sent a request to Halsey to dispatch some of his fleet carriers to help out. Although not exactly pleased with the request, Halsey nevertheless complied, sending some of his carriers in the direction of Lingayen Gulf. Fighter squadrons of Hellcats and Corsairs from the Third Fleet carriers arrived on the scene the next day (7 January) and went after the enemy warplanes with a deadly vengeance. Halsey's dive bombers also plastered every enemy airfield within range of Lingayen Gulf, with the result that the air raids began to abate somewhat by the afternoon of invasion day.

In his history of the invasion, Morison described 6 January 1945 as a "gruesome day" for all hands in Lingayen Gulf. Such a blow was especially hard to swallow after the great naval victory at Leyte Gulf, which led many of the men to believe the Japanese were whipped. Now, the kamikazes appeared to herald a serious prolongation of the conflict. For the Divine Wind, this terrible day of 6 January was the most successful of the war, thanks to the large number of planes utilized. One source claims that a total of 21 American and Australian ships involved in the Lingayen operation were hit by kamikazes during a 24-hour period. The Americans claimed to have destroyed as many as 80 enemy aircraft during the same timeframe.

The following day (7 January), Japanese aircraft again launched a series of raids, both conventional and suicidal, against the assault force convoy that was still making its way to Luzon Island. One of their primary targets, of course, was MacArthur's flagship, the *Boise*. The first air raid came before daylight while the armada was cruising through the South China Sea west of Mindoro Island. At 0645, a bomb splashed 1,000 yards off *Boise's* starboard quarter. The plane that dropped it was heard passing overhead, but flew away unseen in the darkness. The ship's radar had failed to detect it because the Japanese pilot made his approach by hiding among friendly aircraft that were operating in the vicinity. About 20 minutes later, just at sunrise, the radar detected more bandits at a range of eight miles. A "Nick" was spotted diving on the flagship from 5,000 yards out. The cruiser's starboard AA battery let loose with a fierce barrage, forcing the attacker to withdraw. At 0840, another attack was mounted by a "Nick" racing in at 240 knots from an altitude of 3,000 feet. The cruiser rammed up her own speed to 20 knots as her 5-inch and 40-mm guns furiously blasted away at her assailant. Although her gunners hit the dive bomber, the enemy pilot managed to drop a bomb from 1,500 feet, which luckily missed the ship, and then beat a hasty retreat. The whole incident took less than a minute. Almost immediately, another "Nick" surprised the *Boise* by diving on her out of the sun from 5,500 feet, but the assailant was spotted by a keen-eyed lookout when it was only about five miles out. The lookout cried out the alarm: "Meatball at 10:00 o'clock," and *Boise's* 5-inch and 40-mm AA guns opened up when the bandit got to within 3,000 yards of the ship. A CAP fighter shot down the kamikaze before it could reach the cruiser.

There were more air raid alerts throughout the afternoon of 7 January. At 1814, other ships on *Boise's* port bow opened up on an "Irving" dive bomber that was some five miles away from her position. The kamikaze crossed ahead of the formation, turned and came back in. It was hit by 40-mm shells while trying to crash dive onto the *Phoenix,* and was blown apart in mid-air over the cruiser, one piece falling in flames to starboard and the other to port of that ship. Radioman Chalmers Hallman related that this kamikaze came so close to the *Phoenix* that one sailor, thinking it was going to crash into the cruiser, jumped overboard. Hallman lamented, "The tin cans searched for him, but all they found was his lifejacket and shirt. It was believed the ship's screws got him."

Minutes later (1825), *Boise* spotted an enemy plane flying high overhead, hiding among the clouds. It apparently had been escorting a kamikaze that was shot down just minutes before. This Japanese pilot did not try to attack; instead, he fled when the cruiser's AA rounds began bursting around his aircraft. One kamikaze, however, managed to get through the flak and crashed into LST-912, causing some damage and killing four men.

The devil birds continued their strikes on the fleet into the night. At about 2215, a Japanese destroyer and several motor torpedo boats approached to attack the convoy. A destroyer went out to engage the enemy vessels. She illuminated the Japanese destroyer with star shells and then opened fire on it. The enemy warship exploded and sank at 0300. In the records of this attack there is no mention of the fate of the Japanese torpedo boats, but they apparently caused no significant problems.

More of the same was in store for the *Boise* and the other ships throughout the next day, 8 January. The action began long before daylight with an air attack at 0300. A group of enemy bombers flew over about 10–15 miles northwest of the *Boise's* position, dropping flares to illuminate their targets, and were taken under fire by other ships. The USAAF CAP shot down four of the bombers before they could cause any harm.

At dawn, as the convoy approached Luzon Island, they were attacked by a group of kamikazes that came in low over the island and then climbed up to altitude. Plummeting down from out of the sun, the suicide planes headed for the escort carriers, but were jumped by the CAP. A fierce dogfight erupted, and over the next hour, the American pilots shot down six enemy aircraft. One bandit evaded the CAP fighters and swooped down to bomb the USS *Marcus Island* (CVE-77). His bomb missed its target, but the pilot then turned toward another escort carrier, the *Kadashan Bay* (CVE-76). The suicide plane took several hits from the heavy AA barrage that was thrown up by every ship in the area, but even so, with smoke and flames pouring from his aircraft, the Japanese pilot exploded into the jeep carrier in a giant ball of flame. With a huge hole in her hull, the baby flat top was soon five feet down by the bow. The damage control parties worked furiously to put out the fires and plug the hole to keep the crippled carrier from sinking, but she was knocked out of the fight. *Kadashan Bay* remained inactive in Lingayen Gulf for the next three days before being towed back to Leyte.

Another kamikaze broke through the fighter cover and the umbrella of flak to crash into the USS *Callaway* (APA-35), which was crewed by U.S. Coast Guard personnel. The "Zeke" fighter slammed into the area of the ship's bridge in a shower of shrapnel and burning aviation fuel, killing 29 crewmen and wounding 22 others. Cool and skillful work by the damage control party doused the flames and kept the ship from sinking. Miraculously, none of the 1,188 GIs on board were injured, and the *Callaway* remained on station to accomplish her mission of landing the soldiers the next day.

The devil birds' attacks continued without let up. At 0808, *Boise's* radar detected a bandit 30 miles out to the west at 5,000 feet and approaching at 200 knots. As the "Nick" came within range, she opened up with her portside 5-inch guns, scoring several hits on the attacker, which was also taking fire from other ships nearby. The damaged suicide plane turned and came in straight for the *Boise* on the port beam, but it was blown apart and fell into the water about 3,500 yards short of the ship.

Late in the afternoon, *Boise* and TU-77.1.2 joined TF-79, Vice Admiral Theodore S. Wilkinson's Lingayen Attack Force, and while preparing to pass into Lingayen Gulf, another raid by a flight of six enemy planes took advantage of the setting sun. At 1816, a kamikaze was shot down by a fighter plane about eight miles southeast of her position. A minute later, another hostile plane was splashed by an American fighter about nine miles to the south. In all, the CAP shot down four of the enemy suicide planes, but the others that managed to get through the air cover continued to press the attack.

At 1847, *Boise* took position at end of the column of ships steaming into Lingayen Gulf. Three minutes later, her radar picked up two enemy planes approaching at 50 miles. One of these made a suicide dive on the *Boise* at 210 knots from 10,000 feet. At 1856, the destroyer screen opened fire on the kamikaze attacking the cruiser from the northwest. Two minutes later, *Boise* took the suicide plane under fire with her 5-inch guns when it approached to 9,000 yards, scoring many hits on the attacker as he barreled on in. After about 45 seconds, *Boise's* scorching AA fire got too hot for the Japanese pilot, so he veered off and crashed into the port quarter of an escort carrier, the USS *Kitkun Bay* (CVE-71), which was only about 1,000 yards away. The baby flat top was heavily damaged and suffered 53 casualties, 17 of whom were killed. She remained afloat, and was towed out to sea so that the next morning, under her own steam, she was able to join the other escort carriers operating off Lingayen Gulf.

AA fire from ships in Lingayen Gulf, 10 January 1945. Photo taken from USS *Boise*. (NHHC, 80-G-304355)

According to Morison, whose eloquent prose would lead one to believe that he had been an eyewitness (one historian asserts he was riding aboard the *Boise*, but neither Morison's history nor the ship's records confirm that), wrote that as the sun sank into the South China Sea on the evening of 8 January:

> ... the soldiers and sailors steaming north witnessed one of those sunsets that poets wrote about in happier times. The sea was smooth, and the orange and scarlet glow suffused over a cloudless aquamarine sky seemed too brilliant to be real. A gentle breeze rippled through the convoy, cooling the steel plates of the transports and giving all hands a refreshing breath as they came on deck during the second dog watch. Men laid it away in memory's locker as one of those rare impression of natural beauty that survive when the horrors of war are forgotten.

The sunset seemed to herald a pleasant end to what had been one hell of a day for the ships in the invasion fleet, but the devil birds were not yet done with them and returned to press their attack. At 1905, *Boise* shot down an attacking suicide plane, which splashed into the water about two miles astern of the cruiser. The all-clear did not come until 1937. In his journal entry for 8 January, Hallman crowed about the *Boise* shooting down two planes that day. He reported seeing a twin-engine "Betty" bomber, which had been trying to crash dive on a destroyer, go down in the "drink" about 200 yards off the cruiser's port beam.

More of the same was in store for them on the day of the invasion (S-day). Well before dawn on 9 January, five American battleships, *Mississippi, California, New Mexico, Pennsylvania*, and *Colorado* (BB-45), together with the heavy cruisers *Louisville, Portland, Minneapolis*, and five light cruisers, *Columbia, Denver, Montpelier, Phoenix*, and *Boise*, were on station in Lingayen Gulf ready to begin the pre-landing bombardment. In addition, two RAN heavy cruisers, *Shropshire* and *Australia*, as well as several Aussie destroyers were on hand to support the landings.

The *Boise* crew had barely finished their breakfast when they were called to battle stations to repel an air attack as the ship began evasive maneuvers. The first enemy planes assaulted the fleet at 0650. All the ships in the anchorage opened fire on them, but none came within range of the *Boise's* guns. While they were fighting off the Japanese planes, fires were seen to break out on the beach from an air strike by American bombers. At 0700, about half an hour before sunrise, the big warships began shelling the beach; *Boise* did not join in the pre-landing bombardment that day because MacArthur was on board. Oldendorf's formidable fire-support group of battlewagons and heavy cruisers had been softening up the beaches of Lingayen

USS *Mississippi* (BB-41) shelling beaches of Lingayen Gulf, Philippines, January 1945. NHHC, 80-G-301229)

Gulf with their big guns for two days, although SWPA HQ had received solid intelligence that the Japanese had largely abandoned the landing zones and pulled the majority of their forces back into the mountains. This intelligence had not been shared with the navy, which expected to encounter shore batteries and other beach defenses. In reality, there were fewer than 20 enemy gun emplacements around the gulf, with most of them positioned on the eastern shore. Therefore, the naval artillery barrages were largely wasted, but the pounding that the big guns gave the landing areas undoubtedly put the soldiers' minds at ease, and they were able to land with almost no opposition.

During the pre-landing shelling, as the GIs were preparing to go ashore at 0745, two "Zekes" were spotted by lookouts after they had sneaked in over the mountains undetected by radar. One made a power dive on the *Boise* at a speed of 300 knots from an altitude of 9,000 feet. She began blasting away at the assailant with her 5-inch guns, but as it got closer the 40-mm battery took over, and finally the 20-mm guns joined in the shooting. The AA barrage was so ferocious that the pilot turned away from the cruiser in search of a softer target, but almost immediately both Zeros were shot down by the combined fusillades from several ships. Three bombs exploded in the water about 4,000 yards from the *Boise*, which had ceased firing. The smoke watch expressed disbelief that they had missed the Zeros because the sky was so filled with flak that he could barely see them.

Avery reflected that as long as the 5-inch guns were firing, he did not worry too much, because the enemy threat was still relatively far away. When the 40-mms began pounding out their pom-pom beat, however, he started to get nervous. But once the 20-mms started chattering away, he always tried to get out on deck to see what was happening because that was a sure signal that the kamikazes were right on top of them.

The *Boise Chronicler* commented that he was glad they were at least allowed to fire at attacking enemy planes that day. One of these planes crash-dived into the USS *Columbia,* hitting her forward director; *Boise's* deck crew saw this kamikaze slam into the "Gem of the Ocean," which was only about six miles away at the time. Hallman noted in his personal war journal that the kamikazes "sure played hell with our Navy." By his count, over the course of several days the *Columbia* was hit twice by kamikazes as were *Australia* and *Shropshire*. Hallman also mentioned that the heavy cruiser *Louisville* and the battleships *Mississippi* and *California* were struck by suicide planes during this period.

Actually, the crash-dive suffered by *Columbia* on 9 January was the third time the "Gem " had been struck by a kamikaze in as many days. The last attack caused extensive damage, killed 24 crewmen and wounded 68, this in addition to the hands she lost in the earlier attacks. While larger ships such as cruisers and battleships could better withstand hits from the kamikazes, that *Columbia* survived three such devastating hits is practically a miracle. The "Gem" again showed her astounding spunk and remained in the fight, continuing to carry out her fire support duties. She finally departed Lingayen Gulf in the evening after the landings were completed. Her crew's heroism and determination in saving their ship and completing their mission earned them the navy's Unit Commendation. While Morison praised *Columbia's* "remarkably bold and efficient crew," the heavy cruiser HMAS *Australia* showed equal toughness in withstanding five kamikazes hits during the Lingayen operation. She was severely damaged and suffered heavy casualties, but also remained on station to carry out her assigned bombardments.

Amidst the noise and confusion of the constant air raids on the morning of S-day, the troops began boarding their landing craft at 0755 in preparation for hitting the Luzon beaches at San Fabian and Lingayen. As the troops were being loaded, all hands on the *Boise* were wondering how the GIs were feeling and what they might be thinking at that moment. Less than an hour later, the landing craft were heading for the beach. Suddenly, at 0910, a hush fell over Lingayen Gulf as the warships stopped their shelling while the landing craft stood into the shore. Twenty minutes later, the first assault wave hit the San Fabian beaches; succeeding waves followed on schedule. That first day, 68,000 assault troops of the U.S. Sixth Army, commanded by General Walter Krueger, stormed ashore on Luzon, meeting little resistance. Over the next few days, the number of soldiers unloaded on the beach rose sharply to 203,608. The army established a 20-mile-long beachhead, captured the coastal towns, and pushed about five miles inland in very short order. Although enemy opposition to the landing had been light, the Japanese would put up a hell of a fight in the days and weeks to come, struggling tenaciously to hang onto the largest and most valuable island in the Philippines.

"A Right Guy"

Throughout the morning of 9 January, General MacArthur watched the action from the flying bridge of the *Boise*. The TBS-50 was connected to speakers so that everyone on the bridge and throughout the ship could hear what was going on across the gulf. Much of the radio chatter had to do with the air battle; the kamikazes continued to harass the ships throughout the landing operations. At 1100, another attack began in which a destroyer escort sitting nearby was slammed by a suicide plane. The kamikazes struck terror into the hearts of the sailors and Marines on the ships in Lingayen Gulf, but there was at least one man on board the *Boise* who appeared to have nerves of steel, even in the face of the devil birds that were seeking to kill him above all others. That man was none other than General MacArthur.

Like many of the men on the *Boise* and the other ships in "MacArthur's Navy," Avery idolized General "Mac." He asserted that the supreme commander never displayed the least sign of fear, and would frequently go out on deck during air raids to watch the action. With shrapnel falling like rain, the general wore his Filipino field marshal's cap, as my father called it, instead of a steel helmet, his eyes shaded by the signature aviator's sunglasses. When bombs exploded close aboard, or kamikazes went roaring by, "Mac" never flinched nor missed a puff on his oversized corncob pipe. Such bravery and coolness under fire earned him the enduring respect and admiration of his men.

William Breuer's book on the retaking of the Philippines relates a great story that illustrates MacArthur's legendary ability to remain cool under fire as well as something of his sense of humor. On the first morning after *Boise* departed Leyte Gulf (5 January), GQ rang out, calling all hands to battle stations to repel an air raid. The cruiser's AA guns kicked up a deafening noise as they fired on a Zero that was diving very fast on the ship, wailing a high-pitched whine as the wind rushed past it. All eyes were glued on their assailant as it closed in. Suddenly, when it was less than 100 yards off, the fighter plane was blown apart by the flak. The huge blast from the exploding aircraft rocked the *Boise* violently. Through all the excitement, MacArthur remained in his cabin. When his personal physician went in to check on him, the general appeared to be sleeping. Believing MacArthur was pretending, the doctor timed his breathing at 16 breaths per minute, a rate associated with sleep. The doctor then woke the supreme commander and asked, "General, how in the hell could you sleep at a time like this?" To which MacArthur replied, "Well, Doc, I've seen all the fighting I need to, so I thought I would take a nap."

Avery later informed his wife that his ship had transported General MacArthur back to Luzon and that he had directed the fight from her decks. This of course was a couple of months later, which was the first time the crew were even allowed to hint that the CINC had been aboard. Avery related that they had remained at their battle stations for five days straight, adding, "We sure had the Brass hats aboard. We could hardly man our battle stations for falling over a General. I almost ran over General Doug once going to my battle station."

Avery later recounted a more detailed version of this story. One day, GQ sounded, catching the young petty officer from Georgia at a point on the ship that was quite far from his battle station. As he ran through the ship, he took a short cut up through the superstructure past the senior officers' quarters, an area that was off limits to enlisted men. As he was sprinting along the deck, the CINC opened the door of his cabin and stepped out right in front of Avery, who nearly knocked the "Old Man" off his feet. The field marshal's cap fell off the general's head and rolled across the deck. Avery, shocked and frightened nearly out of his wits, helped the supreme commander regain his footing and passed him his hat with its visor covered with more "scrambled eggs" (gold braiding) than the young sailor had ever seen, all the while stammering an apology. But General MacArthur merely smiled and replied calmly and graciously, "Carry on, son." Avery immediately took off running again for his battle station as the *Boise*'s AA guns roared in anger at the swarming enemy planes. He always said he was thankful it had been MacArthur he had run into and not some shave-tail ensign, who would surely have clamped him in the brig. Avery closed his brief mention of this up close and very personal encounter with the general in his letter to Anne by proclaiming in admiration, *"He sure is a right guy."*

Throughout his time on the *Boise,* MacArthur kept in close touch with his Filipino guerrilla forces in the Philippines by radio and through messengers who slipped ashore at night from American submarines to retrieve valuable intelligence on the enemy's positions and activity. On S-day, he communicated by radio with Filipino guerrillas on Luzon, who gave him updates on the enemy's movements. From the information he was receiving and from what he could see with his own eyes from the cruiser's decks, MacArthur was visibly pleased with the progress of the landings and knew the Allies would carry the day.

Around midday on 9 January, a PBY Catalina touched down in the bay near the *Boise* and taxied alongside. Lieutenant General Richard K. Sutherland, MacArthur's chief of staff, got off the plane and stepped into a whaleboat to transfer to the ship. He had come to give his boss a status report on the battle. Although the landings were going well, the soldiers were meeting some opposition. At 1245, *Boise* received a message from the beach that troops in the area known as White Beach were encountering mortar fire; three men had been killed, several were wounded, and some of their vehicles were destroyed. At 1335, several more generals boarded the ship to confer with the CINC.

At 1300, the kamikazes renewed their attack. This time the battleship *Mississippi* was struck by a suicide plane, inflicting several casualties, but little material damage. Moments later, it was again HMAS *Australia*'s turn. The devil bird clipped one of her stacks, damaged the superstructure, and blew some holes near her waterline. This was the fifth time that the formidable heavy cruiser was mauled by kamikazes during the operation. Nevertheless, she defiantly signaled with characteristic Aussie grit, that she was "battered but unbowed."

After meeting with his generals, MacArthur decided to go ashore for a firsthand look at how the invasion was proceeding. At 1344, *Boise* closed to within five miles of the beach in preparation for MacArthur and his staff to go ashore. As she moved into position, the *California* passed near enough to her for all hands to see that she had been hit by a suicide plane on her after director. At 1400, a landing craft (LCVP) came alongside to take MacArthur ashore. The all clear sounded a few minutes later, and at 1407, "Mac" and his staff left the ship to tour the beachhead. When he returned to the ship at 1723, wet to the knees, it was clear to everyone that he had been forced to wade through the waves to reach the shore.

At 1813, despite the constant air raids, *Boise* dropped anchor in the gulf, just five miles off the town of Lingayen. Within minutes it seemed as if every ship in the harbor was shooting at enemy warplanes. There were so many bandits in the air that the transport area where *Boise* was anchored had to be covered by a smoke screen for AA protection. Even after sunset, the Japanese planes continued to press

General MacArthur leaving USS *Boise* to go ashore at Lingayen Gulf, January 1945. (NHHC, 80-G-304340)

their attacks relentlessly, something they rarely ever did. AA fire could be seen all around throughout the evening. At 1905, *Boise* herself fired on an enemy plane attacking from the northwest, but in the dark, it was impossible to see whether she hit it. The all clear finally sounded at 2009, and *Boise* secured from GQ. But as it turned out, the enemy had a great deal more in store for them that night.

That same evening, HMAS *Australia* and the cruisers *Columbia* and *Louisville* joined a convoy of ships that pulled out to return to Leyte Gulf. The three cruisers were going back to repair the extensive damage they had suffered at the hands of the kamikazes.

Suicide Boats and Swimmers

In the early morning hours of 10 January 1945, the Japanese introduced a new suicide weapon, when a group of speedboats armed with HE charges slipped into the anchorage to attack the Allied ships. The suicide boats first struck at 0348, damaging an LST that was lying 8,000 yards from the *Boise*, and again swooped in close aboard at 0420, damaging two destroyers with hand-launched explosive charges. Shortly thereafter, the USS *War Hawk* (AP-168), a navy transport ship, was rammed in the suicide attack, which blew a 25-foot hole in her side, leaving 61 men dead. She appeared to be in the process of abandoning ship when an underwater explosion was felt and heard by all hands aboard *Boise*. This blast came from LCI-974, which was struck by one of the suicide boats and subsequently sank less than a mile from the cruiser. A plane was also heard passing low overhead, but was not seen as the warships had begun covering the transport area with smoke. As it turned out, *War Hawk's* crew did not abandon ship, but quickly undertook repairs to keep her afloat while fighting off enemy air attacks during the day. With a temporary patch and power restored, the damaged but feisty transport ship limped out of Lingayen Gulf on 11 January to return to Leyte. During the voyage, she barely escaped yet another attack by a kamikaze, which her gunners shot down, spraying fiery debris across the ship's bow.

The suicide boat attack continued in the early morning darkness. At 0536, the USS *Philip* (DD-498) illuminated and began shooting at an enemy speedboat heading directly at the *Boise* at a distance of only 2,000 yards. The boat was blown to pieces just before it reached General MacArthur's flagship, thanks to the excellent marksmanship of the destroyer's 20-mm guns. Such was the confusion caused by the attack in the dark and smoke that initial damage assessments varied. The *Boise Chronicler* complained that those suicide boats "really raised hell with our ships." He reported that they sank two destroyers and a destroyer escort. According to Hallman, the enemy sank an LST, an LCI, and a large transport, while (inaccurately) the *War Hawk* was damaged and had to be abandoned. He also noted that the suicide boats damaged another LST and two destroyers, and summed up with the comment, "We had quite a time." Later that morning, *Boise* learned that three other transports had been sunk during the night attack by the suicide boats.

After that hair-raising incident, things calmed down a bit. At 0558, two officers and 28 wounded sailors from LCI-974 were brought aboard *Boise* for medical treatment for fractures and lacerations. They were patched up, given morphine, and then transferred to the USS *Monrovia* (APA 5).

Piecing together an accurate account of this suicide boat attack is difficult. Visibility was limited due to the extremely dark night, so confusion reigned, leading to several conflicting versions of events. The darkness and the smoke screen prevented the ships from getting a definitive handle on the number of aggressors involved, and as a result, estimates were erroneously low. As best we know, the Japanese had a flotilla of some 70 plywood speedboats, each with a crew of one to three men, in Lingayen Gulf. The boats were armed with two depth charges, a light machine gun, and small arms. They slipped in and rammed into a target ship or released their depth charges close aboard. At least 10 vessels were attacked in this manner, eight or more of which were apparently either sunk or damaged. The final tally of destruction caused by the

Japanese suicide boats appears to have been one LCI sunk and another knocked out of action for the rest of the war, three LSTs and the *War Hawk* seriously damaged, and one destroyer, the USS *Robinson* (DD-562), suffered light damage. According to Japanese sources, almost the entire group of special attack boats was destroyed in the raid, so they were unable to mount any further operations in the gulf.

No sooner had the suicide boat attack ceased when Japanese warplanes struck the anchorage like a swarm of enraged hornets, about an hour before sunrise on 10 January. They especially sought out the *Boise,* where General MacArthur was quartered. At 0634, the ship's 40-mm guns began firing at an enemy plane that was diving on her at a distance of less than three miles. With visibility hindered by the smoke screen, the Japanese plane dropped down to 200 feet before it released a bomb that splashed less than 60 yards from the CINC's flagship. Ten minutes later, another dive bomber plunged down on the *Boise,* straddling her with bombs to port and starboard. Again, her gunners were unable to see this attacker in the dark and the smoke screen, but the seemingly charmed cruiser came through the air raid undamaged, although one sailor was slightly wounded by shrapnel from the bomb blasts.

After wolfing down a quick breakfast of hot dogs, the crew returned to their battle stations and expected to remain there all day. At 0700, a Flash Red signaled another air raid. The warships in the anchorage threw up a heavy curtain of flak, but one destroyer escort was hit by a kamikaze.

Meanwhile, the ground war on Luzon continued to rage. The cruisers began shelling the island again at 0930, blasting Japanese troop concentrations that had come within range of their guns. That morning, the army reported that the invasion was going well; American forces were three days ahead of schedule and meeting only scattered resistance.

As if the special attack units of suicide boats and devil birds weren't enough to deal with, another new threat suddenly emerged from the waters of Lingayen Gulf. At 1015, two Japanese swimmers with explosives strapped to their backs were captured and taken aboard a transport ship for questioning. At 1230, as General MacArthur was again leaving the *Boise* to go ashore, the word was passed to all hands that Japanese personnel were swimming out to the ships with explosives and boxes covering their heads. Marine sharpshooters were assigned to walk the *Boise*'s decks, and rifles were also handed out to the gun crews on the 5-inch mounts. Their orders were to shoot at any and all floating objects they spotted. My father told me that once when he was napping on deck to escape the intense heat down below, he was abruptly awakened by a rifle shot fired close to his ear by a Marine who was shooting at a wooden box floating near the ship, which might have concealed a suicide swimmer. Avery was temporarily deafened by the shot and later complained that he never completely recovered his hearing in that ear. He recounted that the enemy terrorists would climb up a ship's anchor chains and start slinging hand grenades around until they were shot dead or else blew themselves up. Some historians have dismissed the "rumors" of suicide swimmers as unfounded, arguing instead that they were surviving crew members of the suicide boats. It made little difference to the men on board a ship whether the enemy personnel who climbed up the anchor chain had survived the sinking of a suicide boat or had swum out to the ship from the beach. Either way, the attackers were willing to die in an attempt to inflict as many casualties as possible on the Americans. Fortunately, their courageous efforts largely failed.

The lull in the air raids abruptly ended with a Flash Red at 1300. The destroyer *O'Brien* was slammed by a kamikaze crashing onto its fantail, but luckily no one was injured. Amidst the confusion of combat, a U.S. Navy Avenger torpedo bomber (TBF) flew over to drop a written message on a battlewagon. The American pilot undoubtedly did not appreciate it much when the ship's nervous AA gunners opened up on him.

Once MacArthur had returned aboard after another inspection tour of the beachhead, *Boise* got underway with her task unit, TU-77.1.2, to pass the night at sea with the escort carriers' task group. Lingayen Gulf was presumed to be too hot for MacArthur to remain there overnight after the suicide boat raid of the previous evening.

As the cruiser pulled out of the gulf, the USS *Edwards* came alongside at 1855 to transfer mail and passengers from CINCSWPA, but the operation was interrupted by another air raid. Two enemy planes swooped down on the ships, and the destroyer dropped the lines and moved away. The *Boise* fired on the attackers, shooting down one of them and driving off the other. The *Edwards* then pulled back alongside and passed the mail bags, but before the passengers could be transferred, more enemy aircraft attacked, forcing the destroyer to break off once again as the cruiser rammed her speed up to 25 knots. There were four enemy aircraft in this second group, at least one of which was a kamikaze. The suicide plane flew directly over the *Boise,* attempting to crash dive on her, but the scathing AA barrage she threw up was too hot for the Japanese pilot, so he jumped over the *Boise* and crashed into a transport ship, the USS *DuPage* (APA 41), that was just astern of her.

During the evening air raids, the AA fire around the area blazed hot and heavy. *Boise* lookouts spotted a large explosion on the beach at 1912 that was thought to have been from the crash of a downed enemy aircraft. Things eventually quieted down, however, and the crew secured from GQ at 2010. It had been another busy day of heavy air raids. The "Noisy *Boise*" had been the first ship to fire on all incoming bandits, shooting down at least two of them and earning Admiral Kinkaid's compliments for her excellent gunnery. One can be sure that her distinguished passenger also appreciated her gunners' skill, which kept the kamikazes at bay.

The Japanese resumed their air strikes on the Allied ships in the early morning of 11 January, but as far as *Boise* could see, no ships were hit. At 0808, as *Boise* moved back into Lingayen Gulf to take up her station. She proceeded on her way to anchor five miles off the town of Lingayen at 0849. Most of the day was relatively quiet, but GQ sounded at 1815, and the ships in the harbor began making smoke. This heralded yet another air raid, but the men of the *Boise* had "no dope" on any damage that might have been done to the ships. Just before nightfall, a Zero sped toward *Boise* from out of the setting sun. The cruiser opened fire on the kamikaze, but because of the smoke screen they were unable to see if they hit it. Other ships in the vicinity, however, reported that the suicide plane had been shot down. Just minutes later, a "Val" was spotted three miles out and closing very fast. *Boise* took the bandit under fire until it flew out of range without her gunners being able to see if they scored any hits on it. This incident marked the last of the enemy air attacks on the *Boise* that night. The all-clear sounded at 2020.

After slowing a bit on 11 January, the kamikazes renewed their attacks in force before dawn on 12 January. The first air raid alert came at 0614, and *Boise*'s crew scrambled to their battle stations. The ships began laying a smoke screen so that when the sun broke over the horizon at 0730, the fleet was shrouded in smoke. Twenty-five minutes later, the ship was jumped by three *Nakajima* Ki-44 "Tojo" fighter aircraft approaching at 210 knots over the island at 6,000 feet altitude. She began blazing away at the attacking formation with the full array of her portside AA battery of 5-inch, 40-mm, and 20-mm guns. The withering fire from the *Boise* and the other ships in the area broke up the bombing run, and the "Tojos" fled the scene. After five minutes, she checked fire momentarily, but resumed shooting at an enemy fighter coming at her dead ahead. At 0806, another of the "Tojos" made a run on the port side, and despite heavy flak managed to release its bomb, which narrowly missed the ship, exploding only 200 yards astern. Another suicide plane came screaming in at 1,000 feet, penetrating to within 1,500 yards of the *Boise* before she shot it down with assistance from other ships; another "Meatball" was also shot down and crashed near the beach. Throughout the engagement, the cruiser was taking evasive action at high speed while making smoke to cover herself and other nearby ships. After about 45 minutes of swatting away at the "Tojos," it was all over, and the all clear sounded at 0842.

On the morning of 12 January, Lieutenant General Walter Krueger, CO of the U.S. Sixth Army, returned to the *Boise* to confer with MacArthur. Later that afternoon, Admirals Kinkaid and Theodore S. Wilkinson (CTF-79) also came aboard to meet with their boss. In these meetings with his senior officers, the CINC stressed the importance of pushing on to Manila as soon as possible, to liberate the city and the American POWs imprisoned there. In a 1944 meeting with the Joint Chiefs of Staff, MacArthur had promised that his forces would take the capital city within two weeks of landing on Luzon. He believed that the enemy would evacuate the city rather than attempting to defend it, which indeed was the Japanese commander's intention. But it turned out, his orders were disobeyed by a subordinate.

After three years of Japanese occupation, Filipinos were overjoyed at the sight of the Allied fleet in Lingayen Gulf and American soldiers storming ashore. Civilians swarmed onto the beaches to welcome the Americans, waving American flags that they had kept hidden from the enemy, and to help unload the supplies from the landing craft.

A truly remarkable event occurred on the *Boise* that illustrates the Filipino people's intense loyalty to the United States during World War II. Around midday on 12 January 1945, *Boise* received a signal from the beach that a sailor named Estanislas Bandong was requesting permission to come aboard. Both the deck officer and the yeoman on duty happened to remember Bandong, recalling that the Filipino mess steward had been left behind when *Boise* hastily departed Manila at the outbreak of the war in early December 1941. Permission was granted for him to come aboard, and the sailor reported back to his ship after being stranded in the Philippines for three years. He was carrying his leave papers from 4–8 December 1941 and still wearing part of his uniform.

Bandong's story is nothing short of high drama. When *Boise* arrived in Manila on 4 December 1941, Bandong, one of some 20 Filipino cooks and stewards in the officers' wardroom, had been granted leave to visit his family who lived nearby. When the cruiser and other navy ships in Manila Bay were suddenly ordered to leave port, Bandong was recalled from leave, but he could not get back before the ship pulled out of Manila on 6 December. Left behind, he signed on with a merchant ship, serving on board until the merchantman was sunk. The Filipino swam ashore only to be captured by the Japanese invaders who held him prisoner for a time. Avery, who was greatly impressed with the man's courage and loyalty, related that after Bandong managed to escape from the Japanese, he hid out for a time and then joined the Filipino resistance, until the day in January 1945 when he saw his own ship anchored in Lingayen Gulf. Officer's Mess Steward Second Class Estanislas Bandong was warmly welcomed aboard later that day (12 January) by the skipper, Captain Downes, who determined that given the circumstances, no punishment was warranted for his having been AWOL for over three years. Vince Langelo, who was serving on *Boise* in December 1941, relates this tale in some detail in his book, which includes a photograph of Downes welcoming the sailor back aboard on 12 January 1945.

There were more enemy air raids on the Allied ships in Lingayen Gulf on 13 January, but they did not pose a direct threat to the *Boise*. At 0615, she went to GQ, as the ships began laying a smoke screen over the anchorage. About a half hour after sunrise (0730), the deck crew watched as the CAP shot down an enemy plane over the beach.

At 1415, MacArthur and his staff left the ship, and transferred his flag to his new headquarters ashore at Dagupan, Luzon. This completed *Boise*'s assignment of transporting the CINC and serving as his HQ afloat. He left behind with the CO an autographed photo and a letter of appreciation for the *Boise*. Copies of both were made and distributed to all hands.

Although fewer in number than on previous days, air raids continued throughout the day up until dark. At 1701, the *Boise* crew went to battle stations because a "Val" had been reported in the area, but within minutes, the enemy dive-bomber was shot down by the CAP about 20 miles away. Finally, the all clear came at 1955, essentially heralding the end of the major kamikaze threat to the U.S. Navy in the Philippines. By then, the Japanese were running out of aircraft and pilots. Realizing that the Divine Wind had failed to stop the invasion, they began withdrawing the bulk of their remaining air strength to Formosa.

The *Boise Chronicler* wrote that so many aerial attacks had been made

Portrait of General Douglas MacArthur distributed to the crew of USS *Boise* when he left the ship at Lingayen Gulf, January 1945. Inscription reads "To the USS *Boise*: A gallant ship, a gallant crew, and gallant officers. Douglas MacArthur." (Original is the property of the author)

against the ship that he could not detail them all. By his count, *Boise* had undergone 31 air raids since the beginning of the Lingayen Gulf operation. Hallman's journal records that they were under constant air attack, and Avery wrote that they were at their battle stations for five days straight.

The kamikaze attacks during the Lingayen operation had been intense, terrifying, and deadly. In his 5 February action report on the Luzon operations, *Boise*'s skipper summed up his ship's record of air defense in the month of January 1945. During the period of 9–13 January, the cruiser fired on 15 enemy planes, expending 350 5-inch AA common rounds, 52 5-inch VT fuse rounds, 3,315 40-mm service rounds, and 1,306 20-mm service rounds. In every case but one, other ships were also shooting at the same attackers, so Captain Downes claimed no sure kills, i.e., aircraft that were knocked down solely by his own guns. However, he did claim five sure assists in bringing down planes that were also under fire from other ships. The skipper reported that on 8 January, while operating in the South China Sea, her AA batteries damaged a "Nick," a "Val," and another unidentified type of plane. On 11 January, her 5-inch and 40-mm guns hit a Zero in Lingayen Gulf, and on 12 January her AA gunners damaged a "Tojo." All of these damaged aircraft were seen, or were reported, to have crashed after being fired on by the *Boise* and other ships in the fleet. The "old man" declared that in three other cases, *Boise*'s searing AA barrages forced would-be assailants to turn away to seek softer targets.

Captain Downes reported a problem that plagued his SK air search radar, which was hampered in tracking incoming enemy aircraft by the fact that Lingayen Gulf was almost landlocked. *Boise* was unable to search for bandits using the 360-degree Plan Position Indicator (PPI), so full use was made of the A scope, which provided range to the target for his weapons control system. Her radar frequently picked up bogies over land only to have them fade into the land mass after just one or two plots. As it was necessary to maintain a full 360-degree search, the SK could not be kept trained on a bearing to pick up the bogie when it came out of the fade or climbed above the land mass. This frequently allowed attacking aircraft to close on the ship's position without further detection except for the sharp eyes of the lookouts. Downes said that some means of elevating the SK beam was needed. He also complained that the smoke screens had often left *Boise* exposed while other units were effectively covered. As the largest combat ship visible, the risk to her (and to her distinguished passenger) had been "unduly great." He urged that combat ships be furnished ample supplies of smoke pots to supplement the smoke screens laid by the screening vessels.

Avery later informed his wife that the men of the *Boise* had remained on their battle stations for the better part of five days straight during the Lingayen operation. According to the CO's action report, *Boise* went to GQ at least 11 times during the period 9–13 January specifically due to air raids, and all hands were forced to man their battle stations for long hours every day. On 9 and 10 January, the crew remained at battle stations for over 14 hours each day. The next few days were similar. On 12 January, they were at GQ for more than 13 hours; on 13 January, for over 12 hours. By comparison, 11 January had been a pretty good day since the crew had to remain at their battle stations for only eight hours. Despite the terror and anxiety produced by the kamikaze threat, the skipper reported that all hands performed their duties and stood up well to the stress and strain, showing no ill effects. *Boise* suffered only one casualty during the entire operation—a man was wounded in the foot by a 20-mm shell fragment fired from another ship. The wound was not too serious, so the injured sailor remained on board after the shrapnel had been removed by the ship's surgeon. As for the wounded crewmen from LCI-974 that were treated on board the *Boise*, 13 were stretcher cases and 17 men were ambulatory. The wounded sailors were treated for fractures and lacerations, patched up, and given morphine before being transferred to another ship.

The Divine Wind that swept across Luzon Island and Lingayen Gulf during 4–13 January exacted a heavy toll on the Allied fleet. The kamikaze planes and suicide boats sank 24 ships and damaged 67 others. The carnage they caused was horrible, and casualties, both dead and wounded, were heavy. As time went by, Allied AA defenses steadily improved, and once the element of surprise had been lost, the effectiveness of the special attack tactics declined significantly. Ever greater numbers of suicide aircraft and fighter escorts had to sortie to achieve substantial results. The attrition of Japanese warplanes and pilots was such that by 7 January 1945, their offensive capability was largely spent. Sporadic attacks by small groups of planes continued, but by the middle of the month, even these ended. During the entire Philippines campaign, the IJAAF launched some 400 aircraft on 61 suicide missions, while the Japanese navy sent out 436 kamikazes on 107 missions. The Japanese claimed that 154 vessels were hit by army suicide planes and 105 by navy crash divers, but as usual, the enemy's statistics were grossly exaggerated.

Given the fact that she was such a high priority target for the enemy, it seems almost miraculous that the *Boise* was not hit by a suicide plane or boat, and suffered only one minor casualty during the brawl at Lingayen Gulf. Luck was certainly important, but in all fairness, great credit must be given to her excellent AA gunnery, which drew praise from Admiral Kinkaid, the Seventh Fleet commander. The war diary's pages and the accompanying AA action reports are filled with accounts of attacking planes being forced to veer off in search of easier targets by the fiery curtain of steel that the scrappy cruiser threw at them.

Avery had only the highest praise for his ship's gunners, both in shore bombardment and in repelling air attacks. He singled out one in particular, who was a true "Dead-eye Dick" with a single-mount 20-mm cannon. Avery loved to watch this man shoot, and whenever possible, he would find a place on deck where he could observe him blasting away. He recalled that on one occasion, when a kamikaze was barreling straight in on the *Boise* with guns blazing, this "ole boy" locked on the devil bird along with every other gun on that side of the ship. The flak was so thick that it seemed you could not stick your hand out without getting it shot off, yet the kamikaze kept on coming, skimming along just a few feet above the water. The 20-mm sharpshooter had the kamikaze dead in his sights and was really pouring it on him. He then flipped down his gun sight, stepped out to one side of his gun, and continued shooting from the hip, knocking pieces off the Japanese aircraft with every shot. Finally, when it seemed the suicide plane would surely ram into the ship, the Japanese pilot decided he'd had enough and peeled off, crashing into the side of a nearby transport ship. With gunners of that caliber manning her AA batteries, it is perhaps less surprising that the old "Noisy *Boise*" escaped unscathed from the firestorm of death and destruction kicked up by the Divine Wind in Lingayen Gulf.

With Japanese warplanes largely gone from the skies over Luzon, and the U.S. Army pushing far enough inland that naval gunfire support was no longer needed, many of the warships on loan from the Third Fleet were released, and the Seventh Fleet cruisers were deployed to cover the six escort carriers of "Taffy-3" (TG-77.3) that was operating in the South China Sea to protect the Mindoro-Lingayen supply line. At 0130 on 14 January, *Boise* sortied from Lingayen Gulf with *Phoenix, Denver,*

Montpelier, and eight destroyers. The column of ships raced along at high speed to rendezvous with Taffy-3 at 1017. For the first time in 10 days, they enjoyed a day with no air attacks, causing the *Boise Chronicler* to exclaim, "What a relief!"

For the next two weeks (14–28 January), *Boise* operated with the task group of escort carriers in the South China Sea, about 100 miles west of Luzon and Mindoro Islands, which were covering convoys entering and departing Lingayen Gulf. On 18 January, *Boise* and *Phoenix* put into Mindoro to refuel and replenish their ammunition. During their overnight stay at the island, *Boise* received 122 bags of mail, which all hands were happy to get. The twin bobtail cruisers left Mindoro the next day to rejoin TG-77.3. Their mission now was expanded to include defending the approaches to Mindoro and Lingayen Gulf against possible surface attack and to interrupting "Tokyo Express" runs to Manila, should the enemy attempt to reinforce or resupply their forces there. Mercifully, their two weeks with the "baby bird farms" on the Mindoro-Lingayen Line were uneventful, so the men of *Boise* got some desperately needed rest after their trying ordeal at Lingayen Gulf.

Meanwhile, General MacArthur's troops were tightening the noose on Japanese-held Manila. As the GIs that had landed at Lingayen Gulf were driving down across the central plains, a smaller amphibious landing was made on Luzon some 45 miles southwest of the Philippine capital on 15 January. Two additional landings were made on the main island, in which the *Boise* played a minor role. The first was the Zambales operation (29–30 January) just north of Subic Bay, the site of the American naval base situated about 60 miles northwest of Manila. The landings at Zambales were designed to block off the Bataan Peninsula to keep the Japanese from retiring there to mount a prolonged resistance. The second landings were made at Nasugbu, Batangas province (31 January), on Luzon's southwest coast just below the mouth of Manila Bay. *Boise* was assigned to TU-77.3.1 for both operations with the task of covering the aircraft carriers while they conducted air operations in support of the landings, and standing by to provide fire support for the troops as needed. Both operations went smoothly with few losses of men, aircraft or ships, and the men of the *Boise* basically took it easy as they watched the escort carriers launching and recovering planes that were flying bombing missions and providing air cover for the soldiers on shore.

Although the Japanese had withdrawn the bulk of their airpower from Luzon, enemy submarines still lurked in the area, posing a threat to the American warships. Around noon on 30 January during the Subic Bay operation, an anti-submarine patrol plane spotted a Japanese sub on the surface some 60 miles northeast of *Boise's* task unit. Two destroyers and two destroyer escorts were dispatched to kill the sub. No information regarding the outcome of their mission was found. The day after the Nasugbu landings, a Japanese sub again came calling. While the task unit was steaming towards Mindoro Island at 1954 on 31 January, *Boise* made radar contact on a surface target bearing 123° T, range 19,700 yards. Two destroyers from the screen,

USS *Bell* (DD-587) and USS *O'Bannon* (DD-450), were sent to investigate, and the column changed course to avoid contact. At 2004, the target faded from the radar screens of *Boise* and the destroyers, so it was believed to be a Japanese submarine. Just two minutes later, the tin cans picked up a sonar contact and began dropping depth charges. At 2036, a new destroyer escort, USS *Ulvert M. Moore* (DE-442), was sent in to help the destroyers with her state-of-the art sonar equipment that was far better than that of the other two ships. The hunt continued until just after midnight, when the destroyer escort finally "killed" the sub with "hedgehogs," an anti-submarine weapon that was much more effective than depth charges at sinking submarines. With the submarine threat eliminated, the task unit continued on to Mindoro unmolested.

Boise anchored at Mindoro in the morning of 1 February with all hands hoping to get some good chow; they were sick of the beans, rice, and "buggy" bread that had been the staples of their diet for the past several weeks. For the next week (1–7 February), they were joined by the light cruiser *Cleveland* (CL-55) and had a chance to relax and enjoy recreation parties on the island, where they found a large torpedo that had run up on the beach. While Avery and his shipmates were able to rest and enjoy some free time, the men's thoughts turned to home, and they dreamed of returning there soon. There was scuttlebutt about the possibility that they might be heading for the United States, to which Hallman responded, "Here is hoping." But it was not to be, at least not for several more months. At 1800 on 8 February, the task group left Mindoro for the old naval base at Subic Bay, arriving there on 9 February. As they pulled into the anchorage, the crew could hear gunfire, so they knew the enemy was not far away. Four days later, the cruiser headed out to help retake the island fortress of Corregidor in Manila Bay, which was a crucial part of the plan for liberation of the Philippine capital.

CHAPTER EIGHT

The Battle of Corregidor and Manila

As American troops advanced across Luzon, the Japanese were hunkering down in Manila and other parts of the main island. The Luzon campaign had gone well since the Americans first landed at Lingayen Gulf on 9 January 1945. By the end of January, the GIs pushing southwards through the central plain were approaching Manila. Meanwhile, on 31 January, an airborne operation dropped three parachute regiments just south of the capital. The paratroopers then began to drive towards the city, encircling the Japanese forces that were dug in there.

By 3 February, U.S. Army units and their Filipino allies were entering the outskirts of Manila in the face of stiffening Japanese resistance. Retaking the heavily garrisoned city would prove to be a far more difficult task than anything they had previously faced on Luzon. The city was garrisoned by three Japanese army battalions and 16,000 sailors and Marines of the naval defense force under the command of Rear Admiral Iwabuchi Sanji. The supreme commander of all Japanese military forces in the Philippines, General Tomoyuki Yamashita, ordered the city's evacuation, but Sanji defied his superior, and instead commanded his forces to dig in and prepare to fight to the death.

The battle for the Filipino capital would drag on for nearly a month as the Americans fought house to house to dig out the Japanese occupation forces. General MacArthur sought to save the beautiful, old Spanish colonial city, which he loved, and its civilian population, by tightly restricting the use of artillery and air support. Unfortunately, this only made the soldiers' tasks more difficult and dangerous, and in the end, devastation of much of the city could not be avoided. When it finally fell to the Americans on 4 March, Manila was less a city than a smoldering heap of ruins. Over 100,000 Filipino civilians were killed in the capital city. Some were caught in the crossfire between the opposing forces fighting in the streets, but thousands more perished as the result of Japanese atrocities—the rape, torture, and brutal executions of men, women and children that have become known as the Manila Massacre or the Rape of Manila.

Corregidor–Bataan Operation

To facilitate the recapture of the capital and complete the liberation of Luzon, control of Manila Bay was crucial. Thus, the Americans mounted an operation to take and hold the entrances to the bay and the southern end of the Bataan Peninsula around Mariveles Harbor. Corregidor Island, together with several islets strung across the entrance to Manila Bay, guard the sea approach to Manila. Corregidor, a tadpole-shaped island four miles long by 1.2 miles wide, divides the entrance to the bay into north and south channels. During the Spanish colonial period (1570–1898), Corregidor Island had served as a fortress, prison and customs house for the royal government, and it was from here that the famed Manila galleons set sail for Acapulco, Mexico, with their rich cargoes of silks, porcelain and other goods from China, Southeast Asia, and the East Indies destined for Mexico, the rest of Spanish America, as well as Spain itself. The steep and rocky island, nicknamed "The Rock," was heavily fortified, having served as a major U.S. Army base during the American occupation of the Philippines from 1898 to 1942. The subordinate islets of La Monja, El Fraile (Fort Drum), Caballo (Fort Hughes) and Carabao (Fort Frank), were also fortified by the Americans.

Boise took part in the Corregidor–Bataan operation as a unit of Fire Support Group (FSG). TG 77.3, commanded by Rear Admiral Berkey, consisted of three heavy cruisers, the light cruisers of CRUDIVs 12 and 15, and the destroyers of DESRON-21, augmented by the USS Abbot (DD-629). CRUDIV-15 was designated as FSG A (TU-77.3.1), and consisted of the Phoenix, Boise, and four destroyers. FSG B (TU-77.3.2), under the command of Rear Admiral Ralph S. Riggs, USN, comprised three Cleveland class light cruisers from CRUDIV-12, namely the Denver, Cleveland and Montpelier, plus five destroyers. The reserve FSG C (TU-77.3.3), under the command of Commodore Harold B. Farncomb, RAN, comprised the heavy cruisers Shropshire, Portland, Minneapolis, and an escort of six destroyers. The three FSGs assisted TG-78.3, commanded by Rear Admiral A. D. Struble, USN, which included the transports, amphibious assault ships, minesweepers, and other support units of "MacArthur's Navy." In addition, there was on hand a PT unit (TU-70.1.5) of 12 motor torpedo boats under the command of a Lieutenant Taylor. Dog Day for the landings at Mariveles at the mouth of Manila Bay was 15 February 1945, with H-hour set for 0900.

In the preliminary stage, 13–14 February, Berkey's TG-77.3 covered the minesweepers which were clearing mines from Mariveles Harbor and the entrance to Manila Bay, and also participated in the pre-invasion bombardment of the southern Bataan peninsula, Corregidor, and the associated forts on La Monja, Caballo, Carabao, and El Fraile islets scattered across the mouth of the bay.

Boise's specific role in the Corregidor operation consisted of five functions: (1) participating in the pre-invasion bombardment on the two days prior to the landings and knocking out enemy shore batteries as required on D-day; (2) covering minesweeping operations north of Corregidor Island on D-1 and D+1 days; (3) using her scout planes to spot for enemy gunfire and floating mines and to provide anti-submarine patrol on D-day; (4) delivering call fire for the army as needed; and (5) acting as Fighter Director Ship for the CAP and coordinator for USAAF air strikes on the "Rock."

Intelligence for the operation was good in most aspects, but was seriously flawed by a gross underestimation of the enemy garrison's numbers. A Japanese soldier captured during the operation gave the enemy troop strength on Corregidor as about 3,000 men. This figure proved to be much more accurate than the 300 to 850 estimated by American intelligence reports, upon which troop allocations for the operation had been based. In reality, the Japanese forces on the "Rock" numbered at least 4,700 men, most of whom were naval troops, according to Japanese sources. Other estimates have put the enemy personnel numbers as high as 6,000.

The Japanese were well-entrenched on the strongly fortified islands in the bay, where they were believed to have heavy artillery ranging from 5-inch to 16-inch guns. The Rock itself was a maze of tunnels and caves that sheltered field guns, ammunition, and personnel. For this reason, MacArthur's plan of attack called for a thorough bombardment by the navy's big guns (the army's respect for which had increased enormously over the previous two years), interspersed with aerial

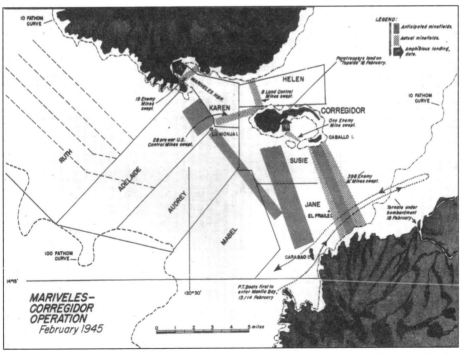

Battle for Corregidor–Mariveles Harbor, 1945. (U.S. Coast Guard Headquarters, *The Coast Guard at War: The Pacific Landings, Vol. VI.*, p. 172)

bombing by the USAAF. The defenses of Corregidor and its subordinate islets were in fact subjected to this combined softening up before the troops actually landed. The Fifth Air Force alone flew some 2,000 sorties, dropping a total of 10,000 tons of bombs on the Rock.

By this stage of the Luzon campaign, the bulk of Japanese airpower in the northern Philippines had been largely eliminated or evacuated to Formosa, leaving the Americans in control of the skies. Thus, no enemy air threat developed during the Manila Bay operations, much to the sailors' relief. Nonetheless, just to be sure there were no surprises, a CAP of USAAF fighter planes was kept aloft during the operation, with *Boise* serving as fighter control ship to direct the CAP. The Japanese again utilized suicide boats manned by one or two men and packed full of high explosives. Dozens of these suicide boats were concealed in caves or tunnels beneath Corregidor Island from which they launched attacks on the Allied ships in the early morning of D+1 (16 February).

The American intelligence data on enemy minefields in the bay proved to be solid. Large numbers of mines were found in the locations that had been pinpointed, with the south channel of Manila Bay particularly heavily mined. In addition, controlled (circuit-fired) minefields were laid in Mariveles Harbor and in the north channel.

At 0800 on 13 February 1945, *Boise* got under way from Subic Bay with *Phoenix* and the four destroyers of FSG A to shell Corregidor, the other islets, and the Bataan Peninsula. Also, along for the show were the light cruisers *Denver, Montpelier,* and *Cleveland* of FSG B. As the cruisers approached Manila Bay, USAAF A-20 Havocs were bombing the Rock. *Boise* went to GQ at 0915 and launched two scout planes to spot fire for her and the two destroyers operating with her. She and *Phoenix* went in first to carry out their assigned bombardment. As the twin cruisers moved up at about 1010, a large column of smoke could be seen rising above Corregidor as a result of the bombs dropped by the A-20s. For some two and a half hours, *Boise* shelled assigned targets on Carabao Island, Corregidor, and the small islets of Caballo and El Fraile, expending 264 6-inch and 280 5-inch rounds before she ceased fire at 1334. Her salvos blew up a building that blazed for two hours and triggered a large explosion and oil fires on Corregidor; her gunners also scored direct hits against Fort Drum on El Fraile Island. When *Boise* completed her assigned bombardment, she was relieved by the *Cleveland* and withdrew to the holding area to wait for the *Phoenix* to complete her firing runs. After the *Brooklyn* class twins had completed their bombardment, the *Cleveland* class cruisers and destroyers of FSG B got their turn at bat and battered Corregidor until about 1600.

The absence of return fire from the Japanese shore batteries on Corregidor fooled some into thinking that perhaps the planes had knocked out the enemy's heavy guns. Admiral Berkey, however, was under no such illusions and was "exceedingly perturbed" that the enemy had not shown his hand by returning fire and revealing the precise locations of the gun emplacements. To Berkey's mind, this could only spell trouble in the coming days. With the day's shooting finished, at 1513, *Boise* and *Phoenix,* with TU-77.3.1, departed for Naval Station Subic Bay for the night. As they pulled out of the area, *Boise* transferred control of the CAP to the *Montpelier.* After arriving back at Subic Bay, the men had a chance to enjoy a movie on the fantail that evening, a welcome respite before having to go back and do it all over again the next day.

Before daylight on the morning of 14 February, *Boise* sortied from Subic Bay with FSG A to shell Corregidor for the second time. She would again serve as fighter director ship for the day's operations. This time, however, there was a great deal more excitement than on the previous day. The Japanese shore batteries broke their silence, interrupting American shelling of assigned targets several times during the morning. Ships operating to the south of Corregidor were fired on by heavy artillery positioned at different points on the Rock, as well as by guns emplaced on Carabao and Caballo Islands.

The fire support ships were accompanied by the minesweepers, whose job was to clear the area behind the island so that the cruisers could get in to blast the other side of the Rock. *Boise*'s main tasks for the day were to cover the minesweepers while they cleared the minefields and provide counterbattery fire to knock out Japanese artillery positioned on Corregidor and the subordinate islands. All morning the cruiser shook with the thunder of her 6-inch and 5-inch guns that hammered the enemy batteries that were firing at Allied ships and minesweepers. The Japanese gunners on the fortified islands and in caves on the south side of Corregidor specifically targeted the minesweepers, hitting them hard. When *Boise* spotted muzzle flashes in the mouths of caves on the Rock or on the subordinate islands, she quickly silenced them with deadly accurate gunfire. The cruiser occasionally had to check fire for air strikes by USAAF A-20s and B-24 Liberators.

Boise turned her guns on a small coastal steamer sighted just off Corregidor at 0842, but luck was with the Japanese vessel. It got lost from view in the smoke and dust kicked up by an air strike on the Rock, and while the cruiser was forced to check fire, the little craft managed to escape. At 1138, she spotted another small Japanese craft steaming past Corregidor and began shooting at it with her 6-inch rifles. After hitting the ship several times, she checked fire and refocused her attention on shore batteries on the Rock until ceasing at 1205. After a very busy morning, *Boise* retired to a position five miles southwest of La Monja Island to standby for calls for fire support.

At 1329, the USS *Fletcher* (DD-445) was covering the minesweepers when she was struck in the forecastle by a shell from a shore battery on Corregidor. Lookouts spotted this gun which was located in a cave or tunnel in the side of a cliff, and barrages from the *Phoenix* and two destroyers promptly slammed the door shut on it. At 1351, the minesweepers again came under fire, and the USS *Hopewell* (DD-681) was sent up to engage the offending shore batteries. The minesweeper YMS-48 was hit by shells from Corregidor, and the *Hopewell* rushed to her assistance. When the destroyer was seriously damaged by a direct hit, two other destroyers, the *Nicholas* and the *Taylor*, were sent in to help and take the *Hopewell* in tow. At 1417, Berkey ordered a cease fire for planes to lay a smoke screen over the minesweepers in the northern area. He also ordered the *Fletcher* to recover stranded minesweeper personnel under cover of the smoke. As the destroyer approached the area, she sighted muzzle flashes from shore batteries and reported the coordinates. Berkey then ordered all ships of TG-77.3 to open fire on the gun emplacements. When the army planes had laid the smoke, *Fletcher* completed her mission of recovering the crew of the burning minesweeper and then sank the little vessel, which was unsalvageable, with gunfire. About an hour later, the destroyers returned to Subic Bay to discharge the casualties and remove the crippled *Hopewell* from harm's way.

Boise was ordered back in at 1445 to relieve *Phoenix*, alerting all ships that a flight of A-20s was coming in to bomb and strafe Bataan. When the air strike on Bataan was completed, *Denver* was ordered to begin bombarding Mariveles. *Boise* and her destroyers received orders to engage assigned targets in that area at 1459, but before they started shooting, a damaged A-20 Havoc bomber ditched in the waters of the bay, 2,000 yards off *Boise*'s port beam. She immediately dispatched her destroyers to pick up the air crew, and in less than 15 minutes the *Taylor* had lifted the survivors out of the water. At 1517, *Boise*'s guns roared as she opened fire on her assigned targets around Mariveles as well as an area on Corregidor's north shore just west of Morrison Point. Four minutes later, her secondary battery joined in, blasting the same targets with 5-inch projectiles. After shooting for about 15 minutes, *Boise* observed an explosion and large fire in her target area, indicating that her projectiles had found their mark. Shortly thereafter, she was relieved by the *Montpelier* and moved to a position north of La Monja Island.

The ships checked fire at various times during the afternoon to allow for air strikes. At 1557, as she proceeded to a new station 3,000 yards south of La Monja, *Boise* advised all ships that a group of P-47 Thunderbolts was coming in to bomb and strafe Corregidor. The ships interrupted their bombardment again about an hour later for a flight of B-25 Mitchell bombers to make a low-level bombing run over Corregidor. At 1716, *Boise* signaled the ships that all aircraft were clear of the Rock and naval shelling could resume.

Japanese shore batteries were not the only threat to minesweepers and the covering ships during the Corregidor-Mariveles operation. Enemy mines continued to cause trouble, even in areas that had been swept and were believed to be clear. The USS *La Vallete* (DD-448) was covering the minesweepers and shooting "floaters" (unmoored mines drifting on the surface of the water) near the entrance to Mariveles Harbor when she struck a mine at 1758. Another destroyer, the *Radford* (DD-446), quickly took the disabled destroyer in tow, but she too hit a mine. The *Taylor*, which had also moved up to assist the stricken *La Vallete*, was ordered to stand clear of the harbor to avoid further mishap, and shortly thereafter, three minesweepers were sent in to aid the two damaged destroyers.

Boise and *Cleveland* were released at 1825, and the former turned over control of the CAP to the *Montpelier* as the two cruisers got underway for Subic Bay. *Boise*'s crew had been at battle stations all day, and fired 578 6-inch and 401 5-inch projectiles. When they got back to Subic Bay, the crew was finally able to relax and enjoy another movie. Radioman Hallman wrote: "The last four nights we have been having movies topside, while about fifteen miles inland the doughboys (GIs) and Japs are ferociously slugging it out. Artillery gun flashes are easily visible."

Early the next morning (15 February), *Boise* weighed anchor and got underway to support the landings at Mariveles on the Bataan Peninsula opposite Corregidor. The Mariveles operation was a small landing compared to others the cruiser had supported. At 0625, she went to GQ and moved into position 2,500 yards from La Monja Island, joining a line of fire-support ships standing 500 yards apart that stretched from La Monja almost to Bataan itself. A few minutes after sunrise, *Boise* began observing shell splashes from Japanese artillery. Her assignment for the day was to spot and knock out shore batteries, while *Phoenix* and the tin cans conducted the pre-landing bombardment around Mariveles Harbor. Other cruisers in the battleline covered the north side of Corregidor with their main batteries and assisted in shelling the Mariveles shore with their off-side 5-inch guns. Air strikes on enemy positions resumed that morning; at 0800, USAAF P-47 Thunderbolt fighter-bombers began bombing and strafing targets on Bataan. H-hour was pushed back to 1000.

At 0900, a flight of P-38s swooped in to bomb Corregidor while the assault forces were entering Mariveles Harbor. Enemy shore batteries across the channel on the Rock began firing on the transport ships as they were pulling into the harbor. *Boise* spotted gun flashes on Corregidor's Searchlight Point and saw the shells splash near the transports. She immediately smothered the enemy guns with a heavy barrage from her main battery, and blasted another gun emplacement on Wheeler Point with her 5-inch guns. Thereafter, she pounded both of the Corregidor batteries with single-gun salvos at the rate of one per minute until the landings were completed and the transports had withdrawn. The Japanese shore batteries were completely silenced during the shelling. *Boise* checked her fire from time to time during air strikes by P-38s and B-24s that struck various points on Corregidor and around Mariveles. Finally, the LCIs launched a blistering rocket attack just before the first wave of troops reached the shore in Mariveles Harbor. Thanks to all the naval and aerial bombardments that softened up the Japanese positions on the mainland, the GIs met virtually no opposition and got ashore according to plan.

The heavy cruiser task unit was finally brought up at 1219 to blast the Rock with their big 8-inch guns. A lot of ordnance was expended that day, with *Boise* alone firing 107 6-inch and 129 5-inch rounds. The ferocious plastering of Corregidor by gunships and war planes prompted the *Boise Chronicler* to comment, "I don't see how there could be a live Jap on the place." Little did he know that the enemy was so well-entrenched that many, perhaps most, survived the bombardment of the island.

Boise's hungry crew wolfed down a lunch of cheese sandwiches on their battle stations, the only food they would get until later that night. Air strikes by USAAF P-38 Lightnings, A-20 Havocs, and B-24 Liberators continued throughout the afternoon in preparation for the army's assault on the Rock the next day. P-47s swooped in to bomb and strafe as well, using fire bombs, "para-frags," and skip bombs. The latter two devices were small bombs designed to allow the planes to make low-level bombing runs with improved accuracy while not imperiling the aircraft. The para-frags were fragmentation bombs attached to a parachute that slowed the fall of the device. With the skip bomb, the pilots could drop the device in such a way that it bounced or skipped across the ground and into the mouths of caves and tunnels where Japanese guns and troops were hidden to protect them from conventional bombardment.

That night, *Boise* and the other light cruisers did not return to Subic, but remained on station west of Manila Bay just in case the GIs on the Bataan beaches needed help. The next day, troops were set to land on the Corregidor itself. During the night, the Japanese sent a number of small (17-foot) suicide boats over to Mariveles from Corregidor. Made of wood, the fast, little boats were almost undetectable by radar and thus managed to sneak up on the armored support craft (LCS-Ls) that were guarding the entrance to the harbor. The suicide boats attacked the screen at the mouth of Mariveles Harbor at 0315 (16 February), sinking three of the LCS-Ls. One of the defenders destroyed five of the suicide boats with machine guns before being knocked out of action by a sixth. Just after daylight, three more enemy suicide boats were sunk by American destroyers. Although they were standing by, *Boise* and her sister cruisers were not called back to take part in this scrap. Official Japanese documents record the date of this attack as 15 February, the day the landings were made at Mariveles. They claimed that 50 of the boats attacked the invasion fleet, damaging a cruiser, a destroyer, and two transports, but they failed to interrupt the landing operations.

The Jump on the Rock

A coordinated assault consisting of an amphibious landing and an air drop of troops on Corregidor Island took place on 16 February. At 0700, *Boise* took her position off Corregidor with the other fire support ships for the pre-landing bombardment. She launched her scout planes to operate with the PT boats in spotting and rescuing paratroopers who might miss the island and come down in the water. At 0720, the cruisers and destroyers of Berkey's TU-77.3.5 began pounding the Rock with HE shells. After 20 minutes, they completed their turn at bat and withdrew to a position five miles southwest of La Monja Island to stand by for calls for fire support. At 0809, A-20s began strafing and bombing Corregidor to close out the pre-landing bombardment.

Earlier that morning, just after sunrise, USS *Claxton* reported that she was surrounded by floating mines five miles west of La Monja Island. At 0819, *Boise* detailed one of her Kingfisher reconnaissance planes to spot mines for the destroyer. Those lethal devices had to be cleared from the areas in which the ships and landing craft would be operating.

At 0830 a vast fleet of C-47s flew over, from which some 1,200 American paratroopers of the 503d Parachute Regiment jumped on Corregidor. It was "a wonderful sight," according to the *Boise Chronicler*, who declared, "There were troop-carrying planes as far as you could see." The C-47s made short runs, coming in very low at about 500 feet, and eight paratroopers jumped from each plane on every pass. The planes then circled around and repeated the operation until they unloaded all the airborne troops. The designated landing zones were two areas on Topside—the old parade ground and a small golf course on the top of the Rock—which were difficult targets to hit given the high wind conditions. Most of the paratroopers made it, but some were killed or injured when their parachutes failed to open, while others were blown past the island by the wind and dropped into the water where they were picked up by PT boats and other small craft. The *Boise Chronicler* described the scene:

> Some of the chutes didn't open, and we could see the small black objects fall to the ground. They landed on the very top of the rock. The spot was only one fourth of a mile square and some of the men failed to land and went into the sea. Our PT boats were running all around picking them up.

Avery also watched the paratroopers jumping onto Corregidor, and his heart swelled with pride at their amazing skill and daring. He also sadly recalled seeing men plummeting to earth with their unopened parachutes trailing behind them, while others drifted slowly down into a hail of heavy machine-gun and small-arms fire from the Japanese garrison on the island.

The first drop, completed at 0943, caught the Japanese defenders totally by surprise. A second drop was made at 1230, which brought the total number of airborne troops to land on the island to 2,050, but the casualty rate was so high that a third drop scheduled for the next day was cancelled; the remaining paratroopers were ferried over to the island by landing craft. Between the parachute drops, an amphibious force began landing on the tail end of Corregidor at 1028.

At 1005, *Boise* and two destroyers, *Taylor* and *O'Bannon*, went out to cover the minesweepers operating in the north channel. At 1154, *Boise* dispatched the *Taylor* to the southeast sector and the *O'Bannon* to the northeast to cover the shores of Bataan and Corregidor during the minesweeping operations in the area. She also sent one of her Kingfishers to spot mines in the water and gunfire from shore batteries on Bataan. At 1253, the cruiser reported mortar fire coming from La Monja Island,

and Admiral Berkey ordered the *Taylor* to take out the mortars. At 1440, the *Boise* crew watched with their hearts in their throats as the American flag was hoisted over Corregidor Island for the first time in three years. General MacArthur was present for the flag raising ceremony and to congratulate the brave paratroopers. Although it was an emotional, uplifting moment, the battle to retake the Rock was far from over. The Japanese defenders retreated into a maze of tunnels and caves from which they put up a determined, fanatical resistance. It would take another 10 days for the GIs to clear out the enemy from most of the island and for Corregidor to be declared secure. The enemy soldiers that could not be dug out of their hiding places were finally sealed in with concrete and left to starve. The same was done with those hiding in tunnels on the smaller islands near the Rock.

Air strikes continued during the afternoon of 16 February; at 1517, a group of USAAF P-51 Mustangs dive-bombed a nearby area. At 1632, Berkey sent the destroyer *Abbot* up to work with *Boise* in protecting the minesweepers, replacing the *Taylor* and *O'Bannon*, which were allowed to return to base. At 1637, one of the minesweepers radioed that she was taking machine gun fire from the north side of Corregidor. Fourteen minutes later, she again reported fire coming from a spit of land at the north end of the island and pinpointed several tunnels along the waterline with camouflage netting still intact, apparently untouched by the naval bombardment. The minesweepers completed their operations in the area at 1750 having cleared only seven mines. Many areas that had been thoroughly swept in previous days were believed safe, but this later proved not to be the case. It eventually became necessary to close an area of the north channel to all ships except shallow draft vessels.

Shortly after sunset, *Boise* and *Phoenix* were released for the day and pulled out with two destroyers to take up station west of Manila Bay for the night. The men of the *Boise* once again secured from GQ after dark. The twin cruisers were ordered to stand by overnight in case they were needed and to be ready to bombard the Rock early the next morning. Neither ship had fired a shot all day, but their crews had thrilled to the show staged by USAAF planes as they dropped tons of bombs on enemy positions.

The attack on Corregidor continued on 17 February with everything going pretty much as planned. Just after daylight, *Boise* launched a reconnaissance plane to search for floating mines in the north channel to the west of Mariveles Harbor. At 0745, the CAP reported to *Boise*, which continued to serve as fighter director and coordinator between USAAF bombers and the warships in the area. At 0816, her scout plane reported a man floating on a log about 2,500 yards from the ship. The *Abbot* was sent to investigate and found three Japanese personnel in the water. Berkey ordered the enemy soldiers taken prisoner and sent two PT boats to help in picking them up. The PTs delivered the captured Japanese to the Admiral, one of whom revealed that he had been educated in the United States and declared he was willing to talk. The POW was taken aboard the *Phoenix* where he was interrogated, and the information he provided was sent to the SFCP. Another report mentioned an English-speaking Japanese POW, also captured that day, who claimed to have been born in Los Angeles. He provided information on the location of some gun emplacements on Corregidor and the tunnels underneath the Rock where the suicide boats were housed. This second report may refer to the same Japanese prisoner mentioned in the *Boise*'s war diary.

Another air strike was made on the Rock at 1050 by a flight of P-47s that bombed and strafed the northeast end of the island. *Boise* stood by all day waiting for call fire from the troops on shore. But she got only one chance to shoot when the SFCP requested fire support for some soldiers who got pinned down by an enemy machine-gun nest south of Morrison Point. As always, the cruiser's gun crews were glad to be of help to the army, and at 1419, began laying down fire from both batteries for 14 minutes. Although the results of this shooting were not reported by the SFCP, *Boise* assumed that the machine guns were knocked out because no further requests for fire support were received from the area. At 1545, the P-47s swooped back in for another bombing and strafing run on the eastern side of Corregidor. At 1725, with her day's work completed, *Boise* left station and returned to Subic Bay, wrapping up her participation in the retaking of Corregidor.

Boise's CO, Captain Downes, reported that his crew remained at their battle stations all day long for five consecutive days during the Corregidor–Bataan operation. They shelled Corregidor and the subordinate islands as well as targets on Bataan during the landings in the Mariveles area. Although several U.S. Navy ships were hit by enemy artillery fire and two struck mines, *Boise* once again came through the fight unscathed. In general, her skipper rated the Japanese shore batteries' fire as inconsistent and rather poor, leading him to speculate that the gun emplacements might have been damaged by the heavy naval and aerial bombardment. It was sometimes difficult to tell because the shore batteries were generally smothered by naval gunfire before they could get off a second salvo. The major exception to the poor showing was on the west and northwest sides of Corregidor, where the enemy's gunfire was rated as excellent by Downes. A few shell splashes were observed quite close to the ships, and one ship was hit several times without anyone ever seeing a splash. These guns were located in caves to protect them from the aerial bombing and could only be put out of action by direct hits from the warships or skip-bombing by the USAAF. Berkey's action report for the Mariveles-Corregidor-Manila Bay operations concurred with Downes's assessment of the poor quality of enemy fire from the south side of the Rock, which usually missed its targets by hundreds of yards. He rated the guns on the northern face as much better, observing that they scored hits on the ships with a "minimum waste of ammunition."

Berkey noted that the pre-attack intelligence reported that Corregidor was lightly garrisoned with only 200–300 Japanese troops, but that assessment was grossly flawed.

The American attackers encountered a garrison of about 20 times that number, and the defenders put up a formidable fight. The admiral further commented:

> … the nearly concurrent landings on Corregidor and Iwo Jima are timely reminders that the Japs are still wily antagonists we cannot afford to underestimate in any respect…. On Corregidor, as on Iwo Jima, there was a tendency to underestimate the number of Japanese present and likewise the formidability of their defense. The numbers on Corregidor were apparently limited only by physical room, for the density was even greater than that on Iwo. The natural defenses at the mouth of Manila Bay when considered from all aspects—from mines through Q boats (suicide boats?) to gun emplacements on favorable slopes—give ample reason for consolation that our losses, though dear at any cost, were very low considering the strength of the enemy defenses that were overcome.

Almost the entire Japanese garrison on the Rock was wiped out. About 20 survivors crawled out of the caves and tunnels to surrender to American forces on the island in early January 1946.

The capture of Corregidor and Bataan was followed by a lull in the action for the navy. Fighting was still going on in the streets of Manila itself, however, but the ships were not involved in that brawl. During this hiatus, the *Boise* remained at Subic Bay from 18 February through 4 March, interrupted only by a three-day run up to Lingayen Gulf (25–28 February). They spent their time during this break in typical navy fashion, making repairs, cleaning, and repainting the ship, but they also had a chance to rest, catch up on their mail, and think of home and family. Avery complained to his wife in a letter dated 2 March that they had received no mail in February, but could not write much because they had run out of stationery and stamps and the latter were being rationed five per man. He went on:

> We aren't doing much these days, mostly laying around…. We are having recreation parties (two cans of beer) now. We go over [to the beach] for beer and a good swim, also our food is very good now. We also have movies at night.
>
> It is so hot out here that we sleep on topside at night. The nights are nice and cool, pretty moon and stars so bright and close and peaceful that it looks like you could almost reach up and pick a few. It is hard to realize there is a war going on then. After I lay down and get fixed for the night, my thoughts turn to you. I wonder what you are doing, if you still love me as you once did….
>
> Then I think of all the wonderful times I have spent with you, and of the wonderful times yet to come, of my next leave with you, of our home and future after the war.

After more than a year in the Southwest Pacific, the stress and strain of combat were being felt. Avery declared:

> Darling when I write and tell you my morale is low, etc. and I gripe a lot to you in my letters, don't worry about me for I'm alright [*sic*]. I have to tell someone and because that someone is you, I feel that you understand me and love me. But don't ever fear that I'll do something wrong, etc. that will reflect on you or my folks. I'll die first.

The fall of Corregidor and the retaking of the Bataan Peninsula cemented American control of Manila Bay and assured the capture of the city. General MacArthur returned to Corregidor on 2 March and was on hand when the city finally fell two days later. With the Philippine capital back in American and Filipino hands, MacArthur summoned a provisional assembly of prominent Filipinos to the Malacañang presidential palace where he declared the Commonwealth of the Philippines to be restored and turned the islands' government back over to the people. In his declaration, the general told the assembled dignitaries: "My country kept the faith. Your capital city, cruelly punished though it be, has regained its rightful place—citadel of democracy in the East."

The liberation of Manila, however, did not complete the Luzon campaign. Fighting on the island dragged on until the end of March 1945. By that time, all areas on the main island of any strategic or economic importance were free of Japanese occupation.

General Douglas MacArthur in the Philippine Islands (Manila?), August 1945. (USNARA, USA C-2413)

Nevertheless, hostile forces remaining in the field on Luzon and on some of the central and southern islands still numbered over 115,000 men. These Japanese troops continued to fight from their isolated mountain strongholds for months. In some cases, resistance continued even after the Empire's surrender on 15 August 1945.

CHAPTER NINE

Wrapping it up in the Southwest Pacific: Mindanao, Borneo, and California, March–June 1945

The U.S. Army's bitter struggle to wrest control of the island of Luzon from the Japanese continued while troops were detached to liberate islands in the central and southern regions of the Philippine archipelago that had been bypassed earlier. These islands were still held by significant Japanese ground forces and a few air units, which had to be neutralized. They would provide strategic locations for air bases that would allow the USAAF to extend its range of operations over the South China Sea to cut Japanese shipping lanes along the southern coast of China and in the Dutch East Indies. As a first step, it was decided to base warplanes on the Zamboanga Peninsula of Mindanao to spearhead the attack on Borneo, where the Japanese still had possession of that island's important oil fields. Therefore, an amphibious assault on Mindanao Island was launched on 4 March 1945, the same day that Manila fell to the Allies.

The Zamboanga Operation, Mindanao Island, 8–12 March 1945

Boise pulled out of Subic Bay on 4 March 1945. She accompanied an invasion force whose mission was to land troops from the U.S. Eighth Army's 41st Infantry Division at San Mateo Point near the city of Zamboanga, on the tip of the peninsula that forms the westernmost part of the island of Mindanao. She was part of the Cruiser Covering Group (TG-74.3) commanded by Admiral Berkey, supporting TG-78.1 under Rear Admiral Forrest B. Royal, USN, who was in overall command of the Zamboanga Attack Force. Jig Day, the code name for the date set for the landings, was 10 March 1945, with H-hour at 0915. Intelligence reported large numbers of Japanese troops on the peninsula and strong defenses around Zamboanga. To soften up the landing sites, pre-invasion naval bombardments by Berkey's cruisers and destroyers were scheduled for the two days prior to the landings. Aerial bombing by USAAF and Marine Corps air groups had begun on 1 March.

At 0810 on 7 March, Admiral Berkey's TG-74.3, with *Boise*, *Phoenix* (flag), and six destroyers, weighed anchor at Mindoro Island. *Boise* was designated as fighter director ship to coordinate the USAAF aircraft that provided fighter cover for the task group during the voyage. Four P-38s made up the CAP that remained over the ships all day until they were relieved at 1825 by two P-61 "Black Widow" night fighters, which stuck around for another hour. After the last of the fighters departed, the column continued steaming toward Mindanao on its own.

Since Japanese aerial attacks had practically dried up, little trouble was expected on that score. Indeed, the first day's sailing was quiet. The only noteworthy incident came at 1720, when destroyers from the screen sighted a sailboat. The USS *Jenkins* (DD-447) went out to investigate and found 23 Filipinos in the boat, which was flying both Philippine and U.S. colors. They proved to be friendly and were allowed to continue on their way unmolested.

Boise's task group arrived off Mindanao's Zamboanga peninsula at 0210 on 8 March. The crew went to GQ at 0600 and remained at their battle stations all day, finally securing at 1700. At sunrise, the men got their first look at the area. Many were struck by the extraordinary natural beauty of the southwest tip of Mindanao Island. The lovely scene struck a deep chord in Avery's emotions, as he expressed in a letter home, "This was beautiful country at this point. Pretty green fields and houses, it made me homesick." The author heard him say on occasions, when he reflected back on the war, that he was saddened by the knowledge that their big guns were about to rip apart much of that verdant, pastoral countryside.

The crew found that their job of shore bombardment during the operation had by now become a familiar routine. They bombarded assigned targets in the days prior to the landings, provided counterbattery fire to cover the minesweepers as they cleared the waters of the landing zone, and then delivered call fire to assist the GIs once they were ashore. In a letter, Avery commented that the Zamboanga operation was "… very much like the usual run of invasions. We shot up the beach pretty bad before the soldiers went ashore."

USAAF bombers made air strikes on military targets in and around Zamboanga before the naval bombardment began. American warplanes frequently returned to strike the area hard throughout the operation.

All hands were immensely relieved by the one thing that was remarkably different in this invasion—the almost total absence of Japanese air power over Zamboanga. Only one enemy aircraft was seen during the entire time that *Boise* was present. On the morning of 8 March, a *Nakajima* Ki-44 fighter appeared in the sky, but was quickly shot down by the CAP, which was provided by Marine Corps fighter aircraft flying out of a makeshift airfield located in recently captured territory at the northern end of the peninsula. With no threat from the air, the fighters were available to provide close air support for the soldiers on the ground, a crucial mission at which the Marine aviators excelled.

Shortly before the first day's scheduled bombardment began, the USS *Taylor* spotted a small native boat with two men aboard and went over to investigate.

The destroyer picked up a *moro* (Moor in Spanish) from the boat, but the intelligence boys got nothing useful from the Filipino Muslim, who claimed to have no knowledge of the enemy. This was most likely untrue. The Muslim people of Mindanao and Sulu had a long history of opposing all foreign invaders of their islands, beginning with the Spanish, then the Americans, and most recently the Japanese. They certainly had no love for the latter, who treated them brutally and with great cruelty, but while some *moros* sided with the Americans in their effort to drive the Japanese out of the Philippines, others did not, preferring to remain on the sidelines while the two foreign "invaders" fought it out with each other. In fact, some Muslim groups fought against both Japan and the United States.

In preparation for softening up the beachhead, *Boise* hoisted out one of her Kingfisher reconnaissance planes to spot fire for her gunners and those of her two destroyers, *Abbot* and *Fletcher*. When aerial bombing temporarily ceased at 1100, the cruiser initiated her task unit's scheduled bombardment, opening fire with the main battery at an assigned target area on Caldera Point, northwest of Zamboanga City. Within 15 minutes, her lookouts reported seeing a large explosion in the vicinity of the target, which probably came from a fuel depot or an ammunition dump. She continued lobbing salvos onto the same target with her secondary battery's 5-inch guns until 1137. Meanwhile, the men topside could see American bombers pounding the beach west of Zamboanga. The cruiser then turned her 6-inch guns on targets at Cape San Mateo, which she blasted for 30 minutes. During that time, American planes also bombed the same area. With the scheduled bombardment completed at 1217, *Boise* stood by to respond to requests for covering fire from the minesweepers that were busily sweeping the channel.

At 1241, *Boise*'s lookouts observed a large explosion near Balisawan, followed by heavy black smoke boiling skyward from what appeared to be an oil fire. Throughout the afternoon other large explosions and fires broke out around the invasion area, many of which were caused by the enemy's destruction of their own ammunition, fuel, and supply dumps. The Japanese also blew up the jetty at Zamboanga to prevent it being used by the Americans. Such acts suggested that the enemy was not at all confident that they could prevent the American soldiers from coming ashore.

Boise spent much of the afternoon watching the destroyers and minesweepers going about their business. At 1630, she moved in to cover an Aussie destroyer, HMAS *Warrego*, and the minesweeper USS *Cinnamon* (AN-50), while they were laying buoys on the Santa Cruz Banks (west-southwest of Zamboanga City) in preparation for the landings, but found there was little need for her services. Later, *Boise* stood by as her sister ship *Phoenix* pummeled Santa Cruz Island for 20 minutes. When the USS *Taylor* was directed to shoot up some enemy planes parked on the eastern airstrip with gunfire, the men of the *Boise* had a front row seat as the destroyer's 5-inch guns blasted the airfield just prior to sunset. With the day's work accomplished at 1930, *Boise*, with TG-74.3, moved off to the west to pass the night.

The next day was for the most part a repeat of the previous day's performance. For my father, however, 9 March 1945 was special in that it was his 29th birthday, his second in the Southwest Pacific. It would turn out to be one of the more memorable birthdays of his life. *Boise* and her two destroyers, *Abbot* and *Fletcher,* were assigned targets for shore bombardment and rotated fire with each ship taking a one-hour turn at bat. Using one of her scout planes to spot fire for her task unit, the big cruiser opened fire with her main battery on a target in the San Mateo area at 0900. After 20 minutes of routine shore bombardment, she observed enemy gunfire aimed at HMAS *Warrego* and the USS *Cinnamon* that were operating near the Santa Cruz Bank. The Japanese artillery piece was firing rapidly, its shells splashing very close to the Aussie destroyer. The cruiser immediately turned her guns on the offending shore battery, directing her Kingfisher over the target area to spot her fire. The first salvo landed short in the water, but subsequent salvos were scored as hits by both the plane and the cruiser's top spotter. The field gun fell silent after the *Boise*'s first salvos landed on it. A destroyer operating close to the beach later in the day confirmed that the gun had been destroyed.

At 0925, another little minesweeper began taking small caliber fire, so *Boise* shifted her secondary battery to pound the area where the machine guns were located. The *Fletcher* also shelled the guns firing on the minesweepers. At 0937, *Boise* switched her main battery back to her assigned target area until she completed her one hour of scheduled shore bombardment at 1000.

While *Boise* was taking a break, B-24 Liberators began high-level bombing in the San Mateo area. During the attack, a major explosion was seen from the *Boise,* which indicated that the bombers had hit an ammunition dump or something of the sort. When a second wave of B-24s struck San Mateo at 1055, everyone was shocked senseless when one of the bombers suddenly exploded in mid-air and fell in flames into the sea. The unfortunate B-24 had been hit by a bomb dropped from a bomber flying above it. Avery, who witnessed the freak accident, described it as a "horrible sight" that left an impression on him for life.

Two men were spotted jumping from the stricken aircraft but only one parachute opened, seen floating slowly down as the fireball that had been the B-24 splashed into the sea. While bombing strikes continued over San Mateo and in the Simonoc area, *Phoenix* sent one of her reconnaissance planes to pick up the survivor from the downed bomber. Berkey described this tragic incident in his war diary entry for 9 March:

> Shortly after noon, a very rare accident dampened spirits when one of our B-24s was struck mid-air by a "friendly" bomb dropped from a higher level. The exploded aircraft was a coffin for nearly all of her crew. Only two men were seen to clear the wreckage, and only one parachute was seen to open. *Phoenix*'s #1 plane, piloted by Lt. j.g. Robert Hugh Smyth, USNR, was diverted from its spotting mission to investigate. Smyth first reported seeing two bodies floating face down. Then he spotted a survivor and "coolly landed" to pick up the bombardier,

2nd Lt. Peter Gondorus, from under the very noses of Jap machine gun batteries on the beach less than 200 yards distant.

During the dramatic rescue, which took less than 10 minutes, a flight of Marine Corsairs made strafing runs along the beach to cover the little Kingfisher while the fortunate young airman was being pulled from the water.

Boise resumed shelling her assigned target at 1246, but the bombardment was interrupted shortly afterwards when she and her two destroyers were sent in to provide close cover for the minesweepers working in the designated landing zone at Cape San Mateo. She took the area south of San Mateo and the Santa Cruz Banks, while the *Abbot* and *Fletcher* took station northwest of the banks. From this position, *Boise* began shelling the airstrip at Wolfe Field with her main battery, but soon switched to let her secondary battery pound the airfield and several other targets in the area.

When the minesweepers began taking fire from the beach east of Caldera Point at 1435, *Boise* moved over to back up her destroyers while jamming the enemy's radio frequency. Less than an hour later, the destroyer *Taylor* knocked out a 3-inch shore battery. *Boise's* Kingfisher spotter plane had to make an emergency landing on the water near the Santa Cruz Banks at 1529 due to a faulty fuel line. The *Abbot* quickly dispatched a whaleboat to take the stricken plane in tow to remove it from harm's way, until a boat from the *Boise* could get over there to haul the little floatplane back to the ship.

Marine F-4U Corsairs strafed the beach from Wolfe Field to Caldera Point again at 1620, and a large fire was observed on that part of the beach soon thereafter. This was just one of many fires caused by the bombardment as well as by the enemy burning supplies throughout the day at various points on Mindanao and nearby Basilan Island. Just before 1800, the Corsairs swooped in again to strafe the beach one final time for that day.

Her day's work done, *Boise* secured from GQ at 1820 and left the fire support station, heading west into the South China Sea to pass the night. Sunset heralded the end to one hell of a birthday for Avery, one that he never forgot thanks to the tragic accident that brought down the B-24 Liberator and killed its entire crew save one.

The amphibious landings at San Mateo came on the morning of 10 March. At 0640, *Boise* launched one floatplane to spot fire, and began blasting her assigned targets before sunrise. The pre-landing bombardment that day was less intense than many others they had conducted. The cruisers checked fire as the landing craft began to head for the shore. USAAF B-25 Mitchells bombed the area around Zamboanga, and B-24s pounded the beaches from high altitude. At 0857, the LCIs let loose with a heavy rocket barrage, and the destroyers saturated the beaches with 5-inch shells as the landing craft were standing in to disembark troops. Close on the heels of the first wave of troops, which landed on schedule at 0915, air strikes resumed on enemy positions in areas around the landing beach.

At 0945, the landing party reported that they were taking mortar fire on their right flank. *Boise* sent a scout plane to seek out the offending mortars, but the pilot was unable to locate them beneath the jungle canopy. More air strikes were called in. Around 1000, there was more high-level bombing to the north and northwest of the beachhead, and as more troops and supplies were ferried ashore, waves of A-20 Havocs bombed Zamboanga. *Boise* counted at least 36 of the twin-engine bombers which departed the area at 1100.

Landing ships (LSMs) near the beach came under fire from shore batteries at 1050, and proceeded to lay a smoke screen to cover the landing craft in the loading area. Two B-25s strafed the area adjacent to the landing zone at 1121, and enemy fire quieted down for a time, but at 1251, an LST reported it was again being shelled from the beach. Planes continued to bomb, and the destroyers continued to pour shells on the enemy gun emplacements. *Boise* received no further calls for supporting fire from the SFCP that afternoon. At 1816, she began recovering her spotter planes, and just after sunset stood out of the landing zone to the northwest for the night. The destroyers that stayed in close to provide artillery support to the troops again took fire from a shore battery just before nightfall.

The troops on shore encountered moderate opposition. Although the Japanese defensive positions were said to have been superior to any the Eighth Army had previously encountered in the Philippines, they were generally found to be empty. Many of their fortified points had been abandoned by the enemy, who became "jittery and thoroughly demoralized by the heavy air and naval bombardment." Hallman thus summed up the *Boise*'s day: "We knocked hell out of a lot of gun positions in our bombardment. Looks like the Seventh Fleet did it again. *Phoenix* and *Boise*."

During the next day's action (11 March), *Boise* again provided counterbattery fire and supporting fire for the troops, as requested by the SFCP. After taking their battle stations at 0600, the cruiser stood by for calls for fire support while the crew watched B-25s bombing and strafing the beaches, destroyers firing on shore batteries, and the spectacular fireworks of a major LCI rocket barrage on enemy positions, which never failed to dazzle those who saw them. At 1037, not having received any calls from the SCFP, *Boise* launched her second Kingfisher to seek out targets for the ship's big guns. At 1050, they located an enemy battery firing from an area to the left of San Roque and saw its shells exploding on the beach. *Boise* let loose on the enemy gun with her main battery at 1109, steadily pounding the Japanese shore battery until 1200, when the ships were ordered to cease fire for an air strike and not to resume until ordered to do so.

At 1215, *Boise* reported to CTG-78.1 that the shell splashes near the LSTs were coming from an artillery piece located to the north of San Roque, and requested permission to open fire as soon as the air strike was completed. At 1300, after four Marine Corsairs swept across the beach on a strafing run, *Boise* again spotted an enemy gun firing from that same area and hitting seaward of the LSTs that were on or near the beach. She also advised that she had a scout plane over the gun and was ready to fire, but the permission to do so did not come. CTG-78.1 again ordered ships to hold fire for another air strike at 1325. Berkey also advised *Boise* that he had not yet received permission to fire on the area where the bothersome enemy battery was located. A flight of B-25s swooped in at 1330 to bomb the beach. Minutes later, when that air strike was completed, *Boise* finally received permission to open fire and began shooting at the enemy gun emplacement with her main battery. She lobbed 44 6-inch rounds into the target area before she ceased fire at 1416.

Although the enemy battery had fallen silent during the shelling by the *Boise*, it was not damaged and soon resumed firing. At 1440, *Boise* reported that her Kingfisher, which was spotting artillery fire for the SFCP, had definitively pinpointed the enemy gun, located in an underground dugout, and was keeping an eye on it. This was in the same area north of San Roque where the guns that had been causing problems all day were located. Over an hour went by before the ship finally received permission from the naval officer in charge of the landing ashore to fire into this area. When it finally came, she began firing at the field gun with single gun salvos from her main battery, and laid it on for 15 minutes from a distance of 14,000 yards. This time, with accurate coordinates, *Boise*'s shooting was right on the money, and the enemy gun was knocked out. Going down for a closer look, her scout plane, which had remained in the vicinity, reported that the bunker in which the enemy battery was hidden had been sealed shut by a landslide caused by direct hits from her 6-inch salvos. After silencing the enemy field gun, *Boise* recovered her scout planes at 1805 and retired out to sea for the night. It had been another good day's work for the men of the old "Noisy *Boise*."

The big cruiser went back in again on 12 March to provide call fire for the army, but stood by all day without receiving any requests for fire support. American planes, however, again bombed and strafed the area heavily. At 1600, *Boise* was released from the operation and headed back to San Jose on Mindoro Island.

Boise's gunnery came in for high praise in her skipper's action report on the Zamboanga operation. According to Captain Downes, after his ship gave her targets a good shellacking, no return fire was noted from any of the target areas, and the plane spotters reported no signs of life in any of them. He also reported that the performance of the Mark-8 radar had been excellent, observing that it was difficult to imagine conducting shore bombardment without it.

The Cebu Landings

After stopping briefly at Mindoro on 13 March to refuel and restock ammunition, *Boise* proceeded to Subic Bay. For the next two weeks, she patrolled back and forth between Subic and Mindoro, with a brief interruption to cover the Cebu operation on 24–26 March. The Cebu landings were part of the operations to clear the

Southern Visayas, the richest part of the Philippines after the Manila area on Luzon. These islands were home to extensive sugar plantations and refineries, as well as commercial centers. Along the coast there were "Hollywood-style houses and other signs of modern life" that coexisted with "primitive conditions in the interior and jungle-covered mountains."

Some 14,500 Japanese troops were reported to be on the island of Cebu, with nearly 85 percent of them concentrated around Cebu City, the Philippines' second largest industrial center. Most of the island's interior was the domain of Filipino guerrillas. The Southern Visaya Islands were deemed strategically important as they offered a convenient staging point for troops redeployed from Europe in preparation for the intended assault on Japan.

Berkey's March War Diary of COMCRUDIV-15 relates that on 24 March, *Boise* sortied with *Phoenix*, the light cruiser HMAS *Hobart,* and six destroyers from Subic Bay en route to the scene of the attack on Cebu City. Later that day, *Boise* and two destroyers were detached from the task group off Mindoro Island and held there in reserve. The Cebu operation was carried out successfully, with Berkey's cruiser division pounding the beachhead for 90 minutes before the landings. The intense naval bombardment forced the Japanese defenders to pull back from the beaches, but was insufficient to explode all the land mines that were strewn everywhere. The need to clear these mines held up the soldiers' advance for nearly two hours. Once the troops were ashore and moving inland, on 26 March the cruisers and destroyers were released, and departed for Subic Bay at 1700. *Boise* and her two destroyers were ordered to return to Subic at 2300 without having participated directly in the Cebu attack. She arrived back at Subic Bay at 0900 the next morning to find three other sidelined cruisers—*Denver, Cleveland,* and *Montpelier*—still riding at anchor in the harbor.

During this welcome break from combat, Avery and his shipmates got a chance to rest, think of home, and dream about the future. In a letter to Anne on 18 March, Avery did just that:

> Today is Sunday, no work, a good dinner, and the best of all we had mail. I'm almost happy. I had four letters from you, one from Genia [his sister]. I also had three Xmas cards…. Darling your letters are wonderful. I feel so good after reading them. Darling I'm so proud of you too. For all the things you are doing for me. There is no one that sticks by me like you do, not even my Mom. Darling I love you so much for it!

The young Georgia sailor sought to calm his wife's concerns about certain habits he had picked up in the navy. He confessed that he had not attended church services that day, but insisted that skipping church was his "only bad habit." Avery downplayed smoking and drinking as vices that "a person usually picks up in an outfit like this during wartime," and told Anne not to worry about them. He promised that he would quit smoking and said that they occasionally were allowed to drink a couple of beers during recreation parties. He told his wife not to worry about him, and assured her that he would never change nor would he ever do anything that would reflect badly on her or on their as-yet-unborn children. He added, "I love you and them too much. I'll sure be glad when the time comes, I can prove it to you and them." Avery kept his promise to stop smoking and indulged in light, social drinking only occasionally.

The news of the war that was reaching the military and naval personnel in the Philippines at this point was encouraging. The war in Europe was winding down. Avery commented that "All the war news is good. It looks as if the Germans are about finished." Many sailors began to think that the war might actually be approaching its end, and they would be able to return home to their families and loved ones. Avery's hopes were raised by the rumors that they would soon be heading home. He said he had no idea how much longer he could carry on unless he got the chance to see his wife again soon. He was hopeful, thinking that it was about time for his ship to return to the United States, but admitted that he was only guessing.

Like many others perhaps, Avery was thinking about his future after the war.

> Darling, I love you more than is possibly good for me. I love you so much that I'm always dreaming and thinking about you. That is the only enjoyment I get out here, thinking about you, dreaming of the future, thinking of Phil T. and Jerri Anne, and making plans for our home and my job after the war. Of course, I'll have to have your advice and point of view on these plans before I carry them out, or maybe I should say before we carry them out.

My father's lifelong dream was to own a farm. He always saved part of his pay during his naval service in preparation for his return to civilian life, in the event that he survived the war. He planned to use the money to buy some land and had asked Anne to look around to see what was available. Now he wrote:

> Did you find out any more about the farms? Let me know as soon as possible. I sure hope we can get a nice one fixed up for you and me soon. It will come in handy when the war is over. We can always have it to fall back on when times get tough, you know.

At times, however, it appeared that talk about the war ending or their getting a chance to get back to the United States was overly optimistic. On 26 March, while the *Boise* was on station off Mindoro Island during the Cebu operation, Avery wrote another letter to Anne, in which he admitted:

> Darling I don't know when we will be coming home. Sometimes I think it will be soon and then sometimes I don't know. I'm just living in hopes. I need you so bad. If I could just talk to you for a little and renew my faith in all that we are fighting for I would be O.K.

On the morning of 4 April, *Boise* departed Subic Bay to make a port call in Manila. During their 24-hour visit to the Philippine capital, the entire crew was allowed to go ashore to tour the ruins of the city, which was once known as the "Pearl of the Orient." In fact, the ship was sent to the Philippine capital to provide as many eyewitnesses as possible to the brutality and destruction that the Japanese had unleashed on the city and its inhabitants during the occupation and the battle for its liberation. The men were ordered to conduct themselves properly and to stay with their group at all times.

The crew was horrified by the terrible destruction that was suffered by the legendarily beautiful, Spanish colonial city. Avery described the place as "shot to hell." The destruction was especially lamentable in the walled city center known as Intramuros. Hallman mentioned the visit to Manila in his memoirs, calling it "strictly a sight-seeing tour with an officer in charge." But, always a typical sailor, Hallman did not miss the fact that the Filipina women in Manila were really "stacked up," and the large number of sunken Japanese ships that filled the waters of the harbor. The next day, the cruiser left Manila and returned to Subic Bay. From there, she proceeded to Leyte Gulf and on to Manus Island, arriving at Seeadler Harbor at 1700 on 11 April.

Boise was in dry dock at Manus from 11 to 16 April. The barnacles were scraped from her bottom and some repainting and other minor repairs were completed. When they arrived at Manus Island, word was passed that Storekeeper Third Class Joseph H. Swartz had been tried by general court-martial on charges of conspiring to steal and sell 10 cases of beer belonging to the U.S. Government. He was found guilty of selling the cases of beer to army personnel and keeping two cases for himself. The court sentenced Swartz to six months confinement at the Naval Annex of the U.S. Army Round Mountain Detention and Rehabilitation Center in Queensland, Australia, and was demoted to apprentice seaman.

While the ship was in dry dock, on 13 April 1945, the men were informed that President Franklin D. Roosevelt had died at his private retreat in Warm Springs, Georgia. Hallman called it "shattering news." Avery was terribly concerned and recalled seeing a big, tough Marine crying like a baby and blubbering, "We won't ever get this goddamned war over with now!" The next day, at 1600, the crew knocked off work for five minutes of prayer for FDR. At 1155 on 15 April, *Boise* held a memorial service for the late president on the cruiser's forecastle.

On pulling out of Seeadler on 16 April, *Boise* got underway for Subic Bay to get back in the war. After a refueling stop at Leyte Gulf on 19 April, she steamed on to Subic, arriving there after a two-day voyage.

Tarakan Island, Borneo, 27 April–2 May 1945

The men of the *Boise* did not have long to wait before being sent back into combat. On 24 April, she departed Subic Bay with *Phoenix*, HMAS *Hobart*, and 10 destroyers. As usual, they were not told where this mission would take them, but the next day the crew learned they were going to invade the coast of Borneo in the Dutch East Indies. This operation was an initial step in General MacArthur's plans for recapturing not only Borneo, but also Java and other strategically valuable islands occupied by the

Japanese. As it turned out, the Joint Chiefs of Staff allowed the Borneo operation, but halted any further advance into the Dutch East Indies, so that Borneo became the last operation in the area.

MacArthur gave overall command of the Borneo operations to Lieutenant General Sir Leslie Morshead of the First Australian Corps. The first objective was to retake Tarakan Island, a small speck of land 18 miles northeast of Borneo in the Celebes Sea. The Japanese had occupied the island early in the war because it possessed valuable oil fields, which now could supply Allied forces in the region. It also offered an airstrip that could be improved and used to support the coming invasion of Borneo itself. The job was assigned to the 26th Brigade of the 9th Australian Infantry Division, commanded by Brigadier David A. Whitehead. Since the Royal Navy wanted to take part in the main event at Okinawa, the naval operations for the Borneo campaign were assigned to "MacArthur's Navy."

During the voyage to Tarakan, *Boise* was once again in charge of the CAP. Although there was no enemy air threat, there was at least one opportunity for the fighter pilots to earn their pay. On the afternoon of 26 April, the task group encountered some boat traffic, all of which were small craft that posed no threat to the warships. At 1600, the destroyer *Nicholas* reported sighting a raft 3,000 yards ahead just off Tawi Island, and was sent to investigate. Later, the destroyer reported that two Japanese on the raft killed themselves when she approached. Another destroyer, the *Taylor,* discovered two more small boats, and went to investigate since they were presumably manned by Japanese. Berkey ordered the *Taylor* to take the enemy personnel prisoner, but to "mow them down" if they resisted capture. He then directed *Boise* to have the CAP fighters strafe other boats that were situated between the *Taylor* and Tawi. At 1640, the pilots radioed that the men in the boats appeared not to be Japanese given their large size and light complexion. *Nicholas* responded that the two enemy soldiers that had committed suicide fit that same description. The CAP was then ordered to fire on the boats. After the fighters strafed the boats, *Taylor* picked up five Japanese personnel who were swimming over to surrender. The prisoners turned out to be a Japanese medical officer, three pharmacist mates (medical corpsmen), and one soldier, all from a Japanese Army medical unit, who reported that they had been fleeing from Bongao Island to Borneo in a small craft rigged with a sail when they were strafed by the American fighter planes. Under orders from Admiral Berkey, the POWs were transferred to the *Boise.* The cruiser received the doctor and the four enlisted men, who were held in confinement on board the cruiser until 3 May.

During this incident, two more sailboats were sighted, and another destroyer was sent to investigate. The *Fletcher* (DD-445) found these sailboats to be manned by Filipino guerrillas, who were allowed to continue on their way.

On 27 April, Berkey's cruiser division arrived off Tarakan (sometimes written Tarekan) Island. This operation, a prelude to the invasion of Borneo that would come a month later, turned out to be a minor event compared to previous invasions. *Boise's* role for the first few days was to protect the minesweepers clearing mines from the bay in preparation for landing troops on the island. The sweeping job was made difficult by the variety of mines present and the strong currents present in the bay. Two of the little minesweepers were damaged by exploding mines before the approach was finally cleared.

The landings on Tarakan were carried out on 1 May 1945. *Boise* helped soften up the beaches for a couple of hours in the morning prior to the troops going ashore. Her main battery was given targets in the town of Lingkas, while the 5-inch battery· was assigned targets along the southeast side of Tarakan Island. After dispatching one of her Kingfishers for spotting fire, the cruiser opened fire with the secondary battery at 0734, followed by the main battery 20 minutes later. During the shelling, both batteries checked fire several times for air strikes over their target areas. The 5-inch battery completed its firing assignment and ceased fire at 0815. Minutes later, the first wave of assault troops landed on the beach and met no resistance. At this point, *Boise* switched her main battery to hit inland targets for a brief time, after which she stood by to provide call fire. During the morning's shooting, she expended 450 6-inch rounds.

The remainder of day was very quiet. *Boise's* planes continued spotting and observation flights over Tarakan. There were no attacks from enemy aircraft, but in the early morning a Japanese submarine launched a couple of torpedoes at the LSTs, one of which received a glancing blow, but suffered no damage. American planes continued bombing runs throughout the day. While most of the troops that landed on the beach were Australian, there were small contingents of American and Dutch forces with them as well, mostly engineers who were there to repair and improve the airstrip and get the oil fields back into operation.

The following day (2 May), *Boise's* planes flew observation flights and spotted gunfire for the destroyers before she and the other cruisers were released to return to Subic Bay. Three destroyers remained behind to provide fire support for the Australian troops ashore. The tin cans remained on station for another week (two of them were there for a month), supporting the Aussies as they drove the Japanese back into the hills. Australian liaison officers, familiar with their army's tactics, were on board to help make the fire from the ships even more effective. The American fire support was greatly appreciated by the Aussie troops, who showered high praise on the destroyers.

Berkey's action report rated the naval bombardment of Tarakan as excellent, although much of it was conducted at extreme ranges, which frequently produced excessive spreads. At ranges inside 11,000 yards, however, the naval gunfire was very effective and silenced the enemy shore batteries very quickly. The only threat posed by the enemy came from shore batteries and mines, but most of the fire came from small arms, mortars, and medium-caliber guns.

Except for gun emplacements on the northeast side of Tarakan near Cape Duoeta (or Djoeata), all batteries were silenced immediately by naval gunfire. At Duoeta Point, however, on the afternoon of 2 May, two enemy guns located on the high ground opened up on the minesweepers, damaging four and sinking another before they were silenced. Fire from these 3-inch (76 mm) guns was evaluated as accurate and devastating. They had been well camouflaged and were undeniably effective. In fact, they were not knocked out until 23 May, when the USS *Douglas A. Munro* (DE-422) blasted them with 5-inch guns and "automatic weapons." One destroyer in TG-74.3, the *Jenkins*, was severely damaged when it struck a mine, but was able to proceed under its own power, with destroyer and tug escort, back to Subic Bay.

Berkey highly commended the cruisers' spotter planes, which again rendered invaluable service, as they did in practically every amphibious operation in the SWPA. The admiral noted that the lack of scout planes on the Australian ships was keenly felt. The planes from the American cruisers had to provide aerial spotting for them as well as for the destroyers, and when operations continued for more than a few days, the pilots were worn out by having to spend so many hours in the air. The task group commander expressed his regrets that on several occasions he had to leave the area of operations because the departure of the cruisers removed the planes that were so useful for aerial observation. Not only did they spot for naval gunfire, but the intelligence information they obtained was most helpful to attack force commanders. In Berkey's opinion, it would be better in future operations to have the planes continuously spotting for call fire from the SFCPs until the operations were brought to a successful conclusion. This, of course, would mean that the cruisers would have to remain on station until the beachhead was consolidated and the troops had advanced inland out of range of the navy's guns.

After what had been a comparatively easy invasion, *Boise* and *Phoenix* pulled out for Subic Bay on 3 May. *Boise* transferred the Japanese prisoners that she had been holding since 26 April, and took on some wounded sailors from the *Jenkins*. Although there were several casualties, only one man was killed. The only naval losses were the two minesweepers that were sunk. *Boise* arrived at Subic Bay on 5 May, and the next day began cleaning and painting the ship to prepare for an admiral's inspection.

By this time, it seemed like the war was truly winding down, at least in the SWPA, and the sailors were thinking of home more and more. With the end of the kamikaze threat, their chances of getting through the war alive had begun to seem pretty good. On the day they got back to Subic (5 May), Avery wrote to Anne, complaining that being separated from her was one of the main reasons "this life out here is so damn miserable." Another reason, of course, was the intense heat of the tropics that never seemed to let up. Avery said the heat drove him crazy to the point that he never wanted to see another summer for the rest of his life. He longed to talk with her and tell her his troubles:

> ... honey, the only time I can get you out of my mind is during working hours and I can't completely forget you then. After working hours and just before I go to sleep at night are the times I think of you most. It is then that I want to be with you more than ever. It is wonderful to think about you and home, peace and quiet again. Darling that is really something to look forward to.

The reports on the progress of the war were all good. Avery reflected, "It looks bad for the enemy. I hope we can soon finish this mess."

The admiral's inspection was held on the morning of 12 May. Admiral Berkey came aboard at 0828 to conduct the annual military inspection, which was followed by the *Boise* putting to sea for AA firing drills, a battle problem (simulation), and a damage control drill. The admiral and inspecting officers from the *Phoenix* gave their sister ship high marks on all drills. *Boise* returned to Subic Bay at 1230, and Berkey left the ship about an hour later.

On Mother's Day (13 May), Avery received three letters from Anne, dated 3, 4, and 5 May. He was overjoyed to hear from her, of course, but it upset him to learn how unhappy she seemed. It hurt even more because he could do nothing about it. He replied:

> It all brings back the thoughts I had after leaving you to join this outfit. You asked me not to leave you, to stay as long as I could, to wait for the draft. But I could not see it your way. I had to go then.
>
> Now I feel like the meanest man living. I'm responsible for all your unhappiness. It makes me feel bad for I know you have had a pretty tough time since I have been gone.
>
> Darling I'm really sorry for I know you are going to hold it against me for a long time. You don't forgive so easy.

Anne had been teaching second grade back home in Eastman, but was thinking of working out of town over the summer. Avery was concerned about this and wrote:

> I don't know what to say about your summer. I'm afraid for you to go away to work some other place. When you are there with your Mom, I don't worry for I know that you are in good hands and they will look after you for me. Please let me know what you decide to do. I'll be worrying my head off until I hear from you. I'm not going to advise you in any way. That would be unfair.

He again talked about how anxious he was to get home to see her. He also missed her parents' farm, which was always one of his favorite spots in the world, and had wondered a lot about how the horses and Sambo (a young mule that had been born on the Taylor place) looked and whether he would recognize them after being away for such a long time. He also wanted to see her father's cattle, and affirmed, "I want a white-faced herd of my own someday."

With the war winding down, Avery was dying to return home soon, one way or another. Even if the *Boise* were not sent back to the United States, he thought perhaps he could get a transfer and some leave during the process. A lot of transfers were coming through at that time. Avery had been on the ship for a long time, so he thought that perhaps he'd get a break soon. He wrote:

I feel like the war out here will be over a lot quicker than most people think … since we have only one war to fight now. We will get all the men and supplies out here now and the brass hats can give it their undivided attention…. Please darling keep your chin up and don't worry. Things will come out O.K. and soon maybe.

The men of Admiral Berkey's cruiser division got a huge morale boost on 15 May 1945, when their sister ship, the USS *Nashville*, pulled into Subic Bay that morning, back from her overhaul in the United States. All hands on the *Boise* were really glad to have her back with them. Two days later, jubilation broke out among the crew when the skipper announced over the PA system that *Boise* would be returning to the United States on 26 June. Hallman commented in his memoirs that it was the most wonderful news anyone ever heard. "The guys were jumping up and down, smiles a mile wide covered every face." Hallman, like most of his shipmates, could not sleep that night for thinking about how wonderful it would be to get back home. For some reason, Avery did not mention this good news in a letter to Anne dated 19 May. It was mostly a love letter in which he said he was daydreaming about the future. He mentioned having received a letter from his mother, who was still grieving over the death of his youngest brother Bo, her favorite who had died in the wreck of the USS *Truxtun* (DD-229) on 18 February 1942 off St. Lawrence, Newfoundland. She told Avery that she kept his blue star next to Bo's gold star at her home.

On 22 May, *Boise, Nashville,* and four destroyers of CRUDIV-15 got underway for Manila. *Phoenix* had gone ahead earlier. Berkey's cruiser division made a port call of three days (23–25 May) in the Philippine capital. They got two liberties, which one sailor described as "not so hot" since everything was so expensive that a small fortune was needed for even a mediocre liberty. It was most likely during this visit to Manila that my father ran across a young American boy with a group of Filipino orphans who were living among the ruins of the city. Avery always had a special rapport with children, and the boy took to him right away, taking hold of his hand as if he never wanted to let go. The child said he had not seen his parents since the Japanese took the city three years before and had no idea where they were or whether they were dead or alive. The little boy spoke Tagalog and translated for the other children and the American sailors. Avery and his buddies gave the children some chocolate and chewing gum, which must have seemed wonderful to those kids after all the suffering and deprivation they had endured. When it came time to return to the ship, leaving that little boy behind was one of the hardest things Avery ever had to do in his life, and he always worried about what had become of the child.

On 26 May, she and CRUDIV-15 returned to Subic Bay. There was now ample time to relax, think of wives and sweethearts, and dream of the future. In a letter to Anne, Avery explained that he had not written for lack of time, assuring her that he wrote every chance he got. He complained that she did not say that she loved him often enough in her letters and begged her to tell him more.

I received your pictures today. Honey I was so proud. I showed them to all my friends and the compliments I got were swell. They all liked them so much. John (Krahling) took the best one. He gave me one of Beverly (his fiancée) and I couldn't refuse him. He said I was sure lucky to have such a pretty girl for a wife.

Darling I'm so proud of you. You are more beautiful than I can remember. When I got these pictures today, I had the strangest feeling I thought I would explode with love for you. Honey I didn't know I could love a person so much. I had almost forgotten what you looked like. For the life of me, I couldn't get a clear picture of you in my mind until today. Darling I love you body and soul.

All the pictures were good. Your Mom's were swell. I told the fellows she was number two girl in my heart and the best cook in the South.

Avery expressed concern about a friend from Eastman, Douglas Martin, who had nearly lost his feet to frostbite during the Battle of the Bulge in Belgium. Martin was brother to Avery's shipmate, Gunnery Sergeant C. F. Martin. Avery told Anne that he wished C. F. and himself could see Doug, and asked her to write to him, "… tell him he will have to come back in cotton picking time. I hope he is O.K. by this time. His feet must have been plenty bad."

On 29 May, Berkey returned again to the *Boise* for an awards ceremony. The ship's company mustered on deck to watch while the admiral presented awards and medals to individual officers and sailors for their performance in the Battles of Surigao Strait and Lingayen Gulf. Berkey praised the crew of the *Boise* for their outstanding performance in both engagements.

Best friends and shipmates, John Krahling (left) and Avery Parkerson (right), USS *Boise*, circa 1944–45. (Author)

A South Seas Cruise with the General

On 1 June 1945, *Boise* departed Subic Bay for a new assignment. They returned to Manila to pick up General MacArthur for a 3,500-mile inspection tour of the central and southern Philippine Islands. *Boise* was MacArthur's flagship again and led a special task unit, TU-74.3.5, which included the destroyers USS *Killen* and USS *Albert W. Grant*. The general had grown quite attached to *Boise* and her crew. As CINCSWPA, he could have chosen any ship in the Seventh Fleet for his tour; it was, after all, his navy. He had ridden into battle aboard two other *Brooklyn* class light cruisers, the *Phoenix* and the *Nashville*, the latter of which served as his flagship for many months in New Guinea and at Leyte Gulf. Perhaps he felt safe on board her since he had witnessed firsthand the excellent gunnery for which she was renowned. Also, General MacArthur was highly image-conscious, and may have considered the international fame that *Boise* had earned would add its luster to his own.

While the ship was at Manila, the crew got another liberty. In the late afternoon of 3 June, MacArthur came aboard, and the three ships got underway for Mindoro Island. MacArthur was accompanied by four U.S. Army generals and other members of his staff, as well as four war correspondents (three Americans and one Australian).

On the first leg of the inspection tour, from 4–8 June 1945, they made stops at Mindoro Island (4 June), Cagayan on Mindanao Island (5 June), Cebu Island (6 June), Iloilo, Panay (7 June), and Puerto Princesa on Palawan Island (8 June), their last stop before the invasion of Borneo. At each stop on the tour, MacArthur went ashore for a few hours, escorted by PT boats. At Mindoro, he traveled into the interior to visit one of his Filipino guerrilla units. According to Vince Langelo's account, at Puerto Princesa, the CINC and his party were taken to a former Japanese prison camp and shown a building where guerrilla reports indicated that 139 Marines had been tortured and burned alive by their captors. MacArthur was horrified and visibly moved by this tale of Japanese brutality.

The Invasion of Brunei Bay, Borneo

The CINC's inspection tour of the Philippines was interrupted when *Boise* and her two destroyers (TU-74.3.5) departed Puerto Princesa on 8 June to join up with the invasion force headed for Borneo. The task unit rendezvoused with the other ships at 1800. The three ships became part of the Cruiser Covering Group, commanded by Admiral Berkey, which was under the overall command of the commander of the Brunei Attack Group, Admiral F. B. Royal, USN. Even though *Boise* served as MacArthur's flagship for the Brunei Bay operation, she was assigned bombardment duties, much to the general's delight, no doubt.

At 0805 on 10 June (Zebra Day), she began shelling assigned targets on the landing beaches in Brunei Bay. An hour later, at precisely 0906, just before the

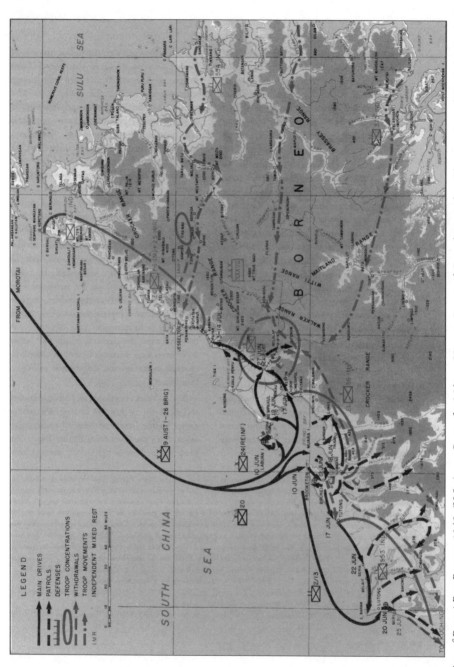

Invasion of Brunei Bay, Borneo, 1945. (U.S. Army Center for Military History. *Reports of General MacArthur: The campaigns of MacArthur in the Pacific, Vol. I,* p. 377)

first wave of troops began landing, *Boise* suddenly lost electrical power aft due to a generator failure, temporarily silencing her two after turrets, two 5-inch guns, one of her radios, and a radar set. The gunnery officer immediately switched his guns to manual control, and power was quickly restored, but the mishap interrupted her firing for about 90 seconds.

Avery vividly remembered this SNAFU (naval slang for a calamity) that caused the ship's guns to fall silent, which was actually more serious than it might seem. The loss of power left her momentarily vulnerable and could have endangered the CINC. Avery knew that he and his shipmates of the Electrical Department were in trouble as soon as the guns did not fire, and everyone suddenly became very anxious. Fortunately, an inquiry showed that the power loss was the result of an unusual problem, which could not have been foreseen, involving the corrosive effects of seawater on part of the cruiser's electrical system. The electricians were therefore exonerated, allowing them all to breathe a little easier. As the troops began hitting the beach at 0915, the main battery ceased fire, followed by the secondary battery 10 minutes later. The soldiers met no opposition as they disembarked on the beaches of Brunei Bay. *Boise* expended 1,030 6-inch and 803 5-inch rounds during the 75-minute bombardment. At 1100, Admiral Royal and Lieutenant General Morshead came aboard to meet with MacArthur and escort him on an inspection tour of the landing beaches. The CINC and his party were escorted by two PT boats and did not return until 1430. At 1435, *Boise* took aboard the survivors from the USS *Salute* (AM-294), which had sunk after hitting a mine on 8 June. The rest of the day was uneventful, and once the general was back aboard, *Boise* retired from the area to spend the night.

On the morning of 11 June, Royal and Morshead returned to escort MacArthur for another tour of the beachhead. *Boise* moved in close to the beach and ordered two PT boats to come alongside to escort the party. At 0850, MacArthur went ashore and returned at 1125. While he was away, Berkey came aboard to present an award to Captain Downes. Once Berkey had left the ship and the general returned, she got underway under verbal orders from the CINC. *Boise* and the two destroyers of TU-74.3.5 were released from fire support duties, and left the scene of the invasion to make for Jolo Island, where MacArthur would resume his Philippine inspection tour.

On arriving at Jolo Island on 12 June, *Boise* and her distinguished passenger were greeted by a flotilla of hundreds of small, outrigger canoes that paddled out to meet them. They then moved on to make inspection stops at Davao (13 June) and Zamboanga (14 June). When the inspection tour was completed on 14 June, *Boise* departed for Manila to return the general to his headquarters. When MacArthur disembarked at Manila on the morning of 15 June 1945, he left a farewell message to the skipper, congratulating *Boise* for such a fine job during her service in the SWPA. Captain Downes said that the general's final words to him as he left the ship were: "May God be with you and your magnificent ship until we meet again. Well done."

The experience of serving as General MacArthur's headquarters afloat for the inspection tour was surely one of the highlights of the war for the men of the *Boise*. Avery always talked about him with a mixture of respect, admiration, and awe. During the two weeks of the tour, *Boise* was once again frontpage news all over the country, thanks to the stories filed by the war correspondents who accompanied MacArthur on the tour. The media attention served to further enhance *Boise*'s fame and helped make her name a household word. The crew were elated upon completing their mission for the supreme commander, because they knew they would be leaving for home within a few days. The campaign to liberate the Philippines had been brought to a successful conclusion, even though pockets of resistance remained in remote locations on various islands, where fighting continued until the end of the war. The retaking of the Philippine Islands removed more than 380,000 enemy troops from the war, severely weakening the Japanese army. The Battles of the Philippine Sea and Leyte Gulf had all but destroyed the offensive capability of the once mighty IJN. Enemy air power was so reduced that they had to resort to kamikaze suicide missions to defend their homeland. In his official announcement of the end of the Philippine campaign on 5 July 1945, General MacArthur gave the U.S. Navy and the USAAF equal credit with the GIs for the victory, and declared that by working in unison, the two branches of service had "inflicted the greatest disaster ever sustained by Japanese arms."

Japanese military leaders in the Philippines also paid tribute to the American three-dimensional strategy of warfare. According to General Haruo Konuma, deputy chief of staff of the 14th Area Army:

> The U.S. Navy and American air power made important contributions to American victory in the Philippines by their protection of convoys. Once ashore, moreover, the landing forces were given excellent protection by the supporting naval and air elements. The Air Force and the Navy contributed greatly to the success of the ground forces during and following the initial assaults, and then continued to keep open the routes to supply the land forces.... The basic reason for American victory in the Philippines was America's ability to concentrate and maintain the necessary men and materials in the frontlines while at the same time cutting the Japanese lines of communication. The well-coordinated action of their land, sea, and air forces was also a substantial factor in achieving victory.

In reference to the U.S. Navy's role in the Philippines, another senior Japanese officer, Colonel Shujaro Kobayashi, declared:

> Through the action of submarines and carrier-based Grummans [fighter aircraft], Japanese supply was effectively cut off in the Philippines. The naval big guns also blasted beachheads before invasions, forcing our troops into the hills. Indeed, the American Navy seemed everywhere at once and powerful.

The defeat in the Philippines sounded the death knell of the Japanese Empire. Japanese military officials later admitted that the strategic consequences of the loss of the archipelago were "disastrous in the extreme." The sea lanes linking the industrial areas of the Japanese homeland and their southern sources of oil, rubber, and other strategic raw materials were severed, limiting their war industries to the dwindling stockpiles in Japan itself and reduced supplies from China and Manchuria. The Japanese high command went for broke by throwing all of the air and naval power that they could muster into the Philippines in a desperate, futile attempt to halt the Allied advance that was grinding relentlessly towards the Japanese home islands. Once the "decisive battle phase" had failed to stop the Americans and Australians, all that was left was to fight a war of attrition in hopes of delaying the final invasion of Japan.

Boise played a significant role in the Philippines, an all-out effort that took just nine months. American determination and resolve were greatly strengthened by the victory in the Philippines. They had for the first time driven the Japanese from a vital strategic area, and final victory in the Pacific was now clearly in sight.

San Pedro, California, Here We Come!

The day after MacArthur left the ship, *Boise* weighed anchor in Manila for Leyte Gulf, arriving there on 18 June. She refueled, took on some passengers, and then departed for Pearl Harbor and California, where she was scheduled for overhaul. Hallman said the weather got a little rough after they left Leyte Gulf. The *Boise Chronicler* ended his chronicle of the ship's service in the Southwest Pacific Theater at this point. They made the voyage to Hawaii without destroyer escort. After passing Ulithi Atoll (20 June), *Boise* began zigzagging and ramped up her speed because enemy submarines were known to be lurking in the area. All hands were ordered to remain alert for any signs of a sub, but the voyage proved uneventful.

In the early morning hours of 27 June, *Boise* crossed the International Date Line from east to west. They gained 24 hours so the ship's calendar reverted back to the 26th. She had a smooth trip to Pearl Harbor, where she docked on 29 June with the USS *Hornet* (CV-12) and the USS *Saratoga*, while a band played in welcome. On 30 June, some of the crew got a few hours liberty in Honolulu before their ship departed for California. Although she remained a unit of the Seventh Fleet's Cruiser Division 15, *Boise* was temporarily assigned to the Pacific Fleet for the period of overhaul in California.

The big cruiser docked at San Pedro, California, on 7 July 1945. In his memoir, Hallman wrote, "San Pedro at LAST!!!!!" The ship pulled in at about 0600 and spent the next 12 hours unloading the ammunition from the magazines. *Boise* remained at San Pedro to undergo an overhaul and radar upgrades through the months of

July and August. Although they could not know it at the time, the war was over for the men of the *Boise*.

Shortly after arriving in California, Avery got that long-awaited leave and was able to go home for a visit after over 18 months at sea. After a short time in Georgia, he departed Atlanta on Delta Airlines on 26 July to rejoin the ship. It was very hard for him to say goodbye to Anne at the Atlanta Airport since he had no way of knowing when he would see her again. He was traveling with his Marine shipmate and friend from Dodge County, C. F. Martin, who got bumped off the flight in Dallas along with some others, including several officers. Avery, however, made the connection to American Airlines at Dallas and arrived back at Los Angeles on 27 July at 0344. He hated to leave Martin, but his friend caught the next plane out, and they met up and stayed together in L.A. before reporting back aboard ship. The two Georgia boys found their ship still undergoing refitting. Avery told Anne, "This ship is really torn down. I don't hardly have a place to sleep or eat let alone write," but promised, "I will write as often as I can."

While *Boise* was at San Pedro, the atomic bombs were dropped on Hiroshima and Nagasaki (6 and 9 August 1945), and Tokyo was bombed with conventional weapons on 12 August. The Japanese capitulated on 15 August 1945 (14 August in the United States) to the great joy of millions of people around the world. The official end of the war came on 2 September 1945, when representatives from the Japanese and Allied governments signed the Japanese Instrument of Surrender on board the USS *Missouri* (BB-63) in Tokyo Bay, in a ceremony presided over by General MacArthur. That same day, which became known as VJ Day, Avery wrote to Anne, saying "the Japs signed the treaty making it official."

Boise was still in Los Angeles preparing to sail for its shakedown cruise. All hands had worked very hard to get her ready for sea. Avery rated a 72-hour liberty, but he could not take it because he had no money.

The scuttlebutt was that the *Boise* would be sent to China for patrol duty, but Avery hoped he would not have to go. He had put in for a transfer to shore duty and was waiting to hear whether he would get it. Nevertheless, he told Anne that he would probably be released from the ship after the sea trials, and doubted they would send him "back out there." It was finally beginning to sink in that the war was over and he had come through it alive and in one piece: "I am plenty thankful I got through this war without a scratch. I guess I'm lucky for I saw plenty of action."

Avery now saw the real possibility of his naval service coming to an end quite soon. He was happy to hear how his wife was making preparations for them to have their own apartment when he got home. He wrote:

> Honey I love you so much and am so anxious to come home to you. I start thinking of me and you in our little home, no one to disturb us, and I get so happy and excited I almost pop. We are going to have such a good life together from now on, be so happy, and love each other so that these bad years will be just a bad dream. I mean the war years.

He wrote again on 16 September while he and his close friend, Electrician's Mate Second Class John Khraling, were making another liberty, their first in about two weeks. He told Anne that he was trying hard to get his discharge, but feared they might try to hold him until he could get a relief. As a senior electrician, he was a "key man" on the ship. *Boise* would be leaving port the next day for the shakedown cruise. The newspapers reported that the cruiser was slated to go to New York City for Navy Day, 27 October, and Avery now thought they might keep him aboard until then, as that would be a "big to-do." He said they might even hold him another couple of months, "for I am an important man in this Navy."

On 18 September, in a letter to Anne, Avery wrote that they were now on the shakedown cruise that was slated to last about 10 days; they expected to return to port on the 27th or 28th. He kept up his hopes that he would be discharged when they returned, but knew they might keep him aboard until *Boise* reached the East Coast. Although he admitted it made little difference, he was eager to get off the ship and out of the navy. Steadily, the reality of returning home to her and to civilian life was creeping in, "I sure wish we had more money in the bank for we are going to need it so bad. If I get out around the first of Oct., I want [sic] be able to save much more. I want us to have so many things I just don't know what to do."

He added that he wished he were rich so he could give her all the things he would like to give her and then confessed; "I guess I should thank God, which I didn't do yet, for getting me through this war alive and not worry so much about the money I didn't have. To tell the truth I didn't dream of getting through alive. But here I am and am coming home to you soon."

Avery had hoped to save about $2,000, but that had been impossible, so they would have to plan and think carefully before spending what money they did have in order to make the best use of it:

> We will have to work and plan together. Are you game? I think you and me will make a team that can't be stopped. It is going to be fun fighting for something we want so badly beside the one I love. Will you help me, please do? I am so anxious to get started. I'll be home soon to start.

While standing the "12 to 4 watch" on 23 September, Avery again wrote Anne, to say that they would be at sea for only five more days and then would be going back in. His long-awaited discharge had come through. The list had been posted and his name was on it, as was that of his buddy Hank Labhart from Indiana. Avery would be leaving the ship by 1 October, and he was overjoyed:

> I have been just like an excited kid lately. Darling it is so hard to realize that I am coming home to you to stay. Darling these have been the three hardest years of my life. So, you see I have paid many times over for leaving you to join the Navy. I can still see you standing on those steps at the post office in Macon. You were such a sad picture then and it was so hard to leave you but honey our country was at war and they needed me.

A Midnight Train to Georgia

On 3 October 1945, her service in the war at an end, the USS *Boise* sailed from California for the East Coast via the Panama Canal. For the first time in over two years, Avery did not sail with her. He left the ship at the San Pedro California Receiving Station on 1 October 1945, and spent the next few days in Los Angeles awaiting transportation. The war was finally over, and people were celebrating. He later recalled going to bars where they would shut the doors after the official midnight closing time, and begin serving Mexican beers that had been smuggled across the border. Avery also remembered waking up in a park in the wee hours of the morning and seeing a Marine and a girl frolicking butt-naked in a big fountain.

While *Boise* was making her way to the East Coast via Panama, Avery rode a troop train across the country from Los Angeles to Jacksonville, Florida, where he was to be discharged. He cabled Anne from L.A. on 6 October to say that he would be leaving for Jacksonville the following Tuesday. The trip would take four or five days. He confessed he was "tired of all this" and anxious to get home. He had been in the navy just over three years and had spent two and a half years at sea in the Mediterranean and Southwest Pacific Theaters aboard the "Old Noisy *Boise*." The war was finally over, and Avery was going home.

The Final Years of the USS *Boise*

Electrician's Mate First Class Avery Parkerson was discharged at the U.S. Naval Personnel Separation Center in Jacksonville, Florida, on 15 October 1945. For his service in the Mediterranean and Southwest Pacific Theaters, my father was awarded the American Campaign service medal, the European-North African-Middle Eastern Theater ribbon with two bronze stars, the Asiatic-Pacific Campaign ribbon with two bronze stars, and the Philippine Liberation Medal with two bronze stars. Like all who served during the war, he was also entitled to wear the World War II Victory medal. As was true of most veterans of the war, he never considered himself to be a hero, although he insisted that many of his shipmates and men on other ships with which they served were bigger-than-life heroes. Rather, he felt he had an obligation to help defend his country, so he did his job, fulfilled his duty, and tried to get through the horror of war as best he could.

My father considered himself exceptionally lucky to have survived the terrible conflict without a scratch. At war's end, he confessed that he never dreamed he would make it through alive. He loved the old "Noisy *Boise*," and was very proud of his service, but after the peace was signed, he was ready to put the navy behind him and get on with his life. At age 29, he went home to my mother, got his old job back at the Ocmulgee Electric Membership Co-op (REA), and started a family. Nine months after Avery returned home to Eastman, Anne gave birth to me, Phillip Taylor Parkerson, the boy they had imagined and talked about throughout the long years of war.

Before the couple could have their second child, however, my dad's luck finally ran out. In 1948, he was severely injured in an accident while repairing an REA power line. Avery was the line foreman for the electric co-op, and when an emergency call came in over a holiday, he took his crew to fix the problem so the family would have power during the holiday. My father climbed a pole near the house while the crew was working on the main line down by the road that was some distance away. Avery said he thought the crew had signaled that they had cut off the power in the line to the house, so he removed the thick, rubber gloves that extended to his elbows and grabbed the line with both hands. The 7,000 volts of electricity that coursed through his arms miraculously did not take his life, but it did take his hands. The tremendous shock knocked Avery backwards, and he fell off the pole. Fortunately, his safety belt caught on a metal rung protruding from the pole so that he was suspended and did not hit the ground. The badly burned lineman was rushed to the hospital in Macon, Georgia, but then was transferred to Crawford W. Long Hospital in Atlanta. My father's injuries were so severe that the right hand had to be amputated, and the left, the index finger of which was also amputated, was paralyzed completely in a claw-like position. After my father healed, he went to Newark, New Jersey, for fitting with a prosthesis for his right hand that came with an interchangeable artificial hand and a hook. I was only two years old at the time, and so have only the vaguest memories of him before the accident when he still had his hands.

Although my dad received a small, non-service-connected, disability pension from the Veteran's Administration, it was insufficient to support a family, so he had to work at whatever jobs he could get without a college education and no hands. The OEMC covered all his medical bills and kept him on in the office for a time, but after a year or two, he was laid off with no retirement or compensation. The VA pension carried earning limitations, so Avery could not earn more than a given amount during any particular year or risk losing the secure income it provided, modest though it were. Therefore, my mother became the family breadwinner, and they gave up the idea of having any more children. She was saddled with a heavy burden of caring for a two-year-old and a handicapped husband who could not bathe or dress himself in addition to working full time. Although my dad was a man of unfailing good humor who kept his spirits up most of the time, his handicap left him frustrated at times when he was unable to perform even simple tasks. Avery occasionally commented on the irony of having gone through the war without a scratch only to come home and lose his hands. However, he never indulged in self-pity or showed the slightest indication of feeling sorry for himself. Instead, he went about his life in such a manner that few people even noticed that he was handicapped.

My father lived an exemplary life until his death on 8 March 1994. He was a fine man, a good husband and father, a loving grandfather. A true patriot who loved his country and was proud of his wartime naval service, Avery never forgot his shipmates from the USS *Boise* and kept in touch with some of his closer friends from the war years. His love for his ship never diminished, and he never wavered in his conviction that she was the best ship in the fleet. Daddy would always tell us, "When they needed to get the tough jobs done, they would always call on the old "Noisy *Boise*.""

The Final Years of a Navy Legend

The USS *Boise* sailed from California to New York City to participate in the Navy Day celebrations in late October 1945. Afterwards, she joined the Operation *Magic Carpet*, to transport U.S. Army troops back home from Europe. She actually began the role in this capacity when she passed through the Panama Canal Zone, where she picked up six army officers and 436 enlisted men who she transported to New York City, docking there on 19 October. At the Navy Day program (20–29 October 1945), the legendary *Boise* was one of the star attractions, along with the aircraft carrier *Enterprise* and the battleship *Missouri*, and she once again became

Operation *Magic Carpet*, November 1945, American soldiers observing memorial plaque on USS *Boise* for crew members killed during the Battle of Cape Esperance, 1942. (USNARA 80-G-701627)

front page news. The cruiser was visited by thousands of people who lined up for the chance to walk her famous decks; among those visiting the "Noisy *Boise*" was President Harry S. Truman, who was on hand for the celebration. The *New York Times* said that of the 36 warships participating in the program, it was the *Boise* that became the public's "Navy sweetheart."

With the Navy Day celebration over and some minor refitting completed, *Boise* got underway on 15 November 1945 for her final mission, the only one she made after 7 December 1941 that did not involve combat operations. As part of Operation *Magic Carpet*, she made two trips to France and England to transport American soldiers back home to the United States. After returning to New York from her last *Magic Carpet* voyage, in January 1946 the ship was sent to the Philadelphia Navy Yard to join the reserve fleet. At Philadelphia, *Boise* was moored alongside her *Brooklyn* class sister ships, *Brooklyn, Savannah,* and *Phoenix.* These magnificent cruisers had completed their distinguished service to the United States in the finest tradition of the U.S. Navy.

A post-war official history of the ship, the core of which was written by her CO and dated 11 October 1945, relates that during the 44 months that the United States was at war, *Boise* served 35 months in combat theaters. She operated in the

Troops assembled on fantail of USS *Boise* while returning from France during Operation *Magic Carpet*, November 1945. (USNARA, 80-G-355364)

USS *Boise* at Le Havre, France, for Operation *Magic Carpet*, November 1945. (USNARA, 80-G-355362)

Netherlands East Indies in 1941–42, the Pacific Area in 1942, the Mediterranean Theater in 1943, and the SWPA in 1944–45. The light cruiser engaged in two night surface actions: (1) the Battle of Cape Esperance (1942), for which she was finally credited with sinking, or assisting in sinking, one Japanese cruiser and two destroyers; and (2) the Battle of Surigao Straits (1944), for which she was credited with sinking at least one large Japanese vessel (a *Fuso* class battleship). While in combat zones, she underwent numerous air attacks and shot down seven or more Japanese aircraft. During all these air raids, her AA fire was so fierce that she was never once struck by a kamikaze. She participated in 14 major invasions and shore bombardments, and was only damaged in action once—at Cape Esperance in 1942. According to this early official history, USS *Boise* earned 10 battle stars during World War II: two on the European-African-Middle Eastern Area Service Ribbon and eight on the Asiatic-Pacific Area Service Ribbon. The Department of the Navy's Dictionary of Naval Fighting Ships, however, says the *Boise* was awarded 11 battle stars. That number of 11 battle stars was confirmed by John Edward Andrade, who served aboard the cruiser from August 1945 until she was mothballed in 1946, in telephone interviews with the author. If *Boise*'s correct number of battle stars was indeed 11, then she earned more than any other *Brooklyn* class light cruiser. Among her sister ships, only USS *Nashville* (CL-43) could boast as many as 10 battle stars.

This official summary does not tell *Boise*'s full story. Several noteworthy aspects of that story were omitted. She and her sister ships, *Philadelphia* and *Savannah*, wrote a new page in the history of naval warfare and proved to the U.S. Army the value of naval gunfire in support of troops on shore, when they smashed counterattacks by German and Italian tanks to save the beachhead at Gela, Sicily, in 1943. *Boise* also distinguished herself in the last great surface engagement in the history of naval warfare, the Battle of Surigao Strait in 1944. That historic shootout, when battleships faced off against each other for the last time, marked the demise of the IJN as an offensive threat, just as it marked the end of an era in naval warfare that had begun with the development of naval gunnery in the age of sail. Thereafter, the airplane replaced the big guns as the principal weapon of modern navies. Finally, she became General of the Army Douglas MacArthur's favorite after she carried him back to Luzon in early 1945, and he selected her to take him on his triumphal tour of the Philippine Islands in June of that year. These and other accomplishments earned *Boise* international fame and a prominent place in the history of the United States Navy.

Boise remained in the reserve fleet until she was decommissioned on 1 July 1946 and joined the "mothball fleet." Five years later, she and the *Phoenix* were sold to Argentina and commissioned in the Argentine Navy. Some of their sister ships were sold to Brazil and Chile. *Boise* was rechristened the ARA *9 de Julio*, remaining in service until 31 October 1977, when she was decommissioned for the final time. Her twin sister, the ARA *General Belgrano* (formerly the *Phoenix*) remained in service until she was torpedoed and sunk by a British submarine on 2 May 1982, during the Falklands-Malvinas War, with the loss of 323 men. It is ironic that after the Japanese tried and failed to sink her multiple times, that storied cruiser finally met her demise at the hands of a former ally. The *9 de Julio* did not survive to see the sinking of her gallant sister ship because she was sold by the Argentine Navy and towed to Brownsville, Texas, where she was scrapped in 1981.

Not a single one of the *Brooklyn* class "bobtails" are left today. While there are ship museums for practically every other type of American warship, from aircraft carriers and battleships to submarines, not a single World War II light cruiser was saved as a museum for future generations to visit. When *Boise* was sold to Argentina, the ship's bell and the bronze plaque listing the names of the crew members who were killed in the Battle of Cape Esperance were removed and given to the city of Boise, Idaho. At the time she was scrapped, pieces of her main deck planks were engraved and presented to the "plank owners" (members of the crew serving on the cruiser at the time of her commissioning) at the 1981 reunion of the men of the *Boise* in Chicago.

Although the mighty "One Ship Fleet" was gone, she was not forgotten. She lived on in the hearts of her surviving crew members, like my father, who were extraordinarily proud and honored to have served on the ship they loved and considered the best fighting ship in the world. Few, if any, of those courageous seamen and Marines, who made *Boise* the most celebrated light cruiser of World War II, are left today, but we who listened so avidly to their fascinating tales of war at sea aboard their magnificent warship will carry on her memory for the remainder of our days.

USS *Boise* (CL-47) General Description

Displacement: 9,700 tons at launching; 11,000 tons fully loaded.
Length: 608 ft. 4 in. (185.42 m).
Beam: 61 ft. 9 in (18.82 m).
Draft: 24 ft. (7.3 m).
Power plant: 8 boilers, 4 steam turbines, 100,000 SHP.
Top speed: 33.5 knots (38.6 mph/62 km/h).
Range: 10,000 nm (11,500 statute miles) at 15 knots.
Compliment: 868 men at launching; 1,000+ during the war.

Armament

Main Battery

Mark 16 6-inch/47 caliber (150 mm)—15 rifles triple-mounted in 5 turrets (3 forward, 2 aft), radar-controlled.
Barrel length: 23.5 feet (7.2 m). Weight of gun: 6.5 tons.
Muzzle velocity: 2,500 fps.
Ammunition: semi-fixed, i.e., projectile and powder casing were separate: Armor-piercing (AP)—130 pounds; High-capacity (HC)—105 pounds; Anti-aircraft (AA)—95 pounds.
Powder case—brass canister, 65 pounds.
Rate of fire: 8–10 rounds per minute (or more).
Maximum range: 26,000 yards (14.5 miles/24 km) at 41° elevation (max elevation 60°).
Flight time, AP projectile: 16.2 seconds at 10,000 yards; 77.3 seconds at 26,000 yards.

Secondary Battery (Dual-purpose)

5-inch/25 caliber (130 mm)—8, single-mount guns (4 on each side of the ship), manual or radar-controlled. Backed up main battery for surface action or shore bombardment, also used for anti-aircraft defense.

Barrel length: 10 ft 5 in. Weight of gun: 2 metric tons. Muzzle velocity: 2,100 fps.
Projectiles: 52–54.5 lbs. HC and AA.
Rate of fire: 12–15 rounds per minute.
Maximum range/ceiling: 26,400 ft. at maximum elevation of +85°.

Anti-aircraft Guns

Oerlikon 20-mm cannon—20 guns, single-mount.
Bofors 40-mm cannon—16 guns, 2 quad-mounts and 4 dual-mounts. Could also
    fire a 4 lb., AP round at surface targets.
Rate of fire: 160 AA rounds per minute.
Muzzle velocity: 2,890 feet per second.
Maximum altitude, AA projectile: 22,299 feet.
Maximum range, AP shell (4 lb.): 6,000 yards.

Armor Plating (hardened steel):
Main belt around hull—5.5 inches.
Turrets—6.5 inches on sides, 2 inches on top.
Main deck—2 inches.
Conning tower—5 inches.

Aircraft (reconnaissance):

1. Curtiss SOC Seagull dual-wing floatplane. (up to 4)
Power plant: 550 hp Pratt & Whitney radial engine. 9 cylinders, air-cooled.
Cruising speed: 65–75 knots.
Top speed: 96 knots (110 mph).
Crew: 1 pilot, 1 crewman (radio, observer, gunner).
Armament: .30 caliber machine guns, two; up to 650 lbs. of bombs or depth charges.
Wings: folding, for storage in hangar deck.

2. Vought 0S2N (or OS2U) Kingfisher monoplane. (maximum number 2)
Power plant: 450 hp Pratt & Whitney rotary engine.
Cruising speed: 115 mph.
Max speed: 164 mph.
Range: 805 statute miles.
Max ceiling: 13,000 feet. Crew: 2
Armament: .30 caliber machine guns, two; 650 lbs. of bombs or depth charges.
Wings: non-folding, could not be carried in hangar deck, remained mounted on
    catapults.

USS *Boise* (CL-47) Commanding Officers, 1938–46

Captain Benjamin V. McCandish, USN	August 1938–August 1940
Captain Stephen B. Robinson, USN	August 1940–January 1942
Captain Edward J. "Mike" Moran, USN	January–December 1942
Commander Burnett K. Culver, USN	1942–1943
Captain Leo H. Thebaud, USN	1943
Captain John S. Roberts, USN	1943–1944
Commander Thomas S. Wolverton, USN	1944, interim C.O.
Captain Willard M. Downes, USN	December 1944–August 1945
Captain Charles C. Hartman, USN	August 1945–January 1946

Aviator's Report, Gela, Sicily, 10 July 1943

U.S.S. *Boise*
c/o Fleet Post Office
New York, N.Y.

MEMORANDUM
From: The Senior Aviator.
To: The Commanding Officer, U.S.S. *Boise*.

Subject: Cruiser Plane Spotting and Reconnaissance on "D" Day, July 10, 1943, over Gela Area, Sicily.

1. Lieutenant (j.g.) Harding and myself were launched at 0600. As the convoy had been firing at friendly aircraft since first light, we flew out to sea to gain altitude before venturing over the ships. I was flying the OS2N, the motor of which I found was not functioning properly as it ran hot and the plane climbed very slowly.

2. After reaching 4000 ft. altitude I headed for the shoreline, and Harding stayed over the convoy. I flew along the coastline the length of the area and as I didn't draw any AA fire, I flew inland trying to identify the various targets, at the same time continuing to climb to 6000 ft.

3. It took some time to place and identify targets as the gridded maps we had were not very good for air spotting. Photographic grids are much better. I was beginning to think the scene below was very peaceful when suddenly I was bracketed on all sides by erratic AA bursts. I took evasive action and dodged bursts several miles to reach the coastline. At this time my motor started cutting out as it was icing up severely and due to high cylinder head temperature already indicated I was reluctant to use full preheat and tried to blow the ice out by leaning out,

which temporarily helped. As I reached the coastline the ship asked for spotting on a target in the area, I had just been over. While spotting this target from the coastline my motor suddenly died on me. I started a glide for the ship with the motor intermittently starting and stopping. I put on full preheat and at 3000 ft. the motor caught full again. I returned to the spotting area and Harding and I spotted fire for two or three targets, with an occasional AA burst near when we got too far inland.

4. On completion of these spots I reported the position of a medium AA battery that had been putting bursts too close for comfort and flew towards the eastern end of the area, on an erratic course at all times to throw off the AA.

5. As I didn't meet any AA fire in this area, I flew further inland and south of the town of Nescemi and noted dust on the road and military vehicles moving towards the coast. I reported this to the ship which requested I identify them as friendly or hostile. I then dove down below 1000 ft. a couple of times and identified them as hostile, several being heavy German tanks with considerable lighter equipment also. Each time I dove down the various vehicles fired at me with light AA weapons. About a half hour later I noticed a collection of tanks along the road about three miles from the coast with several deployed along a ridge firing at what I thought were probably A/T units of ours.

6. At this time the ship asked for a target on the tanks and just as I gave them the coordinates, Harding, who was close to me at the time, and I were attacked by two ME 109 'F's. The dove on us once, missed, and then left us as we headed for the ship.

7. We returned to the spotting area and started spotting fire on the groups of tanks. As my gas was down to 15 gallons at this time, I turned the spotting over to Harding and returned to the ship and was recovered at 0940.

8. The plane was regassed [sic], armed with bombs, motor checked and Ensign Roher was catapulted to relieve Harding at 1015. Just after Roher left, Harding was chased back to the ship by several ME 109's, which dove past him to shoot down another SOC in the area. Later I heard this was a Savannah plane.

9. While I was getting something to eat at 1130 Roher returned to the ship as his radio had gone dead. He reported the position of another group of 15 or so tanks, also that he had dropped his bombs near them and met no AA fire. At 1215 I was launched in the SOC, carrying 100 lb. bombs. I located the tanks and while flying at 4000 ft. directly over them I heard AA fire and tracers seemed to go through

my wings. I rolled over, diving erratically and saw several guns firing tracers at me. Some of which were too close for comfort.

10. I gave the ship target coordinates on the tank column and they opened fire. Just after the third salvo, I glanced up and saw two ME 109's diving on me. I turned inside of them just in time to avoid their getting sighted on me, dove for the ship about five miles off the coast and called the ship reporting the attack. At the time I was approximately five miles inland and at 6000 ft. altitude which was too high for effective spotting but the AA fire at lower altitudes forced me up. They next pulled up over me and made high overhead runs from the stern. By turning towards them as they dove, I was able to keep them in sight and thus just before each was about where I judged he would open fire I faked one way and turned sharply the other continuing my dive. They both fired long bursts on these runs but missed, the first plane's tracers being very close and the second wide. Next, they dove below me and came up under me in my blind spot. I watched them as long as I could and waited until the first plane was about where I figured he would open fire. Just as I pulled the plane into a right split S tracers went past me very close and I felt and heard explosive shells hit the plane. The second plane's tracers were much closer this run as one burst passed just below me and one close to my left. I came out of the dive at about 700 ft., nearly on my back and rolled over looking for the fighters again. As I was nearly to the coastline they withdrew. I called the ship and reported the plane was damaged. They told me to return which I did after unloading my bombs on a place in the brush being shelled at the time by one of our DD's where there was apparently a hostile battery.

11. While returning to the ship my radioman-gunner reported he was uninjured, that he had fired a few bursts at the attacking plane while his gun had jammed twice. Further that the theory you couldn't see tracers coming at you was inaccurate as he had seen all of the firing directly at us including the burst that hit the lower left wing with 2 20MM shells. One of these hit the middle of the wing near the wing root and exploded, several pieces of shrapnel entering the fuselage and cutting the gas line from the reserve tank which fortunately was empty at the time. This shell entered the wing at such an angle that it had to pass within a few inches of both the rear seat man and myself. The second shell passed through the wing at the outboard wing struts without exploding though it passed through the wing's main frame member. On returning to the ship, I learned the same ME 109's which attacked me, had shot down another Savannah plane a few minutes before jumping me in which it was reported Lt. Anderson, Senior Aviator of that cruiser was killed.

12. All I got was a scare, a stiff neck from my heavy binoculars jumping around on my neck while taking evading action and a slight scratch on the first finger of

my right hand. Also, an intense desire to fly a plane in which I can do something besides run when attacked or least have adequate armor protection.

13. In summary it is my opinion that cruiser seaplanes as now in use are not suitable for such duties even if given fighter protection, especially as it is necessary to stay down within range of even the light AA fire in order to see bursts of the target area. The plane has no protection whatsoever from flak and the gas tanks are not armored. In other words, the plane is a flying coffin with opposition of any kind. Also, even with fighter protection it is comparatively a simple matter for any fighter to dive on you for one run and get away—Unless you happened to see these first dives, as I did, you would be a sitting shot, as you are flying slow and level and looking at the ground spotting. The rear seat man is watching for aircraft but he can only cover the stern area from his position. Needless to say, attacking aircraft will be after spotting planes as quickly and hard as possible as proven by my and Harding's experiences. All three times we got over the target it was only a matter of half hour or so when fighters attacked us. It was obvious the motorized vehicles and tanks called for air help as the ship's fire bothered them or even the threat of it.

C. G. Lewis

[Transcribed from a photocopy of the original document from the U.S. National Archives, posted on www.fold3.com.]

Description of the Battle of Surigao Strait by *Boise* XO Commander Thomas Wolverton Posing as a Journalist

The following is a transcription of station TMW's broadcast to the folks back home:

This is your roving reporter bringing you an eye-witness account of the tremendous battle now taking place in the approaches to Leyte Gulf, between our own U.S. Naval forces and a Japanese Naval force consisting of battleships, cruisers, and destroyers.

Your reporter is on board through the courtesy of the Navy Department and his local draft board. I thought, of course, that I would be classed 4-F, but I made the mistake of walking down to the examining center in the hot sun. And although the doctor felt my wooden arm, it was warm—being full of sunshine vitamins—and the next thing I know here I was on one of Uncle Sam's crack cruisers—crack, not cracked, though I was not sure the first time I heard that funny sound as though a thousand automobiles were all stalled in traffic and getting impatient to be on the move. Somebody yelled "General Quarters" and everyone started running in four directions at once. I didn't know they had Generals in the Navy but thought he must be pretty important to create so much excitement. So, I start running around with the others. My left leg caught up to my right leg just in time to keep from going down two sides of a stanchion and I suddenly found myself on the main deck. That's a wooden deck where the sailors sleep at night and get a free shower in these tropical climates. Anyway, I found myself there all alone and while I was looking around to see where everybody had gone all hell broke loose! There was a blinding flash of light, somebody slugged me with a blackjack, and about a dozen thugs threw me down on the deck and after ripping off my shirt started beating me. At least, I thought that was what happened, then I looked up and discovered I was right under the guns of one of the turrets. C–! How those guns shoot! Before I could get out of there, I was black and blue and down to a pair of abbreviated trousers and one shoe without a sock. I don't know whether I forgot to put the sock on or whether it was jerked off over my head. Anyway, I crawled over to the lee side—that's the side where they aren't shooting—and after while I caught my breath and started climbing up to see what was going on. Some officer pushed a microphone into my hands and yelled, "You're on the air!" And here I am. And what a sight it is.

The guns of this cruiser are spoutin' smoke and flame like so many dragons breathing fire. And the noise sounds like a dozen summer thunderstorms all rolled into one. Over on both sides of me I can see other ships apumpin' out the shells. The tracers look like a thousand homing pigeons all starting out from widely separated launching points and heading for the same barn door. They look like they are having a race. They all seem to join up and land in one spot. That old Jap ship and the sea around it looks like it was being beaten by a giant flail. And when the shells land on the ship they flare up like Fourth of July firecrackers in the evening's dusk. What a celebration with just a couple of days to Navy Day!

It's the darkest part of night just before the dawn and now there is an eerie witch's fire outlining the superstructure of our target and we discover it is a huge battleship (*Yamashiro*). From the looks of her we can soon scratch her off the list of Japanese ships.

There's a whale of an explosion and flames leap hundreds of feet into the air then subside quickly as they mushroomed upward. That was a torpedo from our destroyers who have been dashing into close range and are worrying the behemoth as terriers might worry a mastiff.

And now they are releasing more carrier pigeons from other cotes and they are flying straight home to other targets. There are two, three, four, no five ships burning now. And even at this distance you can almost hear the screams of agony of the wounded and dying. But it seems very impersonal. Just the little spot of red tracers apparently drifting slowly but inevitably to the target, then the fires springing up to be capped by a huge mushroom of flame then darkness as another ship sinks beneath the sea with only a pail of darker smoke to mark its grave.

We hammer a destroyer mercilessly for a few moments then our guns are still because there are no more targets within our range. We can still see some of them burning and we steam slowly down and polish them off at our leisure. The proud Japanese force that steamed up with such menace to inflict their style of warfare on us now lies beaten and broken fathoms deep beneath the surface of the sea with only bubbling oil, debris, and a few stunned and helpless survivors floating on the surface to mark the spot where their comrades went to join their immortal ancestors. And may it ever be thus when the forces of Freedom meet the evil forces of the Enslavers.

Glub, glub, gurgle, glub!!

I'm sorry, but your reporter, in the excitement of my sudden appearance alongside him, has just swallowed his false teeth. Oh well! He does not need them for bread and water. And by the time he gets out of the brig—you know he failed to man his gun station—the dentist will have a new set for him. This is the Executive Officer signing off for your incapacitated and incarcerated reporter.

[Note at bottom of page in Avery Parkerson's handwriting]

A. F. Parkerson EM 2/c, U.S.S. *Boise*, Div. E.
Battle of Surigao Straits.
"This was written by our Commander."

Battle of Surigao Strait:
CTG 77 Message and Poem

FROM: CTG 77.
TO: COMCRUDIV 4.

THE COURAGEOUS AND AGGRESSIVE ACTION OF ALL UNITS
ATTACHED TO TASK-GROUP 77.2 IN THE BATTLE OF SURIGAO STRAIT
WON A COMPLETE AND SWEEPING VICTORY OVER A LARGE ENEMY
TASKFORCE. SOUND TACTICS WAS IMPLEMENTED BY EXCELLENT
GUNNERY. THE THOROUGH THRASHING ADMINISTERED TO THE
ENEMY SAVED THE DAY IN LEYTE GULF AND PAVED THE WAY
TO TOKYO.
KINKAID.

[Handwritten margin note]

All Hands
Do not turn on any white lights in compartments when G.Q. is sounded whether
surface action, air raid or P.G.Q. Per Orders CMAA & Exec. Officer

A SAILOR'S LIFE

'A Sailor's life is a jolly life,'
As they say in the old Nay-V.
But we're getting tired of the stress and strife
And condition One E-Z.
And the Nippon Vals and Bets so rife
In the gulf of old Lay-T.
If you disagree, just ask his wife; Or his pal in Tenna-C.

The lookout strains in the sun's bright glare
Till his eyes feel almost dead.
Then he staggers off with a glassy stare and
the thoughts run through his head of one at home who has no care
Asleep in a soft white bed.
The bugle blows and you hear his swear
Flash White! Flash Blue! Flash Red!

Then it's grabbed a line and haul like hell
Then take a rest and blow;
Tote that powder; then grab a shell
And strike it down below
Lash it down in place and stow it well
For who can say or know
Which one of these will down a Nell
On the road to Tokyo.

It's 'Commander this' and 'Commander that'
"When can we feed the crew?"
"Where in hell is the blank Tena CAP?"
Condition Three—Watch Two!
Heave around, then try to catch a nap
Comes the bugle call to you
To defend the ship against the Jap
Flash Red! Flash White! Flash Blue!

CIC what is the course?
Range and bearing to the guide!
What's the disposition of that force?
How's the current? What's the tide?
Air Plot, snap to! Get on your horse!
Is that bomber in a glide?
Laugh it off! Cheer up!
Have no remorse! Point Molly's on our side.

When at the end of days so drear
I lay me down to sleep at night
With thoughts of kegs of ice-cold beer
And steak cooked rare and served just right
I'll dream the end of war is here
And in the world of new found light

These words I hope I never hear
Flash Red! Flash Blue! Flash White!

T. M. WOLVERTON Comdr. U.S. NAVY Executive Officer

[Handwritten on bottom of page]
A. F. Parkerson EM 2/c
U.S.S. *Boise*
Leyte Gulf Area

World War II Aircraft Designations

Number in parentheses indicates number of engines if more than one.

United States

A-20—*Havoc*, Douglas, USAAF (2) light bomber and night fighter
B-17—*Flying Fortress*, Boeing, USAAF (4) heavy bomber
B-24—Liberator, Consolidated, USAAF (4) heavy bomber
B-25—Mitchell, North American, USAAF (2) medium bomber
B-26—Marauder, Martin, USAAF (2) medium bomber
B-29—Superfortress, Boeing, USAAF (4) heavy bomber
C-47—*Skytrain*, Douglas DC-3, (2), transport
F4F—Wildcat, Grumman, Navy-USMC fighter
F4U—Corsair, Chance Vought; Navy-USMC fighter
F6F—Hellcat, Grumman; Navy-USMC fighter
OS2U/OS2N—Kingfisher, Vought, Navy, scout-observation float plane (cruisers
    and battleships)
P-38—Lightning, Lockheed, (2)
P-39—Air cobra, Bell
P-40—Warhawk, Curtiss
P-47—Thunderbolt, Republic
P-51—Mustang, North American
P-61—Black Widow, Northrop (2); USAAF fighters
PB4Y-1—Liberator, Consolidated, Navy (4), patrol bomber
PB4y-2—Privateer, fully "navalized" version of the B-24 introduced in 1943
PBM-3—Mariner, Martin, Navy (2) patrol bomber (flying boat)
PBY—Catalina, Consolidated, Navy (2), seaplane
PBY-5A and 6A—Catalina, Consolidated, Navy (2), amphibian. "Black Cats" were
    specially modified versions for night operations and were painted flat black
SB2C—Helldiver, Curtiss; SBD—Dauntless, Douglas, Navy, dive-bombers

SOC—Seagull, Curtiss, Navy, scout-observation float plane
TBF—Avenger, Grumman, Navy, torpedo-bomber. TBM was designation for Avengers built by General Motors

British

Beau fighter—RAF Bristol fighter (2)
Spitfire—RAF Vickers-Armstrong fighter; Safire—RN carrier-based Spitfire
Wellington—RAF Vickers-Armstrong medium bomber (2)

German

FW-190—Focke-Wulf fighter
He-111—Heinkel medium bomber (2)
Ju-88—Junkers medium bomber (2)
Me-109—Messerschmitt fighter
Me-210—Messerschmitt fighter-bomber (2)

Japanese

(By code name commonly assigned by US and Allied forces)
Betty—Mitsubishi Zero-1, IJN (2) high-level or torpedo-bomber
Fran—Nakajima P1Y, IJN (2) land-based, all-purpose bomber
Hamp—Mitsubishi Zero-2, IJN fighter
Helen—Nakajima Ki-49 "Storm Dragon," Army (2) medium bomber
Irving—Nakajima J1N, IJN (2) night fighter
Jake—Aichi E13A, IJN long-range reconnaissance floatplane
Jill—Nakajima B6N, IJN torpedo-bomber
Judy—Aichi D4Y, IJN dive-bomber
Kate—Nakajima 97-2, IJN dive-bomber
Lily—Kawasaki Ki-48, Army (2) light bomber
Nell—Mitsubishi G3M "Rikko," Army (2) medium bomber
Nick—Kawasaki Ki 45 "Dragon Slayer," Army (2) fighter
Oscar—Nakajima Ki-43 "Peregrine Falcon," Army fighter
Sally—Mitsubishi Ki-21, Army (2) bomber
Tojo—Nakajima Ki-44 Shoki, Army fighter
Topsy—Mitsubishi Ki-57, IJN and Army (2) transport
Val—Aichi 99, IJN dive-bomber
Zeke—Mitsubishi Zero-3, IJN fighter

Glossary

AA battery	the guns used for anti-aircraft defense of a warship. On a cruiser, this battery was made up of the 5-inch guns, also known as the secondary battery, as well as 40mm and 20mm cannons.
AA special	5-inch AA projectile supposedly fitted with a variable time (VT) fuse, but actually fitted with a proximity fuse to confuse the enemy. Also known as a Buck Rogers shell.
AA common	5-inch AA projectile without a VT fuse, which made it more versatile for firing at aircraft or surface targets.
Abeam	on a line at right angles to a ship's keel, 90 or 270 degrees to the ship's heading.
aft	near, toward, or in the stern of a ship or the tail of an aircraft.
amidships	a section or a point at or near the middle of a ship.
ash cans	slang term for depth charges.
astern	behind a ship, or at or toward the stern of a ship.
ASW	anti-submarine warfare.
bandit	a hostile aircraft.
Batt I	a cruiser's primary conning station, or location of the helm for steering the ship.
beam	the extreme width of a ship at the widest part.
big blue blanket	U.S. Navy tactic that kept fighter aircraft over Japanese airfields to prevent planes from taking off to attack ships.
bird farm	slang term for an aircraft carrier.
black shoe	term for a navy line officer who is not an aviator because of the black shoes they wear with their khaki uniforms.
bluejacket	a navy enlisted man below the rank of chief petty officer.
brass	senior officers.
brown shoe	term used for naval aviators because of the brown shoes they wear with their khaki uniforms.
bogey	unidentified air contact, possibly hostile.
brig	prison aboard ship or ashore.

broadside	firing all guns, or receiving incoming hostile fire, perpendicular to the ship's course.
bulkhead	a wall or partition of a ship.
capital ship	term used for largest ships in a fleet or task force, such as battleships and aircraft carriers.
captain's mast	non-judicial disciplinary procedure, often meted out by division or unit commanders.
China sailor	a veteran serving in the U.S. Asiatic Fleet with its homeport in Manila.
CIC	Combat Information Center. The center where a ship's radar, communication, and target-plotting technology were concentrated for coordinating its combat capabilities.
class	ships of the same type built to a common design.
commissioning	when responsibility for a new ship is formally invested in its captain and crew.
conn	the act of steering the ship.
conning station	the place where the helm is located on, or just below, the ship's bridge.
court-martial	a military trial or a tribunal consisting of a group of senior officers.
crossing the line	shipboard hazing ceremony during a crossing of the Equator to initiate sailors who had not yet made the crossing (polliwogs).
crossing the T	classic naval maneuver that allows a column of ships to cross the line of advance of an enemy ship column in perpendicular fashion so as to bring its broadsides to bear on the enemy while they are only able to return fire with their forward guns.
damage control	measures taken to keep a ship afloat and in the fight.
D-day	short for dog day, the code name assigned to the kick off date for many amphibious assaults in the Pacific. After the landings at Normandy on 6 June 1944, other code names became more common, e.g., J-day, short for Jig Day.
dead ahead	directly in front of the ship's bow.
degaussing gear	electrical gear that sets up neutralizing magnetic fields to protect ships from magnetic action mines and torpedoes.
department, see division	terms were often used interchangeably.
depth charge	explosive charge used against submarines (see ashcan).
director	the fire control post charged with locating enemy targets and establishing range and bearing of the targets. A cruiser had two directors, one for the forward main battery and a similar one aft.

displacement	weight of a ship or boat as measured by the weight of the water displaced when the vessel is floated.
disposition	an ordered arrangement of two or more formations proceeding together.
division	in shipboard operations, a unit of men and officers grouped together for command purposes and by function. In fleet organization, a unit of ships between a section and a squadron.
dope	rumor or scuttlebutt.
draft	measurement of a ship's vertical extension below the water-line, usually measured at bow, stern, and amidships.
escort carrier	a small aircraft carrier usually built of a merchant ship's hull, designed for planes to cover convoys of ships and for anti-submarine warfare.
Exec	Executive Officer. The second in command on board a ship.
fantail	the rearmost weather deck of a ship, right above the stern.
fire control	the mechanics of directing gunfire or torpedoes. For gunfire, this involves directors for locating targets; "plot" for calculating range, bearing and speed; and spotting, for making corrections in aim.
fish	U.S. Navy slang term for a torpedo.
flag officer	an admiral or a general, so-called because he is entitled to fly his personal flag, which indicates his rank by the number of stars it displays.
flak	anti-aircraft gunfire.
flank	maximum speed ahead. Generally used as flank speed. Also, the side of a formation.
flattop	slang term for an aircraft carrier.
forecastle	forward upper deck of a ship extending to the bow. Commonly pronounced foc'sle.
forward	toward the ship's bow; opposite of aft.
full speed	a prescribed speed that is greater than standard but slower than flank.
funnel	a ship's smokestack (or stack).
Gedunk (or Geedunk) bar	the U.S. Navy/Marine Corps term for a canteen on a large ship that offers coffee, ice cream, and other snacks, and is open for longer hours than the mess. The origin of the term is uncertain, although one theory is that it is derived from a Chinese word meaning "a place of idleness." Candy and other sweets are referred to as gedunk.
general quarters (GQ)	an alarm calling for all hands to man their battle stations, a ship's highest state of readiness for combat.

GI   a term for a U.S. Army soldier, sometimes said to come from "Government Issue," which was stamped on all their equipment.

hatch   a door in a bulkhead or opening in a deck.

hashmarks   stripes on the sleeve of an enlisted man indicating the number of hitches he had served in the navy.

H-hour   the precise time at which a landing or other operation is set to commence.

head   a ship's compartment containing toilet facilities.

hedgehog   an anti-submarine weapon similar to a mortar, that fired 7.2-inch projectiles and was much more effective than depth charges at killing submarines. The device was thrown ahead of the ASW ship and was designed to explode on contact.

hitch   term of service, generally four years.

I-boat   a Japanese submarine of the 2,100-ton class.

IFF   Identification, Friend or Foe. An electronic device to detect the identity of an aircraft as friendly or hostile.

jarhead   slang term for a U.S. Marine. Also, leatherneck or ocean-going bellhop.

knot   a unit of measurement equal to one nautical mile per hour (roughly 1.5 mph).

ladder   stairway on board a ship.

light forces   cruisers and destroyers.

magazine   ship's compartment used for storing ammunition.

main deck   uppermost complete deck of a ship, areas below this are watertight.

material casualty   jams or other problems occurring in naval guns during firing.

maximum speed   the highest speed a ship can attain when using full power.

meatball   navy slang for Japanese warplane with characteristic Rising Sun (red circle) insignia on wings and fuselage.

Mess   a group of men eating together or a dining area on board a ship.

Moro   Moor in Spanish, term used for a Filipino Muslim.

muster   to assemble the crew; roll call.

nautical mile   1.1516 statute miles (6,080.2 feet).

NGLO pron No-glo   Naval Gunfire Liaison Officer, operated with army units ashore for spotting artillery fire.

normal speed   a ship's speed if a signaled speed is not ordered.

old man   term used to refer to the captain or skipper of the ship.

OOD   officer of the deck, officer of the watch in charge of the ship.

overhead	nautical term for the ceiling of a compartment on board ship.
petty officer	naval non-commissioned officer (NCO).
pharmacists' mate	naval rating for petty officers in the Medical Corps, who were known to the Marines as corpsmen.
plot	to calculate range, bearing, and speed of a targeted ship. Part of the fire control system.
polliwog	a sailor who has not yet crossed the Equator and undergone the traditional initiation.
port	the left side of a ship or aircraft looking forward.
quartermaster	navy petty officer performing navigational duties.
R&R	Rest and recreation.
range	the distance in yards from a ship to a target.
rating	an enlisted man's classification according to specialty and grade. For example, Electrician's Mate First Class (EM 1/c).
relative bearing	bearing in degrees measured clockwise in a circle from the ship's bow (000 degrees). Often referred to by the hours on a clock face, with 12 o'clock being straight ahead and 6 o'clock being straight astern.
salty	old and experienced; can also refer to the profanity-laced language used by sailors.
scrambled eggs	the gold braiding on the visor of a senior officer's cover (hat).
screw	a ship's propeller.
scuttlebutt	navy nickname for a water fountain; also refers to rumor and gossip often thought to originate around the water fountain.
screen	the warships that surround and protect the main body of ships, generally made up of destroyers and destroyer escorts.
scoreboard	area on a ship where enemy flags are painted to indicate the number of enemy ships sunk.
sea bag	a large canvas bag used to store clothing and gear.
Sea Bees	nickname for U.S. Navy Construction Battalions (CBs).
SFCP	Shore Fire Control Party, on-shore artillery spotters for naval gunfire.
shakedown	a test cruise for a newly commissioned or overhauled ship.
shellback	a sailor who has crossed the Equator and undergone initiation.
SHP	shaft horsepower, i.e., the power delivered to the propeller shaft of a ship or aircraft.
skipper	commanding officer of a ship, boat, or aircraft.
slingshot	navy slang for a catapult.
slingshot warbird	a scout plane from a battleship or cruiser, because the planes were launched from catapults or slingshots.

slingshot aviators	the pilots and crewmen of the scout planes.
spot, spotting	to check on hits and misses after a salvo is fired and make necessary corrections in range and tracking.
stand in	to enter a harbor or steer towards shore.
stand out	to steer away from shore or leave a harbor.
starboard	the right side of a ship or aircraft facing forward.
station	the prescribed position of a ship in relation to the guide (or lead ship).
stem	the extension of the keel at the forward end of the ship.
stern	the rear end of a ship or boat.
Split S	an aviation term for an evasive maneuver, consisting of a half roll to inverted flight followed by a descending half loop.
TBS	Talk Between Ships, a radio for voice communications with other ships in a task group.
tin can	slang term for a destroyer.
Tokyo Express	name given to IJN night convoys that delivered reinforcements, supplies, and equipment to Japanese forces on islands in the Philippines, the Solomons, and elsewhere in the Pacific.
top brass	slang term for the most senior army and naval officers.
topside	the main deck or top portion of the outer surface of a ship on each side above the waterline. Also, on deck.
top spotter	a crewman stationed on a platform on a mast, or the highest part of the ship, to spot fall of the ship's gunfire and serve as a lookout. The Top is the term for this platform.
Trade School	slang term for the U.S. Naval Academy.
yeoman	navy petty officer performing administrative and clerical duties.
van	the foremost ship or group of ships in a column. Possibly from vanguard.

Abbreviations and Acronyms

AA	anti-aircraft (gunfire, ack-ack)
ADM	Admiral
AGC	Amphibious Force Flagship
AN	Net Laying Ship (minesweeper)
ANZAC	Australian and New Zealand Army Corps
AO	Fleet Replenishment Oiler
AP	Transport
APA	Attack Transport
AP	armor-piercing (ammunition)
APD	High Speed Transport (a destroyer converted into a fast transport ship)
ARM	Aviation Radioman
BB	Battleship
CA	Gun Cruiser (heavy cruiser)
CAP	Combat Air Patrol
CAPT	Captain
CDR	Commander
CIC	Combat Information Center
CINC	commander in chief
CL	Light Cruiser
CO	commanding officer
CRUDIV	Cruiser Division
CTF	Commander Task Force
CTG	Commander Task Group
CTU	Commander Task Unit
CV	Multi Purpose Aircraft Carrier
CVE	escort or jeep carrier
CVL	light aircraft carrier (sized between a CV and a CVE)
DD	Destroyer
DE	Escort Ship (destroyer escort)
DESRON	destroyer squadron
ENS	Ensign

GQ	general quarters
HC	high capacity (ammunition)
HE	High Explosive
HMAS	His/Her Majesty's Australian Ship
HMS	His/Her Majesty's Ship (Royal Navy)
HQ	headquarters
IFF	Identification, Friend or Foe
IJN	Imperial Japanese Navy
LC	Landing Craft
LCDR	Lieutenant Commander
LCI	Landing Craft Infantry
LCM	Landing Craft, Mechanized
LCS(L)	Landing Craft, Support (Large)
LCT	Landing Craft, Tank
LSD	Dock Landing Ship
LST	Tank Landing Ship
LT	Lieutenant
LTjg	Lieutenant junior grade
NCO	non-commissioned officer
NGLO	Naval Gunfire Liaison Officer
NHHC	Naval History and Heritage Command
OTC	Officer in Tactical Command
PAC	Pacific Area Command or Pacific Fleet
PT	Patrol, or motor, torpedo boat
RADM	Rear Admiral
RAF	Royal Air Force (British)
RAN	Royal Australian Navy
RCT	Regimental Combat Team
RN	Royal Navy (British)
SFCP	Shore Fire Control Party
SHP	Shaft horsepower
SNAFU	Situation Normal All Fucked Up
SWPA	Southwest Pacific Area, one of the two theaters of operations in the Pacific
TBS	Talk Between Ships
TF	Task Force
TG	Task Group
TU	Task Unit
USA	United States Army
USAAF	United States Army Air Forces
USACMH	U.S. Army Center for Military History

USMC	United States Marine Corps
USN	United States Navy (used for career personnel, often referred to as Regular Navy)
USNR	United States Navy Reserve
USS	United States Ship
VADM	Vice Admiral
VT	variable time fuse (fitted to navy anti-aircraft shells, also known as Buck Rogers)
YMS	Motor Minesweeper
XO	Executive Officer

Sources

Documents

Anonymous. "USS *Boise* Chronicle, 1943–1945." Undated stenciled edition circa 1945. Copy in Avery F. Parkerson's Navy scrapbook. Author was probably *Boise's* Executive Officer, Commander Thomas Wolverton, USN.

"USS *Boise* Chronology, 1942–1945." Undated stenciled edition circa 1945. Copy in Avery F. Parkerson's Navy scrapbook.

"History of USS *Boise* (CL-47)." Office of Naval Records and History, Ships' History Branch, Navy Department, Washington, DC. No date, but re-stenciled in January 1951. Copy in Avery F. Parkerson's Navy scrapbook.

CINCPAC, War Diary.

USS *Boise* War Diaries, 1942–45

(at https://www.fold3.com, photocopied from originals in the United States National Archives)

War Diary, 1–31 December 1941.
War Diary, 1–31 January 1942.
War Diary, 1–28 February 1942.
War Diary, 1–31 March 1942.
War Diary, 1–30 November 1942.
War Diary, 19 November 1942–31 March 1943.
War Diary, 1–30 April 1943.
War Diary, 1–31 May 1943.
War Diary, 1–30 June 1943.
War Diary, 1–31 July 1943.
War Diary, 1–31 August 1943.
War Diary, 1–30 September 1943.
War Diary, 1–31 October 1943.
War Diary, 1–30 November 1943.
War Diary, 1–31 December 1943.
War Diary, 1–31 January 1944.
War Diary, 1–29 February 1944.

War Diary, 1–31 March 1944.
War Diary, 1–30 April 1944.
War Diary, 1–31 May 1944.
War Diary, 1–30 June 1944.
War Diary, 1–31 July 1944.
War Diary, 1–31 August 1944.
War Diary, 1–30 September 1944.
War Diary, 1–31 October 1944.
War Diary, 1–30 November 1944.
War Diary, 1–31 December 1944.
War Diary, 1–31 January 1945.
War Diary, 1–31 March 1945.
War Diary, 1–30 April 1945.
War Diary, 1–31 May 1945.
War Diary, 1–30 June 1945.
War Diary, 1–31 July 1945.
War Diary, 1–31 August 1945.
War Diary, 1–30 September 1945.
War Diary, 1–31 October 1945.

USS *Boise*, Action Reports

(in War Diaries, 1943–45, https://www.fold3.com)

Action Report, 16 August 1943, Shore Bombardment, Gela Area, Sicily, July 10–12, 1943. Also contains a memorandum from the Sr. Aviator to the *Boise* CO, "Reconnaissance and Spotting on 10 July 1943, Gela, Sicily," and memorandum from Gunnery Officer to CO, 19 July 1943, "Notes on bombardment of Sicily, 10–12 July 1943."

Action Report, Shore Bombardment, Capo Calava Area, Sicily, August 12, 1943.

Anti-Aircraft (AA) Action Report, 18 August 1943.

Action Report, 21 August 1943, Shore Bombardment, Cape Milazzo, Sicily, 14 August, 1943.

Action Report, 28 August 1943, Shore Bombardment of Palmi, Italy, 17 August, 1943.

Action Report, 24 September 1943, Operation *Avalanche* (Invasion of Western Italy).

Action Report, 29 January 1944, Shore Bombardment of Area "Aberration".

Action Report, 1 May 1944, Bombardment of Humboldt Bay in Support of Landing Operations [18 April 1944].

Action Report, 2 May 1944, Sawar-Wakde Bombardment night of April 29–30, 1944.

Action Report, 18 May 1944, Bombardment of Wakde-Toem Area in Support of Landing Operations [17 May 1944].

Action Report, 31 May 1944, Biak Bombardment in Borokoe-Mokmer Area in Support of Landing Operations at Bosnik [27 May 1944].

AA Action Report, 4 June 1944, Northeast of Biak Island.

Action Report, 5 July 1944, Noemfoor Bombardment in Support of Landing Operation on Kamiri Airstrip.

Action Report, 18 September 1944, Bombardment of Galela Bay Area, Halmahera Island in Support of Morotai Occupation.

Action Report, 30 October 1944, Bombardment of San Ricardo Area, San Pedro Bay, Leyte Gulf, in support of Leyte Landing Operation.

Action Report, 30 October 1944, Report of Action in Surigao Strait on morning of 25 October 1944.

AA Action Report, 21 October 1944, Leyte Gulf.

AA Action Report, 22 October 1944, Leyte Gulf.

AA Action Report, 26 October 1944, Leyte Gulf.

AA Action Report, 3 November 1944, Leyte Gulf.

AA Action Report, 5 December 1944, Leyte Gulf, 1705 hrs.

AA Action Report, 6 December 1944, Leyte Gulf, 1833 hrs.

AA Action Report, 10 December 1944, Leyte Gulf, 1703 hrs. (first run).

AA Action Report, 10 December 1944, Leyte Gulf, 1706 hrs. (second run).

AA Action Report, 13 December 1944, Mindanao Strait, 1755 hrs.

AA Action Report, 13 December 1944, Mindanao Strait, 1850 hrs.

AA Action Report, 15 December 1944, Mindoro Island, 0856 hrs.

AA Action Report, 15 December 1944, Mindoro Island, 0857 hrs.

AA Action Report, 20 December 1944, San Pedro Bay, Leyte Island, 1849 hrs.

AA Action Report, 7 January 1945, Mindoro Strait, 0707 hrs.

Second AA Action Report, 7 January 1945, Mindoro Strait, 0840 hrs.

Third AA Action Report, 7 January 1945, Mindoro Strait, 1823 hrs.

Fourth AA Action Report, 8 January 1945, South China Sea, 0808 hrs.

Fifth AA Action Report, 8 January 1945, South China Sea, 1850 hrs.

Sixth AA Action Report, 8 January 1945, South China Sea, 1905 hrs.

Seventh AA Action Report, 9 January 1945, Lingayen Gulf, Luzon, 0745 hrs.

Eighth AA Action Report, 9 January 1945, Lingayen Gulf, Luzon, 1905 hrs.

Ninth AA Action Report, 10 January 1945, Lingayen Gulf, Luzon, 0634 hrs.

Tenth AA Action Report, 10 January 1945, Lingayen Gulf, Luzon, 1901 hrs.

Eleventh AA Action Report, 11 January 1945, Lingayen Gulf, Luzon, 1855 hrs.

Twelfth AA Action Report, 11 January 1945, Lingayen Gulf, Luzon, 1912 hrs.

Thirteenth AA Action Report, 12 January 1945, Lingayen Gulf, Luzon, 0705–0806 hrs.

Action Report, 5 February 1945, Report of Operations Incident to Amphibious Assault and Landings on Luzon Island, P.I., 1 January–31 January 1945, inclusive.

Action Report, 26 February 1945, Report of Operations in Support of Amphibious Landings on Southern Bataan and Corregidor Island, P.I., 13–17 February 1945, inclusive.

Action Report, 18 March 1945, Report of Operations in Support of Amphibious Landings at Zamboanga, Mindanao, P.I., 8–12 March 1945, inclusive.

Action Report, 10 May 1945, Report of Operations in Support of Amphibious Landings at Tarakan Island, Borneo, 24 April to 5 May 1945, inclusive.

Action Report, 14 June 1945. Report of Operations in Support of Amphibious Landings at Brunei Bay, Borneo, 8–11 June 1945, inclusive.

CINCPAC, War Diary, Solomon Island Campaign, Report of 2nd Savo Action, night of 11–12 October 1942.

COMCRUDIV 15. War Diary, 1–30 November 1944, at https://www.fold3.com.

COMCRUDIV 15. War Diary, 1–31 March 1945.

COMCRUDIV 15. Action Report, 27 March 1945, Mariveles-Corregidor-Manila Bay Operations, 13–18 February 1945.

COMTaskGroup 74.3. Action Report, 17 May 1945, Tarakan Operations, Northeast Borneo, 27 April–5 May 1945.

COMWNTF, VADM H. K. Hewitt (USN), Action Report Western Naval Task Force The Sicilian Campaign, Operation "*Husky,*" July–August 1943. https://www.history.navy.mil/library/online/sicilian-campaign.

Parkerson, Avery F. Collection of letters to Anne Parkerson from USS *Boise,* 1943–45. Originals in possession of the author.

Starnes, James. USS *Boise* (WW II), video of interview discussing *Boise*'s sortie from Pearl Harbor towards Tokyo in 1942. https://www.witnesstowar.org.

Starnes, James. USS *Missouri* (WWII), video of interview discussing *Boise*'s opening fire on Japanese fleet off Guadalcanal [Cape Esperance] in 1942. https://www.witnesstowar.org.

Starnes, James. USS *Boise* (WWII), video of interview discussing his participation in the invasion of Sicily and facing the German air force. https://www.witnesstowar.org.

USS *Savannah*, Action Report during assault phase of invasion of Sicily in the Dime Attack Area, Operation Husky, 19 July 1943.

Wolverton, Thomas. "My Night." Mimeographed article on battle of Surigao Straits written by *Boise*'s Executive Officer, 1944. Copy in Avery Parkerson's Navy scrapbook.

Personal Interviews with *Boise* Crew members

Andrade, John Edward. April 12, 2012. Andrade served aboard *Boise* from August 1945 until she was mothballed in 1946.

Moneymaker, Dr. Garnett. July 13 and 24, 2013. Moneymaker served aboard *Boise* from 1941–44.

Printed and Electronic, Primary and Secondary Sources

Andrade, Dale. "Luzon, 1944–1945." Brochure of the U.S. Army Center of Military History. https://history.army.mil/brochures/luzon/72-28.htm.

Breuer, William B. *Retaking the Philippines: America's return to Corregidor and Bataan, October 1944–March 1945.* New York: St. Martin's Press, 1986.

Brokaw, Tom. *The Greatest Generation.* New York: Random House, 1998. E-edition.

Bustin, Steven George, *Humble Heroes: How the USS Nashville CL-42 fought WWII.* North Charleston, South Carolina: Booksurge Publishing, 2007. E-edition.

Cressy, Glenn. *The Pearl Harbor Conspiracy That Involved the USS Boise and Led to WWII.* Amazon-Kindle e-book, January 26, 2011.

Cressman, Robert J. *The Official Chronology of the U.S. Navy in World War II.* Naval Historical Center, 1999. https://www.ibiblio.org/hyperwar/USN/USN-Chron.html.

Dailey, Franklyn E., Jr. *Joining the war at sea, 1939–1945.* 2012. https://www.daileyint.com/seawar/.

Dull, Paul S. *A Battle History of the Imperial Japanese Navy, 1941–1945.* Annapolis, MD: United States Naval Institute, 1978.

Garland, Albert N., and Howard M. Smyth. *The Mediterranean Theater of Operations: Sicily and the surrender of Italy.* Washington, DC: U.S. Army Center for Military History, 1993. https://history.army.mil/html/books/006/6-2-1/index.html.

Hackett, Bob, and Sander Kingsepp, *Sensuikan! Midget submarines based in the Philippines, 1944–1945.* 2006.

Hara, Tameichi. *Japanese Destroyer Captain: Pearl Harbor, Guadalcanal, Midway—the great naval battles as seen through Japanese eyes.* Annapolis, MD: Naval Institute Press, 2011.

Hornfischer, James D. *The Last Stand of the Tin Can Sailors: the extraordinary World War II story of the U.S. Navy's finest hour.* Bantam Books, 2004. E-edition.

Hornfischer, James D. *Neptune's Inferno: the U.S. Navy at Guadalcanal.* New York: Bantam Books, 2011.

Hoyt, Edwin P. *MacArthur's Navy: The Seventh Fleet and the battle for the Philippines.* New York: Orion Books, 1989.

Kelly, C. Brian. *Best Little Stories of World War II: More than 100 true stories.* 1998. Google Books, 2010.

Krall, Frank. USS *Shubrick* DD-639. Personal War Diary of Frank Krall. http://www.ussshubrick.com/sicily.htm.

Langelo, Vincent A. *With All Our Might: The World War II history of the USS Boise (CL-47).* Austin, Texas: Eakin Press, 2000.

"Maconite says Pacific Fight Gunfire Topped Invasion's." *Macon Telegraph & News,* July 23, 1944.

Mininger, Stella. *A War to Remember: Chalmers H. Hallman Radioman RM 3/C; USS Boise CL-47.* New York: Writers Club Press, 2003.

Moneymaker, Garnett. "The wartime diaries of Dr. Garnett Moneymaker." Ed. & tr. by Dr. Henry Shapiro, 2011. https://www.cs.unm.edu/~shapiro/money-maker_diary.html.

Morris, Frank D. *"Pick Out the Biggest:" Mike Moran and the men of the Boise.* Boston: Houghton Mifflin Company, 1943.

Morison, Samuel Eliot. *The History of United States Naval Operations in World War II—Leyte, June 1944-January 1945.* Vol. XII. Annapolis, MD: Naval Institute Press, 1958. Second printing 1986.

Morison, Samuel Eliot. *The History of United States Naval Operations in World War II—New Guinea and the Marianas, March 1944-August 1944.* Vol VIII. Annapolis, MD: Naval Institute Press, 1953.

Morison, Samuel Eliot. *The History of United States Naval Operations in World War II—Sicily, Salerno, Anzio, January 1943-June 1945.* Vol. IX. Urbana & Chicago: University of Illinois Press. 2000.

Morison, Samuel Eliot. *The History of United States Naval Operations in World War II.—The Liberation of the Philippines: Luzon, Mindanao, the Visayas, 1944–1945.* Vol. XIII. Boston: Little, Brown & Company, 1959.

Neufeld, William. *Slingshot Warbirds: World War II U.S. Navy scout-observation airmen.* Jefferson, N.C.: McFarland & Company, 2003.

Sears, David. *At War with the Wind: The Epic Struggle with Japan's World War II Suicide Bombers.* New York: Citadel Press, 2008.

Taylor, Thomas, and Robert Martin. *Rangers: Lead the way,* 1997.

Thomas, Gerald W. *Torpedo Squadron Four: A cockpit view of World War II.* Doc 45 Publishing. 2011.

Tomblin, Barbara Brooks. *With Utmost Spirit: Allied naval operations in the Mediterranean, 1942–1945.* Lexington, KY: The University Press of Kentucky, 2004.

Tully, Anthony P. *Battle of Surigao Strait.* Bloomington: Indiana University Press. 2009.

U.S. Army Center for Military History. *Reports of General MacArthur.* 2 vols. Facsimile Reprint, 1994. Original printed by Gen. MacArthur's Headquarters in Tokyo, 1950.

Willmott, H. P. *The Battle of Leyte Gulf: The last fleet action.* Bloomington: Indiana University Press, 2005.

Woodward, C. Vann. *Battle for Leyte Gulf: The incredible story of World War II's largest naval battle.* New York: Skyhorse Publishing, 2007.

Index